A History of the World Since 9/11

Also by Dominic Streatfeild

Cocaine: An Unauthorized Biography
Brainwash: The Secret History of Mind Control

A History of the World
Since 9/11

Disaster, Deception, and
Destruction in the War on Terror

DOMINIC STREATFEILD

BLOOMSBURY PRESS

NEW YORK • BERLIN • LONDON • SYDNEY

Published by Bloomsbury Press, New York

All papers used by Bloomsbury Press are natural, recyclable products made from wood
grown in well-managed forests. The manufacturing processes conform to the environmental
regulations of the country of origin.

LIBRARY OF CONGRESS CATALOGING-IN-PUBLICATION DATA HAS BEEN APPLIED FOR.

ISBN: 978-1-60819-270-0 (hardcover)

First published in Great Britain by Atlantic Books in 2011
First published in the United States by Bloomsbury Press in 2011

1 3 5 7 9 10 8 6 4 2

Printed in the United States of America by Quad/Graphic, Fairfield, Pennsylvania

For Jojo

Contents

Introduction

At first glance Turkish Airlines flight TK1202's passengers appear ordinary enough: football fans, perhaps, attending an away game. But there are signs. Eastern European accents. G-Shock watches. Crew cuts. When the men lean forward to open their tray tables their T-shirts ride up their arms, revealing tattoos: daggers, wings, numbers. Not football fans. As the aircraft makes its final approach, they point out of the windows at a Disneyesque palace in the middle of an artificial lake. '*Slayer!*' they grin, giving each other the thumbs-up. '*Camp Slayer!*'

Inside the terminal building Kellogg, Brown & Root contractors mill about.

'No cellphones!' barks a sergeant. 'Those checkpoint guys see you with something electrical, they gonna think you detonating something.'

A brief burst of activity ensues as 150 cargo-panted Americans frantically disentangle themselves from various electrical appliances and stow them in their flight bags. iPods and phones safely out of sight, they form a straggly line to wait for their armoured buses and security details.

We don't have an armoured bus or a security detail.

'We can get them,' Haider, my fixer, says. 'But they'll mark us out as a target.'

Instead, we borrow a battered Hyundai.

Beyond the airport's security perimeter the scale of the destruction becomes apparent. Everything appears to have been shelled. Every building, every wall, broken; in their place, rusty rebar cables contorted like palsied fingers. And rubble. Here are the state courts, burned;

there's the old parliament building, wrecked. Government ministries are identifiable by the blast barriers protecting them: the more important the ministry, the higher the walls. The entire city is coated with a layer of fine concrete dust.

As we move into town, Haider points out sites of interest: the Ministry of X – bombed in 2004; the Department of Y – blown up a year later.

'It was around here somewhere, wasn't it?' he asks the driver.

A couple of years ago, the pair pulled over to help two men lying on the pavement. Perhaps they were wounded?

They weren't. Their heads had been sawn off.

Everywhere, garbage. *Tons* of it. Orange peel, shattered photocopiers, plastic water bottles, old drinks cans. On every corner watchtowers, concertina wire, sandbags; light machine guns peeping through camouflage netting, armoured personnel carriers. Iraqi troops in sunglasses, berets perched on their heads like soufflés in that crazy Saddam-style. Checkpoints beautified with plastic flowers. Beside them, signs:

STOP

USE OF LETHAL FORCE AUTHORIZED

DO NOT ENTER OR YOU MAY BE SHOT

Baghdad, 2009. Crucible of human civilization. Gateway to democracy in the Middle East.

Historians like to break up human progress into bite-sized pieces. It's a useful technique: segregated and labelled, historical eras offer prisms through which to view the past, making it easier to comprehend. Typically, they're bookmarked by inventions: the wheel, the steam engine, the atom bomb. Intellectual movements fit nicely, too: the Reformation, the Enlightenment, Modernism. Each innovation provides a paradigm shift, ushering in a way of thinking previously inconceivable but, after its emergence, unignorable.

Occasionally, waypoints are provided by momentous events. A happening of sufficient magnitude (the argument goes) jars the historical process decisively, severing the connection between past and future, sweeping away the old and paving the way for the new. The Flood in Genesis, the birth of Christ, the attack on Pearl Harbor – all 'watershed' moments. Bookmarking such events not only provides useful academic waypoints, it also offers another important service: reassurance. With the sweeping away of the old comes trepidation. The birth of a 'new era' provides a link to the past: there have been epochal events before. Things have changed rapidly, and not always for the better. We have survived them. We will again.

The impact of American Airlines Flight 11 into the North Tower of the World Trade Center at 8.46 a.m. on 11 September 2001 was immediately labelled a watershed event. Seventy-six minutes later, after both the South Tower and the Pentagon had been hit, United Airlines Flight 93's calamitous descent into a field in Shanksville, Pennsylvania, marked the end of the attacks – and the start of a still-ongoing attempt to define what, exactly, they meant.

Certainly, the strikes were unprecedented. For George W. Bush, they marked a change of political eras 'as sharp and clear as Pearl Harbor'. Secretary of State Colin Powell agreed. 'Not only is the Cold War over,' he explained, 'the post-Cold War period is also over.'

Around the world the media reiterated the global significance of the event, most famously *Le Monde*. 'Today,' stated the French newspaper, 'we are all Americans.' Perhaps Richard Armitage, Colin Powell's deputy at the State Department, put it most pithily: 'History starts today.'

Intuitively, all of these statements made perfect sense. The magnitude – and audacity – of the 9/11 attacks were staggering. All, however, was not as it seemed.

For politicians, as for historians, predictively labelling eras is a hazardous procedure: history is littered with declarations of new eras that have somehow failed to materialize. In the aftermath of the attacks it seemed reasonable to assume that 11 September would trigger a new way of thinking.

Did it?

In a hundred years, when schoolchildren discover what happened at the start of the twenty-first century, what will they think? Will they see the photographs of the collapsing towers, turn the page and forget them? Or will they learn that history stopped, then restarted in some new, fundamentally different direction?

Will 9/11 be a chapter or a footnote?

Things that work in Baghdad: nothing. The water is brown. The power cuts out ten times a day. The phones are disconnected. Mobile networks and Internet connections function intermittently. Transport and sewage: broken. In the hotel restaurant a mournful waiter sits alone watching TV. No coffee. No food. No customers. Duct tape over the windows prevents glass shards from flying into the room in the event of a detonation outside.

Only the Black Hawks appear unaffected. They pass overhead every few minutes: one, in the lead, keeping an eye on the city; the second higher, a hundred metres behind, keeping an eye on the first. Above, surveillance aircraft watch over the helicopters and, above them, satellites look down on all of us.

We drive to the Green Zone to pick up press passes. There are no plastic flowers. Entry is via a labyrinth of concrete blast walls manned by foreign contractors. On the outside, Ugandans. Further in, Peruvians. Here, too, everyone watches someone else's back. Somewhere in the middle of all this, protected by the Ugandans and the Peruvians, is the US military.

'Shouldn't the American army be protecting itself?' asks Haider. 'Isn't that the point of an army?'

Ugandans and Peruvians are cheaper. That's why they're on the outside, where most car bombs go off. Searches. X-rays. Frisks. Body scans.

WELCOME TO THE GREEN ZONE

NO PHOTOGRAPHY

NO CELLPHONES

In the press centre we are interrogated. Where are we from? Who are we interviewing? Who are we working for? We fill in forms, hand over passports and credentials. We are fingerprinted and photographed from a variety of angles, then told to return in a few days. We are not allowed to wander around. We trace our way back through the concrete maze, climb into our Hyundai and go home.

Outside the hotel at night, bursts of automatic gunfire. Who's shooting? What are they shooting at? No one knows. The shots whistle past. In the distance, too far away to hear, an explosion lights up the sky. The power cuts out. A generator starts. The lights go back on. The Black Hawks pass overhead.

Understandably, the first post-9/11 reaction was shock. Why had the United States been targeted? How had this happened? Could it happen again? Within days, however, this sense of insecurity was overwhelmed by a counter-wave of certainty. America had been attacked because it was free. The perpetrators were cowards. They were evil. We would *get them*.

Almost from the beginning, another ingredient was present, too: idealism.

'The kaleidoscope has been shaken. The pieces are in flux,' Tony Blair told the Labour Party Conference three weeks after the attacks. 'Soon they will settle again. Before they do, let us reorder this world around us.'

The slate had been wiped clean; now was the time to make a few changes. Now was the time to implement the policies we had always wanted, but never had the chance. In this sense, what 9/11 really offered policymakers was an *opportunity*. Rereading speeches of the time, the repeated use of this word is striking: 'opportunity'. America had been struck. Innocence had been lost. What could be salvaged? What could we gain?

This equation – uncertainty, certainty, opportunity – paved the way for everything that happened next. Administration spokesmen announced that the United States was working on the dark side; that the gloves were coming off. Now was not the time to err on the side of caution. If the goal was the greater good and the dissemination of freedom, how could that be wrong? In the light of 9/11 and the need to protect its citizens from the 'existential threat' of Osama bin Laden, the United States could have made a rational-sounding case for almost any policy decision.

It did.

In short order, America and her allies invaded Afghanistan, then moved on to Iraq. In the process, international alliances – NATO, the United Nations – were sidelined. Inside the country, civil liberties were curtailed. US citizens were incarcerated without trial or access to lawyers. Telephone lines and Internet hubs were tapped. Dissent was quashed. Outside it, suspects were kidnapped, 'rendered', then tortured and – in some cases – murdered.

To those of a cynical disposition, it was the rhetoric that gave the game away. Once the administration got the hang of it, there was no incongruity in referring to hunger-striking prisoners as engaging in acts of 'voluntary starvation', suicide attempts as 'manipulative, self-injurious behaviour' – or even, in one famous case, 'asymmetric warfare'. It was entirely reasonable to assert that the Coalition of the Willing held a majority in the United Nations; that the invasion of Iraq was not only legal but necessary.

Objectors could easily be placated with a false dichotomy ('either we act on asylum seekers or let them all in and hang the consequences'; 'either we invade Iraq now or let Saddam hand nuclear weapons to al-Qaeda'). A little verbal dexterity was necessary, but, then, the world had changed. Old rules, drafted in a more innocent time, were no longer sufficient – not with Bin Laden on the prowl. They had to be changed, or at least reinterpreted. The law was, after all, a fluid thing.

Haki Mohammed detests Americans.

'I hate them,' he announces nonchalantly, exhaling a plume of cigarette smoke at the ceiling fan.

He leans forward and rests his elbows on his knees. Three years ago US troops kicked down his door, searched his house and accused his family of being terrorists. They had been misinformed: actually Haki was a security guard whose job was to protect one of Baghdad's leading hotels. Although he spoke little English, he managed to come up with a phrase he thought might placate the soldiers.

'We are not terrorists,' he told the NCO in charge of the raid.

The soldier, who had heard this kind of thing before, clubbed him in the face with a rifle butt, breaking his front teeth. When Haki showed him his official identity card, the soldier didn't appear overly concerned.

'He said, "Oh, sorry," then he left.' The Iraqi stubs his cigarette out in an overflowing ashtray. 'We didn't believe them from the beginning,' he says. Then as an afterthought: 'I hate the British, too.'

Outside, on the streets, no one makes eye contact. No one wants to talk. In the ministries, workers need permission from supervisors, supervisors need permission from directorates. Directorates need permission from someone else we never manage to locate. 'We'll call you back,' they all croon. 'We'll come by the hotel and see you.' Then they vanish.

'Do many journalists come here to interview you?' I ask the head of one directorate.

'No,' he says. 'None. And, if I'd known you were coming, I'd have told you not to: it's too dangerous, driving around Baghdad like that.'

Well, now we're here, I suggest, perhaps we could talk?

'I think,' interrupts an assistant, 'it would be better if you came back tomorrow.'

Back into the Hyundai.

In the evenings we sit on the hotel balcony drinking bottled water, waiting for something to happen. Nothing does. Journalism in Iraq is like being stuck in Flann O'Brien's *The Third Policeman*, where the end reveal is that the protagonist is in hell, reliving the same day again and again. Iraq is *Groundhog Day*, with guns. But then, in Baghdad, the only thing worse than nothing happening is *something* happening.

No coffee in the hotel, no water in the taps, no staff in the restaurant, no guests in the rooms. No power in the plug sockets, no return calls. No photography. No cell phones. Use of lethal force authorized. Do not enter or you may be shot.

There's a school of thought that views terrorism as an act of provocation. Violence is involved, of course; civilians die. According to this theory, though, the actual deaths themselves are incidental. The true aim of the terrorist atrocity is not the carnage it creates. The real objective is to push the target into a reaction – preferably an *over*reaction – that might conceivably further the protagonists' goals.

Admittedly, atrocities committed by al-Qaeda are different. The organization seems to relish the prospect of civilian casualties: if they're not Muslims, they have no right to life. Ignoring this homicidal ignorance for a moment, however, the organization's goals are broadly similar to those of other, more conventional, terror groups: disruption. Fear. Publicity. Recruitment.

Seen in this light, 9/11 was not simply an atrocity but a political act with a political goal. Al-Qaeda's aim in striking America was not to kill a few thousand financial workers but a more insidious prodding: Bin Laden wanted to provoke the United States. He was out to wake a sleeping giant. Results were immediately gratifying.

Initially, war was declared on the terrorists responsible. Shortly afterwards, it was expanded to include terrorists everywhere, even those who had not been involved. Finally, war was launched against anybody who might become – at some point in the future – a terrorist. Extraordinary times called for extraordinary measures. The 'War on Terror' was, according to George W. Bush, a 'new and different war . . . on all fronts'. It required a 'new and different type of mentality'.

'[The war] may never end,' Vice-President Dick Cheney admitted to a journalist days after the attacks. 'At least, not in our lifetime.'

For the first time in the alliance's history, NATO invoked Article 5 of its founding charter – an attack on one was an attack on all – and joined the fray. Nations that declined to assist in the struggle were themselves classified as hostile.

The President's ruminations on the theme led him further into the trap.

'Our responsibility to history is already clear,' he announced on 14 September: 'to rid the world of evil'. A two-bit organization in a Third World country had succeeded in provoking the most powerful nation on earth, and her allies, into war.

Somewhere, in a cave on the Afghan–Pakistan border, a tall, bearded Saudi was hugging himself with glee.

Nearly a decade on, Iraq remains the true monument to 9/11. That's why we're here. For two weeks, we hunt government ministers, military-types and *Sahwa* – former insurgents now providing security for their own districts. The only guys who actually want to talk are the latter: having been granted amnesty from prosecution for previous crimes, they have nothing to lose. Then, a catastrophe.

One Saturday morning, the Iraqi army arrests *Sahwa* leader Adel al-Mishedani. There is a shootout not far from the hotel. A number of Iraqi soldiers are killed. Suddenly, the amnesty looks shaky.

Immediately, our *Sahwa* contacts go silent. If there's any chance of prosecution, no one wants to talk. Our lead interviewee flees to Syria; others head for the countryside. With time running out, we spread the net further. Who knows former insurgents? Who has relatives that belong to the right tribes? Who knows someone who might know someone? Just as we're becoming desperate, we get a nibble.

Cousins of cousins have found someone. A rendezvous is arranged. The moment we arrive, the phone rings: the location has changed. The procedure is repeated a number of times as we run around town attempting to attend meetings whose locations change the moment we get to them. After four or five such incidents, Haider's friend, G., loses patience.

'We're here,' he tells the man on the other end of the phone. 'Where are you?'

'We know where you are,' comes the reply. 'We're watching you.'

Then, further directions to another spot.

'Why all the secrecy?' asks G. *Sahwa* are never usually this cautious.

'Perhaps,' concedes the voice. 'But we're not *Sahwa*. We're someone else.'

Tanzhim. *The Organization.* Al-Qaeda. Two weeks in Baghdad; the only people who want to talk are the ones everyone else is looking for.

Administration officials recognized that al-Qaeda represented a uniquely twenty-first-century threat. The problem, it seemed, was something to do with globalization. Prior to the Internet era, a bunch of disgruntled Arabs in the Middle East may have threatened the Gulf states; 11 September proved that they now threatened the rest of the world, too. Our own technological advances had been hijacked and used against us. 9/11 demonstrated, as never before, that the door of globalization swung in both directions.

When it came to our response to the attacks, the door swung in both directions, too. The moment the War on Terror was launched, all aspects of the new conflict were destined to spread. Those behind it saw this as a good thing: how could a war fought for democracy and freedom be anything other? Not everyone agreed. To many, the Global War on Terror was an aggressive campaign to export American power and, with it, the kind of hypocrisy that had prompted the attacks in the first place. It was likely to prove counter-productive. Worse, the campaign would have far-reaching reverberations. In all likelihood, these reverberations would outlast not only the war itself but also the administration that had launched it.

Were they right? Here are the stories of eight of those reverberations. Some you may already know. Others will be less familiar. None has a happy ending.

This is not an account of what happened on 9/11. This is an account of what happened next. It's scarier.

I

Rage

I don't care what the international lawyers say. We are going to kick some ass.

George W. Bush, September 2001

Stroman's madder than hell, but he's not insane. He certainly isn't fixing to get himself shot. The moment the attendant reaches under the cash register for his .22, it's time to act. And he's quick! If Stroman hadn't come prepared, he'd be in real trouble. His gun recoils violently, upwards and to the left. A flame a foot long shoots from the barrel.

The bullet, a copper-coated .44, strikes the attendant just above the left collarbone. Coming as it does from a range of just two feet, the vast majority of the muzzle velocity remains intact. The collarbone fractures and the slug moves on, breaking the first three ribs, penetrating the left lung, then shattering three more. It travels 8½ inches through the victim's torso, coming to a rest just beneath the skin of his lower back. The attendant collapses.

Stroman will later state that he was somewhere else when all this takes place. Not that he will deny the crime (he admits this immediately), rather that the adrenaline, the shooting and the flame that leaps from the revolver's barrel *affects* him in some way. Time neither slows nor accelerates, but rather does both simultaneously, so that, while the flame emerges from the barrel in slow motion, like in a movie, everything else appears to take place instantaneously.

'It's like I was floating above the room,' he says. 'Like someone else was doing it.'

This dissociation may account for Stroman's inability to recall what happens next. But that's clear. It's all on CCTV. He shoves the revolver back in to his waistband and shouts at the attendant: 'Open the register!'

Reaching over the counter he scrabbles about frantically, apparently trying to get to the cash, failing and knocking the keyboard on to the floor. 'Open the register NOW or I'm gonna kill you! OPEN IT! OPEN IT!'

Nothing happens.

Stroman's desperation is now palpable. He reaches for the revolver again.

'I see that gun down there! Open the register or I'm gonna blow your brains out!'

A glance at the window – *is someone coming?* – apparently persuades him not to make good on his threat. Instead, he turns, disappears through the door, climbs into a silver Ford Thunderbird and accelerates across the garage forecourt. As he does so, a regular customer, Sam Bradley, pulling in to the station, is forced to swerve to avoid a collision. Stroman brakes sharply, turns around, eyeballs Bradley and then, incongruously, waves a thank you. He pulls out into the traffic and heads south, towards Interstate 30.

What thoughts are going through Stroman's mind at this point? Elation? Probably. Exhilaration? Certainly.

'Ye-es!' he says. 'God bless America!'

The Shell station is now silent apart from the attendant's radio, which is broadcasting an interminable weather forecast. The attendant is going into shock. Worse, he is bleeding into his own chest cavity; his left lung is filling up with blood. Although nothing can be seen on the CCTV tape, we can hear him rasping, struggling for breath. Occasionally, there is a scuffling sound behind the counter. What's he doing back there?

It seems reasonable to assume the attendant is not aware of – is certainly no longer listening to – the weather forecast. Crime-scene photographs of the station's checkout area, in no particular order, reveal a state of unimaginable carnage. There is blood, of course, seeping through the rubber matting. There is the .22 on the floor, its magazine partially ejected – presumably a result of the fall. On the counter there is the cash register, its drawer still tightly shut; beside it, a carton of Texas Lotto tickets. Then, back on the floor, there is the telephone, off the hook. It is clear from the state of the phone that the attendant has tried to place a call.

We can make a fair guess as to the destination of that call. Some of the numeric keys have blood on them. There's a distinct fingerprint on the number 1, a bloody smear to the bottom right of the keypad, below the 9. The attendant has dialled 9-1-1.

Polunsky Unit Death Row Inmate #999409's correspondence is plastered with US flags. Occasionally, it comes on stars-and-stripes writing paper. Elaborately courteous, the letters are couched in biblical imagery, topped and tailed with little prayers. *Guardian Angel, Beacon of Hope,* runs one, *Empower me to endure and cope.* Sometimes there are attachments: *True Americans, American Me,* ruminations on patriotism. Other times, press cuttings and photographs: himself, his children, a wedding. Occasionally, however, there are little indiscretions, slips, that hint at something less polished.

'If you are not happy with the way our country and beliefs are,' #999409 writes in February 2008, 'then you should pack up and get the hell out.' Later, he continues: 'My uncles and forefathers shouldn't have had to die in vain so that you can leave the country you were born in to come here and disrespect ours and make us bend to your will.' Four months after this, an aside on my plans to visit Iraq: 'Why the hell would you want to go to sand land and interview them ragheads is beyond me.'

On the face of it, this is a simple story. On 4 October 2001, Mark

Stroman, a convicted felon, killed Vasudev Patel, a gas-station propri-etor. The full ramifications of the Patel/Stroman incident have yet to be played out, but when they are two wives will be widowed, six chil-dren orphaned. It's a tragedy, certainly, but hardly a complicated one. Like so much of what follows, however, the truth is harder to pin down.

Is Stroman a patriot or a racist? 'Evil' or misguided? Was his crime very American or very un-American?

'I did what every other American wanted to do,' he told KDFW-TV shortly after his arrest, 'but didn't have the nerve.'

Is that true?

'I'm very, very sorry.' How about that? Scratching the surface of this story reveals a seething mass of contradictions, an orgy of serpents – and all draped in the American flag.

Many, including Stroman himself, would later argue that Patel's death was the result of events that took place in Washington and New York on 11 September 2001. To an extent, they were right. But there was more to it than that. All of the elements necessary for the murder, bar one, were in place well before 9/11. The roots of Vasudev Patel's murder, and the various tragedies that would follow it, lay further back in time.

From the moment he was born on 13 October 1969, it was clear that Mark Anthony Baker's mother was ill prepared for parenthood. Sandra Baker was a high-school dropout; the pregnancy had been unplanned. She was just fifteen years old. Things never improved. When Mark was a toddler, she ran away from home. A year later, a call from the local hospital alerted the family to the fact that she had been found, preg-nant with twins, inebriated in a gutter. That her husband Doyle Baker was not the twins' father (they were later given up for adoption) was no great surprise: he wasn't Mark's father, either. Nor was he the father of Mark's two half-sisters. What he was, was a bully.

Doyle Baker maintained a not-so-secret predilection for beating Mark, slapping him around the head and, on occasion, hitting him in the face with a cowboy boot. He frequently berated the boy for his misdeeds, both real and perceived. If Mark got into a fight at school and lost, Doyle would beat him up as a punishment. When Mark was naughty, he was locked in his bedroom for days at a time. Even outside his room, he was not allowed to use the furniture in the house in case it got dirty. Sandra's sister Sue would later testify that Mark's parents lived 'in their own world' to the extent that 'nothing is important to them except them'.

Then there was the alcohol. Sandra and Doyle drank heavily, often as a precursor to fighting. One Christmas Day Mark's grandfather Robert came for dinner to find no sign of the children. Doyle informed him they had been locked in their rooms for the day and would eat their dinner there.

Mark's grandfather 'came unglued'. 'I'm sorry, Doyle,' Robert told him, 'but it's Christmas. You are not going to do this to these children.'

But the Bakers *were* going to do this to these children. Sandra repeatedly told Mark that he was worthless and she wished she had got a dog rather than had a child. On one occasion, she sat him down and informed him that she had been $50 away from having an abortion while pregnant with him. She should, she told the thirteen-year-old, have borrowed the money.

Unsurprisingly, Mark followed his mother's example and took to running away from home. After climbing out of his bedroom window, he cycled to the house of the only relative he felt actually cared for him: his grandfather. The journey took thirty minutes by car, but far longer by bicycle. Mark was eight when he first made it. Other forms of escape followed. In 1980, aged eleven, he was excluded from school. He got into drugs, smoking marijuana from the age of eleven or twelve, messing with harder drugs shortly after.

He cut classes repeatedly and was made to resit grades so many times that, when he reached the eighth grade, he was four years older than his classmates. By now he was uncontrollable, a hazard to those around him. Teachers characterized him as 'acting out'. There was nothing he would not do to attract attention. The more appalling the behaviour, the more of it he received. He provoked strangers into fights, had a swastika tattooed on his chest, and told friends that Hitler had had the right idea. Here, it seemed, was a young man with a unique talent for breaking things.

When Mark was sixteen, he again emulated his mother's example, dropping out of school and becoming a parent himself. On his wedding day, Sandra refused to sign the marriage certificate, revealing for the first time that his real father was not Doyle Baker but Eddie Stroman, a friend of his grandfather's.

In 1990, Mark (now Stroman) was finally convicted of theft and sent to jail for two years. By the time he emerged, his wife had left him, his grandfather had died, he had a criminal record, no job and an eighth-grade education.

Stroman's attorneys wouldn't bother denying in court that their client was a racist. Evidence to the contrary – presented with some glee by his prosecutors – was overwhelming. There were the *Southern Nazi* T-shirt transfers, and the '*If I Had Known This, I WOULD HAVE PICKED MY OWN COTTON*' sticker on the back of his Thunderbird. There were the unprocessed 35 mm negatives from the glove compartment (preschool children saluting a Nazi flag) and the photographs of Stroman and a friend, one pretending to choke a black man, the other holding an AK-47 to his head. Jesus, the guy had a swastika tattooed on his chest!

From the look of it, racism was something Stroman appeared to have spent the best part of his life advertising. At one point, even his own lawyer described him as a 'racist dog'.

The attorneys probably made the right call, figures Kevin 'Bear' Hartline, Stroman's best friend. Stroman, he tells me when we meet in Dallas in June 2008, is a '100 per cent hardcore racist'. Virtually all of his friends agree.

'Yeah, he was pretty much prejudiced. He didn't like niggers,' says one. 'But, I mean, who *does*?'

Through the bulletproof glass of the Polunsky Unit's death-row visiting centre, Stroman himself is expansive on the subject, his views pretty much in tune with the common-sense rhetoric of right-wing nationalists the world over.

There are the assumptions that, somehow, racial minorities are not 'proper' Americans; that non-Caucasians are flooding into the country and outnumber Caucasians, or soon will; that 'the' immigrants are 'taking advantage' of American charity. Behind these beliefs, unmentioned, lurks the heady notion of racial purity, coupled with a fear of contamination not a million miles removed from the domain of the closet eugenicist.

Perhaps naively, I tell Stroman I find it ironic to hear these views in the United States, a land of immigrants established with the sole purpose of eliminating intolerance. Wasn't it, after all, American tolerance that allowed him to emblazon his own curious brand of nihilism on his T-shirts (*Fuck you, you fucking fuck* was one presented at his trial)? Wasn't it American tolerance that allowed him to demonstrate his own intolerance – in the form of the black doll hanging by its neck from the rear-view mirror of his Thunderbird? The tolerance only seems to work in one direction.

Pushed on the subject, Stroman agrees that, if there had been no Italians in America, there would be no pizza; if there were no Mexicans, there would be no tacos; and that without the Germans there would be no hamburgers. 'And without the Chinese . . . ?' I venture.

Stroman shakes his head. 'I don't like Chinese food,' he says.

If Stroman's attitudes towards blacks were harsh, they were considerably more lenient than his feelings towards other ethnic minorities. At least blacks were American. The bottom of the food chain was reserved for those who weren't. The only thing worse than a nigger was a *sand nigger*.

This attitude is common among his friends, a number of whom tell tales of purported injustices regarding recent immigrants. The Asians come over here, they say, and receive government grants for cars, apartments and businesses. They buy up all the convenience stores and gas stations and motels. They drive Americans out of business. Then they invite their relatives over and multiply like rabbits – or, more appropriately if you hold this world view, viruses.

Initially, these opinions are expressed in a jokey fashion.

'You just want them to speak clear English when you're asking for a pack of cigarettes!' explains one of Stroman's friends. 'Repeat yourself fifty times and they still don't understand! Everybody thinks that way: come over here and speak *English*!'

Attitude is another bugbear.

'These people,' says Ronnie 'Shy' Galloway, 'they come from other countries, and they come here – especially the sand niggers – they don't know how to treat people. They talk to you real bad.' Shy shakes his head. 'I done come across people in Texas: Taliban, whatever you wanna call it. Same way! They don't know how to treat people. So I have a problem with 'em myself.'

It's a surprising admission, coming from a black man like Shy.

Traditionally, America's most recent immigrants are supposed to disappear into the community and pay their dues for a generation or two, or at least until they've learned to speak the language properly. Asians, however, tend not to play by these rules. They invest; they work; they buy up corner stores and gas stations where they are highly visible. Most of all, they succeed. They jump the queue. How do these guys make so much money so fast? They must have some unfair advantage, some kind of winning lottery ticket.

'They let too many people in here,' complains Shy. 'Give 'em loans, build 'em houses. Man! I been here all my life! I got to save my money, get it myself! That's the problem with the United States!'

For Shy and his friends, the issue is not simply that immigrants are successful, it's that their very presence constitutes a dilution, a corrosion of the values that make the United States a great nation: a strike at the heart of America itself.

'Look at the hotels!' explains another former employer. 'All the hotels, the motels, the convenience stores. They own them! From India, whatever!'

Through the glass at Polunsky, Stroman agrees. 'What is there left,' he asks, 'that's actually *American?*'

Perhaps it's a question of how you define 'American'. In February 1982, while Stroman was busy getting into drugs and dropping out of school, a young Indian man flew to Texas looking for work. Vasudev Patel wasn't some economic migrant looking for a free ride. He had a good degree, a bachelors in accounting from the University of Gujarat. In India, where 13,999 out of every 14,000 fail to attend higher education, this put him in the top fraction of the top 1 per cent of the population.

Despite the fact that there were no grants available for new arrivals, he immediately found himself an apartment, lodging with friends in Dallas, and a job as a janitor. The salary, $2 an hour, was meagre, but it was a start. He took the job, pocketed the cash and set about looking for something better. It wasn't long before he found it. On the basis of his degree, Patel was offered a job on the night audit desk at the Hyatt Regency Hotel.

He didn't give up his day job, though. By day he cleaned, by night he kept the hotel books. Soon he swapped the cleaning job for a better one at the Dallas Zoo, where he worked as a cashier. Things were on the up. Eighteen months after his arrival, when he was confident he could prosper in America, he flew home to find a wife.

For most Indian girls, the fact that Patel had a university degree, that he was earning good money and that he was on his way to becoming an American citizen would have made him extremely eligible. Alka, however, was not like most Indian girls. She wasn't interested in America. She wasn't interested in the marriage lottery.

'I didn't want money,' she says. 'I didn't want a handsome man: if they're handsome to look at but not handsome inside, then you have a problem.'

The meeting, arranged by Alka and Vasudev's parents in the summer of 1983, lasted just half an hour. The pair briefly discussed their likes and dislikes and agreed to the match. Patel, it seems, ticked the right boxes. The couple married later that year, and, when Vasudev finally got his green card in 1985, Alka flew over to Texas to join him.

The early days were tough. There was no money. There was no car. If the Patels wanted to go somewhere, they walked or took the bus. On top of the cash shortage was Vasudev's workload: two separate commutes to two separate jobs, eighteen hours a day, seven days a week. Then home to help with the kids.

As if Vasudev didn't have enough on his plate, in 1992 he decided it was time to stop balancing other people's books and start balancing his own.

The couple investigated potential concerns, before eventually settling on a rundown gas station at the junction of John West and Big Town Boulevard in Mesquite, an eastern suburb of Dallas. The Patels pooled all their cash, borrowed from relatives, stretched their credit cards to the limit and bought the business. They then set about transforming it.

When they bought the station in 1992, it was failing. There were no regular customers. This, Alka knew, was a serious problem: in America, she reasoned, people are always in a hurry. If there is a queue, they go somewhere else. But loyal customers will wait: if you treat them well, they will come back. Who knows? They might even help you out one day.

The station was spruced up and repainted and the Patels installed a convenience store. They cultivated customers, so that by 2001 there was a steady stream of regulars. Vasudev Patel, a man who had arrived in America with no cash, no references, no wife and no job, was saving enough money to ensure that his children would be able to study medicine at some of the country's top universities.

Patel came to the United States seeking the American Dream. It took him twenty years, but he found it. Then, at 6.45 a.m. on 4 October 2001, Mark Stroman walked in.

Although his defence attorneys would never manage to garner much support for it from the jury, there was a different side to Stroman. He was intelligent, had a quick wit and considerable charm. His grandfather Robert had also managed to instil in him a cast-iron work ethic. Tom Boston experienced this first hand. Boston, who had a policy of employing former convicts at his auto body shop on Garland Road in Mesquite, hired Stroman in 1992 when he was released from prison. He instructed him to wear a long-sleeved shirt to cover his tattoos and smartened him up.

'You got a second chance,' Boston told the young parolee. 'Don't screw it up.'

The results were extraordinary. 'Bear' Hartline recalls a visit from the newly made-over Mark shortly after he landed the job. He didn't recognize his oldest friend. Convinced the guy in the suit at the door was an FBI agent, Hartline assumed the Feds were out to arrest him, hid in the back of the house and refused to come out.

'Mark just took the ball and ran with it,' says Boston. 'He surprised even me: became boss manager at the shop. Dealt with the employees. Put money in the bank for payroll.'

Stroman kept the customers happy and made sure deadlines were met. Above all, he *worked*.

'In twenty-two years in the business,' recalls Boston, 'he was probably one of the best. Just because of his ambition. His drive.'

Simultaneously, Stroman's personal life took a turn for the better. A new girlfriend, Shawna, and a baby daughter, Cassandra, appeared.

'One thing I can say,' says Shy Galloway, 'he was *crazy* about that girl. She looked just like him. That man loved his daughter.'

For Stroman, however, old habits died hard. The body-shop industry tended to attract undesirables: bikers, tattoo nuts, speed freaks. He had a new audience. Worse, he now had enough money to be able to indulge his passion for illicit drugs. Since school, he had always enjoyed narcotics: most mornings he smoked a joint in the car on the way to work. But his special favourite was crystal methamphetamine. Meth was a versatile drug that could be eaten, snorted or smoked. Apparently, it was impossible to overdose on. Stroman took to dissolving it in water, heating it in a spoon and shooting it directly into the vein. He loved the rush crystal meth gave him, plus – a huge bonus – it helped him to work harder.

The drug gave him the edge at Tom Boston's shop. The work was done so fast because Stroman was on speed, and encouraging the other employees to take it, too. Each evening he would buy half an ounce and ask who wanted to work overtime, distributing it to volunteers. The next morning the work would be done, but they would be exhausted, necessitating another half an ounce so they could get through the day.

George Dodd, who later employed Stroman as a granite cutter, recalls him as 'addicted' to crystal meth. 'He'd get all wound up. He'd be happy at first. You could go two or three days like that. He'd go real, real strong. But then, when you're coming down, you know, it's gonna get ugly.'

'Ugly' was about right. Stroman figured that the trick to shooting crystal meth was not to let the drug wear off. The result was more shots, larger doses and 'tweaking': irrational behaviour, edginess and paranoia.

'Not good,' he recalls. 'You think you're doing everything normally, but you're not – and you're wondering why everyone is looking at you. Not good at all.'

He should know. Back in the 1980s he and his wife were in an argument on speed. Things got ugly. She ended up getting stabbed in the throat.

In the end, even Stroman, whose appetite for the drug was almost heroic, would have to stop. It took him four or five days of constant use, but eventually he'd get to the point where he couldn't go on, and would collapse and sleep for two or three days straight. The moment he woke up, he'd show up at work and start the process again. By the mid-1990s, he had lost nearly half his body weight.

The old school trait – acting out – lingered on, too. There was a lot of attention seeking, usually in the form of tall stories and racist outbursts. Stroman would show up for work with black eyes and pomegranate-coloured knuckles, boasting of glorious fights. He flew a confederate flag in the back of his car and drove around black neighbourhoods, looking for trouble. Asked at weekends what his plans were, he would reply that he was off to the housing projects in South Dallas, 'hunting niggers'. No one was ever really sure whether he was serious.

'There were two sides to Stroman,' recalls Boston. 'He cared about his daughter. I heard him out several times about how he cared so much about Shawna and his daughter. But then he kind of put on this persona to where he was always playing Billy Baddass. Always wanting attention. Very Nazi-like. I mean, very "I hate niggers, I hate this, I hate that." At heart he was very sensitive, but he wanted to be free and go play at the same time – and the two don't mix.'

Friends learned to take Stroman's tales with a pinch of salt. They thought he was playing the hard man to get a reaction. At the same time it was clear that he had an extremely short fuse. It wouldn't take much to push him over the edge.

Prior to the Patel shooting there were warnings. Stroman's came in the form of a repetitive bad trip that started in 1999. There was a large room, with friends on one side and strangers on the other. Television screens in the ceiling were broadcasting events from his life. Everyone was looking at him; he could sense the hostility. There was a palpable sense of doom, an unbearable certainty that something was about to go very wrong. But he could never work out what it was.

He would start to struggle, to get himself out of this unfriendly place, but the more he tried to escape, the more he was drawn back in. Every now and again he would emerge for a brief taste of reality – see Bear, grab a few breaths – and then, as if he were trapped in a revolving door, he would start to swing back again. He became frantic to get out, but there was no escape.

Stroman didn't realize at the time that the trip was a premonition. All he knew was that it was so unpleasant, left him so anxious, that after he'd had it a few times he stopped taking LSD. He gave up the drug, just like that. It was a shame, really. He'd always enjoyed acid before. But it was no big deal: the moment he stopped taking LSD, the paranoia seemed to evaporate. Shortly afterwards, however, the crystal meth began taking its toll and his life entered a downward spiral.

For Stroman, 2001 started catastrophically. On 23 January, the 303rd District Court of Dallas County ruled that his child-support payments were in arrears. If he failed to pay them, the Attorney-General's office threatened to suspend all of his state licences. A court order was issued instructing employers to withhold disposable income. The total sum due was $39,359.40.

That was $39,359.40 that Stroman didn't have.

Hell, he didn't even have the $68 court fee.

Things were not going well at home, either. Unimpressed by his drug use, Shawna left him, taking with her his beloved daughter, Cassandra. Despondent, he hooked up with Sherry, a bartender at a biker bar, the Texas Trap. The relationship was tempestuous: from the start they were unable to decide where to live. He had his own place, but she wanted him to move in with her. The moment he did, they split up. He found another place, a house belonging to a friend called 'Smo' Smolensky, who was out of town. At that point, Sherry decided she wanted to move in with him.

Smo allowed Stroman to live in his house on the condition that he covered the rent. For some reason, this didn't happen. When the bank decided to foreclose on Smo for non-payment, he hightailed it back to Dallas. Since Smo was one of the leaders of the Scorpions biker gang, this was a serious problem. Stroman fled, abandoning his possessions. Never one to back down from a fight, however, he baited the Scorpions, driving his car up against the front of their club to block the main exit and lobbing a homemade bomb through the door. The biker gang threatened to blow him up in retaliation. He took to sleeping in his car.

By the summer of 2001, all of Stroman's friends had noticed he was in a bad place.

'That was just a bad time for Mark,' recalls Boston. 'He was doing a lot of drugs at the time. I didn't really know where he was staying. I knew that he was kind of down and out . . . I'd seen the guy cry several times, and he wasn't that kind of guy. I saw him just depressed. I felt really bad for him.'

'He became real distant, and just – he was trying to put up a good front that he was happy and normal,' says Bear. 'I could tell, and he mentioned it about the child support and all that shit, but he never let it come across that it bothered him as much as it really did.' After one visit, Bear told his wife Sheila that something appeared to be very wrong with his friend.

'He was reaching out, I guess, wanting to talk about it,' says Sheila, looking back.

Stroman told another friend, Bob Templeton, about his problems with the Scorpions. He also mentioned that he was having difficulties meeting his child-support payments, but didn't reveal that he was

$40,000 in debt. Nevertheless, when Bob's mother heard that he was in trouble, she offered to help.

'See if he needs a place to stay,' Carolyn Templeton told her son.

'Really?' said Stroman when Bob passed on the offer. 'You don't mind?'

Carolyn didn't mind: Mark was unfailingly polite and helpful when he visited. He got on well with her husband, Billy. Most importantly her Great Dane, Sara, had taken a liking to him. This in itself was unusual: 'She was very picky and choosy. And dogs don't lie.'

Even secure in a new house, things failed to improve. On 14 July 2001, Stroman was picked up in the Texas Trap when a policeman responded to a report that there was a bald man carrying a concealed firearm inside. The .45 automatic shoved down the back of his belt was illegal; moreover, as a convicted felon, he was not allowed to carry a firearm at all. This was big trouble. He was arrested and charged. After two days in jail, the Templetons came up with the $1,000 bond needed to release him, and he was freed.

That was another $1,000 he owed.

The bad luck fell like rain. At the end of August, Stroman took a job refitting a kitchen in Garland. While fetching the granite worktop for the bar, he left his car in the wrong place and received a parking ticket. When he lifted the granite worktop – worth $3,000 – to fit it, it broke in half. The next day, fetching a replacement piece, he was awarded another ticket in the same place. At lunchtime, when he popped home for a break, he found Sherry in bed with one of the Scorpions.

Stroman's friends were now aware that something was seriously wrong. The signs were unmistakable. Richard Wood, his employer, bumped into him outside the granite shop, trying to change the oil filter in his truck. The cap was stuck, and when Stroman tried to prise it off with a screwdriver he punctured it and the oil flooded out. He started shouting and screaming, then pulled a shotgun from the trunk of the truck and shot both barrels simultaneously into the air. Because the shotgun had been sawn off, and because the stock had been cut down to make it into a pistol, he sprained his wrist.

'That month, two months!' says Boston. 'It just kept coming and coming and coming. He was about ready to pop.'

In August 2001, Shy Galloway was at Garcia's Garage on Garland when Stroman asked him if he'd like a little work. The job was lucrative, but illegal: he was planning on robbing a gas station. Stroman would drive past the store to make sure there was no CCTV, then the pair would go in together. It was, he said, an 'easy take'. And there were no real victims: the owner of the station was a sand nigger. Shy wasn't impressed.

'That's not my style,' he told his friend. 'I don't need that.'

But Stroman, $40,000 in debt, did need it. Badly.

Not long afterwards, Shy was on the corner of Garland Road and Northwest Highway when his friend pulled over and honked his horn. When he leant in to the car, Stroman told him he should have accepted the offer: he'd taken $20,000, 'living off the land'. He showed Shy a hockey goalkeeper's mask, a note demanding money and a set of false licence plates. He also showed him a large gun, a chrome-plated Smith and Wesson .44 Magnum.

Shy was wary. 'Be careful, man,' he told his friend.

Once again, the Stroman bravado kicked in.

'He said, "Shy, when you read about me, I'm gonna go down BIG! I'm gonna make headlines!"' recalls Galloway. 'I thought he was shooting the shit, you know? But I knew he was robbing. I knew he was robbing.'

Stroman should have known better. Shy Galloway was famous for his loose tongue. Sure enough, the next time he visited Tom Boston's shop, he couldn't resist sharing his exclusive news.

'I saw Mark,' he told his employer. 'He was in his car.' The story tumbled out: Stroman was robbing Ay-rabs. He had a mask. A note. A big gun. If Shy expected Boston to react, he was disappointed.

'I completely brushed it off. Just never thought twice about it,' he recalls. 'Knowing all these cockamamie stories, the story just went in one ear and out the other.'

But it was such a strange story that, while Boston brushed it away, he didn't forget it.

Money problems, drug problems, girlfriend problems, biker-gang problems, crime, guns and a tattletale: for Stroman, the ingredients necessary for a serious outburst were now in place. All that was missing was a trigger.

Alka Patel was at home when the telephone rang. Vasudev was at the station as usual, the radio playing in the background.

'Something's happened,' he told her. 'Turn on the TV.'

She did as she was told, but only briefly: after five minutes she began to feel sick and turned it off. The first thing Vasudev did when he got home that evening was turn the television back on. He couldn't watch for long, either.

'This is so sad,' he told Alka. 'Why would anyone do this?'

The greatest tragedy of all was that this was likely to be just the start.

'Whatever revenge they have with each other,' he said, 'they're just going to kill innocent people.'

Stroman was also at work when he heard the news. He downed tools, jumped into his Thunderbird and raced home to find Bob and Billy Templeton sitting in the den.

'Have you SEEN this?' he asked as he burst through the door.

Bob said nothing, just pointed at the TV. Billy, a former policeman, had some experience of this sort of thing.

'That's no accident,' he mused. 'Those are *terrorists*.'

At that moment the World Trade Center's South Tower collapsed.

To Stroman, the true horror of 9/11 lay not in the planes' impact, or even the razing of the buildings: it was watching the jumpers. Death itself didn't frighten him – it was the *process* of death, the suffering that preceded it.

'Those people who fell from the towers, they suffered,' he would later explain to a reporter from KDFW-TV. 'Those people who tried to take back that plane over Pennsylvania, they *suffered.*'

Perhaps it was the thought of this suffering that kept him glued to the screen all day. He didn't return to work. He sat and watched TV. All the stations were the same: first came the real-time footage, then the replays, then back to the live feeds.

Rummaging frantically for appropriate precedents, newscasters dredged up the same metaphor again and again: Pearl Harbor.

There were similarities. An airborne operation, a sneak attack, many dead. At the same time, however, the attack was strangely redolent of the Cold War: sleeper cells in the United States, a faceless enemy, the President airborne, the Vice-President in a bunker. Even the term applied to the wreckage was pilfered from the Cold War period: 'Ground Zero', the core of a nuclear detonation. The attack was unprecedented, catastrophic. Nothing would ever be the same again. Not for Mark Stroman, anyway.

Shortly after his arrest, in an attempt to explain his actions, Stroman circulated a handwritten manifesto to the Press. Titled 'TRUE AMERICAN', it gave an insight into his thinking at the time, regarding what was to become the key point of his legal defence: that he was a patriot, acting in self-defence during wartime. In the document he pulled out all the stops, describing the United States as 'The land of the free, home of the brave, the land of the Pilgrims [sic] Pride, land for which my forefathers died.' America was 'the land of milk and honey', 'this great country', 'our country, my country'.

Stroman was not alone in his predilection for saccharine, patriotic imagery. As the dust cloud settled over lower Manhattan, public figures called for 'moral clarity', then outdid each other in the search for increasingly eloquent ways to explain what had happened. Like the Press, the most apposite image the politicians could come up with was Pearl Harbor. Second World War metaphors proved strangely reassuring: back then, things were simpler. We knew who we were, and who our enemies were. Back then, the war was clearly someone else's fault. We could fight the enemy abroad, then go home. Back then, we *won*.

Commentators struggled to portray the magnitude of the attacks' significance. 9/11 was not a mere historical event, it was 'the day the world changed'. New York became 'our city', Rudolph Giuliani 'America's mayor'. 'History began today,' proclaimed the newspapers. Biblical imagery was rolled out in force, as if it might vaccinate against the sense of insecurity that had gripped the nation. Casualties of the attack did not die tragically or pointlessly, rather 'made the ultimate sacrifice' in the name of freedom. Firemen were heroes. Policemen were heroes. Victims were heroes. Everyone was a hero.

This flood of patriotic imagery opened the way for escalation. 9/11 wasn't about short-sighted foreign policy, globalization or aggrieved Arabs. It was about *evil*.

'This will be a monumental struggle of good versus evil,' explained President George W. Bush on 12 September 2001. 'But good will prevail.'

A week later, he elaborated.

'The advance of human freedom, the great achievement of our time and the hope of every time now depends on us,' he told Congress. 'We have found our mission.'

The battle lines were drawn: freedom and fear were at war. This oversimplification – heroes and villains, good and evil – led unerringly to a false dichotomy.

'Every nation in every region now has a decision to make,' warned the President. 'Either you are with us, or you are with the terrorists.'

Like a poker player who has just lost big to a complete novice, the United States raised the stakes and bet the house. History had called.

Civilization was at risk. With stakes this high, what else could we do but declare war?

The result was a patriotic bonanza. On 11 September 2001, Walmart's sales of US flags leapt 2,000 per cent. The next day the figure was up to 4,000 per cent. By early October, 80 per cent of Americans were flying the flag at home. Stroman certainly was: he went out and bought a new flag to fly from the back of his truck.

A Presidential Prayer Team, launched in late September, boasted that by mid-December more than a million Americans were praying daily for their Commander-in-Chief.

With the country at war, it now became impossible to question government policy without being labelled unpatriotic. Those who pointed out that the White House's rhetoric was edging uncomfortably close to that of the Islamists who had perpetrated the attacks were shouted down. At one point, Tom Daschle, the Senate Majority Leader, asked for clarification regarding the goals of the War on Terror.

'How dare Senator Daschle criticize President Bush while we are fighting our War on Terror!' exclaimed Trent Lott, the Senate Minority Leader. 'He should not be trying to divide our country while we are united!'

Daschle's impudence was branded as 'disgusting' and 'giving aid and comfort to the enemy'. He had, apparently, 'chosen to align himself with the Axis of Evil'.

Predictably, talk of retaliation was common. 'REVENGE,' crowed an editorial in the *Philadelphia Daily News*. 'Hold on to that thought. Go to bed thinking it. Wake up chanting it. Because nothing less than revenge is called for today.'

Others were even more explicit. Columnist Ann Coulter delivered her verdict on 9/11 and what should be done about it in the *National Review*:

This is no time to be precious about locating the exact individuals directly involved in this particular terrorist attack . . . We should invade their countries, kill their leaders and convert them to Christianity.

Coulter later apologized for this rant, but followed it up with an acidic riposte to those who claimed that Americans might do well to consider the reasons they had been targeted on 9/11.

'They hate us?' she asked incredulously. 'We hate them! America does not want to make Islamic fanatics love us. We want to make them die.'

The solution to the al-Qaeda problem was simple: the application of overwhelming firepower.

'I say bomb the hell out of them,' concluded Democrat Senator Zell Miller the day after 9/11. 'If there's collateral damage, so be it. They certainly found our civilians to be expendable.'

Alongside the increase in rhetoric and flag-flying came more sinister forms of patriotism. On 12 September – the same day President Bush announced the 'monumental struggle of good versus evil' – Chicago's largest predominantly Arab mosque was surrounded by an angry white mob chanting 'Kill the Arabs!'

Police advised Muslim schools to close for a week, and worshippers not to attend Friday prayers for their own safety. The impulse behind such protests was stated most bluntly in the graffiti (presumably scrawled by a member of the Boston Fire Department) at the World Trade Center site:

Kill all Muslims
9-11-01
BFD

At first people began spitting at foreign-looking individuals and pulling the veils from Muslim women in the street. Then things got worse. In Indianapolis, an Afghan man was set on fire. In New Jersey, a Pakistani was beaten unconscious. In Phoenix, vigilantes threw home-made bombs into the backyard of an Iraqi family. Salt Lake City's Curry in a Hurry restaurant was burned to the ground.

Ironically, those most often in the firing line were Sikhs, not Muslims: they wore turbans, like Osama bin Laden. Opinion polls at the time indicated that the hostile mood was far more widespread than was ever admitted. Popular surveys held at the end of 2001 showed majority support for the assertion that Arabs in the United States should be forced to carry special identity cards, even if they were US citizens. One poll asked whether all individuals of Middle Eastern appearance should be required to wear some form of visible identification indicating that they had been vetted by US authorities; half of those who responded agreed.

Like most Americans, Stroman had not heard of al-Qaeda before September 2001. Even when he did, he wasn't especially curious as to why the United States had been targeted. In his mind the organization was filed under the blanket term 'Ay-rabs'. This in turn was a subsection of another heading in his cognitive Rolodex: 'Foreigners'. It was not a term of endearment. 9/11 confirmed all of Stroman's worst suspicions. Not only were the sand niggers among us, not only were they taking advantage, but they were a *threat*. No doubt right at that moment there were cohorts of Ay-rabs around the United States booking themselves into out-of-the-way flying schools, learning how to pilot – but not to land – international jet airliners. Sitting and waiting for another strike was no longer an option. Now was not the time to err on the side of caution.

Immediately after the attacks, Stroman started telling friends what he was going to do about al-Qaeda. Shy Galloway recalls a conversation in which he announced his intentions.

'He's gonna take care of all these Taliban, all these sand niggers. He said, "I'm gonna rob 'em, do whatever it takes."' Galloway thought this was pretty much par for the course: more Stroman tall tales. 'I think he's shooting the shit, you know? He said he was going around every convenience store . . . "Wherever there's a sand nigger, I'm gonna take 'em down."'

Sometimes the tales drifted into the past tense. George Dodd, who employed Stroman at the time, remembers him alternating tales of what he planned to do with accounts of retaliatory derring-do that had apparently already taken place: 'We were all talking about how we thought it was crap, you know, what happened, 9/11, and he said that he'd shot at some place or something. Front of a church or something like that.' Like Galloway, Dodd put it down to bravado. 'I never heard about it in the news. I just said, "You're full of shit."'

But Stroman wasn't full of shit. And he was about to prove it.

Vasudev and Alka Patel were on the forecourt of the Shell station one evening at the start of October when they received their warning. A friend, Ranjid, showed up, having driven all the way from Arlington.

'There's a man going around Dallas after 9/11,' he said. 'And he's killing people.' But he wasn't just killing *people*. He was killing Asians.

Vasudev didn't believe it. It sounded highly unlikely: who would want to kill gas-station attendants? What did they have to do with 9/11? The Patels were from India! India had no connection to al-Qaeda. And he was a Hindu, not a Muslim. There was no reason why he should be targeted. Besides, the Patels had been in the neighbourhood for more than ten years; all of their customers knew them. They were regulars, friends. Beneath the 9/11 Remembrance Flag fluttering over his garage forecourt, Vasudev was adamant.

'Nothing's going to happen,' he assured his friend.

Ranjid nodded. 'Just be careful.'

But Vasudev was always careful. That was why he kept a .22 semi-automatic under the cash register.

*   *   *

Stroman probably would have laughed had he known of the existence of Vasudev's .22. Since childhood, he had maintained a strict meritocracy when it came to firearms, at the top of which lay 'more' and 'more powerful'. For this reason, when he moved in with the Templeton family in the summer of 2001, he was in his element. Bob Templeton was a gun collector; his father Billy, a licensed dealer. The house was crammed full of arms: for Stroman, moving in was like winning the lottery. Aside from the enjoyment he derived from handling the weapons, he was reassured by their presence.

'I can sit there and lay back on the couch and look at all them guns,' he told Bear Hartline when he moved in. 'I just feel so safe.'

He wasn't alone. In the days after 9/11, domestic sales of arms and ammunition in the United States rose by 10 per cent. National Rifle Association membership enquiries leapt more than 100 per cent. In the six months after the attacks, the FBI handled 130,000 more applications for the right to carry a concealed weapon and 455,000 more checks for gun purchases.

On the face of it, there was nothing wrong with this: the US Constitution guaranteed the right to bear arms as a means of self-defence. Post-9/11, however, Stroman's understanding of 'self-defence' shifted. If anyone thought that after 3,000 Americans were murdered so brutally he was going to hang around twiddling his thumbs until someone attacked *him*, they were sorely mistaken.

Again, he was in tune with many Americans. According to the US government's official line, it now became acceptable – necessary, even – to retaliate in advance of being attacked. Arabs in the United States were arrested. Phone lines and Internet hubs were tapped. American citizens were detained. This was war – with a difference.

'The best defence against terrorism,' explained Secretary of Defense Donald Rumsfeld on 16 September, 'is offence.'

History had restarted. The old rules were out of date. The gloves were coming off.

'The only path to safety is the path of action,' President Bush instructed cadets at West Point. 'Our security . . . will require all Americans to be ready for pre-emptive action.'

Stroman missed the speech on TV, but it didn't matter. He was already on board.

Every day since purchasing the Shell station in 1992, the Patels had followed a routine. Vasudev would start work at 5.30 a.m., cleaning up the station, turning on the radio and opening for business. At 6.30, he would ring Alka, so she could prepare breakfast for the children and take them to school.

Alka was already up when Vasudev called on 4 October 2001. A good thing, too: his brother and his kids were staying, so, in addition to dropping off her two children at school, she had his children to deal with. Three different school-runs. She had just completed the first and returned home to collect the next child when the owner of the gas station across the street telephoned. Something was going on, he told her. It looked like there had been a robbery.

'Is my husband OK?' asked Alka.

'He's fine. But you need to come over.'

Alka arrived at the station to find the forecourt ringed with crime-scene tape. When police refused to allow her in, she became concerned.

'Where's my husband?' she asked an officer. 'Is he all right?'

He was fine, he replied, but had hurt his hand. He'd been taken to Mesquite Community Hospital. Not to worry, though: he'd walked into the ambulance and was talking at the time.

Acting on this advice, Alka headed home to drop the other kids off at school. She then drove to the community hospital to see about Vasudev's injured hand. Another police officer was waiting in the lobby.

'Are you Mrs Patel?' he asked. When she nodded, he directed her to the visiting room. A few moments later, a doctor ambled in, looked at Alka, then down at his clipboard.

'You already know your husband's dead, right?' he asked.

Alka was so shocked she didn't know how to respond.

'If I had known that,' she said, 'do you think I would even be able to come here?'

While Alka was struggling to accept the fact that Vasudev was gone, Stroman was cruising around town in his Thunderbird. He was becoming increasingly agitated. He was itching to tell someone what he'd just done, but it was still early and no one was around. What was the point of having a secret if you couldn't share it?

At 10.30, he pulled into Garcia's Garage at 11606 Garland, where he found the owner Jesse Garcia moving cars out of the shop for the day. Stroman was actually looking for Shy Galloway, but he hadn't arrived yet, so the pair shot the breeze. After a couple of minutes, he looked at his watch. He hadn't come to make idle conversation. He lit a cigarette and turned away.

'If you see Shy,' he said over his shoulder, 'tell him I came by looking for him.' Then, beside the car, he stopped. This was just too good an opportunity to waste. 'Hey,' he said, 'c'm 'ere.'

As Garcia approached the Thunderbird, Stroman opened the passenger door and lifted out a black bag full of weapons including an AK-47, a shotgun and a machine pistol.

'It's an Uzi,' he told Garcia.

The garage owner, a gun fan himself, was impressed, but concerned.

'Mark,' he warned, 'if they pull you over and find this stuff, they're going to take you to jail.'

Stroman shook his head. 'No,' he said. 'If they pull me over, they're not gonna take me alive. You're gonna see me on TV.'

Garcia passed this off as run-of-the-mill Stroman banter.

'That's what he'd always tell us, me and Ronnie,' he says, seven years later. '"You're gonna see me on TV one day. You're gonna hear about it in the news. I'm gonna be famous."'

Perhaps Stroman sensed that Garcia didn't believe him. Perhaps he couldn't resist it. It was time to spill the beans. He pulled out one more gun, a chrome-plated Smith & Wesson .44 with a long barrel, opened the cylinder and spun it.

'Guess what?' he said. 'I just shot me a sand nigger.'

When Tom Boston's ice maker took a dump at the end of September, some might have thought it was fate. Boston wasn't among them. He was just pissed. He bought a new one. Two days later, that took a dump, too. Now he was really pissed. Boston was heading home along Big Town Boulevard with a third ice maker in the back of his pickup when, approaching the junction, he noticed the crime tape.

'Damn!' he said, to no one in particular. 'I wonder what happened there?'

He pulled over and approached a news reporter, who told him that someone had been shot.

'Who?' asked Boston. The journalist didn't know, but told him it was a young man, and that he was dead. Boston went home, unloaded the ice maker, then headed back along Big Town Boulevard to the body shop. On the way, he passed the Shell station again.

Boston was one of the clients Alka and Vasudev Patel had cultivated since taking over the Shell station in 1992. He was a regular. All those years ago Alka had figured that if you treated your customers well they would come back.

'Who knows,' she had told Vasudev, 'they might even do you a good turn one day.'

Stroman's former employer now had all the pieces of the puzzle.

'I'm on the way back to the shop and I'm thinking to myself – and about three miles further on I just say MARK.' Boston's eyes narrowed. 'Shy saw Mark with a gun . . . No! That's billions to one!' Boston told himself to forget about it, but he couldn't. 'I get to the shop and I tell my wife, "I have this strong feeling. I have no clue why, but I've just got a hunch."'

Boston called a friend at the District Attorney's office. 'Listen,' he said, 'there's a shooting that the FBI's investigating, and it's off a Shell station. I just passed there about an hour and a half ago.'

He then repeated the story Shy had told him a couple of days earlier: the gun, the mask, the cash demand. Refusing to divulge any names, he suggested that if the Shell station's CCTV footage showed a well-built guy with a shaved head and arms covered in tattoos they should call him back. Five minutes later the phone rang. He was summoned to the police station, where the tape was played.

'Is this the guy?' an investigator asked. 'Are you sure?'

Boston didn't even need to watch. 'I can hear the voice,' he told him. 'I know it.'

'Tom,' said his friend, 'this isn't the only one. There's others.'

For legal reasons, I can't tell you about the others. I can't even tell you how many others there were. The murder of Waqar Hasan, shot in the face with a .380 automatic at Mom's Grocery at 10819 Elam Road, on 15 September; the partial blinding of Raisuddin Bhuiuian by a .410 shotgun shell from a Cobra double-barrelled pistol at the Buckner Food Mart on 21 September.

I also can't tell you about the midnight drives, the attempts to shunt cars driven by Arabs – or people who looked like Arabs – off the road. And I can't tell you about a plot to fill a silver Ford Thunderbird with arms, drive it to Richardson Mosque on Abrams Road, and open fire on everyone in the building.

I *can* tell you that in each of these cases the victims – or planned victims – were Asian immigrants. And that in none of these crimes was any money stolen. After Waqar Hasan was shot at Mom's Grocery two thick wads of banknotes under the till were left untouched. And, although Raisuddin Bhuiuian offered the cash register's contents to his assailant, it was refused. Strange robberies, indeed.

I can also tell you how the story ends.

Stroman recognized the 212th Federal Court the moment he was led in. It was the room from his bad LSD trip. Above the front of the court were the TV screens, used to present evidence of the crime. To the left of the courtroom were his friends and family. To the right, relatives of the deceased.

The verdict was a foregone conclusion. Ballistics had matched the bullet to Stroman's gun; the shooting was captured on CCTV from two different angles. His attorneys had very little to offer: not only had he admitted his guilt to the police when he was arrested, but he had also demanded an interview with KDFW-TV and confessed to two further shootings on air.

'They drew first blood,' he told the TV crew. 'They attacked American soil first. I retaliated against the people that I thought retaliated against me.'

Stroman proved quick work for a Texas jury. The first stage of the trial lasted just a day and a half. On the morning of 2 April 2002, he was found guilty of murder.

In the second stage, the punishment phase, Stroman's attorneys had more to work with: his childhood, his parents, his history of drug abuse. It was still an uphill struggle. The jury needed a good reason to grant clemency, because the prosecution had an excellent reason why it should be denied. Stroman had done bad things. He was a bad man.

Evidence of his traumatic childhood didn't cut much ice in court. State prosecutors Greg Davis and Robert Dark discounted it as 'all that same stuff' ('when all else fails, blame your parents for not giving you enough love'). The defendant wasn't some sad, abused child, they assured the jury. Stroman was a 'predator', 'as violent as they come', a man who would 'just as soon kill you as take a breath'. His life was 'a roadmap that leads directly to the death house'. He was a 'cancer on society', 'one of the most dangerous individuals you'll ever see in your life'.

To back up these claims, the prosecutors presented evidence of repeated run-ins with the law, dating back to charges of aggravated robbery in 1981 – when Stroman was just twelve. There followed a roll-call of shame as his wrongdoings were described to the court. Car crimes in 1983; burglary the same year; possession of an offensive weapon in 1985; entering to rob in 1986. At one point he had even stabbed his own wife in the throat. The common link between these incidents? All took place before he was eighteen years old.

No, said Davis and Dark. Stroman might have been dealt a bad hand, but he didn't deserve any sympathy for it.

'He did exactly what he wanted to do,' stated Davis. 'And all along the line he had a choice.'

Stroman's 'patriot' argument was likewise declared worthless. According to the prosecutors, 11 September had offered him an opportunity to settle a few old scores. Sensing, correctly, that the mood in the United States had changed, he had deliberately stepped outside of the law, unilaterally establishing his own set of rules, the 'Stroman Rules', then acted on them. Among them was the fact that 9/11 had destroyed the presumption of innocence: all Asians were now to be presumed guilty and punished.

'He has the rules,' said Davis, 'which would allow him to become a self-appointed vigilante.'

This kind of behaviour, the prosecutor told the jury, wouldn't wash under anyone's description of the law. It was unacceptable and illegal. It was downright dangerous.

The defence tried every available angle, from foetal alcohol syndrome to outright patriotism. But they were unwilling to put all their eggs in one basket. No one argument, it seemed, was strong enough to justify the magnitude of the crime. Simply, the attorneys weren't sure what to argue, because they didn't truly understand why Stroman had shot Vasudev Patel. Beyond the wall of patriotic mumbo jumbo he was spouting to anyone who would listen, Stroman himself seemed not to know.

Two medical experts were called. Dr Judy Stonedale argued that Stroman was suffering from Acute Stress Disorder, brought on as a result of 9/11. This might be the reason he had been unable to recall his own motives clearly, or the sequence of events. It might also be the cause of his comment that when he shot Patel 'it was like someone else was doing it'.

Dr Mary Connell agreed. Stroman, she said, had been paranoid, suspicious, guarded and agitated – 'in extreme distress' – for months prior to 9/11. The attacks, appalling to any normal person, were much more so to someone in his vulnerable state. The eleventh of September was a perfect trigger.

In an aside, Connell was asked about bereavement. Her answer was revealing. 'In any grieving process,' she said, 'there's an initial reaction of shock. There's denial, where the person can hardly believe that this has happened . . . And then there's a tendency to be angry – and very, very angry.'

All of the ingredients for Stroman's crimes were present prior to 9/11. His propensity for guns, for over-reaction, his xenophobia, his hot-headedness, his insular world view and his parochial, inflexible sense of patriotism were already there. They just needed a catalyst to bring them out. Stroman was madder than hell.

The jury didn't care. On 4 April 2002, Stroman was sentenced to death. To the consternation of the court, he stood to attention, held up a US flag, saluted the judge and thanked him for the sentence before being led away.

2

For Those Who Come across the Seas

For those who've come across the seas
We've boundless plains to share;
With courage let us all combine
To advance Australia fair.

Australian national anthem

Karim al Saadi was woken by a surreptitious knock at his Jakarta guest-house door. Bleary-eyed, the Iraqi schoolteacher checked his watch – *1 a.m.* – and slipped open the lock. An agitated stranger was standing outside.

'Abu Badr sent me,' the man whispered. 'It's time.'

Saadi was used to this kind of clandestine summons. He and his wife Halima were seasoned nomads. Since fleeing their home in 1991, they had traversed a substantial part of Iraqi Kurdistan on foot, before bribing their way into Iran, where for nine years they had eked out a living selling T-shirts on street corners.

In June 2001, alerted to the fact they were due to be arrested, they had procured false travel documents and skipped the country, flying to Kuala Lumpur. They had successfully navigated the entire length of Malaysia without passports or visas, then secreted themselves into Indonesia, at night, by boat. Since July, they had been hiding out, avoiding the attention of the authorities, and waiting.

The couple dressed, shouldered their bags and followed the stranger outside. It was time. Abu Badr said so. After a decade of running, the Saadis' journey was finally coming to an end.

On the opposite side of Jakarta, a similar scenario was unfolding. Like the Saadis, Rashid Kahtany and his wife Soham had been living illegally in Iran before hot-footing it to Indonesia. Rashid, too, was an Iraqi schoolteacher. Unlike the Saadis, however, Rashid and Soham were travelling with children: their daughters, nine-year-old Tuka and eight-year-old Duha.

The Kahtanys had also entrusted themselves to Abu Badr's Indonesian network. Not that it was cheap: Badr had demanded $1,500 per adult (at that price, he laughed, children could travel for free). Kahtany, who didn't have the money, had offered a deal, handing over his entire life savings and promising to pay the outstanding $1,000 later.

Badr had agreed. He could afford to: business was good. This one operation would net him somewhere in the region of a quarter of a million dollars. Besides, he figured, there was no shortage of Iraqis willing to part with their cash.

Although the Kahtany and Saadi families had grown up just 120 miles apart, they had never met. In the early hours of 5 October 2001, however, their stories merged: strangers yet neighbours, brought together 5,000 miles from home, on a fishing boat.

The moment he arrived at the beach, Saadi had misgivings. The *Olong* was old and battered – and small: just twenty-five metres long. He asked a friend, an engineer, for his opinion.

'He looked at the engine, and he said it was good,' recalls Saadi. 'He said, "It's OK, the boat's not bad. But this is a lot of people. A lot."'

It *was* a lot of people. By the time everyone was on board, there wasn't enough room for them to sit, let alone lie down. Fewer than half the passengers, mostly women and children, fitted under the canopy. The rest were forced to stand or squat on the outer decks and roof.

'This is dangerous,' Soham Kahtany told her husband as they boarded. Concerned for the safety of her children, she asked other mothers what was going on, and was assured that this was only a ferry to the main trafficking boat, which was too big to come in to the shore. It was a pretty feeble explanation, but it was better than the alternative: that the *Olong* was a death trap. That didn't bear thinking about. Of the 223 refugees now on board, 74 were children. One boy, Mustafa, had been born when his mother was traversing Indonesia. He was just twenty-one days old.

The Iraqis had come a long way. They had spent all their money. They had no documents. They could not retrace their steps. Rashid Kahtany hunched down on the edge of the roofed area, pulled Tuka on to his lap and wrapped his arms around her. Inside, his wife did the same with Duha.

'We didn't have any experience.' He shrugs. 'We didn't know anything about boats.'

Boatbuilding was not the only subject of which the family could plead ignorance. None of them could swim.

Just before first light, the boat's three-man crew hoisted a tatty Indonesian flag and cast off. The helmsman brought the boat around and set a fixed course of 174 degrees. Almost due south. As the *Olong* ferried its precious cargo into the heart of the Indian Ocean, the sun began to rise and there was a brief moment of elation. Some of the refugees shook hands. They had almost made it. Next stop: Australia.

There was a certain irony in the departure date. The fifth of October was the very day that John Howard, Australia's Prime Minister, had chosen to call the 2001 federal election. Meteorologically, the signs were fair. Politically, however, the forecast was dreadful. The Iraqis were sailing into a storm they couldn't possibly have understood, let alone predicted.

Illicit traffic is an aspect of globalization that Western governments are unwilling to accept. We're supposed to be shipping *our* products, infor-mation and democracies to the Third World; they're not supposed to be sending theirs back over to us. But by the time the *Olong* set sail, that was exactly what was happening.

Globalization had rendered borders porous: all kinds of stuff was slipping across. This reverse traffic – 'globalization from below' – proved every bit as unstoppable as that from above. How were we supposed to monitor it? Police it? Conventional notions of borders, border protection and national security had come to seem outdated, even rather quaint.

Australia was not alone in facing the problem of asylum seekers. Everyone wanted to help refugees; what they didn't want was hordes of economic migrants showing up to claim asylum, then living off social security for the rest of their lives. In Australia in 2001, this was what seemed to be happening – just when there was an election coming. It made the Government look bad. And it wasn't a terribly popular government to start with. In fact, it was on its uppers.

At the start of 2001, Prime Minister John Howard's Liberal coalition had been trounced in a series of catastrophic state elections. By March the Liberals' main rival, Kim Beazley's Labor Party, was polling a full nine points ahead. Pundits predicted a landslide: Labor needed only a handful of new seats to win office. They were expected to gain sixty. The Liberals, hailed by press reports as 'simply unelectable' in 2000, were on the way out.

This mood prevailed inside the administration, too.

'Parliament House was a bit like a ship itself,' one senior Liberal insider told me in 2008. 'The rats were all leaving. Almost nobody believed that Howard was going to win that election.'

Even the Prime Minister was a doubter, later admitting that in April and May 2001 he was in 'the depths of political despair'.

Kim Beazley, meanwhile, was supremely confident, telling colleagues they were going to 'surf into office'. His enthusiasm was infectious.

'It looks as though we can't lose,' said his chief of staff. 'Unless there's a war.'

*   *   *

As the *Olong* passed out of sight of land, the refugees scanned the horizon, hoping for a glimpse of Australia. On board the mood was a delicate balance between trepidation and fear: they were nearly there, but this was the most dangerous part of the trip.

For Ali Alsaai from Najaf the balance swung early on, when his five-year-old daughter Banin was violently sick.

'She started vomiting,' he recalls. 'She needed water, but when we gave it to her she just threw up.' Banin then passed out. At that point her older sister, Hawraa, began to vomit, too. 'Diarrhoea and vomiting. The children just cried and cried. And there was no doctor on the boat. Then we got scared.'

When the sun set the situation deteriorated. During the day the air had been warm and the water calm, but after dark the temperature plummeted, the swell grew and the boat began to heave.

Rashid Kahtany shakes his head. 'Very bad,' he says. 'When the night came, that first night, there were big waves. They washed over the deck.' Those on the canopy roof congratulated themselves they weren't ankle-deep in water. Then it began to rain and they got soaked, too.

In the dark, everyone began to suffer from motion sickness. Children cried out for their mothers, who, in turn, cried out for their husbands. But the boat was rolling so heavily that no one could even stand.

'We had one lady,' says Soham Kahtany. 'I thought she was going to die. She couldn't drink anything. She vomited and vomited and vomited. She couldn't even open her eyes. And it was so cold. Very, very scary.'

The mood on the boat now swung decisively from apprehension to fear. In the darkness, the refugees began to pray out loud.

Although the Iraqis felt abandoned, they weren't. Actually, quite a lot of people were looking out for them – most of them on board a Royal Australian Navy frigate 150 miles to the south-east. HMAS *Adelaide* and her commanding officer Norman Banks had received intelligence from the mainland that a Suspected Illegal Entry Vessel – 'SIEV4' – was out there somewhere. It was their job to find out where. Unfortunately for the refugees, however, *Adelaide*'s mission was not to help them reach their destination. In fact, it was the exact opposite.

The first clue the Iraqis received that something was afoot was when they spotted an aeroplane in the early afternoon of the second day. After the horrors of the night before, they crowded on to the upper deck and waved. The crew of the P-3 Orion, *Mariner 1*, turned back for a second look and at 1.14 p.m. a message was relayed to *Adelaide*: a teak-hulled SIEV, flying an Indonesian flag, was a hundred miles outside Australian waters, heading south at a speed of 8 knots. Fifty people were visible on the roof. All were wearing lifejackets. Inside *Adelaide*'s operations room the *Olong* was designated a Critical Contact of Interest. Five minutes later, the vessel's identity was confirmed. *Adelaide* had found her target.

When *Adelaide* caught up with SIEV4 three and a half hours later, Banks launched a pair of rigid-hulled, inflatable boats (RHIBs) to open communications with the asylum seekers. The crews of the RHIBs pulled up alongside the *Olong* and demanded to speak to her skipper. When he failed to appear (he had disguised himself as a woman and was hiding among the families under the boat's canopy), the sailors ordered the asylum seekers to turn their boat around. They refused. The scene was now set for a second night at sea. It was to be considerably more traumatic than the first.

Over the next six hours, warnings were repeatedly passed to the Iraqis that they should alter course for Indonesia. They were having none of it. At 1.43 a.m., the crew of a RHIB threw a written message taped to a water bottle on to the deck. The Iraqis picked it up, took one look and tossed it overboard. Further warnings were passed on in English, Bahasa and Arabic.

'Some Australian navy people spoke Arabic. I think Lebanese,' recalls Rashid Kahtany. 'They spoke to us by speaker from a long distance. They asked me, "Who are you?" I shouted "We are Iraqi refugees!" "You have to return, you can't come to Australia!"'

The asylum seekers had made a decision to feign ignorance and continue south whatever the consequences.

'They shouted, "Stop! Stop!" but we didn't,' says Karim al Saadi. 'We were pushing very hard to reach the ocean of Australia, so they couldn't return us. Everybody was saying to the driver, "Go! Go! Go! Quickly! Fast!"'

The Iraqis were nearly there, and they knew it. The lights of Australia's Christmas Island were visible on the horizon. Such was the excitement, though, that, when the *Olong* passed into the contiguous zone bordering Australia's territorial waters at 2.30 a.m., the Iraqis remained oblivious. They had no idea what 'contiguous zone' meant, either in geographical or political terms.

According to detractors, the Howard government's handling of the asylum-seeker issue in general – and the *Olong* specifically – was cynical, racist and driven by the need for political gain. A perfect example, in fact, of the Government's use of 'dog-whistle politics'.

The idea was simple. Just as silent whistles send out high-frequency tones audible only to dogs, the Government set about broadcasting messages audible only to certain parts of the electorate: blue-collar, dissatisfied-with-the-Liberal-Party voters – specifically those that had abandoned the Government for Pauline Hanson's nationalist One Nation Party. The key message (foreigners = bad, asylum seekers = worse) was designed to resonate with the naturally racist tendencies of this demographic, while going unheard among the general population, and thus avoiding any embarrassing allegations that the administration was playing the race card.

First, however, voters had to be primed to hear the message. The initial step was to create an atmosphere of fear. This was done by overstating the magnitude of the problem. Through the late 1990s, government spokesmen repeatedly referred to 'waves' and 'armadas' of asylum-seeker boats en route to Australia, raising the spectre of a 'national emergency' and an 'assault to our borders'. Immigration Minister Philip Ruddock himself cited evidence of 'whole villages in Iran' on the move. The technique (if that's what it was) was successful: according to a poll in 1998, the average Australian overestimated the numbers of boat people arriving annually by 7,000 per cent.

The next stage was a public-relations offensive designed to excise Australians from their sympathies with displaced persons. 'Refugees', a word with positive – or at least neutral – connotations, was replaced in public discourse with 'asylum seekers', a term which covertly called into question the validity of the arrivals' claims: they were *asking* for asylum, certainly. That didn't necessarily mean they *deserved* it. Plenty of reasons soon emerged why not.

Because Australia voluntarily took in 12,000 humanitarian cases each year, it was easy to portray illicit arrivals as 'queue jumpers'. Why didn't they wait their turn like everyone else? Boat people were thieves, stealing the places of other, doubtless more needy refugees. Since they were dealing with people traffickers such as Abu Badr, meanwhile, it was also easy to portray asylum seekers as 'illegals', lawbreakers and, potentially, criminals. Boat people, said Ruddock, were 'those who are prepared to break our law, those who are prepared to deal with people smugglers and criminals'. And where did criminals and their associates belong? In jail. The only sensible thing to do was lock them all up once they arrived.

Even incarcerated they still posed a threat. If asylum seekers in detention camps protested, it was evidence they were ungrateful for their treatment and undeserving of it; the more desperate the protests, the clearer the evidence against them. When asylum seekers rioted in the Woomera detention facility, it was taken as proof that they were organized, militant and violent: the kind of people, in fact, who needed to be safely behind bars. When they stitched their lips shut, this was presented not as evidence of their desperation, but of their alien, foreign

customs, antisocial habits and true motives: they were trying to intimidate the authorities.

'We are a humane people,' reasoned the Prime Minister. 'Others
know that, and they sometimes try and intimidate us with our own
decency.'

The asylum seekers were exploiting the nation's generosity, using
Australians' humanity as a weapon against them.[1]

Which was exactly what the Iraqis on board the *Olong* were about
to do.

At 3 a.m. Banks passed close by the *Olong's* port side, illuminating the
boat with a signal lamp and ordering the asylum seekers, through a
loudhailer, to heave to. The size of the frigate, and its proximity, had
the desired effect: the Iraqis were transfixed. But still they refused to
turn. It was time to take the threats up a notch.

Banks now trained the signal lamp on to a gunner on the bridge
wing. As the Iraqis watched, the gunner fired a burst of 5.56 mm
rounds into the water just ahead of them.

'Stop your vessel!' instructed Banks. Nothing happened.

After four further bursts, he selected a larger weapon: a 50-calibre
machine gun mounted on the upper deck. At 4.18 *Adelaide* opened up
with the 50-cal. On board the *Olong* the asylum seekers panicked, running
from one side of the boat to the other and screaming.

'We could see their faces,' recalled the gunner, Able Seaman Laura
Whittle. 'The screaming was just horrific. They were yelling, "Help us!"
and at one point it was more deafening than the 50-calibre machine gun.'

Still the Iraqis refused to turn.

---

[1] Philip Ruddock denies any attempt to vilify asylum seekers. 'You're dealing with
language that is itself dynamic,' he told me in 2008. 'It's changing. And the language
you might use will change according to the circumstances.' Of the 'queue jumper' allegation, he commented: 'People who simply show up, they *are* jumping a place in the
queue . . . It's not demonizing them. It's a statement of fact.'

Thirty-five minutes later, Banks upped the ante again, manoeuvring the frigate aggressively close to the *Olong* in an attempt to force the refugees' vessel off course. If they didn't stop or turn, there was going to be a collision.

Finally, the Iraqis flinched.

'The big ship came up to ram us,' says Saadi, 'so we had to turn. If we didn't stop, the ship would have hit us. There was a huge bow wave, and we stopped.'

The manoeuvre, dramatic though it was, was actually a feint. The moment the asylum seekers' boat altered course, a nine-man boarding party scaled the stern and made its way to the helm. By 4.45 a.m., the Australian navy was in control of the *Olong*.

Banks' plan was to alter the boat's course forcibly, to make it return to Indonesia. This proved tricky. No sooner had the sailors made it aboard than the Iraqis ripped out the ship's compass and its communications equipment and threw them overboard. All over the boat Iraqis – terrified at the thought of being returned to Indonesia – began sabotaging equipment to make it impossible for the Australian Navy to send them back. Some pulled planks out of the boat's superstructure. Others set to work on the engine, which began to produce dense black smoke.

Many of the asylum seekers would later blame this on the *Adelaide*: the *Olong*'s engine had been pushed so hard, they argued, that it was overheating. The truth was less equivocal. Actually, it was sabotaged.

'Some people went down to the engine,' smirks Rashid Kahtany. 'They know how to fix it – but they also know how to break it!'

Coolant lines were slashed, rags and plastic thrown on to the engine casing to create the smoke. At 5.19 a.m., despite the best efforts of the boarding party to prevent the boat from being vandalized, the engine finally stopped, handing the Iraqis their first victory.

'They said, "Go back! Return to Indonesia!"' says Saadi. 'We said, "How can we? The engine doesn't work!"'

The Iraqis had won the point, but there was a cost. Stalled in the water, the *Olong* turned across the swell and began to roll heavily. Water streamed over the deck. By now the asylum seekers were angry, panicking and potentially violent. Some started to struggle with the boarding party. What other options did they have?

The first man in the water was not an Iraqi, but an Iranian, Abu Ali.

'He said that he didn't want to see his kids die and that he was going to jump instead and drown,' recalls Ali Alsaai.

When the Iranian was fished out of the water and returned to the *Olong*, Adelaide's crew warned the asylum seekers not to copy his actions: there were sharks, they said. Big ones. It made no difference. Others began to leap in, too.

As the sun rose at 5.39 a.m., Norman Banks, on the bridge of the *Adelaide*, was greeted by a scene of some panic. Two RHIBs buzzed around the *Olong*, plucking asylum seekers from the water. His men were on board, potentially being assaulted. The boat was rolling heavily, her engines stopped. Two hundred and twenty-three asylum seekers, more than half of them women and children, were hysterical.

It was at this point that the incident reached critical mass. The Iraqis, convinced they were going to be returned to Indonesia or drown, now decided to play their final card – sacrificing their own lives for those of their children. Rashid Kahtany recalls the moment precisely.

'Some people on the boat, they said, "OK, the big people, the adults, leave them! But what about the children? Just take the children and leave us!"'

Karim al Saadi was one of the first.

'What are you doing?' he screamed to the sailors in the RHIB below. 'We don't have anything, only women and children!' Saadi turned to the young mother beside him, took twenty-one-day-old Mustafa from her and cradled him in his arms. '*I* see the children!' he shouted to the sailors in the RHIB. 'Don't *you* see the children?' Saadi then lifted Mustafa up to show them the boy. 'Look at the children!' he shouted.

Others followed suit. And so, in the grey dawn of 6 October 2001, just before 6 a.m., the Iraqis raised their children up to the sky.

In what was to prove a supremely bad piece of timing, at this exact moment Norman Banks received a telephone call from his superior, Brigadier Mike Silverstone at Northern Command Headquarters in Darwin. Silverstone, who was gathering information for Peter Reith, the Minister for Defence, requested an update. What did the Minister need to know?

Disagreements over what was said in the course of this phone call have raged ever since. What is not disputed is that Banks was in the middle of an extremely taxing operation. Civilians were in the water. Iraqis were panicking and threatening his men, and a boat was being vandalized: it was quite possible the situation could deteriorate further and that if it did lives might be lost. Banks needed to be controlling the situation, not telling people about it on the telephone. Nevertheless, the gist of his message was clear. The *Olong* was seven or eight miles from the contiguous zone. The steering had been disabled. People were in the water. They were wearing lifejackets. Kids were being held up.

While Banks spoke, Silverstone took notes in a Department of Defence Field Survey notebook. As he listened to the commander, the Brigadier scribbled:

Vessel disable the steering. Men thrown over side. 5, 6 or 7

The two officers spoke for about a minute. When the call was over Silverstone hung up the phone and added another, crucial, word:

Child

Four hours later, Immigration Minister Philip Ruddock made a sombre public statement about SIEV4.

'A number of people have jumped overboard and have had to be rescued,' he told a press conference in Sydney. Then, at 11.15 a.m. Australian Eastern Time, he added the detail that would propel the story to the top of the news agenda. 'More disturbingly,' he said, 'a number of children have been thrown overboard.'

Quizzed about the incident, the Minister admitted his personal dismay. 'I regard these as some of the most disturbing practices that I have come across in the time that I have been in public life.'

The Press immediately clamoured for more information. How many children were thrown overboard? How old were they?

'The sorts of children who would be thrown,' Ruddock speculated aloud, 'would be those who could be readily lifted and tossed without any objection from them.' Not just children, then. Small children. Babies.

To the Australian government, virtually everything asylum seekers did was evidence of their mendacity. If they had money, they weren't proper refugees and thus were undeserving of assistance; if they didn't have money, they were most likely *economic* refugees – and thus equally undeserving.

Asylum seekers who made the voyage from Indonesia without lifejackets were risking the lives of their families and thus irresponsible; if they wore lifejackets, however, it was proof that they planned to throw themselves or their children into the sea.

'Clearly planned and premeditated,' Ruddock told journalists when he broke the news that the passengers on SIEV4 had thrown their children into the water. 'People would not come wearing lifejackets unless they planned action of this sort.'

This kind of rhetoric led to a catastrophic reversal of logic. Asylum seekers weren't innocent victims in need of protection, but *perpetrators* trying to pull a fast one on Australia. Australians were the ones that needed protection, not refugees; specifically, they needed protection *from* refugees. Asylum seekers with their 'prejudices and intolerances' were a threat. And not just a cultural threat, but a health threat, too. Who knew if they had even been vaccinated?

'These people are criminals,' wrote Senator Ross Lightfoot in a letter to the *Australian*. 'If they bring with them communicable, pandemic, epidemic or parasitic diseases (and they are from areas where contagious diseases are rampant), then innocent Australians could suffer.'

Immigrants rife with prejudice and disease. Criminals. States of emergency. Transportation of ethnic minorities. Mass detention. Epidemics. Parasites. The Howard administration was dredging up some toxic parallels. Then, in September 2001, three weeks before the *Olong*'s departure, Australians turned on their television sets and watched the World Trade Center collapse. One final ingredient was added to an already volatile brew.

Although the head of the Australian Security Intelligence Organization later conceded that there was no evidence any terrorist had ever made it to Australia by boat, the notion that the boat people had terrorist links took root immediately. On 12 September 2001, Solicitor-General David Bennett, fighting an asylum-seeker case, reminded the court of the importance of protecting Australia from the sort of people 'who did what happened in New York yesterday'. The distinction between friendly and enemy aliens, he said, had been rendered 'old fashioned' and 'quaint' by the events of the day before.

Talkback radio propagated the message. 'How many of these ... people are sleepers?' presenter Alan Jones wondered aloud that same day.

On 3AK Radio, Defence Minister Peter Reith was asked whether Bin Laden's associates might be hiding among the boat people.

'We shouldn't make assumptions,' he cautioned, before making one himself: the boats might provide 'a pipeline for terrorists to come in and use your country as a staging-post for terrorist activities'.

Prime Minister John Howard agreed. 'There is a possibility some people having links with organizations that we don't want in this country might use the path of an asylum seeker to get here.'

Here was an opportunity. The Australian government had a new weapon in the battle against asylum seekers. With the *Olong* the Government had a story that trumped even 9/11.

'There's something to me incompatible between somebody who claims to be a refugee and somebody who would throw their own child into the sea,' Howard explained on 8 October. 'It offends the natural instinct of protection, and of delivering safety and security to your children.' The Prime Minister's verdict on the *Olong*'s passengers was unequivocal: 'I don't want in Australia people who would throw their own children into the sea. I don't.'

Given the facts of the case as they had been reported, most Australians found it hard to disagree.

By 10.30 a.m., sailors from the *Adelaide* had persuaded the Iraqis to put their children down. They had repaired the *Olong*'s engine and steering gear and had turned the boat back towards Indonesia. The boarding party then departed, passing control of the boat to the asylum seekers. For good measure, they handed over a navigational chart and an orienteering compass scrounged from one of the ship's company: it seemed a bit harsh to put the boat back into international waters without one.

But Banks and his crew guessed that this would not be the end of the story. Repairs to the steering gear might not last, and the weather was worsening. *Adelaide* steamed just over the horizon, out of sight of the Iraqis, but within range so that she was capable of monitoring them – and waited. After a matter of minutes, the *Olong* stopped again.

At 1.30 p.m., the Iraqis hoisted a square white flag and, below it, a black ball, and started signalling, raising and lowering their arms. The *Olong*, dead in the water, was now officially in distress; Banks and his crew were obliged to offer assistance.

The vessel was reboarded and examined for seaworthiness. This time the verdict was damning. The starter motor had been broken and the diesel-rocker case removed. The fuel tank had been filled up with seawater. Moreover, since the engine had stopped, there was no power to the bilge pumps and the vessel was slowly taking on water.

'Most likely unrepairable,' concluded *Adelaide*'s engineers.

Banks passed a line to the *Olong* and began slowly towing the vessel towards Christmas Island. There was no hurry: he had been instructed not to take the asylum seekers ashore or on board the *Adelaide*. Until the Prime Minster decided what he wanted to do next, there was time to kill. The two vessels steamed for twenty-four hours, awaiting instructions.

'We turned a lot,' recalls Karim al Saadi. 'Sometimes I saw Christmas Island on the left, sometimes it was on the right. We went in circles.'

On board the *Olong*, the mood was now calm, the asylum seekers compliant. They thought they were getting what they wanted. But the situation was precarious: in the bilges, the water level was still rising. Banks sent over a number of pumps to empty them, but one after another failed. He then passed over a Peri-jet hose from his flight deck and started pumping the water out until, finally, the bilge-water level dropped to a steady 50 cm. This situation could not last for long, but the fix only had to last until the Government made a decision regarding what Banks was to do with the asylum seekers and an order was relayed down the line. It was an order that never came.

At three o'clock the next afternoon, for no apparent reason, the water levels suddenly started to rise. Banks ordered women and children to be moved to the upper deck. The women begged to be taken on to the *Adelaide*, but were refused. According to the sailors, the Government had instructed them not to rescue anyone unless the boat actually sank. At 4 p.m., the boarding party reported that the *Olong* was taking on a lot more water. An hour later, the boat began to slump. Banks stopped his engines and dispatched his executive officer to take a look. The news was not good.

'I think we're going to lose this one,' the XO reported. 'It's starting to go.'

As the *Olong* slowed to a halt, Karim al Saadi heard a deep groan under his feet. The timbers of the boat's hull were giving way. Things now happened fast.

At 5.08, the *Olong*'s bow dropped and waves started washing over the deck, carrying away the Iraqis' few personal possessions. The asylum seekers, desperate to avoid the water, scrambled from one side of the boat to the other, causing it to list heavily, first to port, then to starboard. Banks ordered the towline to be cut, turned the *Adelaide* around to shelter the ailing vessel and addressed his crew over the ship's intercom.

'The worst – or the most feared – order I would ever expect to give is: "Launch the life rafts!"' he later recalled. 'It was not a difficult decision to make. It was clearly evident that I had to make that decision. But the gravity of those orders was significant and will stay in my mind for ever.'

Doubtless it will stay in the Iraqis' minds, too.

'The soldiers told us to jump into the water,' recalls Karim al Saadi. 'They said, "Jump! If you don't jump, we can't help you!"'

Saadi tried to explain that he and his wife were diabetic, that she was unable to swim, but the response was the same: according to the sailors, they were under orders not to intervene until the boat went down. The asylum seekers would have to jump.

This answer was not reassuring to those with young children. What if the lifejackets didn't work? What if they were too big, and the children slipped out?

Rashid Kahtany was trying to decide whether to leap into the water with his youngest daughter Duha when the deck gave a sudden lurch and they were hurled overboard. It was the first time Kahtany, a non-swimmer, had ever been underwater.

'The ocean was dark!' he says. 'I thought a big fish would come and snatch our legs.'

The moment she saw her husband bob to the surface, Soham assumed he had jumped deliberately, grabbed her older daughter firmly around the waist, took a deep breath and stepped off the boat.

Saadi and his wife were among the last to go. Shaking with fear, they sat on the deck, holding hands. The boat then tilted and the pair slid into the sea together. As Saadi supported his wife, he looked back at the *Olong*, which was now disintegrating.

'The weight of the engine pulled the back of the boat under,' he says. 'It began to break. The engine went under, leaving the wooden hull out of the water.'

It was the end of the line for the *Olong*.

Two passengers were spared the ordeal of jumping: twenty-three-day-old Mustafa and his mother. Recognizing that this was a special case, Banks ordered both to be lifted into a RHIB, which turned away from the sinking boat and headed towards the *Adelaide*, leaving behind it 221 Iraqis and all their worldly possessions, floating around them in waterlogged suitcases.

Although it took the best part of two hours, by 6.45 p.m., the *Adelaide*'s ship's company had increased by 223. An awning was rigged over the forecastle, lavatories were set up, food, water, towels and dry clothes were distributed. Sailors who might previously have displayed animosity towards the asylum seekers now showed their true colours, helping wherever possible. The crew all missed their own evening meals, most without even noticing; many stayed awake through the night running a babysitting rota for the exhausted Iraqi mothers.

'I was particularly proud of that shift in attitude,' Banks told a Senate inquiry later. 'They performed a miracle.' The performance of his company, he said, was 'unparalleled'.

In the case of the seven sailors who spontaneously jumped into the water to assist the asylum seekers, without lifejackets and from a height of twelve metres (equivalent to leaping from the roof of a four-storey building), there seems little doubt this was the case. So impressed was Banks that when he saw photographs of his crew in the water the next morning he immediately added captions explaining that they had been taken during the rescue on 8 October, and that they showed examples of the 'immense courage' of his crew, then e-mailed them to the mainland.

By now both the Government and the Press were up in arms. Newspaper headlines on the morning of 8 October – ASYLUM SEEKERS THROW CHILDREN OVERBOARD, BOAT PEOPLE THROW CHILDREN INTO OCEAN and CHILDREN OVERBOARD: LATEST TWIST ON THE REFUGEE FRONTLINE – left little room for debate about what had happened. Government spokesmen reiterated, to anyone willing to listen, the implications of the asylum seekers' antics.

'Any civilized person would not dream of treating their own children in that way,' said Foreign Minister Alexander Downer. 'They're not types of people we want integrated in our community, people who throw children overboard.'

To the administration, this was another example of asylum seekers trying to manipulate the country in order to get their own way.

'It was clearly their intention to do this,' Ruddock commented, 'and it's clearly their intention to put pressure on us.'

The only way to handle this sort of behaviour was to stand fast. 'This kind of emotional blackmail is very distressing,' agreed the Prime Minister. 'But we cannot allow ourselves to be intimidated.'

The Government was keen to point out that the incident raised the issue of Australia's right to defend itself. It was a line that ran well after 9/11: on 7 October, the same day the refugees had apparently thrown their children overboard, the US-led coalition had started bombing Afghanistan. The world was at war. Didn't Australia have the right to pre-empt an assault on its territory?

'There are those who wish to breach our borders,' Downer explained. 'We're entitled . . . to do our best to protect our borders.'

This argument resonated with the electorate. The next day the *Herald Sun* polled its readers: 'Should boat people who threw their children overboard be accepted into Australia as refugees?' More than 95 per cent voted NO.

And yet, in the minds of some of the country's more astute journalists, there were niggling doubts. The story seemed unlikely: asylum seekers, no matter how perverse, presumably still loved their children. It was one thing to put pressure on a government to take you in; it was quite another to throw your own kids into the sea. Other than the Government's word for it, there was no evidence whatsoever that this had actually happened.

Not until the morning of 9 October. At 9.30 a.m., Elizabeth Bowdler, a journalist from Channel 10 TV, dug up the *Adelaide*'s satellite telephone number and managed to reach Norman Banks.

Yes, he told her, asylum seekers had been pulled from the water, and, yes, children had been involved. He'd held one himself. What Banks didn't realize, however, was that they were talking at cross purposes: Bowdler was fishing for information about children being thrown overboard two days earlier. He was talking about yesterday's rescue.

At the end of the conversation, Bowdler mentioned that she was keen to source some archive pictures of the *Adelaide* for her news piece. Banks suggested the Internet, then dropped a bombshell: actually, he said, there were photographs of the incident itself. Just a few hours earlier, he had e-mailed some to the mainland. Perhaps she might be interested in those?

When news broke that there were pictures of children in the water, Australia's Department of Defence was inundated with calls. Where were they? Could they be released? The next afternoon, with a flourish, they were.

'*You* may want to question the veracity of reports from the Royal Australian Navy,' challenged Defence Minister Peter Reith. '*I* don't.'

Reith also revealed that the Navy had film of the incident, courtesy of the *Adelaide*'s electro-optical tracking system.

'Someone has looked at it and it is an absolute fact,' he concluded. 'Children were thrown into the water. So do you *still* question it?'

The Government had a cast-iron case. The only problem was, it wasn't true. No children had been thrown overboard. None of the sailors had seen any children being thrown overboard. None of the photographs showed children being thrown overboard or children who had been thrown overboard. Neither, as it eventually became clear, did the ship's electro-optical tracking system film.

Close examination of the photographs would have demonstrated this fact. When he e-mailed the pictures on 9 October, Norman Banks had carefully inserted captions stating that they showed Iraqis being rescued the day before. The Children Overboard allegations related to incidents that had taken place twenty-four hours prior to that. The photographs were of the wrong incident, on the wrong day.

But by the time they were released to the Press, the captions and the dates had mysteriously gone missing.

From the outset, there were two groups of people who recognized that the Children Overboard story was untrue. The first was the crew of the *Adelaide*.

Once the asylum seekers had been disembarked at Christmas Island on 10 October, some of the sailors went ashore, where barroom gossip revolved around the media event of the moment: how the Iraqis had thrown their children into the sea. Annoyed at the way that the truth was being stretched to fit a political agenda, the sailors spilled the beans.

Banks had realized 'there was a clear misrepresentation going on' the moment he saw the front page of the *Herald Sun* on 8 October, at which point he had informed his superiors that something was very wrong. When an ABC TV News report two days later displayed his photographs as evidence that the Iraqis had thrown their children overboard, he lost his temper: that very same day he had forwarded statements from crew members who had participated in the incident. None had reported any children thrown into the sea.

'The whole show was wrong,' he told the Christmas Island harbour-master.

That night on the mainland, the same news report also shocked Banks' superiors, who began frantically telephoning each other to discuss what to do next.

The second group that could have put the media right was the Iraqis themselves. But they were being held, incommunicado, in a basketball court on Christmas Island. For a group largely composed of Muslims, conditions were far from ideal: men and women sleeping in the same room, no clean clothes and food of questionable quality. Such was their relief to be back on dry land, however, that most were content. What they really wanted to know was what would become of them now? They had made it to Australian territory. What next?

After nearly two weeks in the basketball court, community leaders were taken aside and informed that they were to be transported to the mainland.

'An interpreter came in and said, "You're going to Australia,"' recalls Karim al Saadi. 'Everyone had to sit down and he called out our names. After that they put numbers on our backs. He said that the aeroplanes were coming.'

Their destination, apparently, was Sydney. Not everyone was convinced.

'Some Iraqi people said, "Don't go! Don't fly!"' says Soham Kahtany. '"They'll take you somewhere else." We didn't believe them.'

'They were right,' Rashid chimes in. 'It was a trick.'

When he arrived at the aerodrome, Ali Alsaai recognized his plane immediately: during his conscription in Iraq, he had parachuted from a C-130 Hercules a number of times.

'It was a cargo plane,' he jokes, 'but the cargo was us.'

Inside, seats had been installed, alongside a makeshift lavatory with a blanket rigged around it for privacy, but a cargo plane was a cargo plane. The asylum seekers were moved in groups of forty or fifty at a time.

Karim al Saadi also recognized the aircraft. He knew right away that it was military. That didn't concern him. He just wanted to know where it was headed – but, whenever he asked, he was told to shut up. Not all of the aircrew were as uncommunicative. In Ali Alsaai's plane the crew announced they were on their way to Sydney, and that the journey would take about six hours. Once airborne the Iraqis became suspicious. The Australian mainland should have been quite close. Why was the flight taking so long? Alsaai, who had been given a specific journey time, soon knew that something was wrong.

'Six hours later I asked, "Where are we?" The officer told me to be quiet. At seven hours, again, I asked, "Why are we still flying?" The same at eight, nine, ten, eleven hours.'

After thirteen hours in the air, the planes finally landed and the refugees disembarked. Those still expecting to see the Sydney Opera House were in for a shock.

'We were in the middle of a jungle!' exclaims Saadi. 'And there were all these soldiers, people with very black faces.' Saadi turned to a friend. 'Where are we?' he asked. 'Is this *Africa*?'

Not only were the soldiers black, but, more worrying for the Iraqis, they all had mouths the colour of pomegranates; occasionally they would spit out a jet of red liquid that the asylum seekers – never having encountered betel-nut juice – assumed was blood.

'Soldiers,' recalls Widad Alsaai. 'Tall black men. With guns. And red teeth. We just looked at them.' She turned to her husband. 'Where is Sydney?' she asked him. 'Is this *Sydney*?'

Hawraa, the couple's eldest daughter, burst into tears. 'Mummy,' she said, 'I don't want to die here! Let's go back!'

At that moment, there was a roar behind them as the Hercules they had travelled in lifted off again.

Plucking up his courage, Saadi turned to one of the guards.

'Mister,' he said, 'where are we?'

'Manus Island,' the soldier replied.

'Where is Manus Island?' the Iraqi enquired.

'Papua New Guinea.'

Saadi thought for a moment. 'Well, where is Papua New Guinea?'

The soldier shook his head and wandered off.

For the Iraqis anything other than Sydney was going to be a disappointment, but Lombrum Naval Patrol Base was beyond all expectations.

'There was nothing there,' says Saadi. 'It was an old World War Two camp. They put in beds and chairs and used plastic sheeting to make rooms. And it was very hot.'

'Very hot' was about right: Manus is two degrees south of the equator.

Soham Kahtany took one look at her new family home and burst into tears.

'We're going to live *here*?' she asked her husband. 'They're putting us *here*? It's a *jungle*!'

Rashid didn't know what to say: he was still trying to work out what country they were in. Like many of the Iraqis, he assumed he was in Africa, because of the ferocious heat and the fact that most of the inhabitants were black.

'There was just this big, big forest,' he says, 'and all these people with no shoes and red mouths.'

Soham was inconsolable: 'I couldn't stop my eyes. I just cried and cried and cried.'

Living conditions were not good. The food was bad, the water was bad, the power was intermittent and it was too hot to move. The accommodation – battered Nissen huts and converted shipping containers – was full of local wildlife, including spiders and scorpions. For those with children this was a serious concern: many of them were sleeping on the floor. Almost immediately, the Iraqi men took to hunting snakes.

'Every day we killed maybe five,' says Rashid Kahtany.

Perhaps they should have left them alone: they might have kept the other pests down. One night Hawraa Alsaai woke up to discover rats scampering over her sleeping parents. From that point on the twelve-year-old cried herself to sleep.

But the most worrisome of all the fauna was the smallest. *Falciparum malaria*, a chloroquine-resistant strain of the parasite, is endemic to Manus. Since there were no mosquito nets or repellents, the results were predictable.

'Everyone got sick,' says Saadi. 'Typhoid or malaria, I don't know. Nobody would eat. Everyone was sweating and throwing up their food. My wife was so sick she couldn't move.'

The Department of Immigration would later state that anti-malarial drugs had been administered from the moment the Iraqis arrived. This has been disputed. Either way, three months after their arrival at Lombrum, doctors at the local hospital confirmed fifteen cases of malaria among the asylum seekers.

Immigration Minister Philip Ruddock denied they had been infected in Manus. One of his spokeswomen commented that boat people often arrived with diseases anyway: they'd probably brought the contagion themselves.

With a daughter who couldn't sleep for fear of rats, a wife who couldn't stop crying, and surrounded by friends who were dropping like flies, Ali Alsaai was now furious. After two days on Manus, he trooped into the reception office and demanded to know what country he was in and how long he was going to remain there. *What was going on here?*

What was going on was that the Australian government was making a stand. In the face of intolerable levels of asylum-seeker arrivals, it had become clear to Philip Ruddock that something had to be done. If Australia came to be seen as a 'soft touch', more boats would show up and the numbers would increase. That, in turn, had further consequences: either he would lose his job or the Government would lose the election – or both.

Ruddock understood there was no way asylum seekers were simply going to stop coming over of their own accord. But if they couldn't be stopped at the point of departure, changes had to be made at the point of arrival. The key problem here was the law. The moment asylum seekers set foot on Australian soil, they had a number of rights. These rights interfered with the Government's business of shipping them back where they came from. Part of the problem was the interference of the judiciary.

'The courts here in Australia have progressively over time worked their way into the system of determining refugees,' Ruddock told me in 2008. The effect, he said, was corrosive: if an asylum seeker was deemed not to be a genuine refugee, he could be deported. But if he got himself a lawyer, he could appeal and appeal and appeal – effectively turning Australia's asylum-seeker policy into a lottery. The process took so long and cost so much money that at the end of the day it was more economical simply to let them in. This, clearly, was an unacceptable state of affairs.

Theoretically, however, there was a simple solution: if the asylum seekers didn't actually *land* on Australian territory, they would be unable to access the courts. Stopping the boat people from touching Australian soil now became the cornerstone of Ruddock's 'Pacific Solution'.

The idea was the result of a fortuitous encounter. 'It was about this time,' recalled Ruddock, 'that a lawyer[2] very close to me said, you know,

---

[2] Ruddock was cagey about the exact source of this suggestion: he told me who the lawyer was, then had second thoughts. 'I've never dobbed her in,' he said. 'You can't include that!'

"Why do you have to allow people who simply get to Christmas Island –
or any of these offshore places – access to the legal system?"'

It was an intriguing question. On the face of it, the answer was
obvious. Australia's outlying islands were part of her Migration Zone,
which meant they were covered by Australian law. But who said the
islands *had* to be part of the Migration Zone? What if they were simply
removed from it?

Bureaucratically, the idea was brilliant. If Australia's outlying islands
were excised from her Migration Zone, asylum seekers landing there
could be deemed not to have triggered international obligations to allow
them judicial access. They would be unable to reach the courts to start
the appeals process that cost so much time and money. In September
2001, Ashmore Reef, the Cartier and Cocos Islands, and Christmas
Island – the most common destinations for boat people departing from
Indonesia – were duly excised from Australia's Migration Zone. Over
the next four years, the Government would seek to excise more than
3,000 of its outlying islands.

But this, in turn, triggered another problem: what to do with the
asylum seekers next? They might not be in the Migration Zone on
Christmas Island, but the moment they were transported to the mainland for processing, they certainly would be, and surely it was not
possible to excise the Australian mainland from its own Migration
Zone.

Another solution presented itself. Perhaps someone else could take
them? In September and October 2001, East Timor, Fiji, Kiribati, Palau
and Tuvalu were asked if they would like to do so. All declined. Two
nations, however, agreed.

On 10 September 2001, the governments of Australia and Nauru
signed a Statement of Principles in which Nauru agreed to host a detention centre for up to 800 asylum seekers for an initial six-month period.
The bankrupt nation was awarded AU$20 million for development
activities – a deal the head of the AusAID Nauru programme would

later describe as an 'unmitigated bribe'. Three months later, the agreement was updated. For an extra AU$10 million Nauru agreed to take
another 400 asylum seekers (this was later increased again to 1,500).
For the world's smallest republic, this was a lot of people. Its population now comprised more than 10 per cent Australian asylum seekers.

A month after the Nauru deal was struck, Australia and Papua New
Guinea signed a Memorandum of Understanding to establish another
processing camp on Manus Island. As was the case with Nauru, Australia
agreed to cover the costs of the detention and processing activities.
And, as with Nauru, there was a sweetener for the helpful government:
Australian aid packages were fast-tracked, including the upgrading of
schools, police housing and a local airport. The Manus detention centre
was opened on 21 October 2001. The Alsaai, Saadi and Kahtany families were the first arrivals.

The Iraqis were now in a precarious position. The determination process
(establishing whether they were bona-fide refugees) was conducted by
Australians. But because it was taking place in a 'declared country'
outside Australia, the operation remained outside Australian law. If
they were mistreated, the asylum seekers could not access or appeal to
Australian courts. The governments of Papua New Guinea and Nauru,
meanwhile, could wash their hands of what was taking place on their
territory, because the areas were being administered by the Australian
government. The Iraqis were shipwrecked in a legal no-man's-land.

International observers were appalled. Amnesty International repeatedly warned that the 'Pacific Solution' contravened international law.
Human Rights Watch (HRW) agreed. 'Australia,' the organization
concluded, 'has taken its own policy of mandatory detention – a prac-
tice specifically found to be a human-rights violation by the United
Nations Human Rights Committee – and exported it to less-developed
neighbours.' This was 'an attempt by Australia to avoid its obligation
under international law'. Oxfam also agreed, dubbing the programme

a 'Pacific Nightmare'. Even the UNHCR, the normally diplomatic United Nations refugee agency, expressed 'strong concerns'. According to the organization, Australia's policy of mandatory, indefinite detention of refugees was 'not consistent with the provisions of the Refugee Convention'. Shipping them offshore was even worse.

Reactions to 9/11 were similar all over the world. Despite the fact that 2001 marked the fiftieth anniversary of the Refugee Convention, immediately after 11 September the nations responsible for its establishment went out of their way to sidestep its obligations. Typical were the governments of Greece (where all Afghan refugees were barred), Spain (whose foreign minister announced that 'the strengthening of the fight against illegal immigration is also a strengthening of the anti-terrorist fight') and the United Kingdom and United States, where laws were passed allowing for the pre-emptive and indefinite detention of foreign suspects.

Outraged individuals beating up foreigners was perhaps a predictable reaction to an atrocity as grievous as 9/11, but frequently these misguided vigilantes were taking their lead from their own governments, which, according to HRW, 'shamelessly manipulated xenophobic fears in order to muster short-term political support'.

HRW was especially critical of Australia. The country's behaviour, it noted, was 'excessively harsh and restrictive', its ensuing legislation 'unprecedented'. Not missed was the fact that the Pacific Solution had been conceived within sight of a general election.

'Surely,' asked Ruud Lubbers, United Nations High Commissioner for Refugees, 'there are other ways to win elections?'

There was a precedent. In the early 1990s, the United States had faced an influx of asylum seekers from Haiti. Like the Australians a decade later, the Americans realized that, if Haitians landed in Florida, they could demand asylum and then gain access to the domestic courts: a situation that was likely to cost a great deal of money. What to do with them? The United States began a search for somewhere close, some-where suitable and, most of all, somewhere *foreign*, where asylum seekers would have no access to American state or federal courts. Somewhere the Constitution didn't apply.

The simplest answer was Cuba. The United States set up a refugee processing zone outside both Cuban law (it was operated by America) and American law (it was in Cuba). Haitians held there had no recourse to any civilian court in either country. But this wasn't an oversight. *It was the whole point.* The camp became a kind of state of exception: a place where no domestic law held sway.

The site for the camp was a military base on the eastern tip of the island: Guantanamo Bay.

Australians may not have been aware of the precedent, but they were aware that, at last, something was being done about the 'illegals'. The result was a sharp upsurge in Liberal popularity. By mid-August, the Government was receiving a 40 per cent approval rating. Two weeks later, this was up to 45 per cent. In September, it leapt again to 50 per cent, with the Prime Minister's personal rating at 61 per cent: his highest in five years. The effect on the Government was immediate.

'The atmosphere changed,' a senior Liberal adviser told me over lunch in Melbourne in 2008. 'There was a very clear surge of energy around the Prime Minister's advisers and around Reith's office and around Ruddock's office.'

Did the Government realize the value of the asylum-seeker issue in the run-up to the federal election? I asked. Did they know they had hit electoral pay dirt?

The adviser erupted into laughter so violent he nearly choked on his food. 'Shit, yeah!'

9/11 also played into the Coalition's hands. On the morning of 11 September, it became clear that the 2001 federal election was to be a 'khaki' (wartime) election. Such was the trauma of the moment, it seems, voters decided to opt for stability over change. In effect, the Prime Minister was handed a huge advantage: his approval rating was likely to leap at this point, no matter what.

This fact was recognized by Labor leader Kim Beazley. 'Well,' he told his chief of staff when news of 9/11 broke in Australia, 'there goes the election.'

Beazley had planned to win the campaign on domestic policies. This proved impossible. Every time he or his colleagues made a speech, media reports were superseded by news of the War on Terror. On 7 October, Beazley announced a financial initiative to assist new parents; that same day, the invasion of Afghanistan began. On 9 October, Labor's banking policy clashed with the commitment of Australian troops to the war.

On 14 October, Beazley and Howard debated live on television. Beazley won the debate and there was a spike in his polls, until it was revealed the next day that anthrax spores had been posted to civilians in the United States and the focus turned back to terrorism.

'We can't take a trick,' bemoaned one Labor insider. Another commented that, no matter what the Party did, 'we're competing for page nine'.

What was especially noteworthy about the 2001 Australian federal election, however, was not the asylum-seekers issue, or even the tragic interruption of 9/11. It was the way the two issues were yoked together. Traditionally, Australia had always conflated its immigration and asylum policies, arguing – incongruously to some – that the right to turn away potential immigrants gave it the right to turn away refugees, too. Now the Government sought to conflate two further issues: asylum seekers and self-defence. Protecting Australia's borders became an extension of the War on Terror. The tactic was a potent vote winner.

'Howard always does things cleverly,' recalled Beazley later. 'The way he expressed this, even though he had advice from the Security Intelligence Organization to the contrary, was: "I could not guarantee that none of these refugees are terrorists." In dog-whistle terms, that was pretty well perfection: you've got a plausible denial and, at the same time, total political effect.'

Then, as if by magic, on 5 October, the very day that John Howard called the federal election, an asylum-seeker boat showed up. This time its passengers were so inhuman they threw their own children in the sea. For the Liberals, the story was a gift.

The Children Overboard story vanished from the Press almost as abruptly as it had arrived. For a week there was little else, then nothing. There were good reasons for this. The military was not talking and the refugees were isolated and out of the way. Outside the Liberal Party, which also went strangely silent, journalists now had no sources.

Kim Beazley wasn't about to argue: from his point of view, the less written about Howard's asylum-seeker policies, the better. If Children Overboard was no longer taking up the front pages, he might get a look in. Sure enough, with the issue out of the way, Labor polls began to rise, and by the Tuesday before the election Beazley had clawed his way back into the race. But then the Liberals had a final, massive, stroke of luck.

On Wednesday, 7 November, the *Sydney Morning Herald* published a letter from Duncan Wallace, a naval psychiatrist, warning that the 'despicable' policy of returning asylum seekers at sea was damaging the service's morale.

'Nearly everyone I spoke to that was involved in these operations,' he wrote, 'knew that what they were doing was wrong.'

That same day the *Australian* newspaper openly questioned the veracity of the Children Overboard story. The paper had sent a reporter to Christmas Island, where she had interviewed locals who had spoken to the *Adelaide*'s crew. 'Whatever you hear,' one sailor had warned a resident, 'the asylum seekers did not throw their children overboard.'

With the election just three days away, here were two of the nation's leading newspapers effectively accusing the Government of lying.

'All hell's broken loose,' Defence Minister Peter Reith told his senior adviser Mike Scrafton that afternoon. This was an understatement. A month earlier, the Minister had declared it an 'absolute fact' that children were thrown overboard, assuring the Press that the *Adelaide*'s electro-optical tracking system film proved it. Now, when he rang the Navy, he learned that the film didn't show this at all.

Reith had been told a number of times that the Children Overboard story was unsubstantiated, but he had never made that fact public, instead sticking to his original brief on the basis that he had never been *formally* advised otherwise: until that brief was rescinded in writing, he could legitimately claim that the original advice held. But it was a thin story. Surely there must be something else? What was actually on the film?

'The Prime Minister wants somebody to go to the Navy headquarters to look at the tape,' he told Scrafton. 'Somebody they can trust.'

John Howard was due to address the National Press Club in Canberra the next morning, where he was likely to be grilled on whether his administration had lied for political gain. What was he supposed to say?

That evening Scrafton reported to Navy headquarters where he viewed the tape, which had been rewound to a spot where an Iraqi asylum seeker held a young girl in the air. Apparently, this had been the event witnessed by Banks during his fateful phone call of 7 October. After watching the film twice, Scrafton rang Reith.

'In my view,' he told the Minister, 'this doesn't show that children were thrown overboard or even were threatened to be thrown overboard.'

It was bad news for the Government, but Scrafton, an experienced bureaucrat, offered Reith a lifeline. 'I think the best you can say in the political context is that it's inconclusive.'

*　　*　　*

The next morning John Howard faced the massed ranks of the Australian press. For someone who apparently now knew – or at least strongly suspected – that no children had been thrown overboard, he gave a bravura argument that the opposite was the case. Like Reith, Howard stuck to the 'I wasn't officially informed' line. Throughout the exchange, he waved a secret report from Australia's Office of National Assessments (ONA). This was the document, he said, which he considered his formal briefing, and which stated categorically that children had been thrown overboard. Virtually all questions about the incident, the photographs and the film were referred back to it.

'In my mind there is no uncertainty, because I don't disbelieve advice I was given by Defence,' said the Prime Minister. 'It's perfectly reasonable and legitimate of me to say what I have said.' It remained 'an absolute fact', he asserted, that children had been thrown overboard.

The Prime Minister later repeated the mantra during various radio interviews. Asked whether anyone from the Navy or Defence had rung either him, Reith or Ruddock to advise that the story was wrong, he stated they had not.

'Nobody rang my office to that effect and I'm not aware that they rang the offices of the other two ministers,' he said. 'At no stage was I told that that advice was wrong.' Again, he cited the classified report from the ONA. 'I have not received any advice from Defence to this moment which countermands or contradicts that . . . I have not been given different advice. If I were given different advice, I'd make it public.'

The denials came thick and fast. 'My understanding is that there has been absolutely no alteration to the initial advice that was given,' he told ABC Radio's Catherine McGrath. 'And I checked that as recently as last night.'

On this last point, at least, the Prime Minister was telling the truth. He *had* checked his facts as recently as last night. The rest of the statements, however, were less credible. The person with whom he had checked his information was Mike Scrafton, whom he had reached on his mobile phone at a restaurant in Sydney. Over the course of two or three separate calls, Scrafton had specifically informed Howard that the film didn't show children overboard, that the photographs were of the wrong incident on the wrong day, that nobody in the military believed children had been thrown overboard, and that the ONA report that had initially concluded children had been thrown was not based on hard evidence from the *Adelaide* at all. In fact, he told Howard, its sources were media reports citing press statements by Defence Minister Peter Reith.[3]

Scrafton's recollections of these calls – later shared with a Senate inquiry into the incident – led to an uncomfortable conclusion. The Prime Minister was lying through his teeth.

Kim Beazley's adviser was jubilant when he broke the news to his boss. 'This is fantastic!' he announced. 'Howard's a liar!' The Labor leader immediately disagreed. Although the film and the photographs didn't actually show any children being thrown overboard, that didn't necessarily mean children *had not* been thrown overboard. If Beazley wanted to prove the Prime Minister was lying, he would have to demonstrate this was the case. With just two days to go before the election, it was a formidable, perhaps impossible, task. It was also one that he had no particular urge to undertake.

One might suspect that the Labor leader, having been handed such a scandal – the Government apparently lying to the electorate just before a federal election – would be euphoric. The opposite was the case. To

---

[3] Howard maintains that Scrafton is mistaken. 'At no stage was I told by Defence, by Mr Reith or by anybody else that the original advice was wrong,' he told Parliament on 12 February 2002. A week later, he denied he had been told that the ONA report was unreliable. However, in 2004, a Senate inquiry into Scrafton's version concluded that his story was 'credible'. 'The clear implication,' it concluded, 'is that the Prime Minister misled the public in the lead-up to the 2001 federal election.'

Beazley, the re-emergence of the story was a catastrophe: now the final two days of the campaign would be taken up debating John Howard's immigration policies: the one thing Howard was keen to plug.

'We had the most dramatic demonstration of the Dick Morris effect,' Beazley later recalled. 'Which is that, if people are talking about your issue, it doesn't matter whether the story is favourable or unfavourable: you benefit.'

The 2001 federal election was 'one of the most remarkable of Australian elections', according to a report from the Australian Parliamentary Library Law and Bills Digest Group. 'A government seemingly on the ropes just months before polling day is comfortably re-elected. Unusually, the major factors in its victory are immigration and international terrorism.'

John Howard went on to serve another six years in office, becoming the second longest-serving Prime Minister in Australia's history. A close friend of George W. Bush, he signed up to the Coalition of the Willing immediately, dispatching Australian troops to Iraq in 2003. Defence Minister Peter Reith – a man castigated by the ensuing Senate inquiry as having 'engaged in the deliberate misleading of the Australian public', and whose behaviour regarding the Children Overboard incident was described as 'indefensible' – left the Government to become a director of the European Bank of Reconstruction and Development. Immigration Minister Philip Ruddock, architect of the Pacific Solution – a man who had spent a large part of his time as a minister campaigning against the 'corrosive' nature of the judiciary – became Attorney-General.

Kim Beazley announced his resignation.

I met the Prime Minister Australia never had in the lobby of his hotel in Canberra in November 2008.

'Yeah,' Kim Beazley sighed. 'We were going to win the election. No doubt about that. I think if the election campaign had proceeded without

9/11 we would have won it. We could have beaten asylum seekers. We probably could have beaten 9/11 without the asylum seekers. What we couldn't beat was asylum seekers *and* 9/11.'

If he had won that election and become Prime Minister, how would Beazley have responded to George W. Bush asking for support in Iraq in 2002?

'From our point of view, it just stuck out that the initial victory would be quick, but the ultimate chaos would be uncontainable – and the distraction and the impact on the Islamic world horrific.'

You wouldn't have sent Australian troops to Iraq?

'No.'

Despite the Australian government's repeated insinuations, the vast majority of the asylum seekers on the *Olong* proved to be genuine refugees. And despite the Prime Minister's assurances that they would not be allowed into Australia, most of them were. It took time, but they got there in the end.

The Kahtanys were accepted into Australia after six months on Manus, Island. They arrived in Sydney a few months later. The Alsaais were also granted asylum within a year – partly, they think, because their eldest daughter became ill on Manus. The Australian government didn't want to be saddled with the death of a twelve-year-old Iraqi girl in an Australian detention facility in the middle of the Pacific Ocean.

Halima and Karim al Saadi were not so lucky. After a year on Manus their claim for refugee status was denied. They were shipped to Nauru, where they languished for another three years. Then, in 2005, Australia suddenly changed its mind, declared that they were refugees and finally admitted them.

The Saadis travelled to the West seeking asylum. Instead of giving it to them, the Australian government incarcerated them for four years. Why? No one seems to know.

'Were they found to be refugees?' mused Philip Ruddock in 2008.

'Or were they people who were found not to be refugees and then just hung on and hung on?'

Perhaps it depends on how you define 'refugee'. Before fleeing Iraq in 1991, Karim al Saadi had spent time in prison, where his finger-nails were extracted and he was tied to a rotating ceiling fan while soldiers beat his legs with wooden bats. Meanwhile, the secret police visited his home. Halima, heavily pregnant at the time, refused to let them in – whereupon they knocked her down and kicked her so violently that she miscarried. This is why the Saadis were travelling without chil-dren. It is why they remain childless to this day.

Interviewed by immigration authorities on Manus Island, Karim did not reveal that he had been imprisoned. He didn't tell them how he had escaped from an underground jail in northern Iraq the day before he was due to be shipped to Abu Ghraib. He didn't draw attention to the fingernails missing from his right hand or the permanent damage to his legs. Nor did he mention Halima's miscarriage.

Why would anyone seeking asylum not tell the authorities such things?

Seven years later, Saadi shakes his head. 'I thought that if I told them I had been in prison in Iraq they would think I was a bad man.'

3

The Wedding Party

We did not start this war. So understand: responsibility for every single innocent casualty in this war, whether they're innocent Afghans or innocent Americans, rests at the feet of the al-Qaeda and the Taliban.

Donald Rumsfeld, December 2001

PATIENCE MY ASS. I'M GONNA KILL SOMETHING
AC-130 SPECTRE gunship motto

Abdul Malik was returning home from work on the afternoon of 28 June 2002 when he heard the shots: staccato bursts of automatic gunfire coming from behind his house. Every now and then there was a pause, presumably while the marksman reloaded, followed by more shooting. Cautiously, Malik crept around the house into his father's pomegranate orchard, where he found his older brother Khaliq reloading a Kalashnikov.

'What are you doing?' Malik asked.

Khaliq looked up and grinned. 'You'll find out!'

He cocked the AK-47, raised it to his shoulder and, laughing, fired another volley into the sky.

Inside the house, something strange was going on, too. Malik found his mother in the kitchen as usual, but she appeared distant, distracted. Informed that her eldest son was firing an automatic weapon in the garden, she didn't seem bothered.

'What's going on?' Malik asked her. She didn't answer. Instead, she pointed to a basket on the kitchen table. Peering inside, Malik saw a pile of small candy parcels, individually wrapped in exquisite cloth – and the penny dropped. The basket was a *dastmal*, a formal acceptance of a marriage proposal given by a bride's family to the groom's. The strange behaviour, the gunfire, the basket of wrapped candies, all now made sense: a member of the family had become engaged. For a town as small as Deh Rawood, Afghanistan, this was a major event. The Afghan wondered which of his three brothers it might be.

'Who is it?' he asked.

His mother raised an eyebrow indulgently and smiled. 'Abdul Malik,' she said. 'It's you.'

Clandestine negotiations regarding Malik's future had commenced a week earlier, when his mother and aunt had visited the Akhond family in the neighbouring village of Chagasyan, half an hour's walk away from Deh Rawood. The object was to vet the family's second daughter, Tela Gul. On paper, a match appeared propitious: both families were members of the Popalzai tribe and were well respected in their villages. Malik's father was a freeholder with a large house; Tela Gul's had not only completed the Haj, he was also a mullah in the local mosque. One of the mosque's attendees was Malik's uncle. There was a connection.

Abdul Malik wasn't the only one kept in the dark about his mother's secret assignation. Tela Gul also was not informed. Unaware the meeting was about her, she served tea to the two older ladies and made polite conversation. Only when they returned two days later did she realize something was happening. This could be serious, she thought. Throughout the second visit her mother could not find her anywhere. Tela Gul was hiding in an almond grove outside town.

The Malik family found initial reports of Tela Gul to be positive. She was polite, well brought up and attractive: an ideal partner for the family's second son.

'She's good,' Malik's aunt told his father, 'a perfect choice for Abdul Malik.'

Tela's family also appeared happy with the match: Malik had a good job, working for the local police force, supporting American operations in Oruzgan Province. In the last week of June 2002 Malik's father visited the Akhond family to hammer out the financial details. Negotiations proved so easy they were completed in record time. Even the dowry was negotiated without difficulty. It was a sure sign the wedding was blessed.

On the afternoon of 28 June, while Malik was still at work, his male relatives marched to Tela Gul's house to demand her hand in marriage. A brief exchange took place, at the end of which her father handed over a symbol of his agreement: a basket full of candies wrapped in fine cloth. The *dastmal*. The men formally thanked Tela Gul's father, grabbed the basket and ran into the street to celebrate. As they paraded home, Malik's father, brothers and uncles raised their weapons to the sky and loosed a series of volleys of automatic gunfire.

'It was a great moment, a happy moment,' recalls Mohammed Anwar, Malik's uncle. 'Everybody was joining in. We were firing into the sky to let everyone know there was an engagement.'

Malik was less enthusiastic. Why had he not been told about this sooner? He wasn't ready for marriage. He was too young.

'Well, it's a bit late now,' teased his mother. 'You're engaged!'

Who was the girl?

'She's from a famous family. A good family. You'll like her.'

When she revealed the identity of his fiancée and described her to him, Malik began to warm to the idea.

'I knew the family,' he recalls. 'I hadn't been to their home, but I knew who they were. They were Popalzai, like us. I had never actually seen Tela Gul, but I'd heard about her . . . It was a very good match. I think we were both happy with it.'

He told his mother he agreed.

Outside, in the pomegranate orchard, gunshots rang out. Abdul Malik's brother had found some more ammunition.

Nine months earlier a conference took place that would have profound effects on the young Afghans' wedding plans. In the week of 8 October 2001 General Tommy Franks, Commander-in-Chief of US Central Command (CENTCOM) met Secretary of Defense Donald Rumsfeld and the Chairman of the Joint Chiefs of Staff General Richard Myers. Ostensibly, the purpose of the meeting was to allow Franks to brief his commanders on progress in Operation Enduring Freedom, the US inva-sion of Afghanistan, after its first week. But Franks had a specific request for his Pentagon bosses. In his opinion, he told the pair, it was time to deploy SPECTRE to Afghanistan.

Why was SPECTRE necessary? asked Myers and Rumsfeld. What did the CENTCOM commander hope to achieve? What were the risks? What exactly could SPECTRE offer in the Afghan theatre?

Franks explained. The origins of the SPECTRE programme lay in Vietnam. In the mid-1960s – recognizing that Special Forces on the ground needed aerial support more accurate than jets dropping bombs from altitude – the Pentagon had commandeered a handful of AC-47 aircraft and modified them. Three heavy-calibre machine guns with rotating barrels were installed, each capable of firing 100 rounds per second. The resultant hybrids – squat, ugly planes, weighed down with ordnance – were designed to fly low over targets, delivering astonishing quantities of firepower, allowing troops on the ground to extricate them-selves in emergencies. However, because the modified AC-47s were so heavy and slow they presented wonderful targets for the enemy. As a result they flew only at night. Special Forces, who seldom saw these mysterious aircraft watching their backs, nicknamed them 'Spooky'.

The North Vietnamese had another nickname. Night-time tracer fire from the AC-47, delivered at a rate of 18,000 rounds per minute, caused great plumes of smoke and the appearance of fire being spat from the sky. The Vietcong thought they were dragons. The roar of the guns alone was enough to precipitate a retreat.

'Do not attack the Dragon!' commanders instructed their troops. 'It will only infuriate the monster.'

Post-Vietnam, 'Spooky' evolved. The AC-47s were swapped for C-130 Hercules transport aircraft – vast, four-propeller beasts capable of loitering over a target for hours on end, out of sight but within earshot. The new generation of gunships, AC-130s (known as SPECTREs), was fitted with an extraordinary range of artillery pieces including 25 mm, 40 mm and 105 mm canons. A single shot from the 105 mm gun could take the top off a tank.

By 9/11, SPECTRE contained the most sophisticated airborne, computer-driven weapons system in the world, allowing its operators to engage targets at night or through cloud cover with pinpoint accuracy. When Special Forces were on the ground, SPECTRE would circle anticlockwise overhead, watching and waiting. At the right moment the AC-130 would launch a wall of fire, covering the target with ordnance – a technique military planners referred to euphemistically as 'target saturation'.

Subjected to an AC-130 attack, nothing survived. The aircraft carried a crew of thirteen, all part of a secretive unit under US Air Force Special Operations Command, known as the 16th Special Operations Squadron (16 SOS). Five of them were needed just to man the cannons.

After Franks had briefed his Pentagon bosses on the capabilities of SPECTRE, he told them his plan. He wanted to escalate the fighting in Afghanistan. It was time, the General suggested, to insert small units of elite Special Forces and CIA officers into Taliban-controlled territory. These guys were highly vulnerable. They needed aerial protection. Something powerful. What better way of guaranteeing their safety than the AC-130s of 16 SOS?

Details of SPECTRE's subsequent deployment remain classified, but it's no great secret that the first gunships flew out of Masirah Island, off the coast of Oman. Masirah had been the staging-point for the 1979 Iranian hostage rescue and had remained staffed, to some extent, by US personnel ever since. Although neither US nor Omani governments ever admitted to the base's use in Operation Enduring Freedom, post-9/11 the Pentagon filled it with personnel and renamed it Camp Justice. From Masirah the initial six AC-130s had a clean 800-mile run into Afghanistan. First operations began on 15 October near Kandahar.

'SPECTRE,' recalls one Special Forces operative, 'was in the house.'

One of the reasons AC-130s were important in Afghanistan was that there were so few troops on the ground. This was the result of a series of policy decisions made in the immediate aftermath of 9/11. It was to have unforeseen consequences.

Shortly after the first plane hit the World Trade Center in 2001, the White House became convinced that war in Afghanistan was inevitable. A number of problems immediately became apparent. A cursory study of history revealed numerous examples of military forays that had come unstuck there. Alexander the Great, the British and, most recently, the Soviets had all failed to hold the country. In military circles Afghanistan was renowned as possibly the most uninvadable nation on earth. Former Soviet commanders, consulted prior to the launch of Operation Enduring Freedom, warned the United States that taking – and holding – Afghanistan was a great deal harder than it appeared.

'With regret,' one Russian commander told a CIA officer in mid-September 2001, 'I have to say you're really going to get the hell kicked out of you.'

The CIA officer disagreed. It wasn't going to play that way.

'We're going to kill them,' he told the Russian. 'We're going to rock their world.'

One thing the Americans did conclude from these consultations was that deploying large numbers of troops to Afghanistan was not a good idea. The more troops they sent, the more the United States would look like a foreign occupier, and the more likely it was the Afghans would resist. That was the Russian mistake.

'The Soviets introduced 650,000 troops,' Tommy Franks told PBS in June 2002. 'We took that as instructive, as not a way to do it.'

There were other lessons to be learned from the Soviets' experience, too. Timing was critical.

'If you do go in, don't stay too long,' Deputy-Secretary of Defense Paul Wolfowitz advised in November 2001, 'because they don't tend to like any foreigners who stay too long.'

As it happened, the notion of sending low troop numbers into Afghanistan, then leaving as soon as possible, gelled perfectly with promises George W. Bush had made prior to his election. In the Bush White House it was generally accepted that President Clinton had wasted two terms in office meddling in Bosnia, Haiti and Kosovo. The result was a swathe of partially reconstructed failed states that were now apparently dependent on US largesse.

'Nation-building', the new president believed, was a failed notion. It cost a lot of money and ultimately it didn't work. Besides, there were better things for the US military to do with its time than to escort children to school. Especially after 9/11.

The White House's plan called for a 'light footprint' in Afghanistan. Special Forces and the CIA would infiltrate the country, recruit allies among the Taliban's enemies, then use them – together with the wholesale application of US air power – to take the country. Once the Taliban was gone, the Afghans would rebuild their nation themselves. The United States would assist, of course, but not with troops.

This way the country would become self-sufficient faster and the United States would not end up stuck with a nation reliant on it for money and guidance. This way, in fact, the United States would not be seen as an invader at all: all it was doing was providing the firepower to remove a dictatorial regime and adding the democracy that would enable the country to right itself. If, after the invasion, peacekeeping operations became necessary, they could be left to other organizations – the United Nations, perhaps, or NATO – better suited to rebuilding sewage plants and monitoring the school-run. The US military, meanwhile, would fulfil its proper task: hunting al-Qaeda, knocking out the Taliban and killing terrorists.

According to President Bush, the history of Afghan invasions was riddled with cases of 'initial success, followed by long years of floundering and ultimate failure'. This White House was smarter than that. 'We're not going to repeat that mistake.'

Not everyone was convinced. Those with first-hand experience of working in failed states recognized that even if the invasion went well – and there was no guarantee it would – the real problems were likely to emerge *after* Kabul had fallen. Breaking things in Afghanistan was all well and good; putting them back together might prove considerably harder. The country, which had been in a state of civil war for the best part of thirty years, was riddled with internal feuds. It had never been effectively ruled. The chances of this vast, under-resourced nation simply sitting up and sorting itself out were minimal.

In the run-up to the invasion Richard Dearlove, the Head of MI6, visited CENTCOM in Tampa, and raised the issue with Tommy Franks.

'He said to Franks, "What do you think is going to happen after we've pushed over the Afghan government?"' recalls a senior British diplomat briefed on the meeting. 'Franks said something like, "Oh, well, I expect that they'll become a democracy, won't they?"'

US diplomats were also concerned about the lack of reconstruction plans for Afghanistan. James Dobbins, who had worked in Somalia, Haiti and Bosnia, and who became the United States' Special Envoy to Afghanistan at the end of 2001, recalls a certain laissez-faire attitude towards the country.

'It became clear not immediately but pretty quickly – almost immediately – that this simply didn't have the same level of buy-in or interest at the higher levels of US government that I had been used to.' To

Dobbins it appeared that the White House thought the invasion would be hard, but the follow-up easy. He was strongly of the opinion that things might work the other way around. 'The idea that Afghans could adequately secure their country after a twenty-three-year civil war,' he later wrote, 'struck me as naive and irresponsible.'

Robert Finn, who became the US ambassador to Afghanistan in 2002, agreed, taking the White House's 'no nation-building' line with a pinch of salt.

'The rhetoric from Washington, which they said many times, was "We're not doing nation-building. We're not going to do this kind of thing." And I said to myself, "Well, of course they're going to do it, because that's what you have to do to solve this problem."'

Military commanders had reservations, too. General Dan McNeill, who led US forces in Afghanistan in 2002, was summoned to CENTCOM prior to his deployment.

'I was told to take half of my headquarters and leave half of it home in case it had to be replicated,' he says. McNeill wasn't convinced this was a smart idea. 'My headquarters had just been though about a year's worth of good training and we had a pretty good team, and yes, it did bother me that I was going to split it roughly in half and leave half of it at home.'

His superiors, Generals Keane and Shinseki, refused to budge. The justification seemed to be that the deployment was a temporary one. McNeill was instructed to do nothing 'that looked like permanence'.

'No Bondsteel,' Keane told McNeill, referring to the huge US military base in Bosnia.

'So I concluded from that,' says McNeill, 'that we were not going to be there long.'

The issue of how long the Americans would stay in Afghanistan did not occur to Abdul Malik. Like most inhabitants of Deh Rawood he assumed the Americans would sort things out. It was clear to the young man, however, that a great deal of work was necessary. The town had been wrecked by the Soviets during their occupation.

As a result, neither Malik nor his bride-to-be Tela Gul had ever attended school. This was a source of disappointment to the young man: originally, he had wanted to be a schoolteacher. Instead, he had spent his childhood being shunted around the country as his parents tried to stop him becoming another casualty of the ongoing fighting. Whenever news of a Russian offensive arrived, the Malik family would load their possessions on to donkeys, then head for the mountains and valleys around town, where they would hide until the fighting was over.

So itinerant was the young man's life that, when World Health Organization representatives visited the town to check on health facilities and to vaccinate children against polio, he was always absent. Malik was never vaccinated. Neither were his friends. Deh Rawood was isolated from the wider community. News from inside the village seldom made it out; news from the outside seldom made it in.

There were exceptions. Reports of the 9/11 attacks shocked the villagers. Malik heard about them on the family radio. He learned from snippets of conversation that Osama bin Laden was behind them, and that Bin Laden lived near Kandahar, protected by the Taliban. Malik's brother Khaliq thought the whole story was implausible. It was a conspiracy, he told Malik: there had been no attacks. The US just wanted a reason to invade Afghanistan. Unsure what to believe, the brothers consulted their uncle Anwar, who pooh-poohed the conspiracy theory.

'It can't be a lie,' he told his nephews. '*Someone's* done this.' One thing was clear. 'If the Taliban don't do what America tells them and surrender Osama,' he told the boys, 'America will topple them.'

The first Americans Malik saw were Special Forces troops accompanying the future president Hamid Karzai, then making his way north towards Kabul. The Green Berets of Operational Detachment Alpha (ODA) 574 travelled light and, initially, incognito.

'We were told they were doctors,' Malik says. 'That they were here in case someone got hurt.'

The behaviour of these six white men in Deh Rawood was a source of great amusement to the villagers.

'They were filtering the water! They were eating packaged food dropped from aeroplanes. We laughed at them.'

One of the villagers gave the Special Forces men local turbans, to help them blend in. Only later did news emerge that there might be more to these strange Americans than met the eye.

'When more Americans arrived,' recalls Malik, 'people realized that they were not, in fact, doctors at all.'

One individual better informed than most was Jan Mohammed, the governor of Oruzgan Province. It was a source of some pride to him that Hamid Karzai had made an appearance in Deh Rawood.

'When President Karzai started the fight against the Taliban, he started it from here,' Mohammed says. He and other leading figures were buttonholed by Karzai, who enlisted them in the struggle to overthrow the Taliban. 'A government will come to power,' he told them, 'that will meet people's demands, provide education, give rights to men and women, build roads, schools and madrasas.'

News of the impending overthrow of the Taliban caused great excitement in Deh Rawood.

'People were very optimistic about the change,' says Khaliq. 'People thought foreigners would come and the situation would change a lot for the better. Everybody was happy. Everybody thought the foreigners would build schools, roads, clinics and hospitals.'

Most important of all, however, was the idea that the Americans might actually be able to stabilize Afghanistan, to stop the fighting that had plagued the country for the last thirty years. If anyone could do it, the villagers said, the Americans could.

'We were pretty sure that the Americans were very advanced and had the best technology.'

One area of technology of particular interest to the inhabitants of Deh Rawood was the ability of the US military to attack targets from a distance with great accuracy. When the Soviets had invaded, they had razed entire towns with poorly aimed artillery barrages. The mujahedin and Taliban were even less discriminating. But the Americans, it was rumoured, had equipment that enabled them to avoid this kind of damage. They could hit anything, accurately, from anywhere. 'America is a very developed country' says Jan Mohammed. 'We heard that Americans can see even small things of four centimetres on the ground.'

A month after the first SPECTRE gunships went into action from Masirah, the modus operandi changed. In early November 2001, 16 SOS deployed to an 'undisclosed location' near Afghanistan with three further aircraft, making a total of nine AC-130s available for Special Forces: almost half of all the gunships in the Pentagon's arsenal.

The crews lost no time in settling in, decorating their tents with US flags and AC-130 paraphernalia. SPECTRE declared one tent door sign. GUNS DON'T KILL PEOPLE. WE DO.

GHOSTRIDERS read another: AC-130 GUNSHIPS: SO OTHERS MAY DIE. Operators photographed themselves autographing heavy-calibre munitions, then posted the pictures on the Internet: EAT THIS, BIN LADEN, COURTESY OF CARLY, BROOKE AND PAM, MISSOULA, MONTANA.

For the AC-130 crews Operation Enduring Freedom offered a unique opportunity. During the early stages of the invasion, Afghanistan was target-rich, almost a shooting gallery. YOU CAN RUN 16 SOS posters warned BUT YOU'LL ONLY DIE TIRED.

16 SOS immediately set about justifying its reputation for absolute, complete destruction. In November 2001, three aircraft and three crews from the 'undisclosed location' flew thirty-nine combat missions in just twelve days. During that period, the aircraft expended more than 1,300 40 mm rounds and 1,200 105 mm rounds. Between October and December 2001, nine AC-130 aircraft flew 225 missions over

Afghanistan, making them the third most deployed weapon in the US Air Force. The secretive, elite 16 SOS was instrumental in every major Northern Alliance attack in the country.

Troops on the ground adored the gunships.

'Extremely competent, extremely talented,' says a captain who led one of the first Operational Detachments Alpha (ODAs) into Afghanistan in the winter of 2001. 'Just a critical part of what we do.'

Special Forces appreciated not only the trail of destruction wreaked by the gunships, but also the near-hysterical fear they created among Taliban fighters. On one occasion in November 2001, during the battle for Kunduz, the captured Taliban Chief of Staff Mohammed Fazal was under interrogation by Northern Alliance warlord Rashid Dostum. Fazal heard the voice of a female AC-130 Fire Control Officer over his radio and asked why a woman was speaking to US troops.

Dostum informed Fazal that it wasn't a woman. It was the Angel of Death, waiting to deploy a killer ray on Taliban positions around the city. Within moments, Dostum explained, every one of his comrades would be vaporized.

Fazal, who had witnessed an AC-130 attack the day before, seized Dostum's radio, called his colleagues, and persuaded them to surrender immediately. The battle for Kunduz ended there.

Although the AC-130 crews didn't know it, the attribute that made them so effective in Afghanistan – their sheer firepower – had prevented them from operating there earlier. In December 1998, the US military had been considering how it might go about assassinating Osama bin Laden. Cruise-missile attacks had proved ineffective, causing significant collateral damage. Perhaps there was a more accurate, but equally lethal option? The Joint Chiefs of Staff suggested a clandestine AC-130 strike to eliminate Bin Laden, kill his followers and destroy their camps around Kandahar.

Head of the CIA's Bin Laden Unit Michael Scheuer was all for it: 'The military as I understand it said, "OK, we're sick of the President going after us on this. Let's use the AC-130s, which can lay down so much ordnance on a particular target that nothing escapes."'

The plan was bumped up to the White House for approval, but, according to those involved at the time, President Clinton got cold feet when the notion of 'target saturation', as understood by an AC-130 crew, was actually explained to him.

'It would kill *everything* from children and men to dogs, horses, cats and everything else,' says Scheuer. 'The President kind of blanched when the impact of an attack of that sort was described.'

That, it seemed, was the problem with the AC-130s: there was no such thing as a nuanced attack. Either the crews stayed home, or they wrecked everything. SPECTRE ALPHA, read another unit slogan. BLOOD-BATH IS OUR WAY OF GETTING CLEAN.

For a brief period after Operation Enduring Freedom was launched, it seemed as if the military planners had miscalculated. With few overt targets worth bombing from the air and few troops on the ground, progress stalled. Journalists and military pundits glowed quietly: *the invasion wasn't working*. The word 'quagmire' began to appear in newspapers.

Then, suddenly, it all came good. The CIA–Special Forces–Northern Alliance triumvirate swept the country, and the Taliban simply fell apart. On 13 November 2001, Kabul was taken, leaving the city of Kunduz as the only Taliban stronghold. Two weeks later, Kunduz fell. One hundred CIA officers and 300 US Special Forces had successfully taken a country the size of Texas, with a population of 30 million people. And they had done it in seven weeks.

The operation was a triumph, particularly for Donald Rumsfeld, whose notions of a faster, lighter form of manoeuvre warfare were completely vindicated. The Secretary of Defense, it seemed, had rewritten the rule book for war. Time for some reverse-gloating.

'It *looked* like nothing was happening,' Rumsfeld told the Press. 'Indeed, it looked like we were in a – *all together now* – quagmire!'

In the United Kingdom, Downing Street published a list of journalists whose predictions about Afghanistan had been wrong. In Parliament Foreign Secretary Jack Straw ridiculed suggestions that British troops would still be in the country in a year's time.

It was at exactly this moment, however, that things started to go wrong.

A side effect of America's decision not to deploy large numbers of troops to Afghanistan was a reduction in its ability to gather accurate intelligence. All too frequently tips handed to coalition troops were not the result of a genuine desire to assist the United States, but to settle old scores. For instance, on 22 December, the day Hamid Karzai was inaugurated as Afghanistan's interim leader, US aircraft located and bombed a convoy of suspected Taliban leaders on a mountainous road outside Kabul. It soon transpired the casualties were not Taliban at all. They were political administrators from the city of Gardez on their way to attend the inauguration. A rival militia leader had blocked the Kabul road, forced the convoy on to an isolated track, then called the Americans and told them a Taliban convoy was coming. Twelve administrators were killed, along with fifteen locals who happened to live in the village next to the convoy when the bombs fell.

The problem of bad intelligence was especially troubling when it came to the most important question of all: where was Bin Laden?

In December 2001, he was apparently hiding at Tora Bora, but, by the time the mountain complexes were taken, he was gone. US military spokesmen downplayed the loss: perhaps he had never been there at all, they suggested. But he had.

'Bin Laden was there. Zawahiri[4] was there. They were *all* there,' says a senior CIA officer engaged in the hunt at the time. They escaped. 'We had the proof. We lost a golden opportunity.'

At the start of the War on Terror, George W. Bush had made a list

---

[4] Ayman al-Zawahiri, widely regarded as Al-Qaeda's second in command.

of al-Qaeda suspects he wanted captured or killed. Now it appeared that many of them had slipped across the border into Pakistan, beyond America's reach. In March 2002, Bush was asked about Bin Laden at a press conference.

'Marginalized,' the President told journalists. 'I truly am not that concerned about him.'

No one believed it. In fact, the President was desperate to capture the al-Qaeda leader. Apart from meting out justice for 9/11, the White House was keen for signs of progress that could be delivered to the Press. The United States had invaded Afghanistan to capture the guys responsible for 11 September. Where were they? How could the most sophisticated military force the world had ever known prove unable to locate a bunch of third-rate bandits on horses in a Third World country?

With Bin Laden gone to ground, the focus in Afghanistan shifted to the Taliban. Here the problem was potentially more embarrassing: it was one thing not to be able to locate a handful of al-Qaeda terrorists. It was quite another, having driven the Taliban from power, to be unable to find any of its senior members. Rumours circulating at the time indicated that the organization's leader Mullah Omar had escaped from US forces on a Honda motorbike. Pakistan's President Pervez Musharraf joked to Japan's Prime Minister that a photo of Mullah Omar speeding away on his bike, robes flowing in the wind, would make a great advertisement for Honda.

After the debacle at Tora Bora, the Bush administration needed some good news. A few high-level Taliban officials might do it. US intelligence officers offered rewards for information leading to their capture, and were promptly swamped with tip-offs. Claims of Taliban hideouts poured in daily. Intelligence officials joked that finding Mullah Omar was like following up sightings of Elvis Presley. Every day there were new leads. He was here. He was there. He was gone. The hunt was made considerably harder by the fact that no one was quite sure what he actually looked like. Hamid Karzai later admitted he wouldn't recognize Mullah Omar if he passed him in the street.

There were some things the US intelligence community knew about Mullah Omar, however, that might shift the odds in its favour. A study of his childhood, for example, indicated that he had a strong affection for the province of Oruzgan – and one specific part of it: Deh Rawood.

Mullah Omar's father had died when he was young and his mother had married his uncle, Maulawi Muzafa. Immediately after his father's death, Omar had moved to the village of Deh Wanawark, a few miles outside Deh Rawood, where Muzafa was the local mullah. There, the future Taliban leader had grown up, and it was from there that he had started the Taliban movement.

This is why, when Hamid Karzai and the Green Berets of ODA-574 had begun the process of liberating the country in November 2001, they had focused on Oruzgan. The region, Karzai informed his Special Forces assistants, was 'the heart of the Taliban movement'. Every major player had family and friends there.

Abdul Malik and his family were well aware of the importance of the region, and their town in particular, for the Taliban. Some of them had met Mullah Omar.

'I knew him when he was very young. He was a bit younger than me,' says Malik's uncle Anwar. 'I grew up with him.' Anwar had shared a room with Omar for four years during the Soviet occupation. His opinion of the future Taliban leader was not high. 'Not that educated. Illiterate. Among his friends he wasn't even in the top ten.'

In a couple of areas, however, Omar excelled. He was certainly brave in combat. And he was a fantastic marksman. When Anwar and his friends challenged him, Omar would demonstrate his aim by shooting single cigarettes off a wall at the edge of town.

'We would put up a cigarette. He would always hit it first time.'

For a while, the two men were quite close. According to legend,

Mullah Omar was wounded in the face by a piece of shrapnel during a Soviet airstrike and extracted his own eye on the battlefield with a bayonet. This, says Anwar, is hokum. He was indeed partially blinded, but was then taken to Pakistan, where the eye was surgically removed.

'I went into hospital to see him,' says Anwar. 'He told me, "I've lost my eye!" He was really worried about losing his eye.'

Anwar reassured the future Taliban leader. 'Don't worry,' he told him. 'Thank God that you are alive.'

But Omar wasn't having any of it. 'Right!' he told his friend sarcastically. 'This injury has destroyed my youth.'

Later, it was a great surprise to Anwar that Omar had achieved such prominence. Of all the young men growing up in Deh Rawood at the time, nobody would have predicted he would achieve high office.

After the Taliban swept the country, the two men met again. Anwar sought Omar's assistance in freeing a friend of his who had been wrongly imprisoned for a petty crime. Omar issued Anwar with a letter instructing the authorities to release their prisoner. When the guards refused, Anwar returned and told him what had happened. Together, the two men marched to the prison, where they located the man, ordered his release and castigated the official responsible. After the incident, Omar had offered Anwar a job in his administration.

'Come,' Omar said. 'Come and join the Taliban movement.'

Anwar refused. It was the last time they would meet.

The exact nature of the intelligence that reached US officials in the summer of 2002 regarding the Taliban presence in Deh Rawood has never been revealed. It probably never will be. What is clear is that sometime in the spring of that year rumours began circulating that Mullah Omar had returned to Oruzgan and, specifically, to Deh Rawood.

In May, the *New York Times* reported from Deh Rawood that Mullah Omar had been sighted. Either he was in the village or in the vicinity.

If these rumours were true, he was almost certainly receiving assistance from family and friends there.

'They will be helping them in the villages,' General Amanullah, the Afghan military commander for northern Oruzgan, assured the *Times*. 'They are of the same tribe or family . . . of course they will be helping them.'

Special Forces from Norway, Germany, Australia and Canada were positioned in the mountains around town to watch the area and report any suspicious activity. It wasn't long before they did. Whenever helicopters approached the area to drop off men or supplies they were shot at. SPECTRE gunships covering the operations reported fire from artillery weapons, including 23 mm machine guns and a 12.7 mm Soviet anti-aircraft gun known as a DShK. The gunfire appeared to confirm the rumours: this region of Oruzgan housed a High-Value Target (HVT). Signals intelligence – phone and radio intercepts – as well as human sources indicated that the HVT might be one of three Taliban leaders: Mullah Osmani, Mullah Barader or Mullah Omar himself. Possibly even all three. Something, it seemed, was going on in Deh Rawood.

US Special Forces drafted a Concept of Operations (CONOP) plan to sweep the valley, passing through Deh Rawood, clearing the area of Taliban and arresting any HVTs they might find. Four Special Forces teams would infiltrate the area by helicopter. Because it was known the Taliban had intelligence sources in the region, the teams were to split up around the village, taking up blocking positions to cut off possible escape routes to the north, on the roads leading to Helmand Province. SPECTRE would cover the operation from the air in case things went wrong.

Things did go wrong. On the flight in, the Special Forces' MH-47 helicopter was engaged from the ground, causing the pilots to change their landing zone. They then tried to put the helicopter down in an area strewn with boulders. While landing, the MH-47's undercarriage caught on the rocks and was irretrievably damaged, along with the helicopter's hydraulics system, which ruptured. Aircrew aborted the mission and returned to base, topping up the hydraulic system by hand all the way.

One Special Forces team did make it to the Deh Rawood area, where they established their blocking position, only to discover they were now alone. They were forced to spend two days hiding from the villagers before they could be exfiltrated.

'The mission they hoped would net a thousand al-Qaeda and Taliban forces netted nothing,' wrote one of the Special Forces operatives involved. 'Not a damn thing.' There was one good piece of news: apparently the team on the ground had picked up a cellphone. It was rumoured to be Mullah Omar's.

Planning immediately started on another raid. This one was going to be bigger. Teams from the 3rd and 19th Special Forces groups were to go in, along with British Royal Marines and members of the US 101st Airborne Division. Deh Rawood would be surrounded, sealed off and swept. This 'large combined arms mission' was given a name: Operation Full Throttle. According to one Special Forces soldier involved, senior planners were convinced that the town 'was hiding hordes of bad guys'.

On 27 June 2002, just two days before Operation Full Throttle was to be launched, the plan changed. The Royal Marines and the 101st Airborne weren't coming. US Special Forces, Navy SEAL teams and a handful of CIA officers were going in alone. And most of them weren't going in by helicopter any more. They were going to drive from Kandahar. Thirty vehicles would traverse 150 kilometres of rough Afghan terrain at night to surprise the Taliban in Deh Rawood. Special Forces were unimpressed by the new plan.

'All the guys knew that, with such a scheme, any fuck-up was going to have very real consequences,' observed one participant. 'And there was a very real chance for a fuck-up.'

*   *   *

While Special Forces were contemplating the wisdom of Operation Full Throttle, Abdul Malik's family was planning, too. Malik's father had finalized negotiations regarding his daughter-in-law's dowry on 27 June, the same day US forces learned of the change of plan regarding the assault on Deh Rawood. The following day the men in Malik's family would pick up the *dastmal* and there would be a private family gathering. Then, on the night of the 30th, there would be a party.

As in the case of his engagement, Abdul Malik would have nothing to do with any of this. The bride and groom were not invited to their own engagement party. Partly this was to ensure they didn't meet, but there was another motive.

'The groom never stays at home, because he is ashamed,' explains his brother, Khaliq. 'Also, so that all his cousins can make jokes about him when he's not there.'

According to Afghan custom, a wedding party would be strictly segregated. A few male relatives were to attend – twenty in all – but their roles were menial: they prepare the food. Other than when serving the meal, they were to be kept apart from the women.

The Malik house was separated into guest and family areas, and the men set about procuring enough meat, rice and cooking pots to prepare the banquet. Deh Rawood was without electricity, so they scoured the village for lights, borrowing four propane gas burners to position around the house. They also borrowed a neighbour's tractor. Its headlights could be used to illuminate the garden. Abdul Malik was sent off to spend the night at his uncle's house, well out of the way of the women. His bride-to-be Tela Gul was left at her parents' home.

Throughout the day of 28 June 2002, children from the Malik household were dispatched on errands around the village. Their mission was to visit all the family's friends and relatives and invite them to the party on the 30th.

*   *   *

The issue of the invitation list to the wedding party remains one of the unsolved mysteries regarding what happened next. For those who were involved, it is *the* unsolved mystery. Because there was one potential guest whose presence at the Malik household on the night of 30 June would have been of very great interest to the US military.

When Malik's mother had told him that his future bride belonged to a 'famous family', she wasn't exaggerating. Tela Gul's father Mohammed Sarwar Akhond, the mullah at the mosque in Chagasyan, had a brother considerably more important than he was. The brother – Tela Gul's uncle – was Mullah Barader, second in command of the Taliban, and generally regarded by the United States at the time as the means of communication between potential Taliban supporters in Oruzgan and Mullah Omar himself.

At the time of the engagement, all kinds of rumours were circulating about Barader. Like the other Taliban leaders, he had fled Kandahar in December 2001, presumably for Pakistan. Now it seemed he was back. In June, he was spotted in Oruzgan's neighbouring province, Helmand. Gossip picked up by local journalists suggested he was hiding somewhere in the vicinity of Deh Rawood and that he was coming into town at night, on a motorbike, to speak to locals and plan for an insurgency against the Americans. The US military appears to have got wind of these trips: in the spring of 2002, Special Forces launched three raids in the area, two of them specifically targetting Barader's house.

Abdul Malik's family is adamant that, although they knew Mullah Barader prior to the US invasion of Afghanistan, and knew that he was Tela Gul's uncle, no one had heard from him since he had fled to Pakistan in the winter of 2001. Certainly he was not invited to the party. Neither he nor his boss – Uncle Anwar's former roommate – Mullah Omar was due to attend the celebration.

It seems entirely possible, however, that others in town – those less well acquainted with the family or possibly with ulterior motives – might have passed a rumour to American forces: Mullah Barader's niece was getting married. There was to be a party. Mullah Barader might show up. Mullah Omar might show up.

Here was an opportunity.

Operation Full Throttle began on 29 June, when around thirty personnel carriers containing the SEALs, the Green Berets and a clutch of CIA officers departed from Kandahar. The teams drove all night, then stopped for the day to rest and prepare for the raid itself on 30 June. As the sun went down, they checked their weapons, donned their night-vision gear and headed off in the direction of Deh Rawood – and, they hoped, the biggest Taliban seizure of the war so far.

Again, things went wrong. Full Throttle called for four twelve-man Operational Detachments Alpha (ODAs) and a team of SEALs to surround Deh Rawood. Another ODA was to be flown in by helicopter to block possible escape routes. A nearby B-Team would coordinate the mission. The idea was to sneak up on the village ('in complete secrecy', according to one officer present), then pass through as quickly as possible, snatching up the HVTs. But, according to another participant, the 'stealth' element of the raid was compromised before the operation began. Thirty vehicles driving through the desert created a cloud of dust visible for miles around.

As the convoy approached Deh Rawood, it was forced along a mountainside, a downhill slope leading into the Helmand River valley. At the end of the slope on the right was an Afghan National Army checkpoint, manned by armed guards. Since the objective of the exercise was stealth, it now became crucial to disarm the guards. More important, however, was to remove their means of communication, so they could not alert potential insurgents in the valley below.

The convoy stopped 200 metres short of the guard house and the troops debated how best to go about this. For a brief period, they wondered whether they should kill the Afghans. Then they decided it might be better just to talk to them. A handful of US troops entered the checkpoint. They explained who they were, what they were doing, and demanded the guards' weapons, radios and cellphones. At this point it became clear something was very wrong.

'We knew you were coming,' one of the Afghan guards told them. 'We were briefed about you.'

He had been told not only that US troops were coming, but how many vehicles there would be. He had already rounded up his men's communications gear and handed it over to Jan Mohammed, the Province Governor.

'Now,' he told the soldiers, 'would you like to sit down and have some tea with us?'

Abdul Malik's engagement party got underway at sunset. More than 200 women showed up with their children. As they entered the house, they passed by the *dastmal* basket and dropped in small-denomination Afghan currency notes, gifts for the groom's family. Then they got on with the serious business of congratulating the women of the household on the successful engagement, and speculating how many children Abdul Malik and Tela Gul might have.

Outside in the pomegranate orchard, the men cooked the rice and meat, lit the gas burners and started the tractor to provide the lighting for the evening. The children, allowed to stay up late for the party, ran around the garden, then climbed up on to the single-storey house's roof to watch the grown-ups below.

After the meal was served, most of the men who had cooked it went home, but Abdul Malik's uncles and brothers stayed on, drinking tea in the garden. One of them then rigged up a tape recorder, cleared a space in front of the house and trained the tractor lights on to it to provide a makeshift dance floor. Someone found a tape of the *Atan*, a traditional Afghan dance, and put it on. Many of the women moved outside and watched the boys dancing. The kids on the roof of the house laughed.

*   *   *

Having realized the secrecy of Operation Full Throttle had been compromised, the Special Forces left the guard house and headed down into the valley towards Deh Rawood. Almost immediately, they came under fire. They shot back, then split up to assume their various positions around the village.

Again, things did not go to plan. According to one team involved, the US Navy SEAL contingent got lost and ended up heading in the wrong direction. After putting them right, the Green Berets checked in with their air cover: two B-52s, a handful of US Air Force fighter jets and two SPECTRE gunships that were circling overhead.

One Green Beret team then discovered that the site they had been given as a potential point to cross the Helmand river was actually impassable. As they wondered what to do next, they were radioed by one of the AC-130s. It warned them that the Navy SEALS, still apparently lost, had seen them, assumed they were Taliban fighters and had requested the gunship to take them out. Fortunately, the SPECTRE crew had been watching the entire process from above and recognized that it was being asked to open fire on friendly forces.

Operation Full Throttle had not got off to a good start. It was about to get a great deal worse.

Abdul Malik's brother Khaliq didn't hear the planes. He was sitting outside under the pomegranate trees in the garden, drinking tea with his cousins. The meal was over and the party well underway.

'It was a great party. The tape recorder was on. Boys were dancing to the music.'

Mohammed Sharif, the groom's father, didn't hear the planes either. The noise level of the party was too high. He was at the door between the two sections of the house to ensure that no men entered the women's area.

A neighbour, Saheb Jan Agha, who was sleeping on his roof fifty metres away, did hear the planes. Over the sound of the music wafting from the Malik household came the drone of jets, followed by the noise of propellers. At first it didn't worry him: for days now there had been aerial activity over Deh Rawood. Then, around 11 p.m., the tone changed abruptly.

'Right in the middle, I heard this loud sound,' he recalls. 'Suddenly they started.'

Khaliq had just finished his tea when the first missile struck the house. The blast broke both his hands and stripped the flesh from his legs. In an instant he looked up to see that many of his relatives were dead. The children on the roof started screaming and the garden filled with smoke. He just had time to count the corpses around him – seven in all – before the second projectile hit. He was knocked unconscious. Inside the house, his father, guarding the door between the two sections of the party, managed to shout that someone should contact the authorities before he, too, was hit. He was killed instantly.

Partygoers attempted to flee. Laik, a local farmer, had been drinking tea outside with two friends when the attack began. One of them was killed in front of him, so he and the other ran through the courtyard towards the wheat fields. Then his other friend was also hit. Laik was one of the first to realize what was going on.

'The Americans were bombing the house. We could not believe it. We were running everywhere to hide.'

On the roof Malik's grandmother Sardara, who had been playing with the children, desperately tried to get them away, dropping the infants to the ground. She then jumped down to help them to safety, but found herself unable to see: the fire from the sky, and the dust from the ground, had created an impenetrable cloud.

For some reason the children had a better view. Fifteen-year-old Nassema later reported what she had seen: 'A piece of iron sliced the woman's neck in front of me. In a split second, her head was not on her body.'

Eight-year-old Kako witnessed the same incident. She heard a sudden explosion, then looked up: 'I saw the pool in the courtyard filled with blood. There were bodies all around. I saw a woman without a head.'

Most survivors describe two attacks, the first on the women's section of the party, the second on the men's. The first explosions were almost certainly blasts from the AC-130's 105 mm canon. Perhaps there were more. Saheb Jan Agha recalls 'continuous fire'.

Once the revellers started to flee, however, the AC-130 appears to have opened fire on them with lighter-gauge weapons: presumably the 25 mm and 40 mm machine guns.

Ahmed Jan Agha, who had been playing drums in the men's section of the party, thought the house was under rocket attack. 'The aeroplanes were shooting rockets at the people running away. They were chasing us.' His account was later corroborated by children who survived, who all told of running into the wheat fields around town to hide, hotly pursued by machine-gun or rocket fire.

Fifteen-year-old Sadiqua made it to a dried-up riverbed outside the house, but the AC-130's gunners caught up with her. She was shot in both legs.

The first on the scene was Uncle Anwar's brother Abdul Bari. By the time he reached the house at around 2 a.m., the actual shooting was over, but women and children were still running around screaming, and the compound remained shrouded in a dust cloud.

He ran into the house, saw the extent of the damage and started carrying bodies – the wounded and the dead – into the garden. Shortly afterwards, however, US Special Forces arrived alongside the building and instructed him to stop. When he refused, they arrested him.

'They blindfolded us. Handcuffed us,' he says. 'People who had been arrested by the Americans were begging for them to help the wounded. We weren't begging for our own release, but begging to help the wounded people.'

According to Bari, they were lined up and told not to move. Ignoring requests to treat the wounded first, the troops instead started interrogating the surviving wedding guests.

'They asked us if we knew Mullah Omar or Mullah Barader.' Bari thought the question was senseless. 'Of course, everybody knew Mullah Barader: he was from this district.' Deciding that discretion was the better part of valour, Bari denied knowing the mullah. 'I said, "No, I don't know him."'

Abdul Malik, spending the night at his uncle's house twenty minutes away, was woken by the sound of guns. He realized the attack was somewhere in the direction of his family home, but it never occurred to him that his own engagement party had been the target.

He tried listening to his police radio for news, but all he got was white noise; apparently the signal was being jammed by the US Special Forces. As day broke, however, the radio crackled back to life and he learned that his house had been damaged. At that moment, a friend hammered on the door.

'Your house,' he told the groom. 'It's been bombed.'

Malik and his friend started to run.

Uncle Anwar also had no idea the family home had been hit. Around 7 a.m., he received an emergency visit from a couple of neighbours who told him he needed to come right away. There had been an attack, they said. A rocket had landed on his house. Two children had been hurt.

'I didn't believe it,' he says. 'There were lots of people there. If a rocket had hit the house, more would have been hurt.'

As his car approached Deh Rawood, it was obvious the devastation was far greater than his friends had admitted.

'Before reaching the village I could see that injured bodies were being moved.'

Anwar got out of the car and started to run, but was stopped by another friend carrying the body of a young woman. It was his niece.

Cars crammed full of injured partygoers sped past – and the scale of the destruction became clear.

By the time Abdul Malik arrived at the scene, the entire compound had been cordoned off by the Americans and helicopters were ferrying the wounded to field hospitals. At nine or ten o'clock, when all of the wounded were on their way to hospital – by car or helicopter – the clearing-up process began.

To those unfamiliar with the notion of 'target saturation', as practised by a US Air Force SPECTRE gunship, the extent of the damage was flabbergasting.

'We had four cows, one dog, one donkey and many chickens,' says Malik. 'They were all killed.'

Abdul Bari was dumbstruck: 'Everything was dead. Human beings, animals, sheep, cows – everything.'

Even the family cat was killed.

Many of the corpses were unrecognizable.

'A few of the dead children, we never found their bodies. We just collected the bits of meat and put them all into one grave.'

Uncle Anwar helped. 'We collected parts of human bodies that were just scattered everywhere. There was blood everywhere. So we cleaned up the blood, and collected all the human meat.'

Jan Agha brought an old blanket from his home and used it to carry the corpses. 'The wounded and the dead were lying everywhere,' he says. 'Pieces of human bodies were in the trees, on the ground, in all the corners.' Agha set about lifting the bodies from the house. 'I carried one little kid who I thought was asleep. But she was dead.'

When news broke in the United States that its military appeared inadvertently to have killed a large number of civilians in Afghanistan, the Pentagon struggled to keep pace. Initially, spokesmen said the incident might have been the result of a 2,000 lb bomb that had gone astray.

'At least one bomb was errant,' a spokesman admitted of Operation Full Throttle on 1 July. 'We don't know where it fell.'

The next day more detail was added. A B-52 had dropped seven precision-guided munitions in Oruzgan on the night of 30 June. One had missed its target by 3,000 yards.

'It does seem as though something went wrong,' Paul Wolfowitz told National Public Radio. 'But we're still trying to get to the bottom of it.'

One Pentagon spokesman suggested that the civilian casualties might have been 'the result of anti-aircraft artillery', implying the villagers had shot themselves.

The image was one of confusion. 'I read in the paper that there was a wedding,' Rumsfeld told the Press. 'But I just don't have the facts.'

Asked about the incident, Pentagon spokesperson Torie Clarke replied that 'there isn't any reason to believe or disbelieve anything'.

Rumsfeld, however, appears to have had a reason to believe *something*: 'Taliban and al-Qaeda training manuals have explained to people how to do disinformation and how to handle those types of things to discredit the United States.'

Certainly, the Pentagon believed the casualty figures coming out of Afghanistan were inflated. They were right. Initial reports indicated that 250 civilians were dead and 600 wounded. The actual figure was 48 dead, 117 wounded.

Special Forces returning from Operation Full Throttle were appalled. They had been on a difficult, dangerous, night-time operation. A clandestine raid had been compromised. It was entirely possible they had walked into a trap. They were lucky to have made it back alive. Now they were hijacked by the liberal press – no doubt the same liberal press that had predicted the failure of the invasion in the first place – and accused of massacring innocent civilians.

'Something,' one wrote later, 'was fishy.'

General Dan McNeill, Commander of US forces in Afghanistan, was also confused as to what had happened. He summoned one of the Special Force officers who had taken part. 'Describe for me directly what happened,' he said, 'what the situation was.' The case was complicated.

'It was awfully difficult,' General McNeill recalls today, 'but after about a day I began to realize that I could put it all together and understand what had occurred.'

Aircraft providing cover for the ground troops over Deh Rawood had been engaged from the ground, apparently with anti-aircraft artillery. Assuming they were under attack, they had returned fire. One of the AC-130s had targeted the wedding party, where, apparently, men were firing rifles into the sky to celebrate.

General McNeill flew straight to Oruzgan to meet the groom's relatives, including Uncle Anwar. He listened to their account of what happened and apologized on behalf of the US military.

Not everyone was in an apologetic mood. Visiting Afghanistan in mid-July Paul Wolfowitz, the Undersecretary of Defense for Policy, was told that President Karzai was livid and that the US embassy had dispatched a Pashtun-speaking officer to attend the consequent funerals and to apologize for the targeting error.

'Why do you assume there was a wedding party?' the undersecretary asked his briefer. 'How do you know?' Wolfowitz suggested that the US response was misguided. 'We shouldn't be so passive in apologizing. We should be more confident.'

A similar response had come the previous February when Donald Rumsfeld had suggested that another friendly-fire incident was not all it seemed. 'Let's not call them innocents,' he told the Press of a group of Afghans shot by US forces. 'We don't know quite what they were.'

Like Wolfowitz, Rumsfeld also appears to have questioned whether the wedding-party story was true, referring to the incident at one point as 'the so-called wedding'. Why assume civilian casualties were innocent? Wasn't there a possibility they might have been guilty?

Publicly, however, Paul Wolfowitz was contrite. 'All the evidence suggests that innocent people were killed there . . . we deeply regret that. Unfortunately, sometimes mistakes are made.' Investigations were underway.

Two weeks later, while the US military was conducting an internal investigation, the United Nations came up with a document of its own: a 'quick, preliminary report' compiled by staff who had visited Deh Rawood on 1 July. To the horror of the US military, it was leaked to the Press. Not only had the United States underestimated the number of dead and wounded in the town, the report suggested, there was no evidence to indicate the AC-130 had been targeted at all, while there was an indication that the US military had 'cleaned the area', removing evidence of the incident, including shrapnel, bullets and blood. The UN report also highlighted discrepancies in the American account of the attack. A further, fuller, report would be released within forty-eight hours.

It never was. The following day the United Nations changed its tune: the report would remain classified, to be shared only with the US and Afghan governments. According to a UN spokesman, the organization had never been involved in an inquiry at all, but was simply 'responding to humanitarian needs'. Commentators assumed the decision to withold the document was the result of pressure from the US administration – not keen, apparently, to have its account of events challenged. More of the same could be expected.

'The more it drags on, the harder it is to prove,' one UN official told the *Times*. 'Probably the people investigating want it to go slowly and die away.'

Perhaps there was some truth in this. James Dobbins, the US Special Envoy at the time, writes of the Pentagon's 'deny first, investigate later' attitude. Dobbins had witnessed an example of it first-hand, following the misguided US air strike on the Gardez convoy attending the presidential inauguration in December 2001. Sharing a car with General Tommy Franks on the way to the ceremony, Dobbins had mentioned there had been an incident. Franks had not heard about it, but the moment he was confronted by the Press he denied categorically it had taken place.

Dobbins was taken aback: 'I don't think this was necessarily a policy. I think it was a tropism,' he says today, 'but I do think that it wasn't until the fourth or fifth time that this happened that they began to recognize that that particular tropism was impinging badly on their credibility.'

It would be easy at this point to blame the Green Berets, the Navy SEALs and the crew of the AC-130 aircraft for what happened at Deh Rawood. The evidence seems clear-cut. They shot people. The wrong people. Lots of them. No Taliban leaders were killed or caught. Worse, no evidence was ever found of the artillery piece that the AC-130 crew claimed had engaged it. Those who have seen the gun-tape footage from the aircraft swear that it shows enemy fire, but these tapes have never been released. US officials are insistent that, while there was background noise about various Taliban officials in the region, there was no concrete intelligence regarding Mullah Barader. Certainly, they didn't know there was a wedding party.

Over the next few years, this pattern would repeat itself: contaminated intelligence, Special Forces on the ground, aerial strikes, civilian casualties. Often the targets were wedding ceremonies. Apparently, coalition troops, unfamiliar with the Afghan custom of shooting during celebrations, mistook it for hostile fire and responded.

'I'd say it's about time we gave up on the wedding-party bombing strategy,' wrote one satirical blogger in 2008. 'We've been following it in Afghanistan for over six years now, and things are worse in that country than when we first started bombing its weddings.'

To blame the military for these incidents, however, is to miss the point. The wedding-party attack is not simply the story of a bunch of trigger-happy cowboys; it represents the end result of a long chain of decisions. At the head of these was the adoption of a 'light footprint' by the White House. The decision not to commit large numbers of troops meant less accurate intelligence. Operations had to be conducted by small groups of Special Forces, often in unfamiliar regions. They needed to defend themselves. If they got into trouble on the ground, aerial bombardment followed. Mistakes were inevitable. When these mistakes were made on board weapons platforms as lethal as AC-130 gunships, results were always going to be tragic.

Throughout the initial period in Afghanistan, the US administration downplayed any suggestion things were going wrong. The Pentagon vetoed the idea of expanding peacekeeping operations beyond the country's main cities, even when they were to be staffed by other NATO countries. European diplomats fiercely disagreed. The Afghans, they argued, needed to see that things had changed for the better; they needed hard evidence. Above all, if the Karzai administration was to govern with any real authority, it needed security. The best way to arrange this was to expand peacekeeping operations – and fast.

'There was a moment in Afghanistan which lasted – I don't know how long – three months maybe, possibly a bit longer,' says a British diplomat, 'in which people knew that the old order had disappeared, but they didn't know what the new order was. And at that moment you could impose something.'

The suggestion was forwarded to the United States both from inside the administration (Special Envoy Dobbins was all for it) and outside. The answer was unequivocal: 'They were not remotely interested.' According to Rumsfeld, those who thought more troops were necessary in Afghanistan were 'mostly on editorial boards, columnists and at the UN'.

In terms of manpower, the Afghan campaign would prove to be one of the worst-resourced stabilization operations in modern history. In Kosovo the international community had committed 19 troops per 1,000 people; in Afghanistan the figure was 1.6 troops per 1,000. Despite George W. Bush's repeated invocation of the Marshall Plan, when it came to troop levels the Afghanistan mission ranked lower than some of the international community's most notable failures: Somalia (5.7 troops per 1,000) and Haiti (2.9 per 1,000).

At the time of the wedding-party incident, the United States had 8,000 troops in Afghanistan: a quarter of the number of uniformed police officers in New York City. Bosnia had received 2,000 civilian police officers to assist with law enforcement; Kosovo 5,000. Afghanistan received none. Attempts to rebuild the country's police, military and judicial systems floundered: the countries assigned responsibility for them made little effort.

'None of the countries, including the United States, did what they were supposed to do in the way they were supposed to do it,' says Robert Finn, America's first ambassador to Afghanistan for more than twenty years. 'They were all individuals with their own failings, and there was no one in charge who could go around and kick them in the butt and say, "You're not doing it right."' NATO members sent troops from time to time, but often restricted the roles they were allowed to play. No one was keen on putting their soldiers in harm's way.

The result was an inability to provide security of any sort in the countryside. Special Forces could clear and sweep villages, arrest and shoot Taliban and al-Qaeda fighters, but they were unable to stay for long. All the Taliban had to do was slip away when coalition forces arrived, then return once they left. As Mullah Omar famously stated: 'The Americans may have the clocks. But we have the time.'

Instability in the countryside made civilian operations to rebuild the country dangerous. Progress slowed down. Afghans, waiting for roads and civilian infrastructure to be rebuilt, became disaffected – and open to recruitment from Taliban members, who started flowing back over the border from Pakistan and bombing coalition troops. More attacks meant less reconstruction, which fed popular disaffection and led to further attacks. The military blamed the civilians for not repairing the country's infrastructure. The civilians blamed the military: if the countryside wasn't safe, how were they supposed to get the place up and running again?

Money was another issue. The initial sum allocated to Afghanistan by the United States in the winter of 2001 was no higher that it would have been had the country still been under Taliban control – a source of surprise to James Dobbins.

'The idea that we'd liberated a country,' he recalls, 'and the aid budget was the same as it was before we'd liberated it struck me as bizarre.'

The international community did little better. Generally, about half the money requested for Afghan reconstruction was actually pledged. Of that half, half never arrived. The money that did often came in the form of credits with donor countries and was administered through middlemen, who took commissions along the way. Financially, the operation was a disaster. Funding for reconstruction in Kosovo in the first year had been $577 per civilian; Afghanistan received just $60. And yet reconstruction in Afghanistan was clearly going to be harder than it had been in the former Yugoslavia.

'In Bosnia they had these nice, tidy Bosnian brick houses, so you just had to go in and paint them and reconnect the plumbing and the electricity and put a roof on and you were back in business,' says Finn. 'In Afghanistan we were starting from scratch.'

Lack of troops, and visible progress, meant that all most Afghans saw of foreign forces in their country was when a bunch of Special Forces kicked down the door and arrested someone – or, worse, started shooting and killed civilians. No Special Forces, no matter how well trained, were going to fix Afghanistan without proper support. This was a problem that SPECTRE gunships were not going to solve.

Critics of the War on Terror might see a metaphor in AC-130 deployments during Operation Enduring Freedom. Like the gunships, US policy was very good at breaking things, but not so good at putting them back together again. The problem was that while breaking things was entirely understandable – necessary, even, at the outset – it could never provide a long-term solution to the problem of terrorism in Afghanistan. After the Taliban, what?

'There was no planning at all, really, for what would come next,' says the British diplomat. 'I thought it was nuts.'

The night after the attack, Abdul Malik moved back into the family house in Deh Rawood, alone. Everyone else was in hospital or dead. Various government figures, including Hamid Karzai, came to speak to him, and to apologize. None would ever tell him why his family had been targeted, or who – if anyone – had been the source of the mysterious intelligence about Mullah Barader that had led to the attack. Malik could never understand how the US military, with all its technological wizardry, had mistaken a wedding party for an artillery weapon. Three months later, while giving a foreign official a tour of the household, he noticed something high up in a pomegranate tree. It was the intestine of one of his relatives.

Malik and Tela Gul were married five months afterwards. The wedding was a downbeat affair: only fifty guests were invited. There was no music.

'We three brothers have decided that, if anyone within our family gets married or engaged, there will be no party,' says Uncle Anwar. 'There will be no music and no dancing. The door of happiness is closed for us now.'

These are the people to whom Hamid Karzai first appealed for assistance when he re-entered Afghanistan in the winter of 2001. These are the people that teased the US Special Forces for filtering their water. These are the people that gave them turbans better to disguise themselves. They feel differently now.

'The presence of Americans [in Afghanistan] is like eating poison for me every day,' says Anwar.

His brother Abdul Bari agrees. Bari's children had been among the group on the roof that night. He discovered six of their bodies the next morning.

'When you see eighteen people from your family killed in one day, and forty-seven bodies of your relatives in your house, how would *you* feel?' he asks. 'Americans killed eighteen members of my family. Americans are my enemy and the enemy of my family. I cannot forgive Americans for what they did.'

The third brother, Qudus, agrees. 'I hate Americans more than pigs.'

This is not barely concealed anger, or even anger at all.

It is rage.

Midway through 2002, at about the time of the wedding party, something rather extraordinary happened in Afghanistan: the US started pulling out its assets.

CIA officers were appalled. 'We had very elaborate administrative structures set up to work on Afghanistan,' recalls one. 'We had a special operations group, a military advisory group, a high-value targets group: we had all these groups that were focused on very specific aspects of fighting this war in Afghanistan, and then – almost literally overnight – the White House wasn't interested in Afghanistan any more.'

For those who knew what to look for, the signs had been there all along. When he was first sent to Afghanistan at the start of 2002, General Dan McNeill had been instructed to leave half of his headquarters at home, including his deputy.

'At that time I wasn't exactly certain of what that was all about,' he says. 'I presumed it had something to do with Iraq. This day I am relatively certain it had to do with Iraq.'

Michael Scheuer, who headed the Bin Laden Unit at the CIA, came to the same conclusion. 'In March 2002, around the middle of the month, we began to lose some of our most experienced officers: Arabic speakers, regional experts,' he recalls. 'It was quite frankly said they were going to get ready for a war with Iraq.'

In August, another officer, based in Pakistan at the time, was recalled to the CIA HQ at Langley, where he was briefed about the project that would become Operation Iraqi Freedom.

'But we haven't caught Bin Laden yet!' he told his briefer. 'We haven't finished in Afghanistan!'

Officials felt differently. 'Afghanistan was really an accidental war for much of the administration. No one wanted to do it. And once it became clear the Taliban was likely to fall, senior Pentagon officials wanted to turn to Iraq as quickly as possible,' Deputy Secretary of State Richard Armitage later commented. 'It was Iraq, Iraq, Iraq.'

Ironically, the astonishing speed and success of Operation Enduring Freedom appears to have persuaded the White House the next mission was viable.

'When we succeeded in removing the Taliban in Afghanistan, we received such a welcome from the Afghan people,' Rumsfeld told Fox News in July 2002. 'I think it's nothing compared to what the Iraqi people will say and do when they're rid of Saddam.'

4

Groupthink 7075-T6

Simply stated, there is no doubt that Saddam Hussein now has weapons of mass destruction.

Dick Cheney, August 2002

Fuck Saddam. We're taking him out.

George W. Bush, March 2002

In September 2000, an intriguing advertisement appeared on the ground-floor corridor of Baghdad's University of Technology:

ASSISTANCE REQUIRED

Sami Ibrahim was on his way to work when he spotted it. Beneath the headline, a technical term stood out:

PITTING CORROSION, 7075-T6

At the bottom of the page was a telephone number. Intrigued, the Professor jotted it down, climbed the stairs to his office and thought for a moment.

Ibrahim had a fair idea who was behind the message. It was no secret the Iraqi military placed advertisements in the country's leading universities from time to time, requesting assistance with technical problems. It was also no secret that academics who solved these problems were looked upon favourably when the promotions season came around. Besides, the Professor was a patriot. If his government needed help and he was in a position to offer it, why not? Sami Ibrahim took a deep breath, picked up the phone and dialled the number.

The advertisement – and the extraordinary sequence of events it set in motion – was the result of a decision taken fifteen years earlier. In 1984, midway through the Iran–Iraq War, Iraq's Military Industrialization Commission (MIC) had decided to move into the rocketry business. At the time the idea made perfect sense: vast quantities of artillery rockets were being expended on the front line. Manufacturing replacements at home would save a lot of money and boost the Iraqi economy.

Sensibly, the first rockets in the programme were to be direct copies of a relatively straightforward system: the Italian-made, helicopter-launched *Medusa 81*. Less sensibly, however, before a single *Medusa* had been successfully produced, the MIC decided to modify the weapon for launch from the ground. The new system, a 48-tube artillery rocket launcher, was christened the *Nasser 81*.

From the outset the project was a disaster. Without the blueprints for the *Medusa* – or any understanding of the design issues behind it – the Iraqi scientists floundered. Prototypes of the *Nasser 81* were hopelessly inaccurate. Part of the trick to making a rocket fly straight lies in the amount of in-flight spin. Iraq's rockets either failed to spin at all or span so fast their motors failed, causing them to drop out of the sky. Western intelligence agencies monitored the programme's development with great amusement.

'They weren't very successful at making rockets!' smirks one ballistics expert. 'They didn't work!'

Baffled by their inability to make rockets that flew straight, the Iraqis gave up trying. The 81 mm rocket programme ground to a halt.

This, however, created an issue. In Iraq, failure tended to be rewarded with punishment. When the *Nasser 81* project stalled, questions about why the rockets didn't work – and who was to blame – triggered a resurgence of interest in the operation. The programme was resurrected. A new set of blueprints was commissioned. This time there was a new problem: the rockets exploded in mid-flight. Once again, progress was halted.

This stopping and starting became the defining characteristic of the *Nasser 81* programme. Again and again it started, ran into problems and stopped. No one wanted to admit they couldn't make the rockets work. Nozzles were realigned, spin was adjusted, propellant changed – but the moment one problem was resolved, another appeared. Over the years, as the design evolved, MIC's *Medusa* slowly transmogrified into another, rather different rocket. Tragically for the Iraqis, this one didn't work, either.

Finally, in September 2000, MIC convened a panel of seventeen experts to examine the problem. After a decade and a half of haphazard progress, the system was now up and running, but it was hopelessly inaccurate. Recognizing that the Iraqi design, which still didn't work properly, was now substantially different from the fully functioning Italian one, the committee decided to return the system to its original specifications and start again. But here they faced a substantial problem.

The rocket bodies for the *Nasser 81* were 900 mm-long tubes with an inner diameter of 81 mm and a wall thickness of 3.3 mm, made from a high-strength aluminium alloy known as 7075-T6. In the 1980s, when the programme had started, Iraq had imported 160,000 of these tubes from Germany. Unfortunately, they had been stored outside and had corroded. Tiny pits and cracks in the aluminium surface transferred heat from the burning propellant along the body of the rocket to the warhead, which caused it to detonate prematurely. Worse, since the rocket bodies were no longer smooth, they tended to stick and blow up in the launchers.

Clearly, something had to be done. Could the corrosion be fixed? The 2000 committee needed advice. In September the MIC advertised for help.

When Sami Ibrahim called the number on the advertisement he was put through to the Ministry of Higher Education. He explained that he had a PhD in chemical and electrochemical corrosion and had seen the notice. Shortly afterwards, a car arrived at the university. Out stepped a courier with a gift: a 7075-T6 aluminium tube.

Ibrahim didn't know what it was or what it was for, but it was clear something was very wrong with it.

'It was severely corroded,' he recalls. 'But the corrosion wasn't all over the place. It was localized. Some of the surfaces were OK.'

Realizing the problem might make a good research project for one of his students, he called them together, showed them the tube and asked if anyone was interested. A young MSc candidate, Mohammed Abbar, raised his hand.

Clearly, the 2000 committee wasn't going to wait for a young post-graduate to complete his thesis, so the Professor stepped in. He examined the chemical composition of the tube, then sliced it into pieces and put them under a microscope. The next time he met the MIC representative, he passed on a few preliminary observations.

'Corrosion is a bit like a disease,' he told his contact. 'It can transfer from one surface to another.'

It was quite possible, the Professor explained, that one of the tubes had been corroded when it was delivered from Germany fifteen years earlier. If that was the case, then storing it outside, in direct contact with the others, would have caused a galvanic reaction, allowing the contagion to spread. Now the entire shipment must be considered suspect. In future, tubes should be individually wrapped to prevent them from contaminating each other. They should also be anodized, ideally with a chromate solution.

Finally, Ibrahim passed judgement on the rest of the tubes. 'We classified them into three classes,' he recalls. 'One: not corroded at all. These could be used. Two: tubes where the pitting factor was not too high. These could be treated. We could deal with it.' The third group, however – the most damaged – was beyond repair. 'The pitting factor was very high. They were not usable at all.'

Not usable at all. Iraq's MIC had a problem. They needed new rocket tubes.

A month after Ibrahim passed on his advice, Garry Cordukes, a Sydney-based aluminium trader, was reading an aluminium forum on the Internet when *he* came across an intriguing advertisement. A Jordanian company, Atlantic Trading and Communications Corps, was looking for aluminium tubing. The note asked if anyone could recommend a suitable supplier and gave the e-mail address of the company's commercial manager, Hussein Kamel.

Cordukes, who owned 50 per cent of a Chinese aluminium extrusion agency, e-mailed Kamel. 'We can extrude aluminium tube,' he wrote. 'Please forward specifications.'

Kamel replied that he was looking for car parts – specifically, dry-sump pulleys and flanges. The latter were tubes of a rather specific size: 900 mm long, with an outer diameter of 81 mm and a wall thickness of 3.3 mm. The thing was, they were for racing cars. They had to be tough. The only alloy strong enough was 7075-T6. Oh, and one other thing. The aluminium had to be chromate-anodized.

Cordukes didn't have the first clue what dry-sump pulleys and flanges were. He didn't really care. He did care about a new customer who was looking to order somewhere in the region of 60,000 pieces of aluminium. There was an opportunity here. The Australian contacted his factory in China to see if they could, indeed, extrude 7075-T6.

'That's a hard alloy,' the production manager told him. 'Usually it's used in the aircraft industry.'

Cordukes explained about the racing cars. 'That could be right,' the manager said. 'It's high-tensile stuff.'

Negotiations over the contract were unexceptional. In December 2000, Cordukes sent Kamel a sample of 7075-T6 by DHL. Kamel said it wasn't quite right, so another was dispatched. This one was closer to the mark. The two businessmen discussed finances and agreed on a price: $10 per tube.

'He screwed me down,' Cordukes admits today, 'but we wanted the business, an entrée into a new market.'

Kamel put in place a letter of credit with the Bank of New York in Shanghai, and on 2 February 2001 the deal was struck: 60,000 tubes for $600,000, to be delivered by cargo ship within eight weeks.

All appeared normal. It wasn't. Unbeknownst either to Cordukes or Kamel, the moment the pair had exchanged details of the aluminium order over the Internet, the tubes' specifications had been intercepted and flagged by a top-secret signals intelligence package known as ECHELON.

Inside the headquarters of the National Security Agency (NSA) at Fort Meade, Maryland, 9,500 miles away, warning lights were flashing.

Like most bureaucrats, Geoff Wainwright read his mail first thing in the morning. Wainwright's mail, however, was rather different to most. A Customs officer for fifteen years, in July 2000, he had taken a new position with the Australian Department of Defence.

Assistant Director of Intelligence for the Exports and International Programmes Branch, Wainwright's job involved liaising with various governmental departments about the import and export of sensitive materials. This threw up a few complications. The new position required him to liaise with officers from Australia's clandestine intelligence services. At Customs, the thirty-four-year-old had been cleared to access *Highly Protected* materials. He now needed to be cleared to the *Top*

Secret level. The vetting process would take six months; in the meantime, he was given a provisional clearance.

Each morning when he arrived at work, Wainwright was presented
with a sealed envelope containing classified cables from all over the
world regarding materials passing through Australian territory. Most
were fairly humdrum. The cable he received in September 2000 was
different.

'A signal had been picked up,' he recalls. 'There was an Australian
company that might be involved in shipping aluminium pipes over to
somewhere in the Middle East.' According to the signal, these were no
ordinary aluminium tubes. They were to be made of a specific alloy,
7075-T6. Although they had been ordered from Australia, they were
due to be manufactured somewhere in China. Wainwright looked at
the signal again. At the top was a code indicating where it had come
from. The United States.

Wainwright had no idea what 7075-T6 aluminium was. So, over
the course of the next week, he asked experts inside the country's
intelligence community why the tubes were so important. Further
investigation led to some alarming revelations: Hussein Kamel was
not Jordanian. Atlantic Trading Corps was not making racing cars.
The tubes were destined for Iraq. Worse, there was the nature of the
tubes themselves.

7075-T6 aluminium tubes, Wainwright learned, could be used as
rotors in gas centrifuges. Gas centrifuges could be used to enrich
uranium-235. Uranium-235 could be used to make a nuclear weapon.
Inside Australia's intelligence community, wheels began to turn.

'There were a lot of meetings on what should happen with this
signal,' says Wainwright today. 'It came across as something that was
pretty important. In Australia, where we are in our part of the world,
not a lot of exciting stuff happens. This one had a bit of a profile to it.
Somebody had to do something.'

Wainwright arranged meetings with the major players in the

intelligence community, briefed them all on the signal and asked their opinions. No one knew what to think.

'All we were going off was that this person in Jordan was asking this Australian middleman to organize something. We didn't even know whether the thing *had* happened, or whether it was *going* to happen.' What to do next? Wainwright had a few ideas. 'Being a Customs officer, my background was to say, "OK, let's go out and talk to this guy: see if this message has any substance."' Everyone agreed.

The question of who should be responsible, however, was more tricky. The export of aluminium tubes didn't fall under the remit of either home or foreign intelligence services. Who should be in charge? Eyes turned to Wainwright: he was part of the intelligence community now. He had a background in Customs. He seemed to be on top of things. Let him do it.

Geoff Wainwright, unvetted and untested in the field, was about to go undercover.

In the United States, there was a quiet debate going on, too. The moment the NSA intercepted the Cordukes–Kamel e-mails, they were passed on to the CIA's Counter Proliferation Division (CPD). The result was a flurry of excitement: just a couple of months earlier, the Division had established a task force on Iraq to discover exactly this kind of information. CPD resolved to continue monitoring the Australian deal, and, in turn, passed the intelligence on to analysts at the Agency's Weapons Intelligence, Non-Proliferation and Arms Control Centre (WINPAC).

WINPAC analysts scrutinized the data to see if the tube specifications fitted the pattern of a nuclear centrifuge programme – and at this point alarms really started sounding.

Gas centrifuges work by spinning uranium hexafluoride at high speed – in the region of 60,000 to 90,000 revolutions per minute. At these speeds the lighter uranium-235 separates out from the heavier uranium-238, allowing for its collection. But achieving such speeds is hard. The tube or 'rotor' containing the hexafluoride must be extremely light and rigid. It must not flex or distort. Only a handful of alloys are sufficiently strong. 7075-T6 aluminium is one. It was for precisely this reason that Iraq was not allowed to import tubes made of the alloy. An Iraqi attempt clandestinely to import 60,000 of them was certainly cause for concern.

For the purposes of running a gas centrifuge, however, it is not enough simply to buy a tube made of the right alloy. The rotor needs to be manufactured to very precise tolerances. Imperfections in the tube wall will cause imbalance, and the rotor will fail at high speeds. Even tiny flaws – a fingerprint on the side of the tube – can cause it to burst. Since the outer edge of a gas centrifuge rotor can spin at speeds in excess of 700 metres per second – more than twice the speed of sound – the results can be catastrophic.

WINPAC analysts immediately recognized that the Iraqi front company was indeed requesting high tolerances in its aluminium tubes. According to the terms of the deal, the composition of the 7075-T6 had to be exact; the length of the tubes could not vary more than half a millimetre; wall thicknesses were to be held within a 0.1 mm tolerance; the depth of the chromate anodize had to be exactly 15 microns.

Hussein Kamel had rejected two samples from Garry Cordukes: the first on the basis that the chromate anodize was too thick, the second because the manganese content of the aluminium was not high enough. Then there was the issue of the packaging: according to the Australian contract, each tube had to be individually wrapped before shipping. Kamel had been very specific about this. Clearly, someone in Iraq was taking a great deal of care over this order.

WINPAC compared the specifications of the tubes to those of the rotors of known gas centrifuges and immediately found a couple that seemed to fit. One, the 'Zippe type', also used rotors of aluminium 7075-T6. Zippe's rotors had a similar inner diameter and thickness, and were manufactured to similar tolerances. Another, the 'Beams' centrifuge, used rotors of a similar length and thickness, too.

The specifications of the aluminium tubes, their tolerances and Hussein Kamel's excessive attention to detail in the order, together with the fact the tubes were obviously being procured in secret, persuaded WINPAC that they were destined for a clandestine centrifuge programme. Iraq was building a nuclear bomb.

For Geoff Wainwright, making contact with Garry Cordukes in Sydney was no great challenge: he was in the phone book. But how to get him to open up? Wainwright joked to colleagues that in the United States the FBI would kick down the aluminium trader's door and cart him off to a secure unit for interrogation. Perhaps he might try something a little more nuanced? Like a coffee?

The problem was, the intelligence about the tubes had come from an intercepted e-mail. Crashing into Cordukes' office and announcing that the game was up would let the trader – and his Iraqi customer – know that their e-mail was being read.

'It was a top-secret signal,' says Wainwright. 'And this was all part of a top-secret intelligence operation. So I had to figure out how I could go and meet this guy and gather more intelligence.' A little tactical misdirection was called for. Wainwright picked up the phone.

'Garry,' he told the aluminium trader. 'My name's Geoff Wainwright. I'm the new guy, the assistant director at the Department of Defence, and I've only been in the job a few months.'

The lies began to flow.

'Part of my job is to get out there and educate people in industry who might potentially export goods to a foreign country, not knowing that it's illegal. I'm going to be in Sydney, and you're on my list of people to talk to. Is it OK if I come and we meet up?'

A few days later, Wainwright flew to Sydney. Cordukes was inter-ested: he assumed that the Department of Defence might be in the market for some aluminium. Wainwright was interested, too: if this deal was as important as the Americans suspected, he was at the spearhead of a significant undercover operation. Potentially, Saddam Hussein was building a nuclear weapon. He must be stopped.

The pair met in the lobby of Cordukes' company building, shook hands, then moved into his office and sat down. Wainwright started his prepared spiel: 'I'm the new guy, I'm just introducing myself, wanted to have a bit of a talk . . .' then he paused.

'As I walk into this guy's office,' he recalls, 'what do I see leaning up against the wall but an aluminium tube! Two weeks of meetings, discussions with people and then I'm finally sitting there in front of the guy who was the subject of the signal – and the actual item is right there!'

With some effort, Wainwright forced himself to look away from the tube and slipped back into character: 'I wanted to have a bit of a talk about the roles that you have, because you might have to export items that might be covered by our legislation.' The former Customs officer handed over some printed material about export regulations, then suggested that, if Cordukes was ever contacted by someone who sounded dodgy, or asked for something unusual, he was the guy to call. Perhaps, Wainwright fished, the aluminium trader had faced such a situation before and been unsure how to act?

Cordukes bit.

'Well, seeing as you've *mentioned* it,' he said, 'I just got this crazy e-mail from Jordan.' A guy named Kamel had been in touch with an unusual request.

'Really?' deadpanned Wainwright. 'That's interesting.' Then he had an idea. 'Hey!' he told the trader. 'I'm only new in this job – but do you think this is something that maybe I should look at a bit closer?'

When Cordukes agreed that it might be worthwhile, Wainwright played a blinder.

'That tube leaning up against the wall over there' – he indicated the tube behind the desk – 'Is that the sort of thing this guy Kamel's after?'

Cordukes admitted that it was one of the prototypes.

'Look, you wouldn't mind if I sort of borrowed that from you? I could take it back to Canberra with me, analyse it with our scientific experts, then let you know whether it's actually something that could be used to make something nasty.'

The aluminium trader agreed: the tube was a reject, anyway. He didn't have any use for it.

Wainwright could hardly believe his luck. 'I thought, "You *beauty*!" I've gone to this meeting and here I am coming back with the tube! The actual evidence that was spoken about in the signal!' He tucked the aluminium tube under his arm, told Cordukes he would be back in touch again, and departed.

As Geoff Wainwright wandered out into the Sydney traffic with one of the hottest pieces of intelligence on the planet under his coat, he wondered what his colleagues would think. It would have been hard to imagine a more successful initial assignment: Cordukes had no idea what was going on, Hussein Kamel had no idea what was going on. Certainly Saddam Hussein had no idea.

'Everyone on the intelligence community wanted to know what was happening. They couldn't wait for me to report back from my first meeting,' he recalls. 'I knew that everyone was going to say, "What happened?" – "Well, hey, guys, guess what? I actually got the object!"'

Wainwright capitalized further on his success. Alongside the prototype tube, Cordukes had passed on some company details. Inside one of the handouts was a photograph of his factory in China. The moment he got back to Canberra, the intelligence officer handed the picture to the Australian Defence Imagery and Geospatial Organization and asked what they thought of it.

By the time Wainwright submitted his report the next morning, Defence Imagery had managed to locate the factory in China, zoomed in on it and obtained detailed satellite photographs of the entire plant – including a clear shot of a pallet-load of the tubes awaiting shipment.

'I turn up to this meeting, and we've turned up with the pipe. We've got the brochure from the plant. We've zoomed in with all the photographs from space,' he recalls. 'We had everything that was in that signal, either photographs of it or the actual sample of it, the interviews that I've written up with Cordukes – all within about forty-eight hours.'

The material was passed on immediately to the CIA. 'Sorry, guys!' recalls Wainwright of the cable accompanying it. 'It's only been forty-eight hours and we didn't have that much time, but here's the tube, here's the factory, here's the photographs. Anything else you guys needed?' He laughs. 'It really blew the Americans' minds.'

The Australian intelligence – the tubes, the order, the interview and the photographs – did blow the Americans' minds. Wainwright's information was utterly persuasive to the CIA. So certain was WINPAC in its judgement that the tubes were for an Iraqi centrifuge project that in early April 2001 the conclusion was included in the CIA's most highly classified intelligence product: the President's Daily Brief. Shortly afterwards, on 10 April, the Agency circulated a Senior Executive Intelligence Brief alerting its own staff to the fact. According to the brief there was little doubt: Iraq was trying to 'jump-start' a nuclear-weapons programme. The tubes ordered from Australia 'have little use other than for a uranium-enrichment programme'.

This wasn't entirely true. There *was* doubt. One of the first things the CIA had done when it received news of the Cordukes deal was to forward the tube specifications to the Department of Energy's national laboratories at Oak Ridge, Tennessee. There was little that Oak Ridge staff didn't know about gas centrifuges: after all, they made the things. Analysts there were uniquely qualified to determine what could and could not function as a centrifuge rotor. A team of nuclear scientists from the facility's Field Intelligence Element was assembled to examine the data. They, in turn, sought advice from a professor at the University of Virginia, Houston Wood III.

'I happened to be in town,' recalls Wood. 'They asked me to come over and take a look.'

The Professor, who had worked on gas centrifuges for more than thirty years, was considered one of the world's foremost experts on the subject. He was led to a secure unit at the facility, handed the tube specifications and left to himself. Within half an hour he was convinced the tubes were not suitable for use in a centrifuge.

'The material was too thick,' he says. 'That was the main thing. The thickness of the wall of the tube made it much too heavy.' In addition, there was the issue of the chromate anodizing. Centrifuge rotors weren't anodized – and certainly not with chromic acid. In Wood's view the story didn't add up: it would have been impossible even for the United States to manufacture a working centrifuge with the tubes, let alone Iraq. 'They just didn't work,' he recalls.

The day after the CIA reported that there was 'little use' for the tubes other than as centrifuge rotors, the Department of Energy published its own assessment. The tube specifications were 'not consistent with a gas centrifuge end use', it stated. 'The procurement activity most likely supports a different application.'

Clearly, an argument was brewing.

Australia was embroiled in the dispute from the outset. The country's Defence, Science and Technology Organization in Melbourne ran tests on Cordukes' prototype tube the moment Geoff Wainwright passed it on to them. Results were disappointing.

'The key thing was: is this something that is really going to be used to enrich uranium?' asks Wainwright. 'And the tests back from the Defence and Scientific Organization said "No". They said, "It's not the right strength. And it's not the right alloy . . . it's not something that we need to worry about."'

Prodded by the United States, Australian intelligence now wondered whether this was true. The tube had been a prototype. Perhaps the ones in China were being made to higher specifications. There was only one way to find out.

Wainwright's second meeting with Garry Cordukes took place in a coffee shop in Botany Bay. Time for a few home truths. All was not as it seemed, the intelligence officer informed the trader. Atlantic Trading Corps was a front company. The tubes weren't for racing cars. They were for military purposes. In Iraq. As for the company's chief executive, Hussein Kamel – was Cordukes aware that 'Kamel' was Saddam Hussein's surname? The aluminium trader thought for a moment.

'Fuck,' he said. 'Are you serious? What do you want us to do?'

Regarding the trade itself, Wainwright instructed Cordukes to proceed: so far, no laws had actually been broken. But perhaps he could do his government a favour. Was there any way he could obtain another sample? Cordukes explained he was shortly off to China to check on progress. 'Happy to,' he told Wainwright. 'How do you want me to get it to you?'

A week later, a middle-aged man in an open-necked shirt was waiting for him in the arrivals hall at Sydney International Airport. Cordukes had two 7075-T6 tubes under his arm. 'I said, "You're from the Defence Department?" He said, "Yup." I said, "You're after these?" He said, "Yup. Thank you very much." Off he went.' It was the last Garry Cordukes was to hear from the Australian intelligence community. It was not, however, the last he was to hear about the tubes themselves.

In the meantime, the Australian had other concerns. The extrusion plant in China was having problems making the tubes. The Chinese didn't know how to apply the chromate anodize that Hussein Kamel had demanded. Normally they pre-treated aluminium by dipping it in a chromate solution, then anodized it after it had been extruded. This order called for something rather different. They were stumped.

Cordukes suggested a compromise: why not anodize the tubes

normally, then dip them in the chromate pre-treatment tanks afterwards? It was hardly a textbook solution.

'I thought it was dodgy,' admits Cordukes. 'But if the things were only going to be used for exhaust flanges, it wouldn't have made a bit of difference.'

Hussein Kamel didn't seem too worried, so Cordukes wasn't either. The only difference the chromate made was that it turned the tubes a green-yellow colour.

However, the process did slow down production. By mid-May, the mill had only managed to make 2,000 tubes out of an order for 60,000. The aluminium was overdue, and an angry Hussein Kamel was demanding delivery.

'For Christ's sake!' Cordukes told the mill. 'Ship what you have. We can continue to work on the rest and ship them in two weeks as a full container load.'

On 23 May 2001, 1,962 aluminium tubes were loaded into a container and moved to the docks. From there they would travel upriver to Hong Kong before making the journey to Jordan. Five days later, Cordukes was called in to the chairman's office in the extrusion plant.

'We've got a big problem,' the chairman told him. The Chinese government, acting at the request of the United States, was demanding that the shipment be halted. The way the Chinese heard it, the United States would take any action necessary to prevent the tubes from reaching Jordan. Cordukes attempted to stop the shipment, but this proved impossible: two days earlier the container had been loaded on to a freight ship, the *Kota Jaya*, bound for Aqaba, Jordan.

By now the aluminium trader regretted ever having got involved in the deal. He called Hussein Kamel in Jordan and informed him that he was not going to forward the bill of lading, without which the tubes could not be collected at their destination. Then, in true Aussie style, he gave the Iraqi a piece of his mind.

'You've obviously fed me bullshit about what you're going to use these tubes for,' he said. 'We're not playing any more. We're not releasing the bill of lading and we're not producing any more tubes. Fuck off!'

But Cordukes was too late. The tubes were on their way.

When the shipment of aluminium tubes reached Jordan in June 2001, the authorities were waiting. A contingent of Jordanian intelligence agents, together with a handful of officers from the CIA's Counter Proliferation Division, seized it.

The availability of hard evidence in the form of 1,962 aluminium tubes appears to have energized the WINPAC analysts. Arguments about the end-use of the tubes shifted gear. One analyst – cryptically referred to by media and government reports ever since as 'Joe T' – led the charge. Joe, who had worked with centrifuges at Oak Ridge before joining the Agency, was regarded as something of an expert on the subject. And for him, there were no two ways about it: this was a nuclear-bomb project in the making.

Joe T's argument had two main premises. One: the tubes were suitable for centrifuge rotors. Two: they weren't suitable for anything else. If the tubes were not intended for a uranium-enrichment programme, why were the tolerances so high? What were they for?

As it happened, a putative answer had already emerged. A month before the seizure of the tubes in Jordan, the Department of Energy had published a Daily Intelligence Highlight which noted that Iraq had purchased 'similar' tubes before 'to manufacture chambers (tubes) for a multiple rocket launcher'. 'Similar' was an understatement. The previous tubes – also made of 7075-T6 aluminium – were 900 mm long, with an outer diameter of 81 mm and a wall thickness of 3.3 mm: identical to those of the Australian shipment.

On 14 June 2001, WINPAC conceded that the tubes might, indeed, be bound for an artillery rocket programme. This, however, it deemed 'less likely' than the CIA's previous assessment. The next month, all was explained: 'The specifications for the tubes,' according to a 2 July report, 'far exceed any known conventional weapons application, including rocket casings for 81 mm multiple rocket launchers.'

In the year following this document, WINPAC issued a further nine reports, each arguing that the tubes were destined for a centrifuge programme. Other than that the tubes appeared to match the Zippe and Beams centrifuges and that they were manufactured to exacting standards, however, no one presented any further proof.

Convinced the tubes were intended for centrifuges, Joe T now started flying around the world briefing foreign intelligence services about the coup. In July, he visited Vienna, where he set about persuading officers of the International Atomic Energy Agency (IAEA) that the tubes shipment proved that Iraq was reviving its nuclear programme.

From the outset, IAEA officers were underwhelmed by Joe's presentation. To them, there was nothing new or exciting about the tubes at all. Inspectors had seen identical tubes numerous times in Iraq.

'At the Nassr facility at Taji, north of Baghdad, we had observed something of the order of 50,000 of these tubes,' says Bob Kelley, one of the agency's nuclear experts. 'Most of them were sitting in wooden boxes. The sides of the boxes had broken; they were spilling out like jackstraws.' At the time, IAEA staff had briefly considered whether they might be used for centrifuge rotors, then immediately ruled out the possibility. 'The assessment was made that, yes, they have 50,000 tubes; no, they're not for centrifuges. Nobody considered them again.'

George Healey, another IAEA veteran familiar with the tubes, concurred. 'We were aware of all these tubes. They weren't anything near the diameter that the Iraqis had based their centrifuge programme on,' he says. 'It was a non-issue.'

Patiently, Joe explained his theory to the sceptical IAEA men. Iraq had a history of clandestine centrifuge procurement, he reminded them. The tube specifications almost matched those of two gas centrifuges – the Zippe and Beams models; the tolerances of the tubes matched; the material matched; the tubes had been procured, in secret, via a known Iraqi front company. All the pieces fitted together.

Once again, the IAEA officers interrupted. Previously, they said, Iraq had relied on different centrifuge models, whose rotors were made out of maraging steel or carbon fibre. Aluminium rotors would represent a considerable step backwards in technology. Previous rotors were also a different size to the current shipment. If Iraq really planned to use these tubes in a gas centrifuge, it would have to start its enrichment programme from scratch and rebuild the centrifuges around the tubes. This task was completely beyond them, and there would be no outside assistance, since no one in the world was currently using 81 mm tubes as centrifuge rotors in a production environment.

IAEA officials were especially surprised to hear Joe's argument, bearing in mind the fact that a pair of the agency's scientists had been to Jordan and examined the tubes immediately after their seizure. The two officers had carried a couple of tubes back to their hotel room, cut them open with a hacksaw and taken some measurements.

'[The tubes'] walls were way too thick and there was a coating on them that shouldn't have been there,' says an IAEA man. 'It wasn't hard for them to see that there was no way that they were directly useful.' The initial judgement had taken the two officers 'about half an hour'. It was that obvious.

But Joe T remained utterly persuaded by his own argument. 'You would talk to him and he would look at you and smile and sort of say, "Well, if you knew what I know, you would know I'm right,"' recalls one officer present at the briefing.

Over the course of the next two years, officials were visited a number of times by the WINPAC analyst or his colleagues. Each time they were subjected to another tirade about how the aluminium tubes could be used in a gas centrifuge; each time, they countered that the evidence just wasn't there. The more they met Joe, the surer they became that he was wrong. About the only thing the CIA man managed to convince the IAEA experts of was that, actually, he didn't have the first clue what he was talking about.

'A so-called expert,' recalls one senior officer present at the briefings, 'practically a layman . . . No matter what good technical argument was put in front of him, he just always worked his way through it to the same answer.'[5]

Another officer was so struck by Joe's initial briefing that he wondered whether the CIA man was trying to start a war.

Like most intelligence debates, the issue of the Iraqi tubes might have simmered quietly behind closed doors for years to no great effect. It didn't.

Two months after Joe T visited the IAEA, nineteen men hijacked four commercial airliners and crashed them into buildings in the United States. By 12 September 2001, everything had changed. Joe T's theory about the tubes was about to be taken seriously.

Perhaps the most corrosive of all 9/11's by-products was uncertainty. A handful of disgruntled individuals had blindsided the most powerful nation on earth. How could this have happened? What if it happened again? Were we *safe*?

The result was a seismic shift in the way Western leaders perceived risk. Faced with an 'existential' threat, immediate, decisive action was required.

'If we wait for threats to fully materialize, we will have waited too long,' George W. Bush warned cadets at West Point in 2002. 'We cannot defend America and our friends by hoping for the best.'

---

[5] At a meeting in January 2002, one IAEA man decided to see how much Joe T really knew about gas centrifuges. 'He said that these tubes were exactly like the Zippe centrifuge,' he recalls, 'so I said, "*Which* Zippe centrifuge?"' When Joe replied that there had been only one Zippe model, the IAEA man pounced. 'No, that's not true,' he told the WINPAC man. 'And you should know that.' Joe appeared unfazed. Officials present were filled with a combined sense of embarrassment – that Joe was so far out of his depth – and shock at his near-evangelical certainty.

Tony Blair felt the same way, famously explaining that the risk of the 'new global terrorism' was one that he simply was not prepared to run, particularly when it came to the nexus of weapons of mass destruction and radical Islam. In a world where inaction was no longer an option, we had to prepare for the worst, and act accordingly.

'This is not the time to err on the side of caution,' Blair warned his constituents in Sedgefield.

This collision of uncertainty ('Are we safe?') and certainty ('We must act') was to have all sorts of unforeseen consequences.

'It's hard to overstate how differently the US policy community and intelligence community saw things after 9/11,' explains one senior US intelligence official. 'For the very first time in our history, we were attacked on our homeland. It was a huge strategic issue and had a huge strategic impact on the ways policymakers and Congress and the intelligence community dealt with many of these issues.'

A senior officer from the CIA's Counter Proliferation Division agrees entirely. 'That sense – worldwide – of vulnerability, was palpable,' he says. 'It was a cold hard slap in the face of what we were all about.'

In the immediate aftermath of 9/11, officers in the Agency's Counter-Terrorism Center (CTC) refused point-blank to leave the office.

'People were working twenty-four hours a day, *everybody* was working twenty-four hours a day,' recalls a CTC officer. 'I balled up my jacket and used it as a pillow and slept under my desk.'

Almost overnight, CTC ballooned from 300 officers to 1,200. Inside the Center, officers showed up with suitcases full of clothes and stayed for days on end. When they got hungry, they broke into the Agency cafeteria and stole all the food.

'It was unlike anything I had ever seen,' the CTC officer continues. 'I thought, "Wow, this must be what Pearl Harbor felt like."' The US intelligence community had failed to detect – or to stop – the 9/11 attacks. It was not going to be caught napping again.

As we now know from numerous accounts by White House insiders, the Bush administration's thoughts turned to Iraq almost immediately after 9/11. In the language of risk, it now became unacceptable to wait and see what abominations the rogue nation might get up to in the future. The discovery that Saddam Hussein – who *might* have had some sort of link with al-Qaeda, who *might* have been developing weapons of mass destruction (WMDs), and who was certainly a menace to the Middle East – was now apparently building a nuclear weapon led to extreme concern. Those aluminium tubes – of little real interest prior to 9/11 – jumped to the head of the queue. Joe T's certainty, infectious to begin with, now spread like a virus.

Three months after 11 September, Houston Wood, the University of Virginia professor, was contacted again by the US Department of Energy. The Department's position on the tubes was unchanged, but it appears that more ammunition was required to pacify the increasingly agitated WINPAC analysts.

Wood was surprised to hear back about the tubes. 'I thought that we had put the issue to rest,' he says, but again he offered his reassurance. There was no way they could be used for a centrifuge programme.

At the request of the Department, the Professor even contacted Gernot Zippe, the grandfather of centrifuge research. Zippe, then eighty-four years old, had produced uranium for the first Soviet nuclear bomb and had designed some of the earliest functioning gas centrifuges. What did the old man make of Joe T's claim that the Iraqi tubes would work in one of his designs?

'The tubes were purported by the CIA to be like the so-called Zippe centrifuge,' recalls Wood. 'We wanted to give him the specific infor-mation . . . and get his opinion.'

Zippe's analysis didn't take long. The day after he received the spec-ifications of the Australian tubes, he e-mailed Wood, agreeing that there was no way the tubes would work. They were the wrong size. They were the wrong thickness. They were anodized. But still the argument went on.

'That's when I began to get angry,' says Wood.

In the meantime, Joe T flew to Australia, where he addressed officers at the headquarters of the Australian Secret Intelligence
Organization (ASIO). He received a warmer reception here than he
had in Vienna. His evidence was, apparently, 'compelling'. But the
Australian intelligence services had a vested interest in the tubes issue
being significant: they had, after all, provided the intelligence in the
first place.

Alexander Downer, Australia's Foreign Minister – still no doubt elated,
following John Howard's surprise victory in November's general election – would later brag to ABC television of the 'little gem' of intelligence that Australia had passed to the CIA regarding Saddam Hussein's
nuclear programme. The little gem was, of course, news of the
aluminium tubes order.

Australia was right to be pleased about its input on the tubes issue.
Despite the fact that its Defence, Science and Technology Organization
had now concluded – twice – that the tubes were probably not destined
for use in a uranium enrichment programme, a lot of good work had
gone into researching the initial tip-off from the United States. Geoff
Wainwright certainly had something to be proud of.

'I wasn't aware of the disagreements on the international level,' he
says. 'But at these meetings I was getting told that the information I
had gathered and collected from Garry Cordukes and the samples and
stuff were going across the White House desk, were crossing George
Bush's desk . . . This was a really big deal at the time.'

At the annual intelligence community conference on proliferation
at the Australian Secret Intelligence Service (ASIS)'s training centre in
the winter of 2001 the tubes were discussed during the formal sessions.
A great deal of back-slapping was involved.

'There was a mood of great accomplishment and excitement that we
had achieved this amazing thing,' recalls one officer present. '[It] was a
very, very rare and significant victory.' The Australian intelligence officers

were heady with success. 'They were very proud of themselves that they'd played a key role in a big event. Almost juvenile in their excitement about it.'

Over the course of 2002, as the issue of Iraq's WMD capability began to take centre stage, battle lines were being drawn inside the US intelligence community over the aluminium tubes. The State Department's in-house intelligence shop, the Bureau of Intelligence and Research (INR), became embroiled early on. Although INR was small (around 150 analysts), it had the reputation of being professional, impartial and, on occasion, outspoken. As the clock started ticking towards war, it became clear to the Bureau's officers that the aluminium tubes comprised an important – probably the most important – issue.

'There were all kinds of reasons you might want to put together to make the argument [for invading Iraq],' says the Head of INR at the time, Assistant Secretary of State for Intelligence and Research, Carl Ford, 'but, from my perspective, the one that really made the difference was WMD. And of WMD, the only one that really was a significant change in our position – and that was the trigger – was the nuclear question.'

Not only did the 'nuclear question' have the most serious implications, but it was also the only one where there was any real concrete evidence: the aluminium tubes.

As the argument heated up, Ford was contacted by one of his analysts in INR's Department of Strategic, Proliferation and Military Affairs. The analyst (who does not wish to be named) was having trouble with his opposite numbers in the intelligence community, all of whom were refusing to admit that the tubes might have applications other than in a reconstituted centrifuge programme. Having liaised with both the Department of Energy and the IAEA, however, he had been assured with near 100 per cent certainty that Joe T's arguments were worthless. Again and again he argued the case that the majority view on the tubes was wrong; again and again he was ignored.

Admittedly, some headway had been made. After a series of fierce battles, Joe T and his cohorts seemed to have accepted that the tubes in their current form were unsuitable for use as centrifuge rotors. But now they seized on a caveat in both the IAEA and Department of Energy reports. Each organization, while stating that the tubes were the wrong dimensions for rotors, had admitted that it *might* be possible to modify them to make them the right size. The tubes could be chopped in half. The walls could be shaved down. The chromate coating could be removed. It was possible.

It was also highly unlikely. Wayne White, Head of INR's Iraq Team, recalls the nuclear analyst trudging wearily into his office and slumping on to the sofa.

'Oh, Wayne!' he told his boss. 'You wouldn't believe it!'

He told White the gist of the new argument. 'Even though these tubes were not up to spec for use in a centrifuge,' White says today, 'that didn't mean they couldn't be industrially *upgraded* up to specification. We thought the argument was ludicrous.'

WINPAC's new argument was highly implausible. Iraq didn't have the ability or the equipment necessary to perform that kind of high-precision work (if it did, it might have been able to manufacture the tubes itself). The argument also undercut the organization's main thesis: that the high tolerances and specifications of the tubes indicated they were bound for an enrichment programme. If the tubes were going to be chopped up and shaved once they arrived, why would Iraq have cared about ensuring the wall thicknesses were accurate to within 0.1 mm? On top of these arguments came a common-sense retort: if Iraq had been looking for centrifuge rotors, why hadn't it ordered the right-sized tubes in the first place?

Once again, WINPAC had an answer: the Iraqis were engaged in a deception operation. Assuming western intelligence would be monitoring the sale of dual-use technology, they had deliberately ordered the wrong-sized tubes to confuse the CIA.

'Maddening!' reports Wayne White of the argument. 'This was the kind of logic – or *illogic* – that was accepted by other members of the intelligence community. Which we found astonishing.'

'I blame that on 9/11,' says Carl Ford. 'What had been very high standards for making judgements on analytical questions – the bar was lowered dramatically. The amount of evidence you had to make a judgement was lowered.'

Ford wasn't the only one to notice the change. From time to time in the run-up to the invasion of Iraq, the INR boss would fly around the world to liaise with foreign intelligence services. 'I travelled to London, and I had people come up to me and say, "Carl, what are you guys *doing*?" I think there were a lot of people in British intelligence who really didn't understand where we were coming from.'

Traditionally, British intelligence officers like to have at least three sources for everything. The Americans appeared to be relying on single sources, and sometimes highly questionable single sources.

'Basically,' says one British intelligence officer, 'they had all disappeared up their own arses.'

On 8 September 2002, fifteen months after their seizure, the aluminium tubes finally broke into the public consciousness.

'US SAYS HUSSEIN INTENSIFIES QUEST FOR A-BOMB PARTS,' ran the *New York Times* headline.

Joe T's theory featured prominently: according to the piece, the tubes' 'diameter, thickness and other technical specifications' indicated they were intended for centrifuges. The views of the IAEA, Department of Energy and INR – that the tubes had nothing whatsoever to do with a centrifuge programme – did not feature at all.

The story contained a rather graphic image designed to highlight the risk of inaction when it came to Iraq: 'The first sign of a "smoking gun",' administration officials told reporters Judith Miller and Michael Gordon, 'may be a mushroom cloud.'

Having leaked the information to the *New York Times*, the Bush administration capitalized on it. That same day, Condoleezza Rice, Dick Cheney, Colin Powell and Donald Rumsfeld all appeared on mainstream TV, citing the article as evidence they had been right about Iraq's intentions all along.

'There's a story in the *New York Times* this morning . . . ,' Dick Cheney told NBC, before assuring viewers the administration knew 'with absolute certainty' that Iraq was procuring the apparatus it needed for a nuclear weapon.

'There have been shipments of high-quality aluminium tubes,' Rice explained to CNN, 'that are only really suited for nuclear weapons programmes.' She then parroted the *New York Times'* image almost word-for-word: 'We don't want the smoking gun to be a mushroom cloud.'

Rumsfeld took the image a step further. 'Imagine,' he told CBS, 'a September 11th with weapons of mass destruction.'

When Houston Wood read the *New York Times* piece, he called the national laboratories at Oak Ridge, Tennessee. 'I said, "Is this something new?" Because I'd been aware of it for over a year and all of a sudden that came out.' The Professor was informed that no, these were the same tubes. 'I was just shocked. I thought we'd put that horse in the barn.'

Even members of the CIA's Counter Proliferation Division were surprised by the way the story had come out. 'There's Dick Cheney on *Meet the Press* saying, "Wow! The *New York Times* says there's these tubes!"' recalls one officer. 'It was circular reporting!'

Having shouted an accusation, the White House appeared to be using its own echo as an independent validation.

'It was very skilfully done,' says Greg Thielmann, INR's director of Strategic Proliferation and Military Affairs at the time. 'Classic manipulation of the public: the administration was exercising its right at the highest levels to declassify whatever it wanted, for cherry-picking the evidence and making its policy case.'

A fortnight after the *New York Times* piece, BBC's *Panorama* reported on the tubes, too. 'Now there's new information that Saddam is seeking centrifuges,' reporter Jane Corbin explained. 'In the last fourteen months several shipments, a total of 1,000 aluminium centrifuge tubes, have been intercepted.'

Former chief UN weapons inspector David Kay was wheeled in to comment. 'I've seen one of them,' he said, before speculating that the tubes' specifications were indicative of a 'German-derived' centrifuge design. That so many tubes had been seized suggested to Kay that Iraq's prospective enrichment programme was likely to consist of a cascade of more than a thousand centrifuges: a 'large-scale programme'.

INR's analysts were under no illusions regarding the reasons for the government leaks. 'There's nothing that frightens the general public more than "nuclear",' says Wayne White. 'At the time we were trying to fathom why the pressure was being applied [regarding the tubes]. It was because they had to have the mushroom-cloud image.'

Greg Thielmann agrees. 'The way the information was presented was to achieve the maximum fright level and the minimum public education level,' he concludes. 'You say this country has "WMD", then you scare the bejesus out of the population by painting pictures of mushroom clouds. It was horrible sophistry, but it was very effective.'

Partly in response to such popular coverage, the US Senate Select Committee on Intelligence now demanded an official account of Iraq's purported WMD programmes. This account, the National Intelligence Estimate (NIE), would become the base assessment underpinning Congress' decision to authorize war. On the issue of the tubes, all of the old arguments fell out: Iraq was hiding its procurement activities (clear evidence that it was up to no good); the tubes were too expensive and too highly specified to be used as rocket casings; their dimensions were similar to those of the Zippe and Beams centrifuges; and, if they weren't, they could be modified.

The NIE also cited the opinion of the Department of Defense's experts on conventional military systems, the National Ground Intelligence Centre (NGIC). In a separate box, NGIC assessed that the tubes were 'highly unlikely to be intended for rocket-motor cases'. They had apparently compared the tubes with a US rocket that also used 7075-T6 aluminium and discovered that the Iraqi tubes were manufactured more precisely than the US system, or any known Russian system for that matter. According to NGIC, the rocket programme was 'a cover-story . . . to disguise the true nuclear end use'.

The result was a foregone conclusion. After three weeks of deliberations, the NIE concluded that 'most agencies assess that Iraq's aggressive pursuit of high-strength aluminium tubes provides compelling evidence that Saddam is attempting to reconstitute a uranium-enrichment effort for Baghdad's nuclear-weapons programme'.

Not willing to endorse the views of 'most agencies', both the Department of Energy and the INR dissented. The tubes weren't suitable for centrifuges, they noted, and there wasn't sufficient evidence to enable clear conclusions to be drawn regarding Iraq's uranium-enrichment programme.

'Only if you believed it before you looked at the evidence did it make sense,' says Ford. 'But if you did it honestly, you had to admit that there was nothing there.'

The Iraqi gas centrifuge programme was a mirage.

To the credit of the NIE's drafters, these disagreements appeared in their own boxes in the Estimate's text. To their eternal discredit, however, they were omitted from the one part of the report that most policy-makers actually read: the Executive Summary. The result was a document that appeared unambiguous. Saddam Hussein was working on a nuclear bomb. The caveats were missing.

Another game of wordplay was going on at the United Nations. In November 2002, the Security Council passed Resolution 1441, stating that Iraq was in breach of its obligations to disarm, and offering 'a final chance to comply'. Weapons inspectors were to be readmitted and Iraq was to produce a full declaration of its WMD programmes. Any false statements would be considered a further breach and would be reported to the Security Council, which would then meet to 'consider the situation'. The resolution made it clear that a breach would lead to 'serious consequences', but failed to specify what they might be. Pointedly, 1441 did not use the phrase 'all necessary means' – the internationally understood phrase for 'war'.

Effectively for Iraq, Resolution 1441 was a trap. If Saddam Hussein suddenly saw the light and admitted he had WMD, he would be in breach of the resolution and subject to further action. If, on the other hand, he denied he had WMD, he would also be in breach – because we knew he was lying. Saddam Hussein 'will be forced either to demonstrate that he is a liar', gloated British Defence Minister Geoff Hoon, 'or expose himself as a threat'. Both outcomes could end in war.

Resolution 1441 was also a trap for its signatories. It did not specifically authorize war against Iraq, because if it had it would never have been passed at the Security Council. The resolution, as was made clear a number of times,[6] contained no 'automaticity'. By signing it, Security Council members thought they were guaranteeing that a further UN resolution would be necessary before war. But 1441 was a rather slippery document. While it didn't contain 'automaticity', it apparently left the door for military action ajar. Four months later, when it became clear that the United Nations would not pass a second resolution authorising 'all necessary means', that door would be opened.

[6] '[T]his resolution contains no "hidden triggers" and no "automaticity" with respect to the use of force,' John Negroponte, the ambassador for the United States, said of 1441. 'If there is a further Iraqi breach . . . the matter will return to the Council for discussions.' The UK ambassador agreed: 'There is no "automaticity" in this resolution. If there is a further Iraqi breach of its disarmament obligations, the matter will return to the Council for discussion as required in paragraph 12.' Colin Powell apparently agreed. 'There is nothing in the resolution,' he assured the Syrian ambassador, 'to allow it to be used as a pretext to launch a war on Iraq.'

Three weeks after the resolution was passed, UN weapons inspectors re-entered Iraq. IAEA officers, already convinced the tubes were not destined for a centrifuge programme, now faced the task of proving it. George Healey began the investigation into the aluminium tubes. 'OK,' he told the Iraqi scientists. 'What was it that you were doing with these things?'

The Press portrayed inspections as a painstaking business, like pulling teeth: Iraqi intransigence meant that the inspectors were constantly fighting for accurate information. If that was the case with some programmes, the *Nasser 81* rocket project was not one of them.

'They literally stood on their heads to provide us with every document, every drawing, every piece of paper and every piece of tube that anybody had used in relation to the 81 mm rockets,' says Healey. 'It was almost overwhelming cooperation.' Iraqi scientists at the National Monitoring Directorate worked around the clock to provide evidence the tubes were for artillery rockets. 'Bent over backwards is probably an understatement,' Healey recalls. 'Nothing was held back. They provided everything that there was.'

For the Iraqis, part of the process involved showing the inspectors all of their old aluminium tubes. Following the advice of Sami Ibrahim, scientists involved in the *Nasser* programme had been instructed to bury the most damaged tubes to prevent the corrosion from spreading. This order was abruptly rescinded.

'They said, "Stop burying them!"' says an Iraqi scientist involved. 'They said, "The ones that you've already buried have to be dug out, and they should go to the Almutasim Factory again." They started counting them.'

IAEA inspectors were shortly inundated with aluminium tubes: buried tubes, stored tubes, old tubes – every week someone would show up with more.

'Tubes guys had standing in the corner of their office – we got them!' recalls Healey. 'I don't think in the end any of us could imagine what else there might be. There was just information overload.'

The tubes team started off with Healey and one other inspector. Within months it had expanded to fifteen people.

'We went through the manufacturing process for rockets in more detail than you can imagine,' recalls another inspector involved with the process. 'We learned how rockets were made, we learned how they were painted, we watched them put in the propellant, we watched them make the propellant, we watched them make the tailfins, we looked at where they were fired on the range.'

One key interviewee was Mahdi Obeidi, the scientist behind Iraq's gas centrifuge project in the 1990s. Obeidi had managed to procure and operate gas centrifuges in the past; if there was a nuclear programme in Iraq, he would have been behind it. Questioned by the IAEA in Baghdad's Hyatt Hotel, he pointed out that Iraq's successful centrifuges had used rotors made of carbon fibre, not aluminium. The rotors had also been nearly twice the diameter of the Australian tubes.

'Look,' the Iraqi told a British inspector, 'you know our [old] centrifuge programme quite well. We never designed centrifuges: we were provided with foreign drawings. How does anybody think that we could start from scratch with an 81 mm tube and design a centrifuge now?' Obeidi glared at the inspector. 'It's ridiculous.'

George Healey, present during this exchange, agreed. 'He was absolutely right,' he says. 'If Saddam himself had come along and ordered them on pain of being shot to start making centrifuges out of these tubes, they couldn't have done it. They didn't have the know-how.'

Gradually, the inspectors pieced together the story of the *Nasser* rocket programme. They learned about the problems with the rockets, the dates the programme had stopped and restarted, and the reasons why. They collected the various blueprints and subsequent alterations. They then combined this information with western intelligence about Iraq's procurement efforts. The pair matched perfectly.

'We got the whole story from start to finish,' recalls Healey. 'All the drawings: the original drawings [of the rockets], the unaltered drawings.

And if you examined the progression of dimensions it was quite clear what they were doing. There was no question about it.'

Inside IAEA, the verdict was unanimous. 'When we got done,' recalls Bob Kelley, 'it was just an absolute certainty that [the tubes] were being used for rockets.'

But absolute certainty in Iraq was one thing; in the United States it was something rather different. After all, WINPAC was absolutely certain the tubes were for centrifuges. The US administration concluded that, if the IAEA wasn't finding evidence of a centrifuge programme, it was because the programme had been hidden. And, if the Iraqis were hiding the programme, it proved they *had something to hide*.

The result was a reversal of the burden of proof: it wasn't for the intelligence community to establish that Iraq had a nuclear programme, it was for others to prove that it didn't.

'With the Iraqi record,' stated Don Rumsfeld in January 2003, 'there is a presumption of guilt and not innocence.'

Saddam Hussein's possession of WMDs became an unfalsifiable assertion: the more the weapons inspectors *didn't* find, the scarier the programme had to be.

Not all CIA officers were convinced that this formulation was correct. 'I remember very spirited debate about those tubes,' recalls one CTC officer. 'The only other person who they could get to say that it was part of a centrifuge programme was some low-level scientist from the Department of Energy. But inside the Agency it was only the one person, and everybody else said, "No, it's just not true."'

The CIA was now under considerable pressure to vindicate its initial judgements on the tubes, and policymakers were making it clear what kind of results they were after. Following the invasion, Dick Cheney in particular would come under fire for his repeated visits to Langley for briefings on the nuclear situation. The Vice-President may have thought there was nothing wrong with asking questions about aluminium tubes, but intelligence officers saw his constant interest differently.

'Believe me, when the Vice-President shows up and has questions and is in the face of analysts at the working level, he is applying pressure,' says Wayne White of INR. 'His mere presence asking questions which call into doubt the conclusions of the analysts and demanding more thorough answers is perhaps the most intense form of political pressure.'

Cheney might not have meant to push the Agency's analysts, but that was what he was doing.

According to former officers, WINPAC wasn't instructed actively to doctor its conclusions, but pressure was implicitly brought to bear, so that doubts concerning the end-use of the tubes were not raised too loudly.

'From March 2002, I don't think there was any question that they needed any intelligence,' says Michael Scheuer, former Head of the Agency's Bin Laden Unit. 'They were going to go to war. I think perhaps what they didn't want was a paper trail of analysis that said they were wrong.'

To seasoned intelligence officers, there was nothing especially unusual about this: whenever politicians were invested in particular policies they tended to view intelligence through rose-tinted glasses to ensure it fitted in with their policy views.

'When intelligence does not provide the backdrop that they would like, they then put pressure on analysts to be – quote – "team players",' says Larry Johnson, a former analyst. 'This was not new. What happened in Iraq was not new.'

What *was* new was where all this was leading.

In the minds of the administration's craftier operators, there was one further possible reason why the UN's inspectors weren't coming up with the goods on Iraq: they weren't trying hard enough. Lacking the necessary mettle to provide evidence that might lead to a real shooting war, the toothless inspection agencies were prevaricating. When it became clear the inspections did not support its circular logic, the United States decided, once again, to err on the side of caution. Rod Barton, a senior Australian weapons inspector with the UN Monitoring, Verification and Inspection Commission (UNMOVIC), experienced the effects.

An intelligence operator for more than thirty years, and now special adviser to UNMOVIC's Executive Chairman Hans Blix, Barton was halfway through drafting a document on Iraq's anthrax programme in October 2002, when he decided to call it a day. Before going home, he printed off a hard copy, stapled the pages together and locked them in the steel filing box above his desk at the United Nations. The next morning, when he retrieved the document, he noticed something strange.

'There was another staple in it, and there were holes where the first staple had been removed.' Barton flicked through the document and discovered that one of the pages didn't match the others. 'Someone had photocopied it,' he says. 'One of the original pages had finished up in their copy, and one of the photocopied pages had ended up in mine.' UNMOVIC's photocopier was somewhat decrepit and left a black streak down every page. Barton's phantom page had a streak; the rest were clear.

Shortly after this incident, information from Barton's draft document appeared in the *Washington Times*. It was obvious someone had stolen it and leaked selected portions to the Press.

Burglary at the United Nations appears to have been a constant threat. 'You couldn't be sure that because something was in the safe it was secure,' says one British inspector at the time. 'I don't think we ever made that assumption. It just got worse at that point.'

Hans Blix himself was targeted a number of times. At one point, he was taken aside by a US official and shown a series of photographs that could only have come from his own files.

Bugging was also rife. The IAEA was bugged. UNMOVIC was bugged.

The UN Secretary-General was bugged. Non-permanent members of the Security Council who might influence a vote on the war were bugged. So dire was the situation that the heads of both IAEA and UNMOVIC refused to discuss sensitive issues in their own offices. Weapons inspectors took to holding meetings in the Vienna Café in the basement of the UN building, or outside on the streets of New York. To the United States, it seemed, the United Nations had become part of the problem, a target itself.

With some justification, UNMOVIC and IAEA officers viewed the bugging, the burglary and the selective leaking of sensitive material as part of a concerted effort to undermine their work. It was quite obvious the United States viewed inspections as a waste of time and the inspectors themselves as suspect. America was on its way to Baghdad: the last thing it needed was a bunch of liberal-types placing obstacles in its way and bleating about lack of evidence.

'We knew absolutely, directly, that [Paul] Wolfowitz was trying to undermine Blix. And Blix knew it, too,' recalls a British weapons inspector. 'The impression I had, rightly or wrongly, was that these people were willing to go to any lengths – it didn't really matter who got hurt or what principles got trampled on – to advance their particular theories.' The inspector shrugs. 'It was obvious that we were an impediment that had to be got over in order to get to war.'

In public, IAEA judgements that the tubes were not for a uranium-enrichment programme were aggressively countered by American officials with allegations that the Agency had proved itself pretty useless historically. When IAEA Director-General Mohammed ElBaradei specifically warned that the organization had found no evidence of a nuclear programme and that the tubes were most likely bound for a rocket programme, US Vice-President Dick Cheney leapt into the fray. 'I think Mr ElBaradei, frankly, is wrong,' he told *Meet the Press*. 'I don't have any reason to believe [the IAEA] any more valid this time than they've been in the past.'

Weapons inspectors were convinced that the United States had a specific motive for its selective leaking of WMD-based intelligence. 'The not-so-good intelligence was very often shared with the Press first,' recalls another senior officer. 'After being upset at the beginning that we were not getting the information directly, we had some understanding that, if the information had been provided to us, we would have laughed at it.'

George Healey, who was busy interviewing Iraqi scientists to prove the 81 mm rocket case, was livid. 'Some of us found what they were doing quite untruthful and disgusting. They were obviously selling an attack to the public. And they were doing it based on lies.'

Part of the problem was that the inspectors weren't finding evidence of WMDs in Iraq.

'[The Americans] gave us something like 48 [weapons] sites. We found nothing at any of them,' says UNMOVIC's Rod Barton. 'You don't just need a plant to make chemical and biological weapons – you need all the other infrastructure. You need the steel factory, the fabrication plant to make the bombs. You need a whole range of things. [Iraq] had nothing like that. Everything was in a worse state of repair than when our inspectors had last been into Iraq in 1998.'

Iraq's 'Currently Accurate, Full and Complete Disclosure', as demanded by Resolution 1441, didn't help. In December 2002, 12,000 pages of WMD-related material were handed over. WINPAC analysts swooped on the documents and pounced on the omissions, immediately noting that there was no mention of the gas centrifuge programme for which the tubes had been ordered. The possibility that there was no gas centrifuge programme doesn't appear to have occurred to them: the case regarding Iraq's WMDs, as Director of Central Intelligence George Tenet told the President later that month, was a 'slam dunk'.

In January 2003, after a White House request for stronger evidence on the nuclear issue, WINPAC decided to prove that it was a slam dunk. A pair of private contractors was hired to put the tubes on to a lathe and spin them, to demonstrate they were capable of withstanding the necessary speeds.[7] Five tests were performed. Four were prematurely halted, but one tube was apparently spun for two hours at a speed of 90,000 rpm. This, it seemed, proved their case.

Intrigued by the WINPAC report, INR analysts decided to investigate. '[My analysts] went directly to the contractor themselves,' recalls Carl Ford, 'only to find out that, yeah, the spin tests worked, but then, when we tried to do it for any extended period of time, they broke down and they could not be reliably used for centrifuges.'

WINPAC eventually admitted that all had not quite been as it seemed. Actually, the total number of tests had been thirty-one (not five), of which thirty (not four) had failed. One tube was indeed spun at 90,000 rpm, but this was done for sixty-five minutes, not two hours. What the agency still failed to mention was that when three tubes were tested to destruction (a more standard procedure for assaying centrifuge rotors) all failed just slightly above 90,000 rpm: a good sign that they would have failed if spun at that speed for any significant period. When the Department of Energy discovered the truth about the spin tests, analysts filed a Technical Intelligence Note asserting that WINPAC's conclusions were wrong: far from indicating that the tubes would make good centrifuge rotors, the tests showed the exact opposite.

This was not the first time WINPAC's certainty had got the better of it. There had been a string of such incidents. Some of the information the organization cited was just plain wrong. Its specifications for the Zippe centrifuge, for example, were incorrect. According to WINPAC, Zippe rotors were 2.8 mm thick, a fact which almost matched the Iraqi tubes' 3.3 mm. Actually the wall thickness was less than

---

[7] Actually, these were not the first spin tests that the CIA had commissioned. On 16 September the year before, a single tube had been spun successfully to a speed of 60,000 rpm – a fact that was included in the National Intelligence Estimate as 'a rough indication that the tube is suitable for a centrifuge rotor'.

1 mm. This might well have been a simple typographical error, but the fact that Department of Energy experts pointed it out to the CIA repeatedly throughout 2001 and 2002 makes this unlikely.

WINPAC had also highlighted the fact that the tubes had been procured in secret through a Jordanian front company as evidence they were bound for a clandestine nuclear programme. This was rubbish. Hussein Kamel had advertised on the Internet for aluminium suppliers; he had openly haggled over prices with Garry Cordukes, and samples of the tubes had been dispatched to Jordan by DHL: hardly the courier of choice for clandestine nuclear technology.

WINPAC had also pointed to the tubes' high cost as an indicator they were destined for something more significant than an artillery rocket programme. According to the organization, 7075-T6 was 'considerably more expensive than other, more readily available materials', and thus a 'poor choice' for artillery rockets. This was also incorrect. Actually, 7075-T6 was the material of choice for low-cost rocket systems. The United States, Russia and thirteen other countries used it for precisely that purpose.

'Cheap as chips,' comments Garry Cordukes, who made the tubes. '7075 is an engineering alloy, so it's more high tensile, but it's not uncommon whatsoever. Nothing unusual about it . . . Total bullshit.'

In addition to these inaccuracies, information that might have undermined WINPAC's arguments was sometimes omitted. For instance, WINPAC had presented the NIE's drafters with a table to highlight the similarities between the Zippe and Beams centrifuges and the Australian tubes. As it stood, the table showed there were indeed similarities between the sizes of the Australian tubes and known centrifuge rotors. But the table did not include the sizes of Iraq's 81 mm rocket tubes, which matched the size of the Australian tubes exactly. This fact was not presented to policymakers or to those drafting the Intelligence Estimate.

When it came to rocket production, the NIE committee was presented with another table designed to show how the tolerances of the Iraqi tubes exceeded those of comparable US rocket systems. Once again, background material was missing. In reality, US rocket-tube specifications ran to another twenty-five pages, none of which was included. Had they been, it would have been clear that the United States demanded higher standards of its rocket tubes than Iraq. Department of Energy experts also noted that the tolerances of the Iraqi tubes – supposedly so high they precluded any use other than in centrifuge systems – were, in fact, lower than those of numerous standard industrial items, such as bicycle-seat posts and aluminium cans.

WINPAC also omitted to tell policymakers that the two centrifuges it thought Iraq was making, the Beams and Zippe machines, had never been used commercially before. Gernot Zippe himself had noted that the yield from his machine was so low it would preclude industrial use.

On top of this selective amnesia came a more direct form of misrepresentation. At various points, WINPAC reported that its spin tests had proved the suitability of the tubes for centrifuge rotors (although they strongly suggested the exact opposite)[8] and that it didn't have the specifications for the Italian *Medusa 81* rocket (when it did). Then there was the issue of the tubes' weight. In July 2001, convinced the tubes were bound for a Zippe centrifuge, Joe T had tried to persuade the IAEA that the tubes' weight matched those of a Zippe machine.

'[We] explained to him that Zippe's rotors included the end caps and the baffles and the bearings,' recalls one IAEA officer, 'and he had only looked at the tubes.' If the end caps and baffle were added, they told the CIA man, the weights most definitely did not match. 'He just went back and recalculated it as if the tubes were thinner – that is to say

---

[8] 'It wasn't true that they didn't have the right information,' according to Carl Ford. 'In this particular case, they simply didn't tell the truth . . . they took and manipulated the data.'

had been machined – and then added in the weight that he had forgotten on the first round.'

As if this weren't enough, when the WINPAC analyst returned to Washington after the meeting, he apparently informed his colleagues that the IAEA had bought his theory. 'After he returned from his visit to Vienna where people told him, "No, we think you're wrong," he said, "I went to Vienna and they agreed with me."'

On 5 February 2003, Secretary of State Colin Powell addressed the United Nations. 'Saddam Hussein is determined to get his hands on a nuclear bomb,' he assured the Assembly. 'He is so determined that he has made repeated covert attempts to acquire high-specification aluminium tubes.'

While Powell admitted he was no expert on centrifuges, he pointed out that it was strange that the Iraqis had procured such highly spec-ified tubes if they were destined for an artillery rocket programme. 'Maybe the Iraqis just manufacture their conventional weapons to a higher standard than we do,' the Secretary conceded, 'but I don't think so.'

Powell told the United Nations that 'most US experts' believed the tubes were to be used as centrifuge rotors; 'other experts and the Iraqis themselves' argued they were for rockets.

Professor Houston Wood was mortified. 'That speech!' he says. 'He put the US people who disagreed with him, or his report, in the same camp with the Iraqis. I was just astounded.'

Wood wasn't the only one connected with the tubes shocked by the presentation. Garry Cordukes was also incredulous. The Australian aluminium trader knew nothing about gas centrifuges, but he knew a botch-up when he saw one.

'If anyone had tested [the tubes] they would have seen straight away, well, this anodizing isn't what it should be.' Cordukes had been surprised that Hussein Kamel hadn't noticed the coating had not been correctly applied, but for the US intelligence community not to notice, too, was mystifying. 'It didn't gel,' he says. 'It just didn't make sense.'

Around the world, experts in the weapons-intelligence community were glued to Powell's presentation. At UNMOVIC headquarters in New York, analysts crammed into 'the bunker' to watch it on the UN's CCTV system. Despite occasional hoots of derision when the inspectors thought something was awry, mostly the room was silent.

'I thought that they had the goods,' admits Rod Barton. 'I didn't believe Powell would say what he did say unless they had fairly strong evidence. I thought they've obviously got something that we haven't seen – and quite a lot of it.'

In Iraq, weapons analysts were watching, too. Mahdi Obeidi, the man behind the country's 1990 centrifuge programme, was also tempted to believe: was there, perhaps, a nuclear programme in Iraq that he didn't know about?

The notion that there was another, super-secret source behind Powell's assertions seems to have been common among both weapons inspectors and intelligence analysts. Even inside the CIA, certain officers believed it.

'What he was saying was not matching up with my intelligence,' admits an officer in the Counter Proliferation Division. 'I'm hearing and reading everything, but I'm just going, "Well, maybe someone is talking to someone in Saddam's inner circle."'

Everyone assumed that someone else had the proof.

No amount of super-secret informants, however, could persuade anyone who had really studied the tubes that they were suitable for centrifuge use. To them, a physical impossibility was being used to justify war; people were about to start dying.

Wayne White was appalled by the Powell presentation. 'I had a serious problem with the nuclear portion of the speech,' he says. 'It just turned my stomach.'

Geoff Wainwright, the Australian intelligence officer whose work had provided the first tubes and details of the order itself, agreed. 'The biggest load of crap I've ever heard anyone get up and say,' he recalls. 'It made me sick.'

At the IAEA, George Healey was equally dumbfounded. 'I just couldn't believe it, that somebody would know that little about what was going on, to stand up at the UN and say something like that.'

Bob Kelley figured it clearer. 'Somebody,' he says, 'mis-briefed Powell.'

Kelley was correct. Somebody *did* mis-brief Powell. In the run-up to his UN presentation, the Secretary of State had been extremely sceptical about the CIA's claims regarding the aluminium tubes. Not only had he been informed in private by Mohammed ElBaradei that they were not destined for a centrifuge programme, but his own Bureau of Intelligence and Research was lobbying hard to remove the issue from the presentation altogether. Carl Ford, INR's Head, had specifically warned Powell that a number of assertions in the intelligence picture contained 'egregious errors' and were 'highly misleading'. With less than a week to go till his date at the United Nations, the Secretary, on the verge of excising all references to the aluminium tubes from his presentation (an act that would have undermined the entire case for war), demanded a briefing from the CIA at Langley.

Sensing they were about to lose the Secretary of State on the aluminium tubes issue, CIA bosses George Tenet and John McLaughlin produced one of the tubes and rolled it across the table to him. As the Secretary examined it, the pair explained that there was no doubt it had been destined for a centrifuge programme. Behind them, WINPAC's experts nodded sagely.

'It was all very convincing,' recalls Colonel Lawrence Wilkerson, Powell's Chief of Staff and right-hand man at the briefing. The problem was, it wasn't convincing enough: Powell still wasn't buying it.

At this point, the CIA men pulled a rabbit out of the hat. At the last minute, Tenet shared a sensational piece of intelligence with the Secretary of State.

'A counterpart in an allied country,' says Wilkerson, 'had just done a test on the aluminium tubes and had got them to go to 98,000 rpm over an hour period of time. No visible deterioration in the walls, metal or anything else.'

The implication was clear: these were no rocket tubes.

More persuasive to the Secretary than the speed of the spin test, however, was the identity of this 'allied country': France. If the French, at that time resolutely against the war, agreed the tubes were suitable for centrifuge use, that was the kind of information Powell would believe.

'Powell had heard that a very respected intelligence service in another nation that incidentally was a major ally of the United States had said that they believed these aluminium tubes were for centrifuges,' recalls Wilkerson. 'The damage was done.'

Somewhat grudgingly, Powell put the aluminium-tubes issue back into his presentation.

No details of these French spin tests have ever emerged. When Powell asked if he could cite them at the United Nations as evidence, he was turned down. Privately, weapons inspectors wonder if they ever took place at all. IAEA officials, normally the first to be informed about breaking news on the tubes, were never even informed that tests had taken place. They certainly were not informed about the results.

Jacques Baute, at the head of the Iraq inspection team at the time, is openly sceptical. A French nuclear weapons expert with excellent access inside his own country's weapons-intelligence community, he was never told about the tests. He is convinced that, even if they had taken place, they would have been worthless.

'The issue of having the tubes spun physically is completely secondary,' he says. 'It would only confirm what the material *was* – but we already knew that it was high-strength aluminium.' Even had the tests ever taken place, and there is no proof that they did, they were worthless. Except, perhaps, in persuading a non-nuclear expert such as Colin Powell of the veracity of the WINPAC claims.

'The Secretary got led down the Primrose Path,' says Carl Ford, Powell's senior adviser at INR.

Lawrence Wilkerson agrees. 'On the aluminium tubes and the nuclear programme in general,' he says, 'he was lied to.'

To INR staff, it was apparent the US administration had formulated a conclusion, then set about proving it. So certain were key figures in the White House that Iraq was reconstituting its nuclear-weapons programme that all evidence pointing in the opposite direction was simply disregarded. Intelligence officers, swept up in the epidemic of certainty engulfing the White House, abandoned their neutrality and became advocates, telling policymakers what they wanted to hear – which was, of course, what they had secretly believed all along. And, all the while, the prevailing wind blew in one direction: towards Baghdad.

'It's hard to think of a more odious and disreputable use by a government of intelligence information than in the case of Iraq,' says Greg Thielmann.

Carl Ford, his boss, concurs. 'I could not believe,' he says today, 'that [the intelligence community] had sunk so low that we would turn out such crap at such an important, vital time.'

The ultimate irony was that Iraqi officials had not really wanted the aluminium tubes in the first place. The military already had two artillery rocket systems that worked perfectly well. It didn't need another. Even before they sanctioned the order for 60,000 aluminium tubes from Australia, members of the 2000 Rocket Committee had agreed that the *Nasser 81* programme was probably a lost cause.

However, in the topsy-turvy world of Iraqi weapons procurement, things appeared to work in reverse. In 1997, the military had received a shipment of 81 mm launchers. By 2000, the pressure was on to make rockets that fitted them. Unable to make the rockets work, the MIC's scientists had drawn a blank: they didn't really know why the things were inaccurate.

Unfortunately, the Committee's political masters would not have tolerated the conclusion 'We don't know.' Something had to be done. There was no time to find the perfect solution. They just needed *a* solution. So the 2000 Committee seized on the first reasonable suggestion it came across: tightening the tolerances of the aluminium tube casings. If the tubes were better made, it reasoned, the rockets might work better.

The piling of questionable assumptions one on top of another; the knee-jerk response of grabbing the nearest available solution; the rejection of inconvenient truths; the tunnel vision; the political pressure; the threat of getting it wrong – it wasn't so much that the rockets were broken, it was more that each link in the procurement process was corroded: the entire system was unstable. The result was a bureaucratic momentum that made it impossible to abandon the project. The tubes order went through.

Had they been aware of the convoluted process by which the Iraqis had come to order 60,000 aluminium tubes from Australia, America's CIA officers might have sympathized. They had a term for this kind of thing. They called it 'groupthink'.

In June 2002, Sami Ibrahim's postgraduate student Mohammed Abbar submitted his MSc thesis, *A Study of the Quality of the Solution in the Aluminium Anodizing Process*. As the Professor had predicted, Abbar's conclusions were clear-cut. Iraq's aluminium tubes needed to be protected with a chromate anodize. Above all, they had to be stored separately: without some form of insulation, one infected tube would contaminate all the others.

Professor Ibrahim had been right. Corrosion was like a disease. Not only was it almost impossible to eliminate, it was also horribly, horribly contagious.

5

Stuff Happens

Freedom's untidy, and free people are free to commit mistakes and commit crimes and do bad things. They're also free to live their lives and do wonderful things. And that's what's going to happen here.

Donald Rumsfeld, April 2003

I really do believe that we will be greeted as liberators.

Dick Cheney, March 2003

Haki Mohammed and his brothers were shovelling manure on their farm in Yusifiyah when the soldier arrived. Dishevelled and clearly distressed, the man had run a great distance. He slumped against a fence to catch his breath.

'Please,' he entreated, 'are you true Arabs?'

The Iraqis, raised in a culture of obligatory hospitality towards needy strangers, immediately understood the question's subtext. The man needed help. Even had he not been a soldier (Haki thought he recognized the uniform of a Special Republican Guard), they were honour-bound to offer assistance.

'Of course,' Haki assured the man. 'What is it you need?'

The soldier held out his AK-47. 'Take it.' He indicated the webbing around his waist, stuffed full of charged magazines. 'Take them all. I don't want them. But I need a dishdash or a robe. Anything that isn't a uniform.'

Then, without any warning, the soldier started to undress.

The Mohammeds were indeed good Arabs. They fetched a dishdash and the man slipped it on. True to his part of the bargain, he handed over his rifle in exchange.

'Here,' he said. 'It's yours.'

The Iraqis raised their hands, indicating that they didn't expect payment for the robe. For a moment the soldier appeared perplexed. Then, without warning, he flung the ammunition and the rifle down on the ground and ran off into the desert.

Bemused, the Yusifiyans examined the fleeing soldier's belongings. He had not been a Republican Guard at all. His uniform, bereft of rank badges, was that of a rarer outfit: Manzaumat al Amin, the Iraqi military's security and protection agency.

A small, nondescript town of a few thousand souls twenty-five kilometres south-west of Baghdad, Yusifiyah is known for its rich soil, which facilitates the production of potatoes famous throughout Iraq for their size and flavour. The singer Farouk Al-Khatib was born here. But that's about it. For those uninterested in either potatoes or Iraqi popular music, there's little of interest: farms criss-crossed by irrigation ditches, a great deal of sand, and not much else.

Nahir Yusifiyah, the crescent-shaped region surrounding the town, is scarcely more exciting. Sparsely populated, the area is mostly given over to piecemeal agriculture: chillies, oranges and small-scale fish farming. Bounded to the west by the Euphrates river, it encompasses the towns of Latifiyah, Mahmudiyah and Iskandariyah – each about as notable as Yusifiyah. Essentially, Nahir Yusifiyah is one of those in-between places: those driving south from Baghdad to Najaf on Highway 8 pass through it; those heading west to Fallujah on Highway 10, above it. Then they move on. Few stop to take a second look.

Yusifiyah's obscurity, however, together with its convenient location –
less than thirty minutes' drive from Baghdad Airport – make it perfect
for certain purposes: hiding things, for example. Things you'd rather no
one ever knew about. *Secret* things.

Sure enough, fifteen kilometres to the south lies a big, big secret.

The secret dates back to 1977, when the then President Ahmed
Hassan al-Bakr ordered the construction of a vast munitions plant outside
town. Built by the Yugoslavs, the factory was originally to be named
after Bakr himself, until Saddam Hussein seized power in 1979. In a
fit of patriotic zeal, the fledgling dictator named it after the Iraqi general
Qa'qaa ibn Umar, who in the seventh century inflicted a most glorious
massacre on the Persian army in the second battle of Qasidiya: Al
Qa'qaa.

Weapons inspectors who visited the facility were dumbstruck by the
scale of the place.

'*Huge*,' comments one senior figure familiar with the site. 'The biggest
chemical plant I've ever seen.'

Covering an area of 36 square kilometres, containing 1,100 buildings
and employing more than 14,000 staff, the site was essentially a secret,
self-sufficient city, ten times the size of New York's Central Park – in
the middle of the desert. It even had its own power station.

'Just enormous,' agrees another inspector. 'The largest explosives
plant in the Middle East.'

For more than twenty years, Al Qa'qaa formed the heart of the
country's rocketry programme, producing the propellants, igniters and
explosives that made Iraq's munitions (including the now infamous
Nasser 81 artillery rockets) go up, then ensured they detonated when
they came down.

Saddam was so pleased with the facility that, when the Iran–Iraq War
broke out in 1980, he built a number of other weapons factories nearby.
Soon, Nahir Yusifiyah was teeming with armaments facilities. To the
south, Mahaweel, a vast explosives-storage site bordered by Um Nassr,

a manufacturing facility for free-fall aircraft bombs; to the south-east, Hatteen, an ammunition filling plant with its own artillery range. To the north stood Al Qadissiya, a small-arms manufacturing facility. Adjacent to it was Al Furat, built to make small arms, but which shortly moved into nuclear centrifuge development. To the east, there were more: Badr (machine tooling for centrifuges), Nida (scud-missile manufacture), Al Amin (gun barrels) and Hakim (bio-warfare). All huge, clandestine weapons sites with their own research staff and agendas.

From the outside there was little to indicate what was going on in Al Qa'qaa. Surrounded by tall earthen walls, all that was visible was a series of chimney stacks producing oxides of nitrogen and huge plumes of acrid brown smoke. Employees in the facility were not allowed to speak about it; nobody else was allowed in. To Yusifiyans, however, it was obvious the plant made military equipment of some sort: repeated explosions emanated from within the walls when things went wrong, and from the facility's test ranges when things went right. Other than that, nothing.

At the heart of this big, big secret lay further secrets, some so huge they bordered on the preposterous. In the late 1980s, the facility was involved in the construction of the largest rifle in the history of the world: a monstrous weapon with a 150-metre barrel and the ability to shoot a 600-kilogram projectile directly into space. The Supergun required ten tons of propellant for each shot – doubtless the reason why research was underway at Qa'qaa, where the explosive material was to be made.

Unfortunately, even this state-of-the-art facility was not up to the task. At the end of the decade, suppliers were sought for a pair of compounds that the facility was unable to synthesize purely: RDX (the basis for a number of explosives, including C4) and PETN (used in small-calibre ammunition and Semtex). The materials, ordered from Eastern Europe via Chile, arrived in shipments of hundreds of tons.

Then the project stalled. In 1991, following the Iraqi rout in Kuwait, inspectors from the International Atomic Energy Agency (IAEA) gained access to Al Qa'qaa, where they found 145 tonnes of pure RDX and PETN. On a whim, one enterprising inspector asked technicians whether they had imported any other explosives of note. Qa'qaa staff exchanged glances and shuffled their feet, before leading him to a series of bunkers containing hundreds of drums of an off-white, crystalline powder. About as highly explosive as high explosive gets, High Melt Explosive (HMX) is used to detonate nuclear warheads. Qa'qaa had nearly 200 tonnes of it. The IAEA moved all the explosives to secure bunkers on the south-west corner of the facility, then closed the doors with tamper-proof seals. And there the 341 tonnes sat for more than a decade.

Of course, inhabitants of Yusifiyah and the surrounding towns had no idea about any of this. In Saddam's time, there were many things one didn't enquire about. But that was before the curious incident of the soldier, the rifle and the dishdash.

For Haki and his brothers, Operation Iraqi Freedom had started in the early hours of 3 April 2003, when they were woken by the sound of low-flying aircraft. Moments later, the first American artillery shells zipped overhead. With pinpoint accuracy the shells eliminated Republican Guard checkpoints and roadblocks around Yusifiyah, effectively neutralizing all threat of resistance.

By sunrise, American tanks were trundling north up Highway 8 towards Baghdad Airport. There was a brief pause outside town as units of the 3-15th Infantry Battalion fought a skirmish at Al Qa'qaa. Yusifiyans held their breath.

'We thought it might be kind of an equal battle between the two armies,' Haki recalls. 'We thought we would win the war.'

If the Iraqis really believed this, they were disappointed. The Iraqi army was never going to be a match for the overwhelming firepower of the United States. Almost immediately, news arrived that American troops were on the outskirts of Baghdad. Two days later, the 3-15th departed to join the Thunder Runs into the capital.

Ali, one of Al Qa'qaa's senior administrators, recalls the invasion well. 'The Americans came in on the 2nd or 3rd of April,' he says. 'There was no fighting. We heard some shooting, but after that it was all over. Most of the soldiers and officers just took off their uniforms and ran away.' One of them had showed up on Haki Mohammed's doorstep.

Having ascertained from his uniform that the fleeing soldier was not a Republican Guard but a member of Manzaumat al Amin, it took Haki next to no time to deduce that he had come from the secure compound at Al Qa'qaa, and an even shorter time to figure that, if the soldiers had left, the site was unguarded. For a quarter of a century, the facility had been off-limits. Here, finally, was an opportunity to find out what had been going on in there.

Haki's neighbours, many of whom had had similar experiences with fleeing Manzaumat guards, had the same idea. 'Lots of people went in,' he recalls. 'They destroyed the fence, and they went in that way . . . There was no army, no guards, nothing.' The period between the guards fleeing and the first Yusifiyans breaching the compound was remarkably short. 'About an hour,' he says.

By the afternoon of 3 April, the largest explosives plant in the Middle East was open to all comers.

A week after the first Yusifiyans breached Al Qa'qaa's perimeter fence, the US 101st Airborne Division pitched camp just outside the facility. There appear to have been no briefings about the site. The soldiers' attention was elsewhere: the 101st was itching to get to Baghdad. As far as the troops were concerned, they were sitting on their behinds while higher-ups attempted to jump the queue, to manoeuvre their own divisions into the capital for a share of the glorious victory. They were missing the show.

And what a show it was. On 9 April, the day before the 101st arrived at Qa'qaa, US troops had taken the capital, symbolically pulling down the statue of Saddam Hussein in Firdos Square. The image, broadcast around the world, delighted the Commander-in-Chief back in Washington. 'In the images of falling statues,' President Bush later announced, 'we have witnessed the arrival of a new era.'

Unfortunately, by the time the 101st arrived in Baghdad on 11 April, the foundations of the new era were looking distinctly shaky. As the troops settled in to the capital, news began to break that the city was descending into an orgy of lawlessness and looting. Reporters told of mobs roaming the city, stealing everything that wasn't nailed down. There were so many that Robert Fisk of the *Independent* witnessed traffic jams of looters in Baghdad. When news emerged that the National Museum of Iraq, unprotected by coalition forces, had been ransacked, the media started asking awkward questions.

Initially, coalition spokesmen appeared unconcerned. The Iraqis were simply demonstrating their hatred of the Baath Party.

'Imagine the frustration of people after twenty-five years of repression by an evil regime,' the British Forces spokesman told CNN. 'They're only letting off steam.'

Three days later, Secretary of Defense Donald Rumsfeld denied that TV footage of looting was representative of the situation on the ground.

'The images you are seeing on television you are seeing over and over and *over*. And it's the same picture of some person walking out of some building with a vase. And you see it twenty times and you think, "My goodness! Were there that many vases? Is it possible that there were that many vases in the country?"' After pausing for the laughter to subside, Rumsfeld became more serious. The main thing to focus on, he instructed journalists, was that the country had been liberated, that Iraqis were free. Anything else was a distraction. 'I picked up a newspaper today and I couldn't believe it. I read eight headlines that talked about chaos, violence, unrest. And it was just Henny Penny:

"The sky is falling!"' Iraq was going through a period of transition, the Secretary explained. Freedom was sometimes untidy. 'Stuff happens.'

Rumsfeld was right on one point. Stuff did happen. And not only at the National Museum of Iraq.

By 6 April, Haki was unable to contain his curiosity any longer. Many of his neighbours had been into Al Qa'qaa and had returned with fantastic stories of all the useful bits and pieces lying about. He decided to take a look for himself. Haki and his cousins and friends piled into a grey Kia minibus, hung a white flag from the window to placate passing American troops, and made their way to the main gate. Finding it open, they drove in to the compound.

Clearly, word of the free-for-all had spread. Hundreds of Yusifiyans were roaming around inside. A few were sightseers, but the majority were there for more nefarious purposes. They were gutting the place.

Some targets were easier than others. Trucks vanished fairly quickly. The first few were simply hotwired and driven away. When locals realized there was no rush, however, they became more brazen, using the stolen trucks to return and carry away further loot. Those unfortunate enough to have missed out on the initial automobile bonanza brought in their own vehicles – tractors, trailers, mules and carts – loaded them up and left. The next day they came back for more.

'Lathes, machine tools, electrical generators,' says Haki. 'They were even taking the iron posts from the buildings. They were taking anything they could find. I saw a big truck – forty-ton capacity, perhaps. I couldn't believe it.'

Al Qa'qaa was assaulted from all sides. From the north-west came the Yusifiyans; from the north-east, the inhabitants of Mahmudiyah. Some of Al Qa'qaa's senior staff lived in an executive employees' compound just west of the town. When the power went out after the Americans passed by, they returned to the complex to fetch an electrical generator. By the time they arrived, two days before the Saddam statue ceremony, Mahmudiyans were operating a market inside the walls, selling and bartering plundered goods. Ali, the site administrator, was flabbergasted at the scale of the operation.

'It was astonishing, the way they managed to steal such big pieces of kit. When the Yugoslavs built the plant, they installed some of the equipment first, then constructed the buildings around it – that was how big some of the machines were. These looters stole them. Some of them were using cranes.' He shakes his head. 'They even took the electrical cables. They dug them up from the ground and took them. The water pipes. Everything.'

Directly to the east of Al Qa'qaa, residents of Latifiyah were slower to act, thanks largely to the efforts of local religious leaders, who instructed them that it was *haraam* – forbidden – to steal from the site.

'In the mosques the imams were saying, "This is wrong,"' recalls Ahmed, a chemical engineer who worked at the weapons plant before the invasion. He shrugs. 'It made no difference. They went in anyway.' Initially, the targets were the same: cars, trucks, air conditioners, electrical goods, machine tools. Once these items were gone, the looters took anything that looked like it might be valuable. 'We had security devices to protect the perimeter fence. There were cameras, and a computer that ran the system. The looters didn't know what they were. They took them all.'

As yet, however, the looters had not discovered Al Qa'qaa's real treasure: the vast stockpiles of HMX, PETN and RDX. We know they had not discovered the explosives because of a somewhat fortuitous event. On 18 April, two weeks after the looting began, a pair of American journalists did.

Over the course of the month that they had been embedded with the 101st Airborne, reporter Dean Staley and cameraman Joe Caffrey had seen more than their fair share of action. The 101st had encountered stiff resistance as it fought its way north from Kuwait, and the journalists, representing TV station KSTP-St Paul, Minneapolis, were fortunate to have been allowed to tag along. Now, however, they were stuck. At the end of the second week in April, the 101st had established a base a mile south-east of Al Qa'qaa, from which they serviced Black Hawk helicopters and ferried military bigwigs around. A week later, they were still there. With no obvious route to Baghdad, the journalists' chances of an exclusive were growing slimmer by the minute. The capital had fallen a week earlier and the war appeared to be winding down. Staley and Caffrey didn't want to appear ungrateful, but they were bored.

So when, on the morning of 18 April, a sergeant and a warrant officer offered them the opportunity to tag along on a trip outside the camp, they were all ears.

'It was a sightsee,' recalls Caffrey. 'Non-sanctioned. They basically decided on a whim, because they weren't assigned to fly that day, to check out the base.'

Staley grabbed his notebook, Caffrey his camera; the soldiers picked up a pair of bolt cutters and the four men piled into a Humvee to see what they could find.

Within a quarter of an hour, they started finding things. Paved roads. Watchtowers. Perimeter fences. And, within them, munitions of every possible shape and size. There were fat bombs, thin bombs, cartoon-style bombs with big fins and, lying in the hot morning sun, bombs that appeared to be leaking corrosive brown material. Some of them were as big as Volkswagens.

More interesting than the bombs on the ground were the bunker complexes that soon honed into view. There were eight in all, each containing seven or eight buildings. Some of the bunkers' steel doors appeared to have been prised open. The soldiers pulled up alongside one and the four men peered in. Approximately the size of a basket-ball court, the building had a cement floor and was relatively cool. Perhaps once, before the power had cut out, it had been air-conditioned. The interior was dark, other than from the light entering through the open doors. Scattered around the floor were mousetraps. The men ventured inside.

Squinting, the journalists managed to make out symmetrical shapes on the floor: rows of warhead tips, stacked shoulder-to-shoulder. As their eyes grew accustomed to the darkness, it became clear this was not the full extent of the ordnance inside the bunker. Everywhere the men looked, there was more explosive materiel.

'There was just row after row of crates with detonators or caps and different things inside them,' says Staley. The reporter turned to his cameraman. 'Oh my God!' he said. 'Look how much of this stuff there is!'

When the adjacent bunker also turned out to be filled with munitions, the soldiers of the 101st became impressed, too. They had no idea about any of this.

'The 101st Airborne, the people we were with, were absolutely ignorant of Al Qa'qaa,' says Staley. 'There was no notion of what [it] was, or what it meant.'

They were finding out.

The men moved on to a third bunker. This time the steel doors were chained shut, so they peered through the gap between them. Then one of the soldiers fetched the bolt cutters from the Humvee and snipped through the chain. Inside, their flashlights revealed that, once again, the building was filled with munitions. The soldiers became more excited.

'These guys were like kids in a candy store,' recalls Staley. 'They were so curious that we became curious as well. Because they wanted to just see what the next bunker held, so they kept going from bunker to bunker to see what all of these munitions were.'

Outside the fourth or fifth bunker, the soldiers, and the journalists, stopped. A length of thin steel wire snaked around the lock, the chain and the hinges of the door, secured by a copper disc the size of a coin. Clearly, the wire wasn't strong enough to keep anyone out. So what was it for? The soldiers wondered aloud whether it wasn't so thin because it was meant not to be seen, that it was a booby trap. In the end, curiosity prevailed. One of them broke the disc apart and the wire fell away. Nothing happened. They walked in.

There were no warheads in this bunker. Only crates of what appeared to be chemicals. And some strange-looking drums.

'There were these round cardboard cylinders that were maybe a foot and a half across and maybe three or four feet high,' says Caffrey. 'Rows and rows of them.'

Cautiously, the soldiers opened one. Inside was a clear plastic bag containing coarse powder. Caffrey went in for a look.

'It was very flour-like, yellow, bright yellow in colour.' He laughs. 'I don't think anybody stuck their finger in it, we weren't *that* keen on it. But it didn't keep us from opening the top of these cardboard cylinders and opening the plastic bags and peeking.'

Further bunkers also contained the yellow, flour-like substance. In fact, the more the journalists looked, the more they found. Many of the buildings appeared to be filled with it: in one corner might be thirty crates or boxes, in the other, sixty or seventy barrels. The quantity was staggering.

One of the soldiers drew his breath. 'What *is* this stuff?' he murmured.

For a moment the soldiers and the journalists had the same idea. Had they accidentally discovered Saddam's WMD? No one knew. But just in case, Joe Caffrey filmed it all.

While Caffrey, Staley and the soldiers were exploring the bunkers outside Yusifiyah, officials at the IAEA were becoming increasingly concerned. Reports of looting had reached Vienna, and if they were even remotely accurate the Iraqi weapons sites they had fought so hard to inspect might be compromised. The results could be catastrophic.

Prior to the invasion the Agency had told the Americans of the dangers of allowing the security situation to collapse. Two weeks after the start of the war, Jacques Baute, the Head of the Iraq nuclear-inspection teams, visited the US mission to advise, again, that the weapons sites needed protection. He specifically mentioned Al Qa'qaa. Just days before the invasion, he told officials, inspectors had inventoried the facility's HMX, RDX and PETN stores and ensured that the seals were still intact. This kind of material, the Frenchman suggested, should be kept out of the hands of looters.

There was no reaction.

Privately, IAEA officials wondered whether the Americans really understood what they were doing. Al Qa'qaa had made the propellant for the Nasser 81 artillery rocket programme, itself at the heart of the administration's case for war. Inspectors had been in and out constantly prior to the invasion. There was no way the United States could not have known that. The site was full of explosives. It was wide open. On 3 May, an internal memo at the IAEA warned that, if Al Qa'qaa was not secured, the result could be 'the greatest explosives bonanza in history'.

Stuff, it seemed, was still happening. And the sheer scale of it was stunning.

Across Iraq, the moment the fighting was over – and often *before* it was over – anything of value that was not guarded was looted. The magnitude of the theft almost defied belief. Fire engines, ambulances, tanks, heavy machinery and artillery pieces were stolen. Electrical masts and power lines were pulled down with cranes, disassembled, smelted and sold for scrap. Entire power plants went missing. So much looted metal was dumped on Middle Eastern markets that aluminium and copper trading prices plummeted.

Prior to the Iraq invasion, the worst looting most UN staff had witnessed was in Somalia, which had peaked at what they referred to as Phase Four, when locals resorted to stripping the tar from road surfaces for use as fuel. Iraq went to Phase Six. Doors were stolen; roofs were stolen; steel joists and ties were stolen; plumbing pipes and electrical wire were stolen; concrete walls were demolished, the steel rebar inside them smelted down and sold. Everything went. In the weeks following the invasion, western staff drove past buildings that mysteriously shrank, storey by storey, until there was nothing left.

'Buildings just disappeared before our eyes,' recalls one. It was almost as if the earth was being wiped clean by some biblical storm.

'You'd end up with just granules of concrete on the ground. Just a slightly choppy surface,' says a senior weapons inspector. 'You might find the odd bolt – but that's about it. *That's* Phase Six looting.'

Often what was not stolen was incinerated. Prior to the invasion, the Americans had planned to resurrect twenty of Iraq's twenty-three government ministries, yet once Baghdad was taken almost all of these facilities were left unprotected. Sixteen were looted, set alight and completely destroyed. Only one remained unscathed: the Ministry of Oil – which was heavily guarded from the outset – sending a strong message to Iraqis about the true motives behind the invasion.

When staff at the Office of Reconstruction and Humanitarian Assistance (ORHA) arrived in Baghdad in April, not only were there no computers, no chairs, no desks, no employee registers and no telephones left, there were no buildings to put them in anyway. Within a relatively short period, the damage to Iraq's infrastructure by looting far outstripped that caused by the war itself.

Ironically, the first major black eye of Operation Iraqi Freedom was self-inflicted. Having decided, post-9/11, that it was now necessary at all times to prepare for the worst, the White House went to war hoping for the best. So convinced was the Bush administration of the righteousness of its plan – that the operation was a liberation rather than an invasion – it simply hadn't bothered to consider what might happen if others didn't see it that way.

Armchair generals pontificate endlessly about the reasons for the chaos that ensued. Not enough troops, say some. Not enough police, say others. Or not enough planning. Ultimately, however, the failure to anticipate the civil unrest in Iraq was embedded in the very *mindset* of the policy to invade in the first place – a mindset of almost evangelical certainty.

To the neocons, liberating Baghdad in 2003 would be like liberating Paris in 1944. Once the fighting was over, the spark of democracy would kindle. Then, like a benevolent virus, it would spread. America would fix the Middle East the way it had fixed Europe when the fighting finished there.

'Write this down,' George W. Bush instructed Republican governors at the White House on 2 September 2002. 'Afghanistan and Iraq will lead that part of the world to democracy. They are going to be the catalyst to change the Middle East and the world.'

The ferocity of the belief that Saddam Hussein had weapons of mass destruction was matched only by the ferocity of the belief that his removal would solve the region's problems.

To adherents of the vision, it wasn't just clear that Americans would be greeted with flags and hugs rather than bombs and bullets – it was obvious. *So* obvious, in fact, that no Plan B was necessary. The result was an example of groupthink that outstripped even the aluminium tubes.

'[The war] could last, you know, six days, six weeks, six months,' Rumsfeld told US troops in Aviano, Italy, six weeks before the invasion. 'I doubt six months.'

Pentagon estimates that the operation would require 500,000 troops were, he said, 'old and stale'.

His deputy Paul Wolfowitz agreed, telling a Congress committee in February 2003: 'It's hard to conceive that it would take more forces to provide stability in post-Saddam Iraq than it would take to conduct the war itself.'

That winning a war might prove easier than handling the aftermath may have been hard for Wolfowitz to conceive, but it was obvious to anyone with experience of peacekeeping operations. Breaking countries was always easier than putting them back together. Inside the CIA, where the intelligence behind the invasion had originated, officers became deeply concerned that things might not work out the way their higher-ups envisioned. One clerical officer, taking notes at a meeting between DCI Tenet, the Vice-President, the Secretary of Defense and the National Security Council, recalls Tenet wondering aloud if this was really the way things were going to play out.

'I remember a representative from the National Security Council saying, "When we cross that border into Iraq, they're going to throw flowers at us,"' he says. 'Tenet had his microphone turned off and he said, "Can you believe these lunatics?"'

Others voiced more dire warnings. The Chief of the Agency's Bin Laden Unit at the time specifically warned that a US-led invasion of Iraq would be likely to provoke an explosive response from potential militants all across the Muslim world. The result might be a defensive jihad, and a great deal of violence. Warnings were met with vitriol. With the country at war, questioning the White House's policies was worse than disloyal. It was unpatriotic.

Outside the CIA, meanwhile, repeated warnings from aid organizations and NGOs – including Amnesty International, the Red Cross, Unicef and the IAEA – that Iraq ran the risk of descending into an orgy of looting and lawlessness were greeted with a shrug by the Bush administration: those guys just didn't get it. They were the same people that had predicted Afghanistan would turn into a quagmire. The opposite had happened. It had been easy. Iraq was going to be even easier. Didn't they know the world had changed after 9/11?

Tony Blair's Special Envoy to Iraq John Sawers recognized the problem within a few days of his arrival in May 2003.

'No progress is possible until security improves,' he cabled the Prime Minister. 'Last week, the Ministry of Planning was re-kitted out ready to resume work; that night it was looted again.' Sawers' assessment of US efforts on the ground was blunt. '[A]n unbelievable mess. No leadership, no strategy, no coordination, no structure.'

Coalition troops were not providing the security framework necessary for reconstruction to take place. Iraqi support for the coalition was fading fast. The clock was ticking.

At the Tuwaitha nuclear plant south of Baghdad, marauders carried away hundreds of drums of radioactive uranium oxide. Iraq's purported pursuit of uranium at Tuwaitha had been one of the justifications for the invasion, yet, once the initial fighting was over, substantial quantities of it simply went missing.[9]

On 16 April, the former US diplomat Peter Galbraith witnessed the looting of Baghdad's Central Public Health laboratory. Looters carried off crates of vials containing live pathogens, including black fever, cholera, HIV and polio. Once again, research into these materials, at this specific laboratory, had been cited as a reason to invade. Yet a young US Marine Corps officer and his platoon stood by, watching. Apparently it wasn't their job to intervene.

'Stories are numerous,' Sawers informed the Prime Minister, 'of US troops sitting on tanks parked in front of public buildings, while looters go about their business behind them.'

The situation south of Baghdad was deteriorating, too. Initially, looters at Al Qa'qaa had targeted consumer goods such as fridges and air conditioners. Although munitions had been taken, no one really knew what to do with them. It soon dawned, however, that they might be intrinsically valuable. Weaponry was rapidly emerging as a second currency.

'My cousins came to me,' recalls Yusuf, an emerging leader in the insurgency, 'and they said, "You need to come with us. There is a complete storage unit we need to take."' The cousins, security guards at the facility prior to the invasion, led him inside, where he stole rockets and launchers. 'We even found some pistols.'

---

[9] For years after the invasion, small stashes of Iraqi uranium oxide ('yellow cake') showed up around the world. Some was found in Turkey in 2003. The following year, another batch was discovered in Rotterdam, buried in a container full of looted SA-2 rocket motors.

Of course, if Yusifiyans were excited about the discovery of a handful of pistols, they were still unaware of the true value of other items on offer inside Al Qa'qaa. That changed with the arrival of the foreigners.

'After the invasion, we started seeing these Arabs, these foreign fighters,' recalls Haki, 'Palestinians, Egyptians, Libyans.' Most Yusifiyans were wary of these new arrivals, but a number of local tribes took them in: 'Karagol, Jenabies, Rowissat . . .'

Yusuf, who belongs to one of these tribes, confirms the story. 'We allowed the Arabs into our houses and our farms. We welcomed them properly. Some of them even married our daughters.' The fact they were Arab strangers was sufficient to ensure hospitality, but these foreigners had extra pull. They were fedayeen. They were al-Qaeda.

At first the foreigners were courteous. 'They told us they had come to rescue us,' Yusuf says. 'There were lots of them – some of them tied to foreign intelligence services. They taught us how to use [our looted weapons].'

They also informed the tribes that some of Al Qa'qaa's contents were considerably more valuable than pistols. The looting now assumed a far more sinister aspect: the mass appropriation of explosive materiel.

The moment it was clear that foreign fighters were willing to pay large amounts of money for munitions, the locals went into overdrive to harvest them from the sites around Yusifiyah. At the Hatteen plant outside Iskandariyah, looters descended on the facility in waves like plagues of locusts. Some of them brought bulldozers.

The first looters to enter Hatteen had been scavengers and two-bit criminals. These new arrivals were more organized. Some showed up with their own technicians, others wore masks; all were armed. Iskandariyans quickly recognized regional Iraqi and even foreign accents among the looters, who were now hunting specifically for munitions. Since the plant had specialized in the production of artillery and mortar shells, they didn't have to look far.

'I saw loads of munitions,' says Abdul, whose house overlooks the facility. 'We saw the vehicles being loaded. Big, huge lorries, trucks . . . There were convoys of cars leaving Hatteen.' Looters soon began squabbling among themselves. Some brought their own guards. Gunfights broke out over who had access to which bunker. 'Many of them were killed.'

The same thing happened at Al Qa'qaa. 'There was a rush for everyone to take their share,' says Yusuf. 'We took ours. Of course, my cousins came in with me. We even took some Arabs, some mujahedin, with us.' With former employees of the facility as guides and the Arab fighters educating them as to what was, and was not, valuable, it wasn't long before Yusuf finally stumbled upon Al Qa'qaa's real treasure. 'There were bunkers inside. Sort of underground. We opened them. We found weapons, launchers and hand grenades. We also found different explosives, such as TNT and C4 . . . We took anything. Everything we could get.'

Yusuf then made a further, intriguing, discovery. 'We found something that we didn't recognize. It was like a powder. It was stored in specific conditions, in special barrels.' Yusuf had no idea what it was. But he thought he might as well take some. Only later would he learn that it was pure, crystalline high explosive.

Following the rush to appropriate munitions, Yusifiyans had to figure out where to store their loot. Many hid it in their homes. This soon led to tragedy. Rival groups fired rocket-propelled grenades into each other's houses, knowing they were full of explosives. Accidents also led to fatalities. One of Yusuf's barns blew up.

After a few such incidents, the powder was decanted into flour sacks, then dispersed and loaded into subterranean potato stores. Portable air-conditioning units were installed to keep it cool. By 8 May 2003, when the Pentagon's Exploratory Task Force arrived at Al Qa'qaa to search for weapons of mass destruction, all of the PETN, RDX and HMX was gone. Having failed to find chemical or biological weapons or to locate the IAEA's sealed explosives, the unit then failed to secure the facility as it left, leaving to further looters the thousands of tons of other munitions that littered the ground.

With much of the materiel from Iraq's largest munitions facilities now safely stashed in potato stores around town, Yusifiyah became a boomtown. The tribes that had accepted the Arab fighters – Karagol, Jenabies, Juangurdan and Rowissat – held all the aces: access to the Arabs meant access to the money. Each potato sack of the explosive formula went for $300 to $500. Abu Sultan, who looted truckloads of munitions from Mahaweel (a subsection of Al Qa'qaa ten kilometres south of the main compound), made a fortune.

'The biggest trade I ever did?' He sucks air through his teeth. 'One hundred and fifty artillery shells, a thousand kilos of TNT and some boxes of mortars that contained a thousand each.' Sultan's take was $30,000.

Yusifyah, the small nondescript town of a few thousand souls famous for its potatoes, changed dramatically. 'People from Yusifiyah had never seen a dollar bill. They certainly hadn't seen a hundred dollar bill,' says Haki. 'But when [the Arabs] arrived, everyone was talking about tens of thousands of dollars. We started seeing people holding bundles of wads of dollars.'

In this seedy, lottery-win atmosphere, locals rushed to spend their hard currency, throwing lavish weddings, buying cars, trucks and houses. Some used their share of the cash to travel. The sensible ones didn't return.

Meanwhile, bored of waiting for the Americans to establish security and tired of living without electricity, sewerage, clean water and other basic facilities, Iraqis turned in their droves to jihadist organizations, then attacked coalition troops. More violence meant less reconstruction, which led to more dissatisfaction, more anti-American sentiment and more violence. The insurgency became self-fuelling.

Throughout the summer of 2003, the bombing campaign increased. In November, with attacks on coalition forces running at more than a thousand a month, a classified Defense Intelligence Agency report finally stated the obvious: the vast majority of munitions used in the attacks had been pilfered from weapons sites that coalition troops had failed to protect. The next month a joint Department of Defense/Intelligence task force agreed: insurgents had access to 'virtually all the weapons systems and ordnances previously controlled by the Iraqi military, security and intelligence assets'.

Although these reports were classified, it was no secret that Iraq's munitions sites had been – and in many cases were still being – looted.

'We had a map that showed, I think, about fifty-five to sixty square miles – if you put it all together – of artillery, small arms, medium arms – all manner of ammunition, spread all over Iraq,' recalls Colonel Lawrence Wilkerson, Colin Powell's Chief of Staff. When Wilkerson questioned why this materiel was not being secured, the reply was brief. 'The answer was "too few troops. We'll get to it when we can, but we're not worried about it because right now things look pretty quiet".' Wilkerson didn't believe it for a minute: 'I had a couple of Marine buddies who were sending me e-mails about it and they were just appalled that they had actually been to this place and had seen what they knew were going to be their enemy hauling out this ammunition.'

Iraqis were shocked, too. Ali, who had worked at Al Qa'qaa for fourteen years, was beside himself. 'All these things were there in bunkers, but the Americans didn't protect them.'

Haki at one pointed noted that the looting at Al Qa'qaa was being watched by American troops. 'There was a bridge at the top, Saddam Bridge, and it was blown up. The Americans made a kind of temporary bridge and put their personnel carriers there. From there they could see Al Qa'qaa and what was going on inside.' To the Iraqi, the American presence was a joke. 'We didn't understand it,' he says. 'They were letting everyone take the weapons.'

A number of Iraqis went out of their way to draw attention to the issue. In September 2003, a month after the bombing of the UN building in Baghdad (an attack in which munitions from Al Qa'qaa appear to have been used),[10] Ali, the plant's senior administrator, was invited to the Green Zone to confer with the US military.

The meeting in the Convention Centre had been called to discuss how best to get Iraqi industries back on their feet. Ali had other plans. After the conference, he pulled the senior US general to one side and explained that he had come from Al Qa'qaa and that it had been severely looted. He then handed the general a dossier containing his senior staff's assessment of the damage. Such was the extent of the looting, the report stated, it had to be assumed that *all* explosive materiel inside the facility – not just the RDX, PETN and HMX – had gone. The total quantity was staggering.

'We told him that we had lost 40,000 tonnes,' Ali recalls. 'The gunpowder, anything that burned energetically, could be used as an explosive, so you could consider that part of the missing explosives. I said to him, "We have lost 40,000 tonnes."' If the general was concerned, he concealed it well, especially when Ali informed him that among the

---

[10] According to Tom Fuentes, the FBI agent who first investigated the UN bombing, the core of the bomb was a looted 500–1,000kg Soviet air-drop device. This was surrounded with layers of further ordnance to create a 'lasagne effect'. The builder of the bomb, Abu Omar al Kurdi, was captured on 15 March 2005. Questioned by UN staff, he stated that his bombs had been made out of materiel looted from Nahir Yusifiyah by a friend, Abu Al Abbas. Generally, they were constructed on farms around Yusifiyah, then driven to their targets at the last moment. Certainly, al Kurdi was around Yusifiyah at the time: Yusuf recalled meeting him. Abu Abbas, already in custody, admitted looting 200–300 rockets and more than 320 cases of plastic explosive from Yusifiyah in early 2003. He buried them at three locations around town. Fuentes was later flown to the site suspected of having been the source of the UN materiel. A military-industrial complex south-west of Baghdad, not far from the airport, it was huge and contained mortar shells, artillery shells and industrial-sized bags of rust-coloured plastic explosive. All of these facts suggest the source of the materiel that killed UN permanent representative Sergio Vieira de Mello was Al Qa'qaa.

looted munitions were a thousand suicide-bomb belts manufactured at Saddam Hussein's orders in February 2003. 'There was no reaction. He took the records and didn't say anything.'

The Americans just didn't seem to care about the looting of Al Qa'qaa. The result was devastating. Wayne White, INR's senior representative on the interagency team for intelligence collection on Iraq from 2003 to 2005, received briefings twice a week from the Iraq Survey Group, which was hunting weapons of mass destruction in Iraq after the invasion. 'Virtually every single site report was the same,' he recalls. '"We came to the site and found it thoroughly looted."' White couldn't believe what he was hearing: 'There was so much of that going on. Practically nothing was guarded. Practically *nothing*.'

Lawrence Wilkerson likewise was appalled. 'It was being dismissed in Baghdad,' he says. 'But my Marine friends were saying, "No, no, no, no, no. They're taking it out intact. They're going to use it. And they're going to use it against us."'

*   *   *

Abu Shujaa sits in an armchair and thinks for a moment.

'One of the operations we did was the attack on the Al Amyria police station. Its name later changed to the Serious Crimes Unit. This was in October 2003. We received information from our intelligence service that one of the high-profile military generals would be there. We decided to use a car bomb.'

Shujaa has proved a hard man to track down. One of the founders of the Iraqi Islamic Army, he leads a clandestine life – moving, hiding, and moving again. After a month of negotiations in Baghdad, we have found him through intermediaries, and intermediaries of intermediaries. Shortly after our interview, he will flee Iraq for Syria. For the moment, however, clad in a tracksuit, the tall, dark forty-five-year-old is talking.

'We used two cars: Nissan Patrol four-by-fours that had previously belonged to the Iraqi Special Services. We wanted to park them close to the entrance of the police station. We took into account the fact that there were schools nearby.

'We used TNT and the explosives taken from the western bunkers of Al Qa'qaa. They had been removed and hidden in western Baghdad, near Abu Ghraib. In total, we used about twenty-four kilos, which we mixed with the formula [powder from Al Qa'qaa] to make the explosions more effective. The formula was available through the farmers to the west of Al Radhwania and the Al Rashid area [Yusifiyah is in this area]. Most of the explosives had been taken and hidden in flour sacks near the railway tracks.'

Shujaa's first car detonated outside the police station at 9.45 a.m. on 27 October 2003. Passer-by Hamid Abbas was killed, along with his daughters Samar (twenty-five) and Doniya (sixteen) and his one-year-old granddaughter.

'The other car didn't explode,' continues Abu Shujaa. 'The explosives were a bit moist. They had been stored in a place that was too humid. Although the amount that had been taken from Al Qa'qaa was very large, we were concerned that we would finish it all if we didn't use it wisely. So after that we decided to mix a little more TNT with the formula, in case it was too humid.'

*　　*　　*

International Atomic Energy Agency staff in Vienna were now livid. Munitions sites in Iraq had been heavily looted, but the Americans would not allow the IAEA to visit them; the Agency was reliant on second-hand news. When nothing was heard about Al Qa'qaa, inspectors chased up the interim government directly. What had happened to the sealed RDX, PETN and HMX? Was it safe?

A year later, on 10 October 2004, the Agency finally received a one-page letter from the Iraqi Planning and Following-up Directorate.

THE FOLLOWING MATERIALS, WHICH HAVE BEEN INCLUDED IN ANNEX 3
(ITEM 74) REGISTERED UNDER IAEA CUSTODY WERE LOST AFTER 9-4-2003,
THROUGHOUT THE THEFT AND LOOTING OF THE GOVERNMENTAL INSTALLA-
TIONS DUE TO LACK OF SECURITY.

The letter contained a table detailing the 'lost' materiel: 5.8 tonnes of
PETN, 141.233 tonnes of RDX and 194.741 tonnes of HMX. At last, the
truth: 341 tonnes of high explosive were missing.

The letter created consternation. What was the Agency supposed to
do with it? The American presidential election was three weeks away. If
the IAEA went public with the news, it would look like the Agency –
supposedly apolitical – was taking a swipe at the Bush administration.
If, on the other hand, it sat on its hands, it would be open to charges of
sabotaging the campaign of Bush's opponent, John Kerry. Potentially, the
letter was a political trap.

IAEA director Mohammed ElBaradei attempted a compromise,
contacting the UN Security Council. The explosives were gone, he told
them. There was every chance the news would leak. Perhaps, however,
it was possible to keep a lid on it for a while, giving the coalition a
chance to try to find some of them before the news broke?

The diplomatic approach came to nothing. On 14 October, the Agency
received a call from CBS's 60 Minutes in New York. The programme
had managed to obtain a copy of the letter. So had the New York Times.
Realizing the cat was out of the bag, the next day the IAEA officially
informed the US-led Multinational Force (MNF) that the explosives
were missing. News of the report made it almost immediately to
Condoleezza Rice and the President. Meanwhile, 60 Minutes and the
New York Times contacted the Agency again, to check facts for the stories
they hoped to run. David Sanger of the Times hastily drafted an article,
while travelling with the President on Air Force One in the last days
of the election campaign. No date was set for its publication.

Then, suddenly, the story leaked. On Thursday, 21 October – thirteen days before the presidential election – Chris Nelson, the author of a respected Washington political online report, received an anonymous phone call. A huge quantity of high explosives had gone missing, he was told. They had been stolen. They were being used to attack US troops. Nelson did some checking, discovered the story stood up and posted it on the Internet that weekend.

David Sanger, still waiting for the editors of the *Times* to publish his exclusive, discovered that the story was leaking on Sunday. Over a mobile phone call from a football field in New Mexico, he encouraged them to put his piece out right away. The article went out the next morning: 'Huge Cache of Explosives Vanished from Site in Iraq'. Shortly after the newspaper hit the streets, Bush's chief political strategist Karl Rove swept into the media area of Air Force One and started shouting at Sanger.

'Rove came and screamed at me in front of all the other reporters,' he says. 'Declared that this had been invented by the Kerry campaign.' Apparently, the report had hit a nerve.

It was at this point that the story of the looting of Al Qa'qaa got really dirty.

With the presidential election just eight days away, it now became crucial for the White House to neutralize the story. If voters suspected that American GIs were dead because of sheer official incompetence, they might be tempted to vote the wrong way. Evangelistic certainty and moral clarity were one thing; US soldiers dying needlessly in the sand in a faraway country was quite another. Had the explosives been stolen? Why had they not been protected? Had there not been enough troops?

The looting of Al Qa'qaa raised a whole swathe of issues the Bush administration was not keen to address. Not this close to an election, anyway.

Over the course of the next week, the White House deployed a number of tactics to make the story go away. On board Air Force One, spokesman Scott McClellan immediately informed journalists that the looting at Al Qa'qaa was an Iraqi problem. The issue, he said, had been the responsibility of the Iraqi government since 28 June, when the United States had handed back powers of administration. This was disingenuous: the looting had taken place *before* the Americans handed power back to the Iraqis. McClellan's explanation never resurfaced – but it bought valuable time for the White House to cook up some proper denials.

The first tactic the administration deployed to counter the *New York Times* story was simply to assert it was untrue. There were different angles of attack. One was that the explosives had not been there in the first place. Various figures were presented to show that the IAEA had got its sums wrong. There weren't, for instance, 141 tonnes of RDX at Al Qa'qaa. Actually, there had been only 3 tonnes. In conjunction with this argument came a second, more formidable one: that the explosives *had* been there, but Saddam had moved them prior to the war. The Pentagon brandished satellite photos of heavy trucks at Al Qa'qaa the day before the US invasion began.

The 'the explosives weren't there' argument appealed to common sense. How could 341 tonnes of explosives simply have vanished when the area was swarming with US troops? Surely someone would have seen something? To bolster its case, the Pentagon wheeled out Colonel David Perkins, commander of the troops that took the area in April 2003. According to Perkins, it was 'highly improbable' the material had been stolen after the invasion. 'The enemy sneaks a convoy of tenton trucks in,' Perkins asked rhetorically, 'and loads them up in the dark of night and infiltrates them in your convoy and moves out? That's kind of a stretch too far.'

Donald Rumsfeld agreed. 'Picture all of the tractor trailers and forklifts and caterpillars it would take,' the Secretary told *Voice of America*. 'We had total control of the air. We would have seen anything like that.'

To prove the weapons had disappeared prior to the invasion, the Pentagon also cited NBC journalist Lin Lai-Jew, who had accompanied the 101st Airborne into Al Qa'qaa. Neither she, nor the 101st, had seen the munitions: proof positive, government spokesmen argued, that the material had already gone. When CBS pointed out that it was equally possible Lin Lai-Jew and the 101st had not found the sealed explosives because they had never actually looked for them, the administration turned a deft somersault and changed its argument again.

Even if the explosives *had* been there at the time of the invasion, it argued, they had probably been destroyed by US troops. Another officer was wheeled out. Austin Pearson of the 24th Ordnance Company had visited the site on 13 April 2003 and removed 250 tons of ordnance, including TNT, detonator cord and white phosphorous rounds. The material had later been destroyed. There were photographs of the operation, Pentagon spokesman Larry di Rita told journalists, 'which we may provide later'.

It's not our responsibility.

The explosives weren't there.

The explosives were moved.

We destroyed the explosives.

Excuses were coming thick and fast. At one point Deputy Undersecretary for Defence for International Technology Security John A. Shaw accused the Russians of having removed them. It was an interesting way of looking at the problem: the United States had invaded Iraq on the basis of weapons it had assumed were present there, because post-9/11 it was necessary to assume the worst and to plan for it. Now there was real evidence that weapons had been present, the administration decided it was best to assume they had never been there.

In addition to rubbishing the factual basis of the story, more subtle, underhand techniques were employed. Right-wing commentators wondered aloud why the issue had surfaced so close to the election. They then provided the answer themselves: it had been leaked by

Mohammed ElBaradei. The head of the IAEA had recently been informed he would not serve a second term. In retaliation, they argued, he had decided to 'cast his vote'.[11] Also implicated, apparently, were the *New York Times* and CBS, which had set out to launch 'an ambush on the President'.

The waters were further muddied by repeated public assertions that the story had already been proven false. According to former Republican senator Fred Thompson, 'the stories have pretty much been discredited'; General Wayne A. Downing, briefly Bush's counter-terror adviser, announced that the story was 'bogus'. *Fox News* took the angle a step further. According to the network, the story was so weak it was now proving 'an embarrassment to the *New York Times*'.

Finally, the administration added a think-point: even if the materiel *had* been at Al Qa'qaa, even if it *had* been looted, the loss wasn't significant. Iraq had been awash with munitions at the end of the war. Some 402,000 tons of armaments had been destroyed. It was estimated that Iraq's total holdings were in the region of 650,000 tons. Compared with this vast figure, 341 tonnes was a paltry 0.06 per cent.[12] The *New York Times* was making a mountain out of a molehill.

At the start of the campaign, President Bush's advisers steered him clear of the Al Qa'qaa issue. But as the election drew closer and the presidential hopeful John Kerry's accusations piled up, Bush and Vice-

[11] Like all good lies, this one contains a grain of truth. Chris Nelson, who broke the story on the Internet, concedes that his anonymous tip-off did indeed come from a source within the IAEA. The source was not ElBaradei. Actually it was an old acquaintance who, afraid the Agency would not report the loss of the explosives, had apparently taken it upon himself to get the story out so that the materiel could be traced and removed from the hands of insurgents. The leak came in spite of IAEA policy, not because of it.

[12] There was some confusion here. Iraq and the IAEA worked in metric tonnes; the United States used the imperial system: 341 metric tonnes is approximately 377 US tons – the figure most reporters and politicians would use in the United States.

President Cheney entered the fray. One by one, the administration's arguments tumbled out. The charges were 'outrageous', Cheney told an audience in Sioux City. The materials had been moved before the war. That same day, he told an audience in Michigan the charge was 'entirely bogus'. The statistics were 'inaccurate': the army had disposed of 250 tons from Al Qa'qaa, 'which included in that amount some significant portions of the explosives in question'.

Cheney had held forth on the quantity of explosives before. A day earlier, in Wisconsin, he had assured an audience that 'three months before our guys even arrived on the scene . . . upwards of 125 tonnes had been removed already. Instead of 141 tonnes of RDX, there were 3'. The charges, he concluded, were 'phoney'.

Bush agreed. The *Times'* and Senator Kerry's allegations were 'wild charges'. The army had disposed of so much ordnance it deserved congratulation, not criticism. 'We've seized or destroyed more than 400,000 tons of munitions, including explosives, at more than hundreds of sites,' he told an audience in Ohio. 'And we're continuing to round up the weapons every day.'

Bush and Cheney then launched the coup de grâce: a counterattack on Kerry himself. The man's information was wrong; he was making unsubstantiated allegations; he was jumping to conclusions without knowing the facts. He was trying to score political points. Worst of all, he was attacking US troops when they were out there risking their lives for freedom.

'I think it's a cheap shot,' Cheney informed the Sioux City audience. 'I think it's criticism of the troops.' Everyone booed Kerry.

The one factor that Bush and Cheney's arguments shared in common was their intellectual dishonesty.

Accusing the IAEA of bad accounting was a cheap shot. There had been 141 tonnes of RDX at Al Qa'qaa. Three tonnes were stored in the south-western bunkers, but the other 138 had been stored at Mahaweel, ten kilometres away. However, they were still under IAEA seal, so were technically part of Al Qa'qaa's holdings. Satellite photographs of trucks at Al Qa'qaa prior to the invasion were likewise a red herring: not only were there only two trucks in the pictures, but they weren't standing outside the bunkers containing the explosives. They weren't removing or hiding anything. They were just trucks.

The common-sense argument – that looting of this magnitude would have been noticed – rested on the assumption that the explosives were taken in one audacious heist. They weren't. Rumsfeld's assertion that air superiority meant the Americans would have detected any large-scale, post-invasion movement was therefore worthless.

There were further flaws when it came to the testimony of Austin Pearson, who had destroyed 250 tons of munitions. Pearson may have removed 250 tons, but it almost certainly didn't come from Al Qa'qaa (white phosphorous rounds, which he claimed were part of his inventory, were stored at Hatteen, fifteen kilometres to the south). By his own admission, Pearson and his staff had never come across any IAEA-sealed material. Contrary to the Vice-President's claims, they were not the same explosives at all.

On the issue of the percentage of munitions at Al Qa'qaa versus those already destroyed, there was a double deception. It may indeed have been the case that the Americans had destroyed 402,000 out of a total munitions reserve of 650,000 tons in Iraq. And 341 tonnes (377 imperial tons) out of 650,000 tons is indeed 0.06 per cent. But as we have seen, Al Qa'qaa's administrators had already informed the United States, in writing, that the sum total of munitions looted from their facility was not 341 tonnes but 40,000. On this accounting, the missing explosives constituted more than 6 per cent of all explosives in Iraq – 10 per cent of all confiscated munitions: a very great deal more than 0.06 per cent, in fact.

Further statistical manipulation was afoot, too. While the missing materiel from Al Qa'qaa was pure high explosive, the 402,000 tons destroyed by US forces included some very heavy objects that contained no explosives at all. '[The Pentagon] was trying to compare the weight of the guns and stocks and metal and all of that stuff,' says a senior weapons-intelligence analyst. 'They were counting tanks and guns and bazookas – metal – as opposed to the raw explosive that can be directly used . . . It's an absolutely dishonest comparison.'

In addition to their factual inaccuracies, the administration's arguments were intellectually incoherent. If the materiel had been moved before the invasion, how could the Pentagon claim that its troops had destroyed it afterwards? If post-war surveillance of the site made it impossible for the munitions to have been moved without anyone noticing, why didn't pre-war surveillance achieve the same thing? How could both the Iraqis and the Russians have moved the explosives? The ad hoc nature of the explanations meant they were contradictory.

No one appears to have noticed. A string of 'authoritative' explanations from 'authoritative' sources effectively threw a smokescreen over the story, making it almost impossible for outsiders to determine what had really happened. Or so it seemed.

Reporter Dean Staley was at work at his new job at North-West Cable News, Seattle, when he heard reports of the scoop. The story seemed familiar. After reading the *Times*' description of the bunkers in question, on Tuesday night he called his old cameraman at KSTP.

'Joe,' he said, 'I think we've been to the place they're talking about.'

Caffrey had been thinking the same thing, too. He'd been watching a report on TV when a little light went on at the back of his head. The moment Staley called, the two men realized they might be sitting on something important. The journalist went off to search his notes for GPS coordinates, which he had jotted down at the time of the pair's joyride with the soldiers from the 101st, while the cameraman hunted down his field tapes to see what they showed.

Within a matter of hours, it became apparent they knew a great deal

more about Al Qa'qaa than the President and his staff. 'It was clear
that these people didn't know what they were talking about,' says Staley.
'The [White House] message didn't jibe with the facts.'

Caffrey's tape, '*Hangar Search #2*', showed everything: the bunkers,
the chained doors, the IAEA seals (still intact until the soldiers snapped
them) and the hundreds of cardboard drums of off-white powder. All
had been shot nine days after the toppling of Saddam's statue. The
film proved the explosives were present at Al Qa'qaa *after* the invasion.

Caffrey's footage aired locally on Wednesday, 27 October, then across
the United States the next day. Weapons inspectors verified that the
footage showed original IAEA seals being broken and managed to iden-
tify the specific bunkers; Caffrey had filmed the breaking of the seal
on bunker #38. They also identified the sealed HMX, RDX and PETN
stocks; in some cases, the numbers on the cardboard canisters matched
IAEA logs exactly. The conclusion was irrefutable: 341 tonnes of high
explosive had gone missing on Bush's watch.

After viewing the tape, David Kay called for an end to the debate. 'I
think it's game, set and match,' the former leader of the Iraq Survey
Group told CNN. Five days before the presidential election, it was official: the emperor had no clothes.

The next morning, Friday, 29 October, Osama bin Laden succeeded
where the White House's spin doctors had failed. The first videotaped
message from the al-Qaeda leader for more than a year, released that
day, pushed the looted explosives story out of the public eye. Four days
later, George W. Bush won a second term in office.

*   *   *

Abu Shujaa lights a cigarette.

'The second operation was in February 2004. We used wires and
coils in this operation to make sure that the radio distortion used by
the Americans would not affect the devices.

'We planted six bombs on the airport highway near the Al Jihad
Bridge. In each of the bombs we put eight kilograms of TNT in addition

to the formula which we had got from Al Qa'qaa. Three bombs exploded. The fourth one didn't. But the fifth and sixth went off thirty seconds later, while the snipers started shooting the Americans. Enemy losses were quite convenient: they lost two Bradleys and one Humvee.'

*   *   *

News of Bush's glorious second victory left Yusifiyans cold. Haki and his neighbours had other concerns. Top of the list came the recently arrived Arab strangers.

For al-Qaeda, Yusifiyah was important not only because it was home to Iraq's largest armaments facilities, but also because it was strategically extremely well positioned. Baghdad was half an hour to the northeast, Fallujah twenty minutes to the west. Over the next few years, when the situation in Fallujah became too dangerous for them, mujahedin fighters would retreat to Yusifiyah to hide. The Head of al-Qaeda in Iraq, Abu Musab al-Zarqawi, personally visited periodically, partly to stock up on munitions, and partly when the situation in Fallujah became intolerable.

'I met him,' boasts Yusuf. 'He came to Yusifiyah quite a lot. It was a safe place for him. If he wasn't in Fallujah, the next best place was here.'

Eventually, when Fallujah became really dangerous, the Arabs settled permanently in Nahir Yusifiyah. For the locals, the situation rapidly became intolerable. Instead of buying explosives, the Arabs simply took them, forcing potato farmers to store the material in their underground bunkers, then killing them later.

'Those guys started ruling the whole area,' says Haki. 'They weren't guests any more.' In fear of his life, the farmer fled to Baghdad to become a security guard.

In 2004, al-Qaeda established a camp inside the Al Qa'qaa complex itself. 'We had a firing range, like a tunnel. It was used to shoot small-calibre bullets,' says Ali. 'It became a training camp for terrorists.'

Anyone entering the facility without permission was killed. Al-Qaeda spread horror stories about its activities, intimidating locals into collaborating. An execution room was set up with a makeshift gallows.

Yusuf was part of the operation. 'We were making up rumours. We used to kill people in terrible ways, torturing them to give al-Qaeda more influence.' Mutilations, murders and decapitations were filmed and copies were distributed around Yusifiyah to discourage dissent. The violence increased. Anyone suspected of attempting to join the Iraqi military or police was executed. Shias were executed. People with Shia names were executed. People who did anything regarded as Shia-*like* were executed. When Haki's uncle was caught smoking a cigarette, al-Qaeda broke all his fingers with a hammer. Then they killed him.

Soon even Yusuf recognized that things had gone awry. The Arabs weren't the cure for anything. They were parasites, an infection that wouldn't stop. 'We realized that al-Qaeda didn't come to rescue us. They were killing all kinds of people, saying they were atheists and that they idolized statues,' he recalls. 'They planted those kinds of ideas in our minds. Now we realize that it wasn't true. What happened here in Yusifiyah is something you can't imagine.'

When he returned from his work in Baghdad in 2005, Haki found the main road into town littered with corpses, bound, tortured and shot. 'We hadn't seen anything like this before in our lives. Whatever I tell you about Yusifiyah at that time, there was more. It was like a horror film.'

By 2005, commentators were dubbing the Yusifiyah region the 'Triangle of Death': the most dangerous sector in all Iraq. Palm-tree plantations were rigged with explosives to bring down low-flying helicopters; soldiers were abducted, tortured and murdered. Bombs went off everywhere.

It was, of course, no coincidence that Nahir Yusifiyah was so favoured by insurgents. It was where all the weapons were.

*   *   *

I arrived in Baghdad on 26 March 2009, keen to get to grips with the Al Qa'qaa story. Almost immediately it became apparent that government officials did not want to discuss it. Apologies were made, rendezvous forgotten, telephone calls ignored. Within a week, I had resorted to driving around town attempting to doorstep interviewees before they had time to flee. Ambushed at his former office, Mohammed Abbas – the man who first informed the IAEA the explosives were missing – chatted amiably until he discovered I was writing about Al Qa'qaa, at which point he decided it was time to leave. The new head of his department, Sami al Araji, declined to answer questions. Privately, I wondered whether this reticence was related to the findings of the official investigation – one half of which had apparently been headed up by Araji himself.

Certainly, the investigation had been a long time coming. The moment news broke in October 2004 that Al Qa'qaa had been looted, White House spokesman Scott McClellan assured journalists on board Air Force One that the Department of Defense had ordered an inquiry. The President, he said, 'wants to get to the bottom of this'. The next day Donald Rumsfeld commented that a 'detailed investigation' was underway. A day later, President Bush himself promised the citizens of Vienna, Ohio, that the investigation was 'important and ongoing'.

Where is it?

Ali, Al Qa'qaa's senior administrator, says it never took place. Certainly, no one contacted him about it. Asked if an investigation could have happened without his involvement, he shakes his head. 'Impossible. If there was an investigation, it would have to go through the correct processes. Our legal department, the head of our legal department, would have represented us. He hasn't been contacted.'

The American investigation, if there was one, also seems to have vanished. Other than a GAO report into securing weapons sites in future operations, nothing.

Perhaps a proper investigation would have turned up the same kind of material I eventually found. Over the course of two weeks in Iraq, twenty-five witnesses described how the looting of Al Qa'qaa and the munitions sites around Yusifiyah had taken place (one informed me, from his rooftop in Iskandariyah, that he could see looting *still* going on at Hatteen). Two of them explained in detail how they had looted and sold explosives from Al Qa'qaa. Two named the tribes responsible for the theft and sale of the high explosive. Three told how they had stored powdered high explosive from the facility in their potato cellars. Two described how they had used the looted material to manufacture roadside bombs.

Perhaps a proper investigation would have contacted members of Iraq's various bomb-disposal units, all of whom admitted – on the condition of anonymity – that the vast majority of their work was the result of looted explosives.

'The explosives were available everywhere,' says the head of one directorate. 'They were the main reason for the violence in Iraq. If they had been protected and guarded, Iraq would be a different story.' Asked what percentage of the violence following the invasion was the result of the looting, he thinks for a moment. 'I'd give it 90 per cent.'

The second-in-command of another unit goes higher: 'I would say 98 per cent.'

By September 2007, 4.6 million Iraqis – one in seven of the country's entire population – had fled the violence. The result was the biggest migration in the Middle East since the creation of Israel in 1948: more refugees, more migrants, more asylum seekers. Iraq's borders simply couldn't hold them.

Perhaps a proper investigation would have tracked down Abu Shujaa, who used the explosives from Al Qa'qaa to kill and maim both Iraqis and members of the coalition forces. Who knows? Perhaps a proper investigation might even have found Yusuf, who was proud to show off his potato cellar, still stacked to the ceiling with flour sacks filled with ten tons of what appeared to be HMX.

Perhaps, however, an investigation that uncovered this kind of stuff would have been politically embarrassing.

When he arrived back in Washington in June 2003, Jay Garner, the first Head of the Office of Reconstruction and Humanitarian Assistance, was greeted by the President in the Oval Office. Bush, all smiles, was basking in the recent swift victory.

'You want to do Iran for the next one?' he asked Garner.

'No, sir,' Garner joked back. 'Me and the boys are holding out for Cuba.'

6

The Egyptian

The war against terrorism ushers in a new paradigm [that] requires new thinking in the law of war.

George W. Bush, February 2002

They caught The Egyptian on New Year's Eve 2003. The operation – discreet, well out of the public eye – was a triumph of simple, effective policing combined with rapid, accurate, communications: a perfect example, in fact, of the kind of international co-operation that European and American intelligence services had striven for since 9/11. It was also a potent demonstration of the necessity for proper border controls.

They found him on a bus at the Tabanovce checkpoint between Serbia and Macedonia. It was a bit of luck, really: a routine travel-document check indicated an irregularity. His passport was not quite like those of his fellow travellers. Macedonian border guards, sensing it merited a second opinion, instructed him to step off the bus. Where was he going? What was the purpose of his visit?

At first The Egyptian played it cool. He was on holiday, he told them. He planned to stay in Macedonia for a week. When it came to more concrete plans, however, he stumbled. He appeared to have no idea where he was going to stay.

'I don't know,' he admitted. 'A hotel?'

The story didn't stack up.

Macedonian officials then played a trick on The Egyptian, telling him to step back on to the bus and proceed to the capital, Skopje, but to report to the central police station the moment he arrived. Craftily, they neglected to return his passport. It was a low-risk strategy. If it checked out, they could return the document to him, apologize and claim incompetence; without it, he wasn't going anywhere.

The Egyptian was smarter than that. A few kilometres down the road, he noticed he didn't have his documents. Realizing that without them he would be trapped inside Macedonia's capital, he brazenly instructed the driver to turn the bus around and return to the border checkpoint. Al-Qaeda operatives often travel with several passports. This character, it seemed, had just the one.

In an astonishing display of nerve, The Egyptian attempted to wrong-foot the immigration officials back at Tabanovce, demanding an explanation for the error: why had they not returned his passport?

There was a problem, the Macedonians confessed. They didn't know exactly what it was, but they were trying to sort it out. Politely, they then suggested a compromise. It would be best if the bus were allowed to depart for Skopje – why keep the other passengers waiting? – while they ran a few routine checks. Once the matter had been cleared up, they promised, one of the officers would drive The Egyptian to a hotel of his choice. No doubt sensing a free taxi ride in the offing, he agreed. The bus departed, leaving The Egyptian alone with the guards. He was ushered inside the border post and his possessions, retrieved from the bus, were unpacked in front of him. Then a young border official started questioning him.

The Egyptian's cover story was uninspiring. He was forty years old. Fleeing Lebanon's civil war in 1985, he had received asylum in Germany. He lived in the town of Neu-Ulm in Bavaria. He had four children. He was a car dealer. Asked about his reasons for entering Macedonia, the Egyptian concocted a sob story. He had fallen upon hard times, he said. Since losing his job a few months ago, he'd been unemployed. His family, broke and living in a single-room flat, was under intense pressure.

There had been fireworks. Following an argument with his wife, he had fled the apartment and, on impulse, booked a bus ticket to Macedonia – where he'd heard the hotels were cheap. He was trying to get his head together.

To the immigration officer, it was a mundane story: exactly the kind of mundane story, in fact, that a terrorist might concoct to tug at the heartstrings of a gullible border official. It was highly unlikely that any of it was true. But then, who could tell? Perhaps even al-Qaeda masterminds had marital problems.

What made The Egyptian's apprehension so impressive was that at the time of his arrest neither his identity nor his story were well known. They still aren't. To this day, virtually nothing is known about him. The few details that have emerged, however, are distinctly sinister. They revolve around his relationship to a group of idealistic college students in Hamburg.

In the winter of 1998, three young men from Egypt, Yemen and the United Arab Emirates rented an apartment at Marienstrasse 54. Outwardly, they were quiet and law abiding; perfect tenants, in fact. Actually, they were plotting. Enraged at Russia's mistreatment of Muslims in Chechnya, they had decided to travel there themselves, to fight. The only question was, how to go about it? They had little experience of this kind of thing: they were, after all, only students. Then, in November the following year, a chance encounter changed things.

Travelling on a German train, two of the students were approached by a stranger. The man had noticed their impressive-looking beards, deduced they were Muslim boys and decided to strike up a conversation. Almost immediately the talk turned to Chechnya. Engaged on their favourite topic, the two men told their new friend that they planned to go there and fight the Russians. The stranger commented that this was most commendable, and that he had a friend who might be able to offer them some advice. He gave them his phone number and told them that if they were interested he could arrange a meeting, then vanished.

When the students returned to Hamburg, they told their friends about the conversation, decided the offer seemed genuine and rang the stranger, who in turn passed on the telephone number of his contact, a Mauritanian businessman called Abu Musab. The friends soon found themselves travelling to Musab's home in Duisberg where, without warning, the Mauritanian began to demolish their plans.

Fighting in Chechnya, he told them, was an extremely bad idea: not only had the Russians closed the borders, making access almost impossible, but, even if they did get through, they had no military experience. What did they hope to achieve? Musab suggested an alternative. If they really wanted to fight, they should fly to Karachi in Pakistan, then travel on to Quetta, where they should report to the office of the Taliban and ask for a friend of his, Umar al Masri.

Later that month, four students from Marienstrasse did just this and found themselves down a rabbit hole. In Quetta, they learned there was no such person as Umar al Masri. The name appeared to be some sort of a code. If the four students didn't understand it at the time, however, their Taliban hosts did, ushering them across the border into Afghanistan and on to Kandahar, where they were introduced to the real goal of their journey: a tall, bearded individual known as the Sheikh.

By the time the four friends returned to Germany in the spring of 2000, the Chechnya trip had been shelved. They had bigger plans. Soon, the Marienstrasse apartment was humming with activity. German intelligence monitored it from time to time, but because the students' records were clean there was no indication they might be a threat. None of their names rang alarm bells. That would change.

Ramzi Binalshibh would later be refused a US visa, but Marwan al Shehhi would make it into the country to fly United Airlines 175 into the south tower of the World Trade Center. Ziad Jarra would also make it through, to crash United Airlines 93 into a field in Pennsylvania.

Mohammed Atta, who would lead the plot, started the attack, ramming American Airlines Flight 11 into the World Trade Center's north tower.

And the man who had started the ball rolling, the stranger on the German train who had passed on his phone number and introduced them to the Mauritanian, was Khaled el Masri: 'The Egyptian'.

At the Macedonian border post, The Egyptian's interrogator was replaced by a young man in his thirties. He was not a border guard. He was an officer in the Macedonian security and counter-intelligence service, the UBK. His questions were more direct.

Specifically, he was interested in whether The Egyptian belonged to any Islamic organizations in Germany. Apparently he didn't. What about mosques? Were there any mosques in Neu-Ulm? The Egyptian conceded that he occasionally visited the local mosque, that he prayed and fasted 'sometimes', but that he had no real contact with Islamic organizations in Germany. When the officer named a few radical German groups, The Egyptian admitted he had heard of them, but pointed out that they were quite famous: lots of people had. Perhaps to test his adherence to Islam, the man offered him a drink. It was New Year's Eve. Would he like some champagne? The Egyptian said that he wouldn't.

At 10 p.m., a group of plain-clothes officers carrying side arms led the suspect out of the office and walked him towards three vehicles, none of which carried licence plates. The three-car convoy took off in the direction of Skopje. It was late, cold and foggy and the road was deserted. When the motorcade reached a military checkpoint, the lead car turned on a blue flashing light; they all sailed through without incident.

In Skopje, the cars pulled up in front of a family-run tourist hotel, the Skopski Merak, just opposite the city zoo. The Egyptian was led out of the car by three officers, into the hotel and straight into the elevator. On the top floor he was ushered into a nondescript suite containing a double bed, a table and four chairs and an en suite bathroom with a Jacuzzi feature in the bath. Still unaware that his identity had been rumbled, at this point he thanked the men for the lift and bade them goodbye. The officers exchanged glances. One of them then locked the door from the inside.

'We're staying here,' they told him. 'With you.'

The Egyptian appeared taken aback. He wanted to sleep, he told his captors. He was tired. Fine, they said: go ahead – but they weren't about to leave him alone.

'Am I under arrest?' he asked one of the officers.

The man shook his head. 'Do you see any handcuffs?'

Then the men began to interrogate him again, more aggressively this time, in English. Who did he know in Neu-Ulm? What mosques did he visit? Who had he seen there? The officers interrupted each other, firing questions from different angles simultaneously in an attempt to confuse the al-Qaeda man.

In the meantime, the phone lines were buzzing.

News of the Macedonian intelligence service's coup was passed on to the United States immediately via the CIA's station in Skopje. A suspect had been apprehended, the Macedonians informed their allies, attempting to travel on a fake passport. When his name had been run through their databases, alarm bells had rung. They'd nabbed Khaled el Masri, 'The Egyptian'. They were interrogating him right now.

Inside the Agency's Langley headquarters, the news was greeted with jubilation. The chief of the al-Qaeda Unit especially was delighted: if this Khaled el Masri really was The Egyptian, one of the key links in the 9/11 plot had been broken.

'We got him!' she told her colleagues.

'She briefed all of us on the case,' recalls one Counter-Terrorism Center officer. 'It was a big counter-terrorism capture.'

The Macedonians were instructed to keep The Egyptian in custody while the CIA worked out what to do next. As it happened, the Agency had a few ideas. One, in particular, seemed suitable.

*   *   *

The programme had emerged a number of years earlier, the result of an offhand comment from President Bill Clinton. In the late 1990s, frustrated by the inability of the intelligence community to do anything about the threat of Bin Laden in Afghanistan, the President had voiced a suggestion to General Hugh Shelton, the Chairman of the Joint Chiefs of Staff.

'You know,' Clinton thought aloud, 'it would scare the shit out of al-Qaeda if suddenly a bunch of black ninjas rappelled out of helicopters into the middle of their camp.'

Shelton had agreed. But the problem, as both men knew, lay in getting to al-Qaeda. Few of Afghanistan's neighbours were likely to allow the US to station a squad of 'black ninjas' intent on assassinating someone in their country. In the aftermath of al-Qaeda operations against US embassies in Africa in 1998, the President had repeatedly pushed for suggestions regarding a workable plan. Cruise missiles had proved ineffective; SPECTRE gunships were too violent. What else was there?

Various schemes were hatched to enable the United States to monitor al-Qaeda with a view to eliminating its leaders, assembled under the codename Afghan Eyes. One plan was to mount a vast telescope on top of a mountain near Bin Laden's training camps, but this was deemed impractical: in any event, the idea was superseded by technological advances, the most promising of which was the development of the Predator Unmanned Aerial Vehicle (UAV). Piloted by remote control and capable of circling over a potential target for hours on end, the Predator enabled operators to monitor events on the ground in real-time.

In June 2000, a plan to launch Predators out of neighbouring Uzbekistan was approved. By July, testing was complete and on 7 September a Predator flew over Afghanistan for the first time, capturing images of a tall Arab in white robes surrounded by a security detail at Tarnak Farm, a known al-Qaeda training camp. A second sighting three weeks later led CIA analysts to conclude that the man was none other than Bin Laden himself. Those involved with the programme were hopeful: once the Predator was armed with missiles, it would offer a real opportunity to get rid of the al-Qaeda leader without risking the lives of US personnel.

Then the operation hit a bureaucratic wall. The CIA and the Department of Defense could not agree on who should foot the bill. Predators cost $3 million each. What would happen if one was shot down or crashed? Then there was the issue of who, exactly, should pull the trigger on the Predator if it happened to stumble on Bin Laden again. Was the Air Force allowed to take out a terrorist in cold blood during peacetime? The CIA wasn't. The only person who did have the authority to make this kind of decision was the President, but by the time news reached his desk it would almost certainly be too late: either the Predator would have run out of fuel or its target would have left.

With the US intelligence community unable to resolve these issues, the Afghan Predator was grounded after just fifteen flights.

Those involved in the hunt for al-Qaeda were extremely frustrated. Why was the United States having such a hard time bringing terrorists to justice? The CIA could *see* these guys, but was apparently powerless to act. How long was it necessary to wait before someone would actually do something? Out of this frustration emerged a rather different programme: maybe they couldn't extradite these guys and they couldn't kill them, but what if they simply snatched them, then flew them around the world and dumped them in court to face justice? Black ninjas or no, Clinton had been right: it would scare the shit out of al-Qaeda. Rendition to Justice – the kidnapping and transportation of terrorists across international borders – was born.

Actually, something similar had been in operation for more than a decade. In 1986, Ronald Reagan had signed National Security Directive 207, launching a secret programme that enabled the CIA to snatch terror suspects from nations either unable or unwilling to extradite them. George Bush Snr had reauthorized the programme in 1993. So

had Clinton in 1995. Three years later, following his 'black ninjas'
remark, the President signed Directive 62, detailing further instructions on 'apprehension, extradition, rendition and prosecution'.

In the context of preventing future attacks, rendition not only made
sense, it worked. Ramzi Yousef, the al-Qaeda operative who had bombed
the World Trade Center in 1993, was taken from Pakistan to the United
States where he was prosecuted; Carlos the Jackal was taken from Sudan
to France, where he was convicted. To the CIA's Michael Scheuer, who
ran the programme for four years, Clinton's 1995 decision had been a
no-brainer: it was just an extension of a decision that had already been
made.

'The rendition operations they did before us,' he says, 'were basically extradition that was done by force.'

During the period before 9/11, the CIA conducted more than eighty
renditions. Half of all targets were al-Qaeda members.

'These renditions have shattered terrorist cells and networks,' Director
of Central Intelligence George Tenet announced in February 2000,
'thwarted terrorist plans and in some cases even prevented terrorist
attacks from occurring.'

Post-9/11, the operation changed. After 11 September, the occasional
snatching of terror suspects was not enough. On 15 September, in a
War Cabinet meeting at Camp David, Tenet presented President Bush
with a draft Memorandum of Notification demanding more powers for
the CIA. The DCI requested 'exceptional' authority to target al-Qaeda
worldwide; covert operations, including rendition and the use of deadly
force could be deployed without Presidential approval. Essentially, the
draft memorandum was a rewriting of Reagan's 1986 Directive, but it
went a great deal further: according to Tenet, he was requesting 'as
many authorities as CIA had ever had'.

George W. Bush was delighted. 'Great job!' he told him.

Two days later, he signed the document, handing the Agency 'the
broadest and most lethal authority in its history'. Tenet went back to

his office and wrote a memorandum to CIA staff. 'There can be no bureaucratic impediments to success,' he wrote. 'The rules have changed.'

One of the first programmes to benefit was Rendition. 'The Agency had a programme that was at that point six years old and very successful,' says Scheuer, 'so the President asked us at that point to step that up.'

The programme was indeed stepped up. It was also revised. Immediately after 9/11, 'bureaucratic impediments to success' were excised: 'Rendition' became 'Extraordinary Rendition'. As The Egyptian was about to discover, there was an important difference.

In the Skopski Merak, a revolving team of nine UBK officers monitored The Egyptian twenty-four hours a day. When he slept, they watched; when he used the lavatory, they watched. After three days of this treatment, the al-Qaeda man became belligerent, demanding to speak to someone from the German embassy, a lawyer, his wife, anybody. When the officers refused, he attempted to escape. Two of the intelligence officers grabbed their pistol holsters. The third drew his weapon and pointed it at the suspect's face.

'Call the German embassy!' The Egyptian shouted. 'I'm a German citizen!'

The intelligence officer recognized a stalling tactic when he heard one. It wasn't going to work. 'They don't want to talk to you,' he said.

A week into The Egyptian's incarceration, a new, more senior, character appeared. Middle-aged and portly in stature, he came with an assistant in tow. He appeared to be playing the good cop, asking the prisoner if he was being well treated and if the food was OK: if it wasn't, he said, he could arrange a take-out from any restaurant in Skopje. The Egyptian told him that his treatment had been perfectly adequate, but that he wanted to go home.

Perfectly understandable, the officer agreed: he wanted the situation to end, too. Unfortunately, that was quite impossible. Intelligence regarding the al-Qaeda man was mounting. His passport was a fake. Witnesses had reported seeing him in Jalalabad, Afghanistan. One of them was being debriefed by Macedonian intelligence at this very moment. The best thing to do, the intelligence officer advised, was to concede that the game was up. A deal might be possible.

For the first time, The Egyptian became curious: 'What kind of a deal?'

The officer told him that if he signed a document confessing to belonging to al-Qaeda he would be transferred back to Germany. When the prisoner became belligerent and refused, he shrugged his shoulders and left.

A couple of days later, the assistant returned. Things didn't look good, he warned The Egyptian. UBK knew that he was a member of al-Qaeda. He was wanted by the governments of both Germany and Egypt. The assistant showed him a long list of accusations. The only option was to confess. When The Egyptian shook his head, the assistant told him that the matter was now out of the hands of the Macedonian intelligence service. It had been passed to the country's president, who would decide what would become of him.

Macedonian officials knew that in such situations al-Qaeda operatives were instructed to exert pressure on their captors. Having been held in the Skopski Merak for thirteen days, The Egyptian went on hunger strike. The suspect appeared to have stamina, eating and drinking nothing for a week. Not that this bothered the Macedonians: clearly the strike was a gesture. Besides, they knew something he didn't. They were about to get rid of their troublesome guest.

On 23 January 2004, after ten days without food, The Egyptian was told that he had won. He would be transferred back to Germany. At around 8 p.m., he was instructed to stand up and a video camera was produced. He was told to address the camera, to state his full name and to testify that he had been well treated during his time in Macedonia. After that, he would be transferred to the airport.

The Egyptian was taken downstairs and marched through the hotel lobby, where a number of plain-clothes intelligence officers were loitering. A white minivan and a black jeep were outside, engines running: his ride to the airport. Then suddenly, the situation took an unexpected turn. As the al-Qaeda man walked from the lobby into the open air, he was grabbed from behind. Two men pulled his arms behind his back. A third handcuffed and blindfolded him. He was stuffed into the back of the jeep.

Half an hour later, The Egyptian was pulled from the jeep, taken into a building and shoved into a chair. He was addressed by the assistant who had spoken to him ten days earlier, who told him that he was to be medically examined. He was led into another room where two men grabbed him and restrained him. When he tried to struggle, they hit him. Another man grabbed his head, rendering him immobile. The men then started cutting his clothes from him until he was standing in his underwear. When they tried to cut that off, too, he struggled violently. This one, clearly, was going to need sedating.

Finally, The Egyptian was pushed to the floor. His arms were pulled back and he felt a boot on the base of his spine.

Even the senior al-Qaeda member was shocked by what happened next. 'I then felt a stick or some other hard object being forced in my anus,' he later recalled. 'I realized that I was being sodomized.'

Actually, he wasn't being sodomized: he was being administered an enema. The operation complete, The Egyptian was pulled up again, shoved into a corner, his feet were bound together and his blindfold removed. A bright flash blinded him temporarily – he was being photographed. When he recovered his sight, he saw that he was surrounded by between eight and ten gloved, hooded men, all dressed in black.

The Egyptian was given a diaper and a dark-blue sports suit with short sleeves. He was blindfolded again and his ears were plugged with cotton wool. Headphones were placed over the top. A bag was then pulled over his head and his hands were chained to a belt around his waist. He was taken outside, shoved into another car, then on to an aircraft, where his captors spread-eagled him, securing his arms and legs to the floor. An injection was administered. The Egyptian passed out.

In terms of rendition protocols, the Skopje job was unexceptional. The hooded men, the cutting-off of clothes, the diaper, even the enema: this was how these things were done. What was unusual about The Egyptian operation was the fact that, from the outset, it had been compromised.

Rendition, and especially Extraordinary Rendition, was always conducted in complete secrecy: even within the CIA, few officers were read into the programme. Not this time. The security breach, which would later prove catastrophic both for the rendition programme and the Agency itself, was the result not of any action by a foreign intelligence service, or even al-Qaeda, but of an amiable self-employed Spanish urban planner in his mid-forties.

Secretary of the Association of Aeronautical Photographers of Mallorca, Josep Manchado had been logging planes landing at Palma International Airport for five years. Since Mallorca was a major tourist destination, there was no shortage of international airliners, but the Association was more interested in unusual aircraft.

'We can see British Airways or Iberia every day,' says Manchado. 'But a plane from Nigeria doing an emergency stop: that's more interesting.'

For the Association – only eight people strong – the hobby was rather like stamp collecting. 'You want to get all the planes in your collection,' Manchado explains. 'Of course, it's impossible, but you try.'

To this end, the spotters would listen in to air-traffic radio frequencies to learn which planes were coming in, and where they were likely to make their approach. Sometimes Association members would travel to Amsterdam, Frankfurt or Miami to photograph aircraft there.

Manchado visited Palma Airport to spot planes on weekends. There were more around then. But on Friday, 23 January 2004, the morning The Egyptian was rendered from Macedonia, he decided to take some time off work. Pedro, a friend from the Association, had heard that an unusual plane – an Austrian Boeing 777 – was coming to Palma. Perhaps they might get some shots of it. The pair arranged to meet in the old control tower, which the Association's spotters had received permission to use for their hobby.

Just after 10 a.m., Manchado drove his Volkswagen to Palma Airport, parked in the employees' car park, shouldered his camera bag and made his way to the control tower, where Pedro was waiting.

'It was quite a boring day,' he admits. 'Nothing special, nothing different.'

Pedro, however, commented that there was an interesting plane in the airport, a private Boeing 737 Business Jet parked in the General Area. He had taken some photographs of it already.

Since around forty private 737s landed at Palma each year, Manchado wasn't entirely thrilled about the plane, but figured that so little was happening he might as well take a look. Pedro told him not to bother. 'It's not a good time to take pictures,' he warned. 'The sun is in the wrong place.'

Manchado ignored his friend's advice. At 2 p.m., he left the tower and headed for the passengers' car park next to the General Aviation area. There, 150 metres in front of him, was the 737.

'It was a very new, clean aircraft. Completely clear, cream colour with only a registration and a line along the side. Nothing else.'

Aside from the plane's registration number, N313P – which Manchado did not have in his notebook – there was nothing unusual about it. Despite the fact that the sun was behind the plane, Manchado snapped a few pictures.

At home the next day, he examined the photographs. As Pedro had predicted, they were overexposed: the 737 was largely silhouetted. But one was usable. Manchado transferred the image on to his computer, then used Photoshop to clean it up. When the picture was as clear as it was going to get, he uploaded it on to the planespotters' website, Airliners.net. Alongside the photograph he posted a date and a description:

A VERY NEW BBJ [Boeing Business Jet], ALSO NEW VISITOR IN PMI [Palma Mallorca International].

After departing Skopje at 0230, Boeing Business Jet N313P flew 1,375 miles. First stop was Baghdad, Iraq. From there, the aircraft headed to Kabul International Airport, Afghanistan. On board, The Egyptian, blind-folded, sedated and secured to the aircraft's floor, was unaware of his destination. That was entirely as it should be: if the al-Qaeda operative was to be interrogated effectively, confusion regarding what was happening, and where he was, would help. The guy behind the recruit-ment of the 9/11 bombers was likely to put up considerable resistance. He was going to need breaking down.

From the moment N313P landed at Kabul, his treatment was cursory and harsh, partly to assist in the softening-up process. Frogmarched off the plane, The Egyptian was thrown into the boot of a car and driven for around ten minutes, then dragged out and down a flight of stairs, his hands held high above his head. When he stumbled or slowed, he was physically picked up and dragged. Occasionally, he would collide with a wall or a pillar. Finally, he was thrown to the ground and one of the hooded men placed a foot on his neck to restrain him, while another removed the chains and the blindfold. Then, as suddenly as they had appeared, the hooded men vanished, locking the door behind them.

Looking around, The Egyptian found himself in an unlit, cramped cell with crumbling plaster on the walls. On the floor was a stained plastic carpet, a dirty military-style mattress and some torn clothes bundled into a makeshift pillow. Through a small opening in the wall near the ceiling, he saw the last rays of the setting sun and realized that he must have been travelling for twenty-four hours.

Thirsty after his ordeal, he peered through the grille in his cell door and demanded water. Outside, an Afghan guard pointed behind him to a small, filthy, plastic bottle in the corner of the cell. The Egyptian lifted it to his face and sniffed. Not only was the water inside dirty and green, it stank. When he put the bottle down in disgust, he noticed that the smell of the water lingered on his hands. Eventually, he took a swig, but the stench, and the acrid taste, were unendurable. The Egyptian threw up.

At this point, the cell door opened and four men wearing black uniforms and masks entered, dragged him into the corridor and to another cell. Waiting inside were three more masked men, one of whom told him to undress. The Egyptian stripped down to the diaper, then stopped. He was instructed to remove it. When he did, he was then told to stand still while he was photographed. One of the men in the masks took blood and urine samples.

Like all al-Qaeda operators, this prisoner appeared considerably less brave now that he was in custody: he complained about his treatment. His cell was cold. The water was rancid. He was told that the Afghans were responsible for the condition of the cell and the water. Then, incongruously, he was asked whether he had any dietary restrictions: would he perhaps like halal food? When he admitted that he would, the men laughed: halal food. What a joke.

The next night the process was repeated. This time there were seven interrogators. One asked if he knew why he was there. 'That's the question I wanted to ask you,' replied The Egyptian, cocky as always.

The man indicated a large file on the table and told him that it was his dossier. 'You attended terrorist training camps here in Afghanistan,' the interrogator said. 'Your passport is forged, and you had contact with important terrorists like Mohammed Atta, Ramzi Binalshibh and others in Germany.'

But the Egyptian wasn't giving anything away. He had heard about these people, he said: perhaps he had read about them in the newspaper. Then he began to whinge again, demanding that his interrogators contact the German embassy. The lead interrogator indicated that this was not going to happen. They weren't going to let diplomats and lawyers on to this case.

'You're in a country,' he told the al-Qaeda man, 'where there are no laws. No one knows you are here. We can do what we want with you.' When he again protested his innocence, the interrogator became angry. 'If the charges here weren't correct' – he indicated the dossier on the table – 'they wouldn't have flown you here from Skopje.' Why else would he be here?

The Egyptian said that he had been arrested because he was a Muslim.

'Everyone claims that when we start interrogating them,' said the man. 'But they're not Muslims. They're terrorists.'

Inside the CIA, officers were aware that rendition skirted the boundaries of international law. But that did not mean it was entirely without merit. According to the US Supreme Court's Ker-Frisbie doctrine, a court was entitled to ignore the details regarding how a defendant was brought to face justice – so long as he was brought to face justice.

Admittedly, snatching a suspect abroad was probably illegal in the country concerned, but that was a relatively minor issue: espionage violated the law, too. That had never stopped the CIA doing it. The question was, did the benefits of bringing the character to court outweigh the unusual methods used to apprehend him? To all concerned, the answer was clear: yes.

'The snatch is something that goes on on the dark side,' agrees Professor John Radsan, assistant general counsel for the CIA from 2002 to 2004. 'But when you bring them back to justice there will be a light side. The person that is snatched will then appear as a defendant in a court, will have lawyers. There is transparency at the back end of the process.' This transparency 'at the back end' was what allowed the programme to proceed.

Prior to 1995, rendered suspects were delivered to face justice in US courts, where due process was guaranteed. With the arrival of al-Qaeda, however, the rules changed. Under President Clinton, it became acceptable to snatch suspects abroad, then deliver them to foreign countries for trial. This raised significant risks of unlawfulness. Many of the countries where these suspects were wanted had questionable human rights records. It was entirely possible that rendered suspects might be tortured after they were handed over. If this happened, the United States' rendition operation would become unlawful: delivering anyone to torture, or the threat of torture, was specifically banned under both the Refugees' Convention and the Convention Against Torture.

President Clinton appears to have struggled with this dilemma. When the programme was updated in 1995, his administration requested assurances from the CIA that no rendered suspect was ever to be delivered to torture. The Agency thought that the White House was being naive.

'We said very clearly,' recalls Michael Scheuer, '"If we turn these people over to [Egypt's] Hosni Mubarak, two months from now, six months from now, you're going to have your State Department condemn the Egyptians for their human rights or judicial issues." We didn't say there was a chance. We said, "They *will* be tortured." Because that's the way those countries work.'

The White House then asked whether it might be possible for the CIA to obtain an undertaking from the receiving country that the suspect would be treated according to the norms of its own legal system. When the Agency confirmed that these people were entirely likely to be treated according to the receiving country's legal norms – that was the whole problem – the point seems to have been missed. The programme received a green light.

Lawyers were less equivocal about this development, especially when one of the first rendered suspects, Talaat Fouad Qassem, having been located in Croatia, was handed over to Egypt. He promptly vanished and was later presumed to have been tortured and executed. Still, however, the programme had safeguards in place. The CIA was only ever to render suspects facing prosecution, and they were only ever to be delivered to trial.

'We had no permission to pick anyone up who wasn't either the subject of a conviction in absentia or had an outstanding legal warrant,' says Scheuer. Even then the process was subject to vetting by lawyers from the CIA and at the National Security Council. Only after leaping through all kinds of hoops could the Agency transport suspects to and from foreign countries.

President George W. Bush's 17 September Memorandum of Notification removed these safeguards. The nature of rendition now changed radically. Suspects were to be snatched, then transported to countries where there were no warrants out for them. The goal of the operation was no longer 'rendition to justice', but what one protagonist refers to as 'rendition to interrogation': they were snatched not with a view to delivering them to court but pre-emptively, to prevent them from doing bad things, and with a view to grilling them for intelligence about what they might have been planning.

Legally, this shift was highly problematic. In John Radsan's terminology, the snatch part of the operation took place on 'the dark side' of the law, and as such was only justifiable if a trial, the 'light side', was imminent. Transporting subjects to Third World countries where no judicial process was planned was very different.

'That's something from the dark side to the dark side,' he says today. The process was 'troubling'.

Other changes were afoot, too. Post-9/11, the Agency was offered the opportunity to get involved in the interrogation process itself.

'For some reason,' says Michael Scheuer, 'the Bush administration believed that if we interrogated these people ourselves we would get more information from them than the Egyptians or Jordanians or Saudis.'

Frequently, high-ranking al-Qaeda suspects were transferred not to other nations' custody but to secret sites administered by the CIA. This way, their interrogations could be conducted properly by US interrogators; this way, there would be no barriers between the US intelligence community and the terror suspects.

This put the Agency in a difficult position. Where were these terrorists to be kept? In a move similar to that of the Australian government's ruling on asylum seekers' rights outside of its dependent territories – which had facilitated the establishment of the Pacific Solution – the United States decided that international treaties regarding humanitarian treatment of prisoners – such as the Convention against Torture (CAT) and the International Covenant on Civil and Political Rights (ICCPR) – did not apply to US citizens outside of the United States. As in Australia, the result was the creation of a grey zone where international law appeared not to apply at all. Provided the suspects were kept well clear of the United States, they were in a legal vacuum. America could do what it wanted with them. A number of potential sites was considered: ships at sea, isolated islands, then friendly nations.

'Black' CIA sites were established around the world where suspects could be held and interrogated indefinitely. The first of these appear to have been in Egypt and Jordan, longstanding partners in the rendition programme. Further sites would eventually appear in Thailand, Pakistan, Poland, Romania, Iraq, Afghanistan and Uzbekistan.

One of them, an abandoned brick factory ten minutes north of Kabul International Airport, was known as the Salt Pit. It was here that The Egyptian was being interrogated. Things were not going well.

After four nights of questioning, when The Egyptian still refused to talk, his interrogators decided to let him stew for a while. They'd had enough of his demands for representatives from the German embassy. He was duly left alone for three weeks without visitors. A period of quiet reflection, it was thought, might bring home to him the gravity of his situation.

Not that The Egyptian was entirely without company. Despite a ban on communication with other prisoners in the Salt Pit, he immediately set about establishing contact, leaving clandestine notes in the lavatory for other al-Qaeda suspects. He also managed to whisper to them when the guards were not paying attention. Late at night, the Salt Pit's inmates recited their names, addresses and phone numbers to each other in the hope that if one was eventually released he might be able to contact the others' families, or perhaps even al-Qaeda handlers, to let them know where they were. Day by day The Egyptian scratched the date on the wall of his cell, so he could keep track of his time there. He also managed to keep a diary, including dates and details of his treatment. When other prisoners informed him that it would be confiscated if the guards found it, he memorized this, too.

In the meantime, there were daily hardships. Food in the Salt Pit was unpleasant. Breakfast was a cup of unsweetened tea and a piece of bread. Lunch consisted of rice, adulterated with foreign objects such as sand, gravel and insects. The prisoners figured that this was done deliberately, to break them. Occasionally, they were given fruit, usually oranges. Invariably, these were so mouldy that inmates were unable to work out whether they were blue or green. Sometimes there was chicken, apparently the pre-picked bones of meals eaten by the Afghan guards.

Many of the prisoners had health problems. It was freezing cold. Diarrhoea was common. Still the al-Qaeda man refused to break. In fact, over time his resolve appeared to strengthen. Repeatedly, he lambasted the Americans through his cell door for their arrogance. He demanded an audience with a German diplomat, demanded to meet the man in charge of the prison, demanded to know why he was being held in Afghanistan, demanded proper food and water, clean blankets and better treatment. When he was ignored, he went on hunger strike again.

This time it was more serious. Somehow, The Egyptian managed to persuade everyone in the Salt Pit to participate. Not all of them were as strong as he was: having been incarcerated for longer, they had less stamina. Six days into the strike, the others gave up. The Egyptian refused, but, following a promised improvement in food quality, he agreed to drink water. Guards noted that he might be beginning to buckle. He complained of headaches. On a couple of occasions, they observed him trying to pray standing up, and saw him collapse. He was becoming depressed, losing hope. This was good. At night, he whispered to his fellow inmates, asking whether perhaps hunger striking was against Islam. This was progress.

Still he held out. By 28 March, after twenty-three days without food, he began screaming '*Allahu akbar!*' at all hours, through the grille of his cell door.

'I am a German,' he told his captors four days later. 'You're Americans and this is not your country. Why did you bring me here?' Repeatedly, he shouted abuse from his cell. 'Did you treat the Americans responsible for the Oklahoma terror attack this way? Is this the peace and civilized manners that you want to spread and teach Afghans and Iraqis?'

If things were not going entirely to plan at the Salt Pit, back at Langley there was at least progress regarding The Egyptian's true identity. Shortly after he had been rendered to Afghanistan, the al-Qaeda man's passport had been forwarded to the CIA's Technical Services division. Macedonian border officials had noted that something appeared wrong with it; as a result, they had concluded it was a forgery. Technical Services' job was to establish whether this was true. By the end of February 2004, the analysis was complete. The passport was genuine.

There are two versions of what happened next. The first, widely circulated in later days, revolves around a growing realization within the CIA that The Egyptian was not 'The Egyptian' at all: his name, Khaled el Masri, *meant* 'The Egyptian'. The 9/11 plotters may have been recruited by a man called el Masri – but it wasn't this one.

The Agency had rendered the wrong man.

One senior officer in the Counter-Terrorism Center briefed on the case at the time confirms that this is exactly what happened. 'There was no proof that he had done anything,' he says of el Masri. 'There was a similarity in the name compared to one of the names of a suspected al-Qaeda terrorist in our databases.'

According to this individual, the head of the Agency's al-Qaeda Unit – a senior female officer renowned for her 'gung-ho' attitude – had seized on the operation and decided, single-handedly, that el Masri was guilty. Other officers had advised strongly that, in these circumstances, where the only evidence available was a simple name correlation, rendition was a bad idea.

'From the very beginning people had doubts,' he says. 'There were people around her saying, "What's your proof? We have no proof that this guy is connected to anything."'

The head of the al-Qaeda Unit was not cowed. 'We'll get our proof,' she assured her colleagues. 'Once we start debriefing him, once the interrogations begin, we'll get our proof.'

The officer, now ex-CIA, was appalled. 'The guy was an innocent,' he says. 'There was never any hard proof that he was anyone other than who he said he was.'

By the spring of 2004, the Agency was aware it had made a terrible mistake. Jailers at the Salt Pit, convinced that el Masri was innocent, had raised the alarm. Even the rendition team sent to pick him up from Macedonia had voiced their doubts, warning the CIA's Kabul station that all was not right. On 31 March, the day he had castigated his American jailers for their treatment of Iraqis and Afghans, el Masri was pulled into another cell and shackled to a chair. Two Americans showed up, without masks this time, to ask why he was on hunger strike. One was the Salt Pit's chief administrator. The American tried to reason with el Masri, promising to send a report to his superiors in Washington.

'This is not the appropriate place for you,' he told him. 'We all agree.'

After another outburst, an American guard shouted at him: 'I don't think you belong here. I will call Washington again.'

But Washington didn't know what to do. Debate inside the Counter-Terrorism Center appears to have heated up at the end of the month, some officers actively lobbying for el Masri's release. 'Is that guy still locked up in the Salt Pit?' asked one. Eventually, even the head of the al-Qaeda Unit agreed that el Masri might be released, on the condition that once back in Germany he was placed under surveillance by German intelligence. This was deemed impossible; el Masri remained where he was.

The Agency was already in a state of quiet panic regarding the Salt Pit anyway. As the debate over what to do with Khaled el Masri raged inside the CIA, another error at the site was referred to the Justice Department for investigation. In November 2002, a young Afghan under interrogation by CIA agents had been left chained to the floor of his cell, naked, without a blanket. The next morning he was dead. News of the death – apparently the result of a decision made by an inexperienced CIA officer – was hushed up and the corpse was buried anonymously. No records were kept. Although the Justice Department eventually decided not to prosecute, clearly this was the kind of incident that could come back to bite the Agency. The el Masri case offered more of the same, only this time it might be harder to hush up. This wasn't some Afghan nobody. This was a German citizen.

In April, according to Jane Mayer of the *New Yorker*, Counter-Terrorism Center officers from within the CIA, shocked that nothing was being done about el Masri, started plotting to obtain his release. When nothing happened, Jose Rodriguez, the Head of the Centre, and James Pavitt, the Deputy Director of Operations, were told that something was seriously awry.

'It's the wrong Khaled el Masri,' a European officer told Rodriguez. Not only had the CIA kidnapped and imprisoned an entirely innocent man in a dungeon in Afghanistan, he had been on hunger strike for a month. Nobody wanted another death in CIA custody. Something had to be done.

But by now el Masri's health was failing. By 8 April, after thirty-five days without food, he was too weak to get out of bed to use the lavatory. Medical examination revealed that during his time in the CIA's custody he had lost 60lbs in weight. The next day, Afghan staff again tried to get him to eat. Again, he refused. At 10 p.m. on 10 April, the Salt Pit's warder and a doctor demanded point blank that el Masri take food, telling him that, if he did, he would be released in three weeks. When they were unable to offer him any proof of this, he refused.

That night, hooded men re-entered el Masri's cell, pulled him out of bed, bound his hands and feet and dragged him to the interrogation room, where he was tied to a chair. One grabbed his head and forced a feeding tube into his nose. Liquid was then pumped directly into el Masri's stomach.

In May 2004, Director of Central Intelligence George Tenet was finally briefed on the el Masri situation.

'Are you telling me we've got an innocent guy stuck in prison in Afghanistan?' the DCI asked his briefer. 'Oh shit! Just tell me – please – we haven't used enhanced interrogation techniques on him, have we?'

Tenet had more to worry about than el Masri's health: he now had to explain to his superiors what had happened. Later that month, he briefed Condoleezza Rice on the situation, suggesting that the best course of action might be simply to return el Masri to Germany and deny everything. After some debate, it was decided this was not a good idea. The German government would have to be informed about the error.

In Afghanistan, the prison director took el Masri into a cell where he was introduced to an American who said he was a psychologist and explained that he had flown from DC to meet the German. At the end of their session, el Masri was told that he would be released soon. He wasn't.

Two weeks later, a new character appeared: a tall German-speaking man in a military uniform. Identifying himself as 'Sam', he said that he wanted to speak frankly. El Masri thought this unlikely. Each time he spoke, Sam appealed to the two Americans accompanying him as to what he should – and should not – say. Nevertheless, it was worth a try. Commenting that Sam appeared to know who he was, but that he didn't know who Sam was, el Masri asked whether the German could enlighten him: perhaps he could state who he was working for and reveal his full name?

'I can't answer those questions,' said Sam.

Had he been sent by the German government? Sam refused to answer. Did the German government know that el Masri was being detained in Afghanistan? Sam refused to answer. Did el Masri's wife know what had happened to him? Sam shook his head.

Over the next few days, Sam appeared regularly, each time assuring el Masri that repatriation was imminent, but had been delayed. Once he brought cookies and a German magazine and asked if he needed anything 'from home'. On 20 May, after nearly five months of incarceration, el Masri lost his temper and told Sam he was sick of broken promises. He planned to restart his hunger strike.

'Please don't,' Sam told him. 'Give me two days. I will talk to my German superiors.' But el Masri had had enough. The next day he stopped eating again. Another meeting took place, with two Americans and Sam, promising that he would be going home within eight days.

Finally, on the morning of 28 May, el Masri's hands were secured with plastic cuffs, his legs were shackled, a blindfold was placed over his eyes and he was led outside into a jeep. After a ten-minute drive to the airport, he was escorted into a shipping container, sat down and instructed to face the wall. His blindfold was removed and his personal possessions were returned. His hands were then retied, he was blindfolded and his ears filled with cotton wool. Headphones were placed over the top. He was driven to an aeroplane, led up the steps and chained to a seat.

After a six-hour flight, the plane touched down. El Masri was bundled into the back of a minivan and driven for around three hours. The van stopped and three new men, speaking with Slavic accents, climbed in. They then drove for another three hours, at the end of which he was helped out and told to turn around. One of the men instructed him to walk away from the vehicle. Under no circumstances was he to look back.

To el Masri, who now found himself on top of a desolate mountain in a country he didn't recognize, the next step was obvious: one of the officers was about to shoot him. He closed his eyes and started to walk. Nothing happened. Behind him, he heard the van speed away. Around the corner he bumped into three armed soldiers who demanded his passport, examined it and asked him what he was doing in Albania without a visa.

The four men tramped to a single-storey building with a flag on top where el Masri was asked who he was. Having lost a considerable amount of weight, grown a thick beard and long hair during the course of his incarceration, he was told that he looked like a terrorist. When he tried to explain what had happened to him, the men laughed and asked him if he thought they looked stupid. No one would believe a story like that.

To the German it was clear the Albanians had struck a deal with the CIA. They clearly knew exactly who he was. On the table in the office was a small stash of food they had prepared for him. Bread, potato chips and cheese: the exact same food, in the exact same packaging, that he had been given on his journey. The officers drove him to Tirana

International Airport and one of them requested his passport and wallet, removing 320 euros. He then disappeared into the terminal, to re-emerge fifteen minutes later with a boarding pass.

El Masri was ushered into the airport and escorted through immigration control, where his passport was stamped with an exit visa: a curious technicality, since he had never officially entered Albania. He was put on to a commercial plane. Finally, he began to accept that he might survive his ordeal.

After 149 days of incarceration without trial, charge or access to a lawyer, Khaled el Masri landed in Frankfurt at 8.45 a.m. on 29 May 2004. Immigration authorities immediately seized on the dishevelled Arab with the long beard who did not in the least resemble his passport photograph and told him that he was an impostor. Only after considerable efforts did he convince them that he should be allowed to re-enter his own country.

El Masri finally made it home to Neu-Ulm that afternoon to find his flat abandoned. The postbox was stuffed full of unopened junk mail, along with month-old warnings from the German authorities that his social security benefits would be cut if he failed to attend regularly scheduled interviews. Inside the house most of his family's possessions were gone; others had been loaded into removal boxes and abandoned. Tired of waiting for him to get in contact, his wife had left him, taking the children to Lebanon to live with her parents.

In the local Islamic Centre, the German found a friend who filled him in on the details. His wife had sold the family car to pay for the plane tickets. El Masri telephoned his family, tried to explain to his children why their father had abandoned them and promised that they would all see each other soon. A week later, he made an appointment with a local lawyer, Manfred Gnjidic, sat down, took a deep breath and told him a long, extraordinary, story.

Disbelieving at first, Gnjidic told him to write down his story, draw a picture of every place he had been during his incarceration and to collate any evidence that might validate his account. As it happened, there was quite a lot: a return bus ticket to Macedonia; an exit stamp in his passport from Albania; a boarding pass from Albania to Frankfurt Then there was the biological evidence. Samples of his hair were sent to the Bavarian Archive for Geology, where isotope analysis indicated that he had indeed been severely malnourished and had spent a number of months in South Asia.

Gnjidic went to the police, who opened a formal investigation into the kidnapping and incarceration of Khaled el Masri, 'The Egyptian'.

The exposure of the CIA's rendition programme began with the planespotting community. Six weeks after 11 September, chatrooms on the Internet were humming with speculation about 'ghost flights'. Tail numbers of suspect planes were exchanged; it wasn't long before mainstream journalists became intrigued.

Their first stop was the US Federal Aviation Authority database, which listed the companies that owned and flew the jets, many of which appeared to operate out of North Carolina. Searches of the companies' public accounts revealed incongruities: their addresses were post office boxes. There were no phone records, business, corporation records or previous addresses. Staff at the companies were middle-aged, but their social security numbers had all been issued after 1998. The mysterious flights appeared to be operated by people who did not exist.

One company that came up again and again was Premier Executive Transport Services Ltd (PETS), based in Dedham, Massachusetts. Its vice-president Colleen A. Bornt was not only untraceable, but changed her signature every time she handled a pen. According to company records, in December 2001 PETS had purchased a Boeing 737 Business Jet with the tail number N313P. To planespotters, the number was familiar. N313P had been spotted in some pretty far-flung places, including Glasgow, Guantanamo Bay, Tripoli, Poland and RAF Northolt.

It had also been spotted in a rather more salubrious location: the Ballearic Islands. Specifically, Mallorca.

Planespotter Josep Manchado was at home when he received the call. 'They were Germans,' he recalls. 'They said they were from television.' Initially, Manchado didn't believe them – they mentioned the CIA – but, when they phoned back with a Spanish translator, he took them more seriously. The journalists had an unbelievable story, they told him. They had a German citizen who appeared to have been kidnapped by the CIA. They were trying to stand the story up.

Verifying a story such as el Masri's was always going to be difficult: certainly, the CIA wasn't about to explain what it had done. However, one thing the Germans did have (from contacts with British and American journalists) was a list of planes that appeared to be involved in the rendition programme. One of them was the Boeing Business Jet N313P. They also had the date of el Masri's abduction from Macedonia: 23 January 2004. The day before his flight to Afghanistan, Josep Manchado had seen and photographed N313P at Palma Mallorca International Airport. Perhaps there was a correlation?

'They told me that they wanted to talk about this picture because they had a man there telling them he had been kidnapped in this plane,' says Manchado. 'They wanted to ask me some questions.'

The story now unfolded fast. With solid proof that N313P had been in Mallorca the morning of el Masri's kidnap, journalists began digging to see what else they could find. Germany's ZDF Television showed Manchado's photograph to Macedonian air traffic control and persuaded them to hand over a copy of N313P's flight plan for 23 January. There it was in black and white: Palma – Skopje – Baghdad – Kabul. The story stood up.

The first stop, Palma, appeared to be a hub for other CIA flights, too. Alerted to the fact that a foreign intelligence service had been kidnapping civilians through Mallorca, the local police were called in.

An enterprising Mallorcan journalist contacted the ground crews at Palma Airport and asked them if they had ever dealt with the Boeing Business Jet N313P. They had. One company, Mallorcair, had catered for seven CIA jets as they passed through the island.

Mallorcair didn't keep records of passengers on the jets, but staff mentioned that the company's minibus had ferried the Americans to their hotel, fifteen minutes drive from the airport. The Agency, it seemed, favoured two Mallorcan hotels: the Gran Melia Victoria, a five-star establishment overlooking the marina, and the Marriott Son Antem. A little cursory digging by police and journalists at the hotels, and they struck gold. The CIA agents had checked in, and paid for their hotel rooms, individually. Reception had logged their names, passport details and credit-card numbers.

A picture of the entire operation now emerged. Boeing Business Jet N313P had stopped off in Mallorca before moving on to Skopje to pick up el Masri and deliver him to Kabul. The rendition team had stayed the night at the Marriott. After he had been rendered, the jet had returned to refuel for the trip back to the United States. Weather on the eastern seaboard was bad, so the flight home was delayed; the crew had spent two nights at the Gran Melia Victoria.

During their time there, a number of CIA staff had made phone calls. The Gran Melia had a list of their home telephone numbers.

If things were going badly for the rendition programme on the journalistic front, they were hardly improving on the diplomatic one. On 31 May 2004, Daniel R. Coats, the US Ambassador to Germany, met the German Interior Minister. There had been an unfortunate mistake, he told him. The United States had accidentally kidnapped one of his citizens. Coats apparently apologized for the error and warned that el Masri might attempt to go public with his story. If that happened, he requested that Germany remain silent on the issue: there was a risk of exposure of clandestine intelligence operations, and a chance that a case like this might open up the US government to legal challenges. Besides, the CIA had hardly covered itself with glory. This was embarrassing stuff.'

Requests for silence on the matter were not destined to achieve a great deal. The CIA's rendition programme was unravelling. Parliaments in Canada, Italy, France, Portugal, Sweden, the Netherlands and the United Kingdom would shortly open investigations into kidnaps of their citizens. The European Union would designate a special rapporteur on the issue. The Press was close behind. By January 2005, Khaled el Masri was all over the newspapers. In March, the *Washington Post* printed a story about the Salt Pit in Kabul, asserting publicly for the first time that an unnamed Afghan had been murdered there in 2002. When it was reported the same month that Spanish police were investigating CIA flights through Mallorca, the Agency launched what appears to have been a damage-control exercise. Yes, Khaled el Masri had been rendered. It was all the fault of a senior officer in the al-Qaeda Unit.

'She didn't know,' an unnamed source told the *Washington Post*. 'She just had a hunch.'

Not everyone agreed with this verdict. One senior CIA officer who helped compile the Agency's file on el Masri views the story as an abomination.

'There is no rendition that was ever conducted on the basis of one piece of information, or on the hunch of a CIA officer,' he says today. 'For someone to say that any single person – especially in the Operations Division – could authorize a rendition off his or her own hook, without enormous input from the legals and probably from the National Security Council, it's just completely wrong.' Someone was not telling the truth. 'A complete lie,' he says of the story. 'I was *there*.'

The story failed to stop the flow, anyway. Throughout 2004 and 2005, a steady stream of accounts about the CIA's rendition operations came out, each revealing more information than the last, each adding to the puzzle and offering assistance to others searching for the truth about the Agency's conduct in the War on Terror.

In 2005, the debate turned towards the courts when the American Civil Liberties Union (ACLU) picked up the el Masri case. To ACLU, rendition was the worst symptom of the White House's persistent undermining of human rights in the War on Terror: despite the administration's tendency to harp on about the importance of international treaties and human rights, the White House was going out of its way to destroy the legal structures that supported the whole process. Warrantless wiretapping, incarceration of foreign nationals without trial, military tribunals, illegal enemy combatants, 'enhanced interrogation', reversal of the presumption of innocence, racial profiling, data mining: these were the true products of the War on Terror. They stank. And the greatest reek of all came from rendition: a government-sanctioned programme to kidnap, transport, incarcerate and torture suspects who were denied legal representation, denied the rights to access a court, denied any sort of legal rights whatsoever.

El Masri was a poster case for all rendition victims, both innocent and guilty. Here was a man whose every human right had been systematically violated. Here was a chance to challenge the entire programme.

For six months, ACLU worked with el Masri and his German lawyer, preparing their case. Finally, on 6 December 2005, they filed *El Masri versus Tenet* in a Virginia courthouse. The defendants were George Tenet, Premier Executive Transport Services, Aero Contractors Ltd of Johnston County, North Carolina (contracted by PETS to operate N313P) and twenty 'John Does', ten of whom were the CIA agents responsible for the kidnap, the other ten being employees of the defendant corporations. Token damages of $75,000 were demanded.

ACLU's timing was flawless. The day the case was filed, Secretary of State Condoleezza Rice began a state visit to Germany. The moment she arrived in Berlin, she was faced with a barrage of questions about rendition. Her position was not helped by German Chancellor Angela Merkel. In a press conference, Merkel stated that she had spoken privately with the Secretary, who had admitted the CIA had kidnapped the wrong man.

'I'm able to say that we actually talked about that one particular case,' Merkel informed journalists, 'and that the American Administration has admitted that this man was erroneously taken . . . the American Administration is not denying that it took place.'

But it was. What the Secretary had actually said – Rice's aides later clarified – was that, *if* mistakes had been made, the United States would work to rectify them. Certainly, she had not made the admission the Chancellor had mentioned. 'We're not sure,' one US official told a journalist, 'what was in [Merkel's] head.'

Rice had been aware the issue would come up during her trip. The day before she left the United States, she had made a public statement at Andrews Air Force Base defending rendition. It included a number of interesting points. In cases where regular extradition was impossible, she stated, 'the local government can make the sovereign choice to co-operate in a rendition'. In these cases, she went on, 'The United States has fully respected the sovereignty of other countries that co-operate in these matters.' But co-operation was 'a two-way street': US intelligence helped to protect European countries from terrorist attacks, saving European lives. 'It is up to these governments to decide if they wish to work with us.'

Overtly, Rice appeared to be suggesting that, if European nations didn't like what the United States was up to, they had every right not to accept their intelligence assistance in the future. Covertly, however, her emphasis on 'co-operation' with the CIA's rendition programme implied something rather different: that the United States had not violated the sovereignty of these nations – not because renditions had not taken place, but because the countries had co-operated. They had known what was going on.

To the administration and the CIA, criticism from Europe on rendition was hypocritical. If European nations had had objections to this kind of thing, they should either have voiced them before they signed up to the War on Terror, or not signed up at all. Instead, they had all looked the other way. Now, here were those same Europeans scrambling over each other to avoid being implicated, feigning ignorance and desperately pointing the finger at the United States.

Michael Scheuer, who designed the rendition programme, was incensed. 'All of the Europeans that we dealt with were eager to have the information that was derived from renditions,' he says. 'None of them, of course, really wanted us to tell them how we got it.'

The issue of how the United States got its intelligence on rendition suspects came centre stage with el Masri. According to the official version, a 'gung-ho' CIA officer without sufficient intelligence had acted alone, on a hunch. The *unofficial* version, however, was very different. Rendition wasn't some kind of lottery. El Masri was not kidnapped simply on the basis of a mix-up regarding his name. There had been a profusion of intelligence about him, some of it predating 9/11.

'Credit records, phone records, travel patterns,' explains one of the officers who compiled the el Masri file. 'We were not the only country, or the only intelligence service, who thought he was someone we wanted off the street.' According to this officer, prior to his rendition intelligence on el Masri had been passed on to the CIA by 'three or four European allies'. The United States had not acted alone in the case of Khaled el Masri.

Not that this ever came out. In Germany and Macedonia, when the question of who in the government had known about el Masri's rendition was asked, the answer was unanimous: no one. Macedonia – which had apprehended him, informed the CIA of his capture, then held him for twenty-three days in a hotel room waiting for a rendition team to become available – denied that anything had happened at all. According to the Minister of the Interior, el Masri had been interviewed by border guards when he entered Macedonia on New Year's Eve 2003, but had been sent on his way and had enjoyed a three-week holiday in the country. Rendition stories, he said, were 'speculative and unfounded'.

German politicians lost no time in denying their involvement, too. Foreign Minister Frank-Walter Steinmeier said he was 'nauseated' by reports implicating Germany in the rendition. 'Let me make it clear,' he told Parliament in December 2005. 'The Government and [security services] did not aid and abet the abduction of German citizen El Masri.'

German intelligence had known nothing of the affair whatsoever – despite the fact that questions to be put to el Masri, as well as background information on Neu-Ulm, had been handed to the CIA; despite the fact that a German, 'Sam', had visited el Masri in the Salt Pit repeatedly, asked him if he wanted anything 'from home' and had accompanied him back to Europe.

Were the Germans informed? The CIA officer who worked on the Masri file laughs: 'I would say if you wrote that,' he says, 'you would not find many people who would contest it.'

The fact was that, while very few knew what, exactly, rendition entailed, everyone recognized that it was going on. The British provided questions for rendered suspects. The Polish and Romanians provided interrogation sites. Germany provided briefings and background intelligence. Macedonia provided el Masri. Everyone let the planes land and refuel. No one turned down the intelligence yield at the end of the process. Everyone was complicit. Everyone was guilty.

Meanwhile, most of these nations seized on the exceptional nature of the post-9/11 threat, then used it as a justification for enacting domestic legislation that aped US policy regarding human rights: restrictions of rights for foreigners and asylum seekers; indefinite incarceration of suspects without trial; withdrawal of the right to an attorney; suspension of habeas corpus; enhanced surveillance techniques. The list went on and on.

'I do not underestimate the ability of fanatical groups to kill and destroy,' conceded Lord Hoffmann in a famous judgment on the incarceration of terror suspects without trial in the United Kingdom in December 2004. 'But they do not threaten the life of the nation.' The real threat to the United Kingdom, he warned, 'comes not from terrorism but from laws such as these'.

Five years later, the Human Rights Council's Eminent Panel of Jurists on Terrorism, Counter-Terrorism and Human Rights agreed. After an exhaustive three-year study of the effects of the War on Terror on human rights globally, the Panel concluded that human rights protections, assembled over the last sixty years, had been corroded to the point where the international legal order was in jeopardy. Especially worrying was that the nations that had previously argued for the primacy of human rights were the very same nations now busily opting out of them. The result was 'perhaps one of the most serious challenges ever posed to the integrity of a system carefully constructed after the Second World War'.

The report ended with a warning. Human rights protections were the cornerstone upon which democracy was built. It was likely to prove far harder to rebuild this cornerstone than it was to break it. 'States tamper with this framework at their own peril,' stated the Panel. 'It is difficult to exaggerate the risk to society as a whole when governments depart from their obligations in this way.' On 11 September – or perhaps more accurately, 17 September, when President Bush signed the CIA's Memorandum of Notification – America had sneezed. The world had caught a cold.

Two years after Hoffmann's comment, another British law lord, Lord Stein, specifically addressed the issue of rendition in a lecture at the Bar Council. 'In operating the system of secret rendition the Bush administration placed itself above the law and placed the individuals concerned beyond the protection of the law,' he stated. 'Since Nuremberg, such kidnapping has constituted a war crime under international law.

Those consciously involved are subject to the universal criminal juris-diction of international law.'

Stein's comments proved prescient when twenty-six CIA operatives were named and indicted in Italy for their involvement in the rendition of a Muslim cleric, Abu Omar, in 2003. Among them were the Italian CIA station chief Jeffrey Castelli and the station chief in Milan Robert Seldon Lady. Although the Italian government never officially demanded the extradition of the American intelligence officers, their names were passed on to Interpol and warrants were issued for their arrest.

'I think,' says former CIA assistant-general counsel John Radsan, 'I probably wouldn't travel outside the United States if I was one of these people.'

Such was the profusion of information changing hands on the Internet that it was only a matter of time before the CIA agents involved in the el Masri rendition were fingered, too. From photocopies of their pass-ports taken at Mallorcan hotels, journalists obtained pictures of the rendition team; from invoices and credit-card slips, they obtained their pseudonyms. Then, by running names and aircraft qualifications through the FAA databases, they correlated these pseudonyms with real names. Those unwary enough to have made calls during the rendi-tion operation were traced via their home telephone numbers.

In 2007, for the first time in any rendition case, German reporters publicly named members of the team: Eric Robert Hume, Harry Kirk Elarbee, Lyle Edgard Lumsden, James Kovalesky. Reporters doorstepped the CIA men, visited their houses, dug further. To prove that information-gathering was not an exclusive preserve of the CIA, inves-tigators demonstrated how much they knew. Hume was thirty-five, had a beard, lived with his father, had two dogs and co-owned a fishing boat. Kovalesky drove a Toyota Previa, collected model trains and had a degree in microbiology. Lumsden, whose friends called him 'Uncle Bud', was born in 1956, served in the US army and spoke Serbo-Croat. His wife's name was Janet.

Eleven American men and two women were duly charged with kidnapping in Germany. None attended court. None will attend court: German authorities refused to forward extradition papers for the team. But it's unlikely they'll be taking vacations in Germany, or Europe, any time soon.

Inside the CIA, the most worrisome aspect of all this was not the hypocrisy of Europeans in the War on Terror or even the public naming of people who had worked for the Agency. What really rankled was that these guys were essentially taking the blame for doing what they had been ordered to do. The way the story played out in the Press, the Central Intelligence Agency, yet again, had broken the law. Not true.

'This isn't something where an Agency officer just wakes up one morning and decides he's going to conduct a rogue operation,' says one officer briefed on the el Masri case. 'It just doesn't work like that. Everything is done once a policy decision is made at the White House.'

John Radsan agrees. 'Don't believe this was some devious operation that the officers came up with on their own, without presidential authorization,' he says, 'without lawyers approving it.' The CIA was following orders.

A number of former Agency staff stress that, while some at Langley had been keen to increase the remit of the rendition programme immediately after 9/11, others had been wary.

'[Post-9/11] there was a level of concern,' says Radsan. 'Concern about secret prisons, the aggressive interrogations – many of these tactics that were adopted after 9/11 . . . They said to themselves, "This stuff will come back to hurt us. We don't do these kinds of things. This is not our forte. We're not a paramilitary organization, we don't run secret prisons."'

Michael Scheuer puts the decision to upgrade the rendition programme down to a lack of any sort of overall plan on behalf of the White House. 'The Executive Branch after 9/11 was in a state of panic, because they didn't have anything they could do to protect the United States,' he says. 'The only game in town was the CIA's rendition programme. The rendition programme was never designed to be anything more than a complement to full US government counter-terrorism policy, but it turned out to be the *only* policy.'

CIA officers for and against extraordinary rendition both agree on one thing: they were only going to do what they were told to do, and they were only going to do what was legal.

'Not only were they ordered to do it,' says Scheuer, 'but they were told on paper, repeatedly, that it was fully compliant with US law.'

When that turned out not to be true, the obvious next step for the administration was simple: blame the CIA. What was so surprising for many Agency staff was not that it happened, but that it took so long.

'We expected from the very first to be sold out by the politicians,' says Scheuer. 'Everyone knew that we would get sold out at some point.'

As usual, the CIA would do what the White House told it to do, then end up being hung out to dry.

Upon joining the Agency, today's operations officers are instructed to take out malpractice insurance, just in case someone orders them to do something that turns out at a later date to be illegal.

Another former senior officer explains. '"What we want you to do is grab this Arab in Milan." So you say, "Yes, sir." You go grab the Arab in Milan, because that's what your instruction was to do. And then you move on to the next operation, not thinking that the politicians haven't engaged with the Italian government to make sure that this is legal, because you think it is legal.' He snorts. 'And now I have to hire an attorney and defend myself in an Italian criminal court.'

Khaled el Masri is unimpressed by the various sufferings of the US intelligence community. For him, the issue remains personal and, as yet, unresolved. When the ACLU filed his case in December 2005, they had planned for him to be present, to make a statement. Together with his lawyer Manfred Gnjidic, he flew to the United States the week the papers were due to be served. He never made it. Apparently still on a terrorist watch-list, The Egyptian was turned away the moment he landed in Atlanta and returned to Germany the same day. No reason was given. He had to make a statement by live satellite link.

The appearance didn't do much good. In March 2006, the US government made a formal claim that the case be dismissed on the basis that taking it to trial would jeopardize ongoing intelligence operations. The court agreed.

A month later, ACLU appealed, arguing that the facts around the el Masri case had been so widely reported they could hardly be considered secret any more. The court disagreed, asserting that its hands were tied by the law regarding state secrets. The appeal was dismissed.

Not that it was entirely without merit. Federal District Judge T. S. Ellis made that clear: if what el Masri was asserting was true, he stated, 'all fair-minded people must . . . agree that El Masri has suffered injuries as a result of our country's mistake and deserves a remedy'. But this remedy would have to come from Congress or the Executive. Once again, when it came to rendition, the judicial system was powerless.

More investigators came on board. In April, the European Parliament visited Macedonia to investigate the case. Two months later came a Council of Europe report on rendition, which reported that el Masri's story was accurate. 'The case of Khaled el Masri,' according to the Council's Special Rapporteur Dick Marty, 'is exemplary.' German Parliament launched an investigation. In November, the ACLU case was formally appealed.

While awaiting the outcome, lawyers learned that German prosecutors had formally issued arrest warrants for thirteen individuals identified as having been on the N313P flight from Macedonia to Afghanistan. The US State Department refused to comment and the Department of Justice refused to assist German investigators. The CIA refused to say anything at all.

In March 2007, three judges from the Fourth Circuit Court published
a unanimous opinion on the el Masri case, affirming the previous
dismissal on the basis that 'central facts [of the case] . . . remain state
secrets'. Again and again the case was batted out of court on the basis
that intelligence affairs were secret and should remain so. 'The only
place in the world where Khaled el Masri's allegations cannot be
discussed,' stated ACLU attorney Ben Wizner, 'is in a federal
courtroom.'

For el Masri, the continuous trail of rejections led to further issues.
In January 2007, he attacked a vocational training officer who was
teaching him to drive a truck. The officer, who had accused him of
missing classes, ended up in hospital. Four months later, attempting
to return an apparently faulty iPod to the shop from which he had
purchased it, he was refused a refund. Concluding that the lady behind
the counter was being disrespectful, he spat at her. Shortly afterwards,
he set fire to the shop, causing 500,000 euros worth of damage. He
was immediately picked up and sent into psychiatric care. According
to his lawyer Manfred Gnjidic, el Masri, who had as yet only received
superficial help regarding his traumatic experiences, had had a mental
breakdown. He received a suspended sentence for arson.

Further court rejections followed. El Masri became despondent. On
11 September 2009, he struck again, storming into the office of Neu-
Ulm's mayor to demand assistance with his case. He was ejected. Half
an hour later he returned, burst into the mayor's office and attacked
him with a chair. Again, he was arrested. Again it was argued that his
actions were the result of his inability to access justice. This time,
however, he was already on a suspended sentence. On 30 March 2010,
he was sentenced to two years in prison. Led out of court, el Masri was
heard to comment, 'Do whatever you want.'

To those involved in the rendition, el Masri's imprisonment was a
vindication, of sorts. Repeated outbursts were evidence of his violent
temperament. Society needed protection from men like this. That his

behaviour might have been the result of his treatment was irrelevant; the world was a safer place without Khaled el Masri on the streets.

Finally, The Egyptian was where he belonged.

Exposed to the media glare, Premier Executive Transport Services shut up shop. On 1 December 2004, the company hastily sold both of its rendition aircraft. Boeing Business Jet N313P was bought by Keeler and Tate LLC, based in Reno, Nevada. Only, the company wasn't really based in Reno, Nevada. According to an investigation by the European Parliament, Keeler and Tate was a 'CIA shell company . . . without premises, without a website, whose only property was the Boeing 737'. The plane's tail number was changed to N4476S.

But old habits die hard. Six weeks after its re-registration, N4476S was caught reliving the glory days in Mallorca. The Association of Aeronautical Photographers of Mallorca was on the case, snapping a series of photographs of the CIA plane. They were immediately posted on the Internet.

7

Friends in Low Places

*All who live in tyranny and hopelessness can know: the United
States will not ignore your oppression, or excuse your oppressors.
When you stand for your liberty, we will stand with you.*
                                    George W. Bush, January 2005

The truck, a khaki ZIL-131, was Russian. This was good: the Russians,
after all, knew a thing or two about industrial machinery. Crucially, they
understood the importance of weight: a heavy truck needed to be *heavy*.
The ZIL was. Nearly four and a half tons unloaded, this one – full of
armed dissidents – was considerably heavier. This also was good: if
you're planning on ramming your way in to a high-security prison,
weight is critical.

Moments before the truck crashed into the prison's isolator gates,
its occupants let out a cry. Witnesses heard a single word: '*Ozodlik!*'
('Freedom!') Government spokesmen would later argue that the raiders
had shouted something rather different: '*Allahu akbar!*'

The discrepancy between these two accounts, though important
later on, was irrelevant at the time: whatever the raiders shouted, at
twenty minutes past midnight on 13 May 2005, the driver gritted his
teeth, revved the engine and dropped the clutch. The vehicle surged
forward.

The ZIL's weight carried it into the gates, which resisted for a moment
before buckling and crashing open, admitting it into the prison

courtyard. The insurgents were inside. The biggest prison break in Uzbekistan's history was underway.

Three floors up in the main cell block, Sardor Azimov was trying to get to sleep. As usual, the prison lights had been turned off at 10 p.m., but it was a humid night and the businessman was having trouble dropping off. Cramped into a windowless cell with four other men and only a pomegranate-sized hole leading into the prison's main corridor for ventilation, he found the atmosphere stifling. The moment he heard the crash of a truck ramming the prison gates, he sat up in his bunk.

'I heard these very loud noises, then gunshots. I thought it might be the beginning of a war.'

Azimov's instinct was correct. According to some, it very nearly was.

Downstairs, in the prison's main corridor, the raiders worked fast, breaking into the administrative offices, forcing open the guards' safes and retrieving the cell keys. They then swept through the building, opening the cells and releasing the prisoners. Within an hour they had reached the third floor. Unable to see anything through their ventilation hole, Azimov and his cellmates listened intently as the units were breached one by one. When the men reached theirs, though, there was a problem. No key. They set to the door with crowbars, prising it from its hinges, flinging it aside and confronting the startled prisoners.

'You're free!' one of the raiders told Azimov. 'Get out!'

In the corridor inmates milled around listlessly, too shocked to react. Then someone suggested it might be a good idea to get moving and they were herded downstairs. Azimov stepped out into the night air and took his first breaths as a free man.

'I was very emotional, very excited. Everyone was. We'd never seen anything like this before.' As the prisoners wandered out of the compound into Eski-Osh Street, Azimov noticed two prison guards, tied up but otherwise unharmed. There was cheering, but also a sense of uncertainty. He turned to a friend.

'What are we supposed to do *now*?'

*   *   *

That night, as the prison break was getting underway, senior officers of the Eurasia Division of Human Rights Watch (HRW) were holding their annual strategy meeting in New York. It wasn't long before the discussion turned to Uzbekistan, where all present agreed the situation was not pretty. This in itself was nothing new. The republic, ruled – apparently in perpetuity – by the dictator Islam Karimov, ranked among the bottom five countries in the world for human rights, alongside some of the planet's most toxic pariah states: when it came to the routine violation of political and civil rights, Uzbekistan lay only slightly ahead of North Korea and Burma. On economic freedom, the country was 149th in the world, alongside Zimbabwe. Currently, 4,000 Uzbeks were incarcerated for political crimes.

Arbitrary detention, beating, rape, electric shock, fingernail extraction, suffocation: there was little President Karimov's Ministry of the Interior baulked at when it came to those it viewed as a political threat. Not long earlier, HRW officers had faced the unpleasant task of viewing the bodies of a pair of men, jailed for religious extremism, who had died after apparently provoking a fight in Jaslyk Prison. Asked why both corpses were covered in burns, the Uzbek authorities declared the men had been trying to convert other prisoners to Islam, and had had pots of tea thrown at them. The truth was more prosaic: they had been placed in vats of water by their interrogators and boiled alive.

It was the kind of barbarity that could happen only in Uzbekistan. Whenever the country came up in meetings, HRW staff sighed. 'Every year when our conversations about Uzbekistan started, there was a standard introduction,' says Sasha Petrov, the deputy director of HRW's Moscow office: 'The situation is bad and getting worse.'

This time the prognosis was unusually dire. Sources in Central Asia had warned Petrov that something was afoot. 'They basically said we are sure that something is going to happen,' he recalls. 'But they didn't give us any details about what it was.' Someone had an idea that there might be an uprising planned for the autumn, but the information was maddeningly incomplete. The tenor of the meeting, however, was clear. 'There's going to be a crisis in Central Asia,' the Uzbekistan officer told her colleagues. 'Something is going to blow.'

HRW staff were especially interested in a number of ongoing Uzbek cases. At the top of the list was a situation that had developed in the city of Andijan, 250 kilometres east of the capital Tashkent. Ten months earlier, a group of influential businessmen had been rounded up and arrested. Initially, charges had related to financial irregularities, but they gradually transmogrified into 'religious extremism' – a catch-all phrase that, under Karimov, could mean anything from being a member of al-Qaeda to generally annoying the President. The men were facing lengthy prison sentences. Some had been tortured. One of them was Sardor Azimov who was, even as the HRW meeting was taking place, being led away from his cell and into the Andijan night.

Azimov was one of Uzbekistan's bright young things. After leaving school in the early 1990s, he had gravitated towards entrepreneurship, bartering, buying and selling in the markets around Andijan. By 1997, he was one of the city's leading traders and was making regular trips abroad to source merchandise: shoes, clothing, office furniture, building materials, there was little Azimov couldn't buy, import, then deliver at a lower price than anyone else. Polite, well spoken and impeccably turned out, the young businessman created a good impression wherever he went. In post-independence Uzbekistan, he was a rarity: a man capable of inspiring – and maintaining – trust. In 1998, he acquired a handful of factories, hired a staff of thirty and moved into production himself. He then bought a spacious house and a new car for cash, got married and began to enjoy the fruits of his labour. He was twenty-two.

Doubtless, Sardor Azimov's success was due to his personal attributes, but another factor was at play. He wasn't working alone. In 1994, he had teamed up with a group of like-minded businessmen who had decided to revolutionize Andijan's economy. Working on a blueprint created by Akram Yuldashev, a local schoolteacher and mathematician, the group had formed a union dedicated to quality, trust and mutual co-operation. The idea was simple: businessmen would pool their resources to create the kinds of enterprises that would flourish. Instead of competing, they would co-operate.

'The main focus was on quality,' says Nodir Mahmudov, one of the group's founders. 'The old Soviet system was rubbish. We made products that people actually wanted. We were ready to make anything – but it had to be good.'

Shortly after the group's foundation, one of its founders set an example by donating a two-hectare plot in Andijan's Bogi Shamol district for communal use. Factories were built and the group began producing baked goods, sweets and furniture. Since quality consumer products were in short supply in Uzbekistan, the enterprises flourished.

'When we started, and started to be successful, other businessmen began to join us,' says Mahmudov. 'Construction people. Handicrafts people. Carpenters. Lots of people.'

Because state-owned banks were unreliable, union funds were kept privately. New business proposals were debated by the group's members. Once one was adopted, all would work together to develop it. There were no formal agreements between members. Everything was done on the basis of trust. The group had no name, but those who belonged called each other 'birodars' ('brothers').

Success came quickly. One of the main tenets of the group was that wages should be paid on time. Since they were not beholden to Uzbekistan's state banks, which often ran out of cash, this was easy to arrange. Quality goods led to greater demand, which led to greater production, which led to more quality goods. The money poured in and wages leapt. By the late 1990s, the union was paying its staff ten times the standard state salary. There were other perks, too. If employees got married, the company paid for the wedding and helped them to raise the cash for a flat.

'We never advertised for workers,' says Mahmudov. 'But our employees told all their relatives and their friends. More and more people started coming to work for us.'

The group then diversified. During their travels abroad, the businessmen discovered that successful enterprises took care of their employees – something that didn't happen in Uzbekistan.

'We understood that we had to look at the social problems in the lives of our employees, otherwise we might not be able to expand the company,' says Azimov.

The group set up a kindergarten, a series of summer camps and a petting zoo where children could learn to ride horses. It also built private doctors' and dentists' clinics and a hospital for staff and their families.

'We started building schools,' says Mahmudov. 'We taught them the construction business, how to drive, how to use a computer. We taught them how to speak English. Girls were taught how to bake and sew.'

News of the Andijan success story spread fast. Businessmen from other cities approached the group asking for advice and in 1995 the union opened branches in Kokand and Tashkent. By the end of the decade, the Government itself was a customer. New colleges and university buildings were constructed by the group. Furniture for bureaucrats' offices came from Andijan. When senior civil servants held parties, the Andijanis would provide the catering.

'They saw that what we were making was good-quality stuff,' says Mahmudov. 'So they started ordering from us.'

It was going so well, it had to go wrong.

In 2003, members of the group were summoned to the Office of Entrepreneurs in Tashkent. Ostensibly, the meeting was an opportunity for the Government to ask the group its views about tax reforms.

Actually, members were grilled about what they were up to. Where was all this money coming from? At this point, the Andijan union over-played its hand.

'We told them all about what we were doing, the social and educational reforms,' says Azimov. 'I explained about the business end of the union, how we had opened a private hospital and a kindergarten and a horse-riding club for kids.' Mahmudov offered the government representatives a proposal. 'We offered our system to the President: if we used this system in Uzbekistan, there would have been no unemployment.'

Whether it was the grandiose nature of these claims or the fact that the group's leaders had recently refused to pay a substantial bribe to the Andijan City Prosecutor's Office is unclear. Either way the Uzbek regime, startled by the group's influence, decided to step in. In a country with widespread discontent, extreme poverty and no avenues for legit-imate political opposition, the union represented a threat. Shortly after the conference, Uzbek authorities demanded the group's business plans and asked where they had come from. The union's leaders said they had been drawn up by Akram Yuldashev. Since Yuldashev was serving time for political dissent and religious extremism, this was all they needed. It was time to take down the Andijan operation.

Over the course of June and July 2004, twenty-three of the most prominent businessmen, including Azimov, were arrested and taken to the Andijan headquarters of the Uzbek secret police (SNB). Initially, the men were told they were under investigation for tax evasion and financial documents were demanded. When the seized paperwork failed to reveal any indictable offences, the SNB changed tack. The busi-nessmen had affiliations with Akram Yuldashev, the jailed extremist and possible terrorist. Weren't they, too, religious extremists? Weren't they, perhaps, terrorists?

When Azimov denied all knowledge of religious or political dissi-dence and insisted that Yuldashev himself was innocent, too, the SNB decided to push harder. He was beaten repeatedly, first with fists, then police batons. His fingers were splayed and put into a vice-like machine that slowly spread them apart and squeezed them. His interrogators then informed him that, if he failed to confess, his wife would be raped. Other union members were given the same ultimatum. Handed a piece of paper with a pre-written confession, Azimov signed without even reading it. They all did.

That Karimov and his henchmen could behave this way was no great surprise to Human Rights Watch. The Uzbek president had been doing this kind of thing, to a greater or lesser extent, since assuming power in 1990.

More interesting was the fact that Karimov was a strategic partner of the United States. He was a special friend.

The mechanics of the US–Uzbek special relationship shed an interesting light on the White House's prosecution of the War on Terror. A shame, then, that so few US officials involved are prepared to go on the record about it. Even those that have retired are generally unwilling to be named, or to discuss it. Presumably this reticence is a result of the fact that, almost from its outset, the relationship was a disaster. Undoubtedly, it ended in tragedy.

Soon after the United States decided to invade Afghanistan in September 2001, planners had faced the age-old problem: how to get there?

'This region is probably the most remote, landlocked area in the world,' explains a senior Pentagon official involved with the planning process. 'So the real strategic challenge was: how do we get air power into Afghanistan to wage modern war?'

The gravity of the situation was not lost on US policymakers, who were shocked to discover just how hard this undertaking might be.

'You look at the map, you look at Afghanistan and where it is,' Condoleezza Rice later told the PBS channel of these initial discussions. 'I think the colour kind of drained from everybody's faces.'

Traditionally, the United States launched attacks from aircraft carriers, but Afghanistan was so far inland that fleets in either the Indian Ocean or the Arabian Sea were too far away. The Pentagon needed access to one of its target's neighbours. Of the six countries that bordered Afghanistan, three – China, Iran and Pakistan – either were not asked or refused to allow the United States to launch attacks from their territory. This left Tajikistan, Turkmenistan and Uzbekistan.

By far the best option was Uzbekistan: the route between the two countries was not unduly mountainous and it was nicely situated above the north-west corner of Afghanistan, home of the Northern Alliance, the Taliban's arch-enemies and thus key allies of the United States. It was perfect.

Operationally, Uzbekistan was important for another reason, too. Before aerial bombing of Afghanistan could begin, Pentagon officials insisted that a Combat Search and Rescue (CSAR) facility had to be available: if a pilot was shot down on a bombing run, without CSAR he would be stranded behind enemy lines. The White House agreed: US personnel in Taliban custody could put paid to the entire operation. Quite apart from the tactical issues, Americans in Islamic hands had crippled the Carter Administration in the 1980s. The political risk was just too high. Since CSAR was conducted by helicopter, it had to be based in a county near the theatre of operations. That meant Uzbekistan.

'Very swiftly after [9/11] it was very clear that Uzbekistan was a very important country,' says David Merkel, a Central Asia specialist and National Security Council member at the time. 'It was critical to have a military presence and have overflight rights.'

Military planners agreed. 'Uzbekistan,' General Tommy Franks informed CENTCOM on 12 September, 'will be vital to the operation.' The country's strategic importance was hard to overstate. According to one Pentagon negotiator involved, Uzbekistan was 'the geographical and political keystone'.

CSAR from Uzbekistan now became the enabling factor for the invasion of Afghanistan. Before a deal was hammered out, little could happen.

'I don't know what H-Hour was in the minds of the planners in terms of when they wanted to conduct airstrikes against the Taliban,' admits Colonel Jon Chicky, CENTCOM'S Uzbek Country Officer at the time, 'but it was important to have these guys on the ground, to support the bombing operations once they began.'

State Department and Pentagon officials laboured around the clock to facilitate access to the country.

'Travel well into the night, meetings sometimes at midnight with [President] Karimov,' recalls a senior Pentagon planner. 'It was a bit chaotic.'

The United States had a number of effective bargaining chips to offer Uzbekistan in return for a base. At the top of the list was security. The Uzbek leader was paranoid about the threat of Islamic extremism and had been banging the drum about al-Qaeda ever since one of the organization's offshoots, the Islamic Movement of Uzbekistan (IMU), had attempted to assassinate him in 1999. At the time, he had requested assistance from the United States, which had suggested a joint operation.

Still smarting from its inability to deploy AC-130 SPECTRE gunships to Afghanistan to kill Bin Laden outright, the CIA had struck a secret deal with Karimov with a view to snatching the al-Qaeda leader instead. Uzbek special forces were recruited for a cross-border raid, then equipped and trained by the United States. When it had become clear a year later that the operation was likely to be a non-starter,[13] the United States had

---

[13] In the case of the Uzbek snatch team, 'the ethnicity was wrong, the language was wrong. They would stick out like a blonde Swedish American in Kandahar', according to one CIA officer involved. Further teams were recruited through Pakistan's Inter-Services Intelligence. Problems here were even worse: 'The Pakistanis took the training and the money as they should from the suckers, and they had no intention of doing anything.'

established an Uzbek base for Predator unmanned aerial vehicles instead, with a view to deploying them over Afghanistan. It was these flights that had led to real-time images of Bin Laden in September 2000; it was their cessation two months later that would lead to the rebirth of the CIA's rendition programme.

Admittedly, these plans had all come to nothing, but post-9/11 the signs looked good for a new agreement: there was already a relationship, and Karimov was as concerned about al-Qaeda as the White House.

'The US and Uzbek positions on this were similar,' explains the senior Pentagon official. 'We both had a terrorism problem.'

Uzbekistan's President Islam Karimov had a couple of other good reasons to strike a deal with the United States. Ever since the demise of the Soviet Union, Russia had been breathing down his neck. A US treaty would send a powerful signal to Moscow that he was his own man. It would also give him political leverage with his neighbours: after all, no one messes with allies of the United States. Then there was the issue of money. If the Americans really needed a base in Central Asia, presumably they were willing to pay for it. Security assurances, political credibility, trade deals, economic assistance – there was a lot to gain here.

United States officials were not blind to the fringe benefits of an agreement, either. Central Asia was home to the largest untapped fossil fuel reserves on the planet, worth trillions of dollars. True, most of the actual oil was in Kazakhstan, next door to Uzbekistan, but a deal with any Central Asian nation was a step in the right direction. If nothing else, it would give the United States a chance to stymie Russia's monopoly of the region's deposits.

On top of this came the issue of Russia itself. Notoriously cagey about US troops positioned near its borders, here was an opportunity to plant a US base right in Russia's backyard. Best of all, in the light of the 9/11 attacks, the Kremlin was powerless to intervene.

*   *   *

Almost immediately after 9/11, it became clear that a deal between the two countries would be struck. But under what terms? By 15 September the CIA was informing President Bush that Uzbekistan was to be 'the jumping-off point' for the Afghan campaign. The obvious choice for a US base was an old airstrip near the border that the Soviets had used during their invasion of Afghanistan in 1979. The place looked as if it had been deserted ever since: the runways were pitted, the land contaminated with asbestos and the hangars full of Soviet-era MiG aircraft. Situated between the towns of Karshi and Khanabad, an amalgamation of the two names led to a US military acronym becoming the base's unofficial moniker: K2.

Not everyone in the White House was enthusiastic about this new friendship with President Karimov. For a start, he was clearly out to drive a hard bargain. Among other demands, he wanted to join NATO (a request that even the United States was powerless to grant). He wanted a mutual defence pact. He wanted economic support. Above all, he wanted some sort of indication that the United States would not achieve its military goals in Afghanistan and then abandon him, either to face an angry Russia, or fleeing Taliban fighters hell-bent on revenge.

'They weren't very easy to deal with, I'll put it that way,' comments one negotiator. 'It got into, quite frankly, "What am *I* going to get out of this?" They wanted stuff from us.'

Others pointed out the risks of making a deal with a man like Karimov. At a meeting on 15 September, Director of Central Intelligence George Tenet not only presented the President with the draft Memorandum of Notification, making extraordinary rendition a reality, he also warned that intelligence and basing exchanges with a few of the countries the US was currently negotiating with were likely to raise awkward issues. Some of these guys had reputations for terrible human rights abuses. They weren't, Tenet warned the President, the kinds of people you found yourself sitting next to in church on Sunday.

State Department officials were also wary. 'You need to be exactly clear what it is you are asking of the Uzbeks,' Secretary of State Colin Powell told the National Security Council on 24 September: 'the bases, the number of people, what are they going to do, how long they are going to be there'.

Condoleezza Rice agreed: wasn't there a risk that Karimov might reclassify every internal political opponent a terrorist and persecute them all in the name of the War on Terror? 'We have to be sure,' she said, 'we know what we're buying into.'

Powell and Rice's warnings would later prove prescient, but Vice-President Dick Cheney had little time for their hand-wringing. 'We need to get al-Qaeda,' he explained. 'Before they get us.'

By 27 September, the White House was impatient with Karimov's demands. US men and materiel were backing up at airstrips around the world, waiting to get into Uzbekistan. In Spain, Sicily and Turkey, military aircraft clogged the runways, unable to proceed any further. They wanted CSAR. They wanted to go.

'Our delegation is not senior enough,' Cheney concluded. 'We need a swing through the area with a high-level person . . . We need a presidential call to Karimov. We need someone to go in and settle it.'

Secretary of Defense Donald Rumsfeld did the deed, and on 3 October Uzbekistan gave CSAR permission with a view to operations commencing the moment the correct equipment had arrived at K2.

Four days after the unofficial go-ahead, a Status of Forces Agreement was signed between the United States and Uzbekistan. Officially, Karimov was allowing the United States to deploy CSAR from his territory. Unofficially, K2 was to be the hub of the entire operation: Special Forces planned the Afghan infiltration there and the first CIA officers and troops into the country all flew through the base to launch the invasion. Later arrivals would include three AC-130 SPECTRE gunships from the 16th Special Operations Squadron: K2 would be the 'undisclosed location' from which the crews would launch their attacks, including the one on the wedding party in Deh Rawood.

Militarily, the deal was unprecedented. For the first time, the United States was inserting troops within the borders of the former Soviet Union. Politically, the deal was equally exciting: after 200 years of Great Gamesmanship, Central Asia's crown jewels had just dropped into America's lap. Here was an opportunity to reshape the strategic balance of the entire region. One hour after the deal was done, the United States started bombing Afghanistan.

'As soon as the agreement was signed,' says Colonel Jon Chicky, 'the planes launched.'

After eight months of interrogation, on 11 February 2005, the twenty-three businessmen were removed from Andijan Prison via a tunnel, herded into police cars, then driven to Altinkus District courthouse, where they were displayed in iron cages.

Over the next four months, they were charged with attacks against the constitutional order, organizing a criminal conspiracy and funding a criminal group. In short, the Government's case was that the men belonged to an extremist political sect named after its founder, the jailed dissident Akram Yuldashev: *Akramiya*.

At the end of each day, the 'Akramists' were sent back to jail, where they were incarcerated separately. Every three weeks, they were rotated to new cells to prevent them from making friends and contaminating the jail's population with their revolutionary extremism.

For a judicial system as rampantly corrupt as Uzbekistan's, finding the twenty-three businessmen guilty presented no real challenge. Not so easy, however, was dealing with the fallout. The men were the city's main employers and their assets had been seized by the Government; thousands of labourers had either been laid off or stood to be laid off in the event of their conviction.

They had also dedicated a great deal of time and resources to building hospitals, surgeries and schools. They were extremely popular. The moment the trial began, their supporters showed up to picket the courthouse. As the trial progressed and numbers swelled it became clear to the authorities that guilty verdicts might be counterproductive: the point of the exercise was to stop these men, not make martyrs of them.

When numbers reached the thousands, the SNB realized it had painted itself into a corner. The lead interrogator summoned three of the businessmen and offered them a deal.

'He told us that we should pay $100,000 per person, and then he would release us,' says Sardor Azimov. The twenty-three were allowed to confer briefly to consider the offer and the three men reported back. 'They said to him, "OK, if you are going to demand this kind of money, you'll have to release one of us, without conditions, to go and get it." We agreed to pay.'

Not so fast, said the SNB. No one was going free. The twenty-three were told that, if they couldn't get the $2,300,000 in one go, they should cobble together as much as they could and pay in instalments. At this point, the businessmen realized they were being played and refused to pay a penny. The interrogator flew into a rage. He showed Azimov the telephone in his office.

'I could take this phone and smash it into a million pieces, so no one could ever use it again,' he told the young man. 'That's what I'm going to do to you. I'm going to pull the whole thing apart so badly that no one will ever be able to put it back together.'

On 11 May 2005, the final day of the trial, more than 2,000 protestors showed up outside the court to stand all day, silently awaiting the verdict. Human Rights Watch had been correct. Something was about to blow.

It was a shame, really. The whole thing had started so well.

Although the US–Uzbek relationship was never going to be a simple affair, initially all looked promising. America hiked aid payments and military assistance to Uzbekistan by a factor of three, and a steady stream of military aircraft ferried materiel and manpower into and out of K2. Far from being the 'quagmire' predicted by the Press, Afghanistan toppled almost immediately. By mid-November 2001, coalition troops had taken Kabul. Behind the operation lay the critical re-supply base, Karshi Khanabad.

The United States–Uzbek Status of Forces Agreement had been a stopgap designed to get the United States into Afghanistan as fast as possible. Once the liberation was underway, it was clear something more formal was needed. To this end, meetings continued through late 2001 and into 2002 to hammer out what, exactly, both sides could expect from the K2 deal.

US delegates approached these meetings with a degree of trepidation: while the base was crucial to the Afghan effort, Karimov's atrocious human rights record rang warning bells. US administrators held no illusions about the republic's president, for whom it was clear that 'preserving national security' and 'staying in power' amounted to the same thing. The White House didn't want to get too close to Uzbekistan. Accessing an airbase in Central Asia was one thing; propping up a corrupt dictatorship was another. The War on Terror, after all, was supposed to be about spreading freedom.

Meetings started on an unexpected note when the Uzbek delegation presented US officials with a draft agreement they had concocted themselves. At the top of the draft was a list of human rights and democratization reforms. It was time, negotiators were told, for Uzbekistan to progress into the twenty-first century.

The Americans almost fell off their chairs. Could it be that Karimov actually wanted to reform his regime? It appeared so. In January 2002, a Declaration on Strategic Partnership and Co-operation (known as the 'Framework Agreement'), using the Uzbeks' draft as a blueprint, was signed by both countries in Tashkent.

'There was optimism, not just at [the] State [Department], but with all of us,' recalls a senior Pentagon official involved. 'It was seen as a good opportunity. And a good sort of indication, a positive indication on the Uzbek side that they might be interested in democratizing.'

To counter the risk of the Uzbek deal going wrong, the United States settled on a dual strategy: funding and supporting Karimov, while at the same time gently encouraging him to democratize. The airbase and the money became levers with which to exert pressure on the country.

'The base gave us some equity,' says Colonel Jon Chicky. 'There was a belief, at least from the military perspective, that the base gave us an opening for the diplomatic side to do things with the Government.'

The State Department was equally enthusiastic: with a little encouragement, Karimov might be guided in the right direction, and the apparent contradiction between strategic interests (access to K2) and democratic interests (human rights) could be resolved. The carrot was money; the stick, the threat of its withdrawal. If the policy worked, the United States–Uzbekistan deal might even pave the way for further relations around the world, and become a template for handling difficult Third World dictators in the future.

Already, however, there were signs that things were going awry. On 27 January 2002, while his negotiators were assuring US delegates they wanted positive reform, Karimov extended the presidential terms of office, allowing himself to remain in power – potentially until the end of his life. Apparently, 9/11 had changed everything.

'At a certain stage of historic change, you need a strong will and a certain figure,' he said, 'and you have to use some authoritarian methods at times.'

US officials, unconvinced by his reasoning, comforted themselves that change was coming; maybe not fast, but the country was at last headed in the right direction. Two days later, Elizabeth Jones, US Assistant Secretary of State for Eurasian and European Affairs, appeared on Uzbek television wishing the President a happy birthday and inviting him to the White House to meet George W. Bush.

Human rights monitors were less credulous. No matter what the United States offered Uzbekistan, they felt, Karimov was unlikely to change his spots. This was, after all, the man who had told the Uzbek parliament that Islamic extremists needed 'to be shot in the forehead', then offered to do it himself.

'I'm prepared,' he announced a year later, 'to rip off the heads of two hundred people in order to save the Republic.'

Arrests of political dissidents continued unabated; prison conditions were still brutal; torture was still endemic; the Press still censored. The difference was that, after signing a deal with the United States, Uzbekistan now had a powerful argument with which to justify its repression.

'9/11 changed the picture,' explains Alison Gill, Human Rights Watch's Tashkent officer. 'The Uzbeks were delighted to continue clamping down on people and cloak it in the language of the global War on Terror . . . It was a field day for them.'

It wasn't only the Uzbeks. All around the world countries involved in counter-insurgency operations, civil wars or repression of their own populations leapt on the War-on-Terror bandwagon. Dissidents, insurgent groups, religious groups, asylum seekers, activists – all kinds of awkward types were labelled 'terrorists' and targeted pre-emptively. Russian atrocities in Chechnya, Chinese persecution in Tibet and torture throughout the Middle East now became legitimate parts of the War on Terror.

In December 2001, Egyptian President Hosni Mubarak cited US policies as proving 'that we were right from the beginning in using all means [to combat terrorism]'.

Even Robert Mugabe had a go. 'We agree with President Bush that anyone who in any way finances, harbours or defends terrorists is himself a terrorist,' Zimbabwe's Information Minister Jonathan Moyo told the Press in late 2001. 'We, too, will not make any difference between terrorists and their friends and supporters.'

In the face of this widespread opportunism, Uzbekistan became a poster case for the US administration.

'How do you balance the immediate operational security imperative of waging war against al-Qaeda against the longer-term interest in protecting human rights?' asks Tom Malinowski, Human Rights Watch's leading Washington DC advocate. 'We identified Uzbekistan as *the* test case.'

Most human rights advocates understood that the United States was going to cut deals with unsavoury regimes in the post-9/11 environment. They also understood that leverage gained by co-operation rather than criticism might turn out be a force for good. They just considered it unlikely. 'I thought it was going to be very, very difficult, but that it was worth trying,' comments Malinowski. 'And we also had to work with what we had.'

To the astonishment of the staff of Human Rights Watch, 'working with what we had' in Uzbekistan paid dividends almost immediately. Karimov readmitted the Red Cross, relaxed some of the laws regarding opposition parties, dropped government censorship and, most surprisingly, in June 2002, publicly invited the UN's Special Rapporteur on Torture, Theo van Boven, to assess the state of the criminal justice system. There was a ray of hope.

Uzbekistan milked van Boven's visit for all it was worth, both prior to and during the trip in November and December 2002. When the report was released two months later, however, the President was appalled. The Special Rapporteur noted 'copious' reports of beatings, suffocation with plastic bags and gas masks, deliberate infection of inmates with contagious diseases, the insertion of needles under fingernails, rape, electric shock, false self-incriminatory confessions, the planting of evidence, arbitrary detention, withholding of the right to legal counsel, lack of respect for the presumption of innocence, rampant corruption in the judiciary and the absence of habeas corpus. Torture, he noted, was systematic ('habitual, widespread and deliberate'), indiscriminate, pervasive and persistent. He also implied that it was sanctioned at the highest levels.

The Uzbeks were horrified: to their minds, they were democratizing rather well. Inviting the Special Rapporteur was unprecedented in Central Asia. Now they were being publicly vilified. The Framework Agreement with the United States had contained all sorts of flowery language about human rights. No one expected to do it all at once.

'A lot of the stuff in there [Karimov] didn't expect to be held to,' says a very senior State Department officer stationed in Tashkent. 'Implicit in the K2 agreement was that the US would sort of give them a bye on human rights.'

The US would. But only to an extent.

After picketing the Andijan courthouse for the best part of four months, friends and colleagues of the twenty-three businessmen showed up on the day of the verdict expecting the worst. Nodir Mahmudov was summoned by the SNB and warned that there was to be no trouble. To placate him, officials suggested there was a real chance that some of the charges levelled against the businessmen were to be dropped and that the prosecutor was not going to ask for the maximum sentences. A couple of defendants might even be freed. But this was dependent on the trial ending peacefully.

'Just stay quiet,' the SNB men told him. 'Don't try anything.'

When it was announced that the verdict would be delayed by a day, the crowd outside the courthouse became restless. SNB officers arrested a handful of protestors and carted them away, further inflaming the situation. The next day, 12 May, saw the verdict delayed again, this time indefinitely. There were rumours of further arrests. Mahmudov decided that enough was enough; after a brief conference with the relatives of the twenty-three and other union leaders, a rally was planned for the following day, 13 May.

It was too little, too late. That night, at around 11.35 p.m., a group of the union's associates launched attacks on police stations, military barracks and government buildings around the city. Weapons, ammunition and hand grenades were seized, along with a number of hostages and a truck: a heavy, Russian-made ZIL-131. An hour after the initial assault, the weapons, the ammunition – and the truck – were used to attack the jail. The goal was the liberation of the twenty-three businessmen, but, in the process of locating them, more than 500 criminals were released. Some of them were handed guns.

Outside Andijan Prison, leaders of the jailbreak spread the word among the newly released prisoners that they were about to march to the city centre, where there would be a demonstration. The plan was to gather in front of the regional administrative building, the Hokimiyat in Babur Square, demand their rights and an opportunity to air their grievances with President Karimov. Those who wanted to come along were more than welcome; others could simply go home.

'There were loads of people in the street,' recalls Sardor Azimov. 'Some went in different directions, but I joined up with the majority and we all headed off to the Hokimiyat.'

As they walked, escapees were lent mobile phones on which to call relatives and friends, partly to let them know what had happened, but mainly to tell them to come to Babur Square immediately to join the demonstration.

As dawn broke on 13 May, Andijanis woke to the news that something momentous was going on in Babur Square. Children skived off school, adults ducked work; everyone went to take a look. By 7 a.m., hundreds of the city's inhabitants were arriving. Protest leaders rigged up a PA system next to the Babur monument so that their demands could be heard. Drinks vendors and other street traders showed up. But they weren't the only ones interested in the proceedings.

President Karimov was woken at 1.45 a.m. with different news: Andijan was under attack. He and his interior minister Zokir Almatov immediately ordered troops on to the streets. Karimov then flew to Andijan where, from 7.30 onwards, he managed the crisis. As troops from the Interior Ministry flooded the area, the two groups, protestors and the Government, came to blows.

According to witnesses, at around 8 a.m., a military vehicle approached Babur Square, stopped near the Hokimiyat, and two uniformed men climbed out. They raised their rifles and fired directly into the crowd, killing a young boy. Enraged, the protestors rushed the car, seized the men, beat them, then took them into the Hokimiyat as hostages. Other officials around the square received the same treatment.

This cycle, a military drive-past, a shooting and retaliation by the crowd, became common throughout the day. Inside the Hokimiyat, hostage numbers rose; outside the number of casualties and protestors went up, too. Streets around the city square were blocked to impede the passage of military vehicles.

Intermittently, the Government attempted to negotiate with the protestors by mobile phone. Interior Minister Almatov, who handled the talks, asked what the group wanted and was told that the release of political detainees, including Akram Yuldashev, was imperative. After conferring with the President, Almatov announced that this was impossible. The best he could offer was safe passage for the protestors across the border into neighbouring Kyrgyzstan. He wanted his hostages back. He wanted the protestors out of the country. That was the bottom line.

Meanwhile, in the square, angry Andijanis queued to use the microphone to address the swelling crowds.

'People started joining us, and started talking about their problems,' recalls Nodir Mahmudov, one of the first to address the rally. 'Pensioners came and said, "I don't get my pension on time"; others started telling about their jobs and their financial problems.'

Two hostages – the state prosecutor and the chief of the tax inspection authority – were thrust in front of the microphone to explain, presumably under duress, that they knew the twenty-three businessmen were innocent all along, but they had been pressured to convict them. The crowd threw stones.

The protest in Babur Square, originally planned to air views about the twenty-three businessmen, was becoming something rather bigger.

Among the crowd, it was rumoured the President was coming to hear Andijanis' concerns, that Karimov would make things right. Every now and again a helicopter would circle overhead, reigniting the rumours: the President was on his way! As the excitement mounted, few protestors realized that government troops were sealing off streets around the square. A handful who attempted to leave were turned back by Armoured Personnel Carriers, and word spread slowly that the crowd might be trapped. By 4 p.m., all access to Babur Square was effectively shut off. Speakers at the microphone warned protestors not to panic, and to refrain from anything that might provoke a government show of force.

'Do not spill any blood! These soldiers are your brothers!' one warned. 'They will not shoot.'

The confidence that nothing bad would happen was echoed by a document written by one of the twenty-three businessmen and circulated through the crowd.

'Dear Andijanis!' it said. 'If we stick together, they will not do anything bad to us.'

But they would.

The UN Special Rapporteur on Torture's report was not the first inkling the Uzbek president had that his relationship with the United States was on the slide. As early as March 2002, the US State Department's Office of Democracy, Human Rights and Labor (DRL), had warned that Uzbekistan was exploiting its role in the War on Terror to justify internal repression. Voices were raised in Congress as politicians began asking why, exactly, the United States was bankrolling a dictatorship that arrested, tortured, incarcerated and boiled alive its citizens.

Although Karimov visited the United States in March that year and received assurances from President Bush that 'we are not going to teach you' about democratization, in reality things were turning out differently.

Much of the pressure coming to bear on the Uzbek administration was the result of adroit lobbying by Human Rights Watch. The way the organization saw it, buddying up with dictators in Central Asia was not a productive way to wage the War on Terror. Ignoring human rights abuses for the sake of political expediency was a mistake the United States had been making in the Middle East for decades. It had led to the rise of al-Qaeda in the first place.

Potentially, the situation was even worse in Uzbekistan. Whatever foreign NGOs might have thought about Karimov's repressive techniques, the republic was facing a very real threat from extremist terrorist organizations, at the head of which were the Islamic Movement of Uzbekistan (IMU) and al-Qaeda itself.

These threats were not imagined. The goal of the organizations was to bring down the Government and establish an Islamic caliphate. Multiple bombings in Tashkent in 1999 had proved that the IMU could hit hard, accurately and with lethal force.

'They did a pretty good job, they were pretty professional about it,' recalls a senior State Department official stationed in the capital at the time. 'It's not easy to blow up five or six bombs within five minutes of each other in separate parts of town. That was serious.'

In their more melodramatic moments, British and American politicians liked to characterize the al-Qaeda threat as 'existential', but the existence of America or Britain was never really threatened in the way Uzbekistan's was.

'It was an existential threat to the Uzbekistan that we knew about,' says the official. 'It sure as hell was an existential threat to Mr Karimov!'

To US administrators there was a greater danger. If the IMU or al-Qaeda succeeded in attacking Uzbekistan with sufficient force, it might spark a civil uprising that could topple the Government. Once that happened, the country was likely to explode into violence. Another failed state in Central Asia had the potential to be catastrophic: now Russia had been elbowed out of the way in Uzbekistan, the United States might be expected to step in to maintain security – but the US military was already busy in Afghanistan, and was gearing up for Iraq. Worse, a major collapse of state power in Central Asia had the potential to spread across borders. If Uzbekistan went, it might take its neighbours with it. An epidemic of failed states in Central Asia could create havoc. That was how wars started.

For all these reasons, it was crucial that Islam Karimov kept a lid on Islamist extremism in his country. The problem was, the way he was going about it – arresting, torturing and incarcerating innocent Muslims – was likely to achieve the exact opposite. Repressing legitimate forms of political dissent paved the way for extremist organizations such as the IMU and al-Qaeda to fill the void.

'Very few cases that I monitored closely showed any real signs of actually being serious extremists,' recalls Alison Gill. 'There are extremists in Uzbekistan, make no mistake, but mostly the people I saw being accused actually had very little connection.'

A case in point was the treatment being meted out to the twenty-three Andijan businessmen – all supposedly members of the phantom extremist group Akramiya (an organization so mysterious that no one, including the businessmen themselves, had ever heard of it).[14] Human rights monitors worried that by arresting and torturing innocent Muslims Karimov was creating the very conditions he was attempting to avoid. US Senate advisers agreed. According to one, the situation in Uzbekistan, and especially Andijan, provided 'textbook conditions for the growth of radical Islam'.

---

[14] Debates about the true nature of Akramiya rage to this day. 'So far as we can tell,' said John G. Fox, Director of the US State Department's Office of Caucasus and Central Asian Affairs, 'the Akramiya group is neither extremist nor terrorist.' Professor Frederick Starr, Chairman of the Central Asia-Caucasus Institute and Silk Road Studies Programme at Johns Hopkins University is less charitable. To him, the group typified the kind of racketeering operation that flourished in Uzbekistan in the 1990s – which did, in some cases, lead to political and religious extremism. As he observed in 2006, 'It's not the Rotary Club of Andijan.'

The Uzbek administration didn't see it that way. Karimov and his ministers were appalled that the United States, with whom they had just signed a special treaty and to whom they had leased, at some political cost, an airbase, was now dumping all over them. This was not at all what they had had in mind when they had signed up to the global War on Terror.

By mid-2003, the Red Cross had pulled out of the country and the World Bank was warning that Uzbekistan needed to change its ways if it wanted more loans. News of prisoner abuses was all over the international press and the UN's Special Rapporteur on Torture was making President Karimov look like a crook. Even the State Department, with whom Uzbekistan had negotiated the basing agreement, seemed hellbent on kicking the country from pillar to post.

As if the United States had any right to lecture Karimov about human rights! Since 9/11, Karimov had allowed his country to become a hub for CIA rendition operations – apparently so that the United States could do the very same things he was currently being castigated for. To the Uzbek president, the scale of the hypocrisy was staggering. Money was coming in, sure, but not much, and probably not enough to justify prolonging the deal much longer. The relationship was beginning to fray.

Officials involved in the US–Uzbek relationship place much of the blame for what happened next at the feet of an old foe: Russia. Deeply suspicious of US motives, the Kremlin had no intention of allowing its arch enemy – or her oil-hungry friends – to remain in the region for long. The only reason Vladimir Putin had permitted the Americans into Central Asia in the first place was that he had been powerless to stop them. He wanted US troops gone.

To this end, Russian officials concocted a disinformation plan designed to sow the seeds of discontent between the Americans and their hosts. The United States, Central Asia's leaders were informed, was not telling the truth about its motives. It wasn't out to fight terrorism, and it certainly wasn't out to help anyone 'democratize'. What it wanted was oil. And the simplest way to get it was to replace Central Asia's established rulers with US-friendly puppets. The CIA, as usual, was up to no good.

When Central Asian nations fell to a series of 'coloured revolutions' shortly after the US invasion of Afghanistan, Russia's predictions appeared to be coming true. In 2003, it was Georgia; the following year, Ukraine; the next, Kyrgyzstan. It was no coincidence – the Russians told anyone willing to listen – that these revolutions had taken place shortly after the United States had arrived. This was the way the US machine worked: just a little push from the CIA, and these revolutions would spread across borders like a plague. If America was willing to invade even Iraq for its oil, no one was safe.

The technique could have been tailor-made for the already suspicious Islam Karimov. Shortly after his overthrow, US intelligence got wind of a conversation between Georgia's ex-leader Eduard Shevardnadze and the Uzbek president. The pair discussed what had happened, and Shevardnadze warned his friend to be cautious of American promises – especially when the White House started harping on about 'human rights' and 'democratization'.

As if on cue, while the Russian poison was doing its work, George W. Bush was re-elected. He immediately talked up human rights and democratization.

'When you stand for your liberty,' Bush told the citizens of oppressed nations in the course of his second inaugural address, 'we will stand with you . . . In the long run, there is no justice without freedom and there can be no human rights without human liberty.'

For Karimov, the President's speech was a wake-up call. The Uzbek president fancied himself canny enough to know that, when George W. Bush said 'democratization', he meant 'regime change'.

*　　*　　*

Ironically, Bush's second inaugural address torpedoed the special relationship inside the United States, too. Seasoned State Department officers were appalled at the emphasis on spreading democracy (was this a policy or a metaphor?). Others were listening closely. Democracy and freedom were on the march: the President had said so. This cast the agreement between the United States and Uzbekistan in a different light. All of a sudden, certain branches of the Executive became immensely interested in human rights issues. Of course, if human rights was the topic, they need look no further than Uzbekistan.

According to the terms of the US–Uzbek Framework Agreement, the United States would offer financial assistance to Uzbekistan, which, in turn, would undertake meaningful political reforms. The United States was offering financial assistance, but the Uzbek regime was stalling on the reforms.

'[Karimov] had signed a declaration,' says Tom Malinowski, Human Rights Watch's DC advocate, 'and it had very, very strong human rights commitments. I saw that, and I thought, "Aha! This is my hook."'

To Malinowski, Karimov was not honouring his part of the bargain. Someone should be told. That someone was Patrick Leahy, chairman of the Senate sub-committee responsible for approving foreign spending. Malinowski took the text of the agreement to Leahy, filled him in on the background and suggested that Uzbekistan be held to its part of the bargain.

'It's hard to argue against holding a country to the promises it has made to the US government,' Malinowski says today.

Leahy agreed. In February 2003, Congress passed a motion stating that, for Uzbekistan to receive US aid, Secretary of State Colin Powell had to certify the country was making substantial progress on human rights. That summer – to much scoffing – he did just that. Human Rights Watch ramped up its lobbying, contacting leading congressmen and suggesting that dealing with the administration was likely to prove politically embarrassing and that what was going on in Central Asia was flat wrong.

'We're not the kind of country that should be in any way associated with people that boil people alive,' says Malinowksi.

It was hard to disagree with this statement, so the following year, when the time came to decide whether to pay Uzbekistan its money or not, it was much harder to get away with simply saying the country was doing a great job: partly thanks to Human Rights Watch, everyone knew that it wasn't.

In Senate hearings on the subject, experts disagreed over the best course of action. If the United States stood up for democracy and human rights, it would doubtless lose its new-found friendship with Central Asia – and its airbase. On the other hand, if it stood by Karimov and K2, where did that leave the President's promises about human rights? What was the point of fighting a War on Terror if your own allies were busy boiling people alive?

The White House now found itself in a fix. Having bound itself to a dual strategy – democratization in Uzbekistan and access to K2 – it had to decide which was the most important. The Pentagon and the regional bureaux of the State Department argued that keeping the base was crucial and that advances on human rights in Uzbekistan, slower than hoped for but apparently significant, justified continued payments to Karimov. The State Department's functional bureaux, meanwhile, especially the Bureau of Human Rights and Labor, held that Karimov's 'reforms' were a sham to keep the United States off its back, and that nothing was being achieved at all. No more money should be passed to the republic.

The result was an irreconcilable split. 'For us, at the DoD [Department of Defense], the most important thing was to maintain a relationship with a country that was geo-strategically important,' recalls Colonel Jon Chicky. 'Our commanders in CENTCOM kept telling us how important the base was. So for our purposes we needed to keep the base open and maintain a relationship with Uzbekistan.'

On the other side, various factions of the State Department became adamant about not doing deals with dictators.

'You had the State Department screaming, "There's no democracy! We can't deal with these people! We have to attach conditions to aid!"' recalls Dr Stephen Blank of the US War College. 'And you have the Pentagon saying, "We have a war to win!" The people that I talked to were completely frustrated. I talked to people from the Pentagon and the NSC and they just couldn't get anything done.'

As the situation failed to resolve itself, further rifts emerged. Lawrence Wilkerson, Secretary of State Colin Powell's right-hand man, witnessed the bureaucratic in-fighting.

'You've got the bureaucratic technique going on,' he says, 'the DoD seeking out allies in the State Department to buttress its position (and finding them in the regional bureaux) and you've got people in the functional bureaux like DRL, seeking out what allies it can find, usually in the NGO community and in Congress, because you've got lots of people in Congress who will fall on any human rights issue and make it their placard for the day.'

For the Uzbek president, the issue of the US relationship was rapidly becoming confusing. On the one hand, Congress and various parts of the State Department were lambasting him for not achieving his human rights goals; on the other hand, he was receiving lavish praise from the Pentagon for his stalwart help in the War on Terror. To make matters worse, in the spring of 2003, Karimov discovered that the President of Kyrgyzstan, next door, was receiving more money for his air base than he was. He wrote a personal letter to President Bush asking for this to be remedied. It wasn't.

The next year, Congress was finally convinced the Uzbek human rights situation was not improving and severed all aid payments: $18 million went unpaid. Suspecting that his airbase was now threatened, a fortnight later US Chief of Staff General Richard Myers flew to Tashkent and announced that the Pentagon would pay the shortfall.

'That will screw the State Department!' he commented as he left the podium. 'That will screw them!'

US legislators were livid. This was not going to happen again. Efforts were redoubled to deny United States funding to Uzbekistan as well as to stop the Pentagon from paying them through the back door.

With US funds to Uzbekistan curtailed, the money tap was finally turned off. It was now harder to argue that the United States was supporting a murderous dictator. But it was also harder to use the promise of further funding to encourage Karimov to engage in political reform. The money was gone: there were no longer any levers with which to exert pressure. The relationship was coming apart. According to one senior Pentagon official involved, it was 'like watching a train wreck in slow motion'.

For Karimov, maintaining a deal with America now looked increasingly pointless. The Uzbek president decided it was time to renegotiate his contract. He was willing to offer long-term access to K2, but wanted clarification regarding what, exactly, the United States planned to offer him in return. Shortly after Congress refused to certify Uzbekistan for foreign funding, Karimov wrote to the United States offering a draft agreement for basing rights to K2 and asking for a decision.

By now, however, the State Department and the Pentagon were gridlocked. The State Department was unable to work out whether human rights or strategic issues were more important in the US–Uzbek relationship. The Pentagon, meanwhile, was in the middle of a Global Posture Review that involved analysing where bases would be needed in the future. Perhaps a US air base in Uzbekistan wasn't necessary after all. With the US decision-making process effectively paralysed, no one knew what to do. Karimov's letter went unanswered. He wrote another; again, no response. From 2004 to 2005, Uzbekistan wrote six separate times, asking what, exactly, the United States wanted. The United States never replied.

'These letters from the Uzbek side to us pointed out the fact, painfully, that we were unable to come to terms with the totality of what our interests were in Uzbekistan,' says a senior Pentagon official of the process. 'We just weren't able to agree how to move forward.'

Unable to decide whether to strengthen the knot or cut it altogether, and distracted by the now daily bombs going off in Iraq, the White House left Karimov hanging.

Until, on 13 May 2005, he made the decision for them.

The situation in Andijan came to a head rapidly. At around 5.20 p.m., a series of military trucks and APCs approached Babur Square from different directions. Simultaneously, soldiers opened fire on the crowd. Panicking, people started to run, only to discover the exits were blocked: there was no way out. Protest leaders acted fast, using the PA system to order the crowd into two groups and surrounding them with government hostages for protection.

Then an opportunity presented itself. It seemed that Ministry of the Interior troops had forgotten to block one of the exits from the square: the main road to the north, Cholpon Street. Two groups of protestors, the first at least 400 strong, the second much larger, started marching up the street. Women and children were shoved to the centre of the groups, men to the outside, holding their hostages in front of them. Most made it away from the square safely until they reached the junction with Parkovaya Street 500 metres up the road. Beside the toy shop, Detsky Mir, government troops had moved two civilian buses into the street and positioned them end-to-end, blocking it completely. Protestors hauled the buses apart, creating a gap a few metres wide, and squeezed through. But it was a trap. The buses created a funnel through which protestors had to pass slowly, making them easy targets.

'The moment we went through,' recalls Nodir Mahmudov, 'they started shooting.'

The first to pass were shot clean through the forehead. As Mahmudov himself went through, at the last minute he ducked; a bullet went directly through his hat.

'There was a hole through both sides,' he says. 'They were shooting to kill.'

Protestors who made it alive between the two buses dropped to the ground and lay still, waiting for the shooting to stop and wondering what to do next.

At this point it started to rain, further confusing matters. The first group of protestors shoved the buses completely out of the road, crashed past them and ran further north towards the Cholpon Cinema. With the buses behind them, the gunfire stopped and everything went silent. Once they reached the cinema, however, and the junction with Baynalminal Street, there was another surprise.

As the first group approached the cinema, they saw that the military had blocked the road with trucks, jeeps and Russian 8-wheel APCs fitted with 14.5 mm machine guns. In front of School Number 15, sandbag barricades had been erected. On the ground, soldiers were prone with guns at the ready. For a moment there was a pause. Then, when the crowd reached a range of about 300 metres the troops opened fire.

'From the APCs there was a sound like *boom-boom-boom-boom!*' recalls one survivor, 'then the automatics: *takh-takh-takh!*'

At exactly this moment the rain turned into a torrential downpour. Unable to see through the rain, unable to flee, facing a hail of automatic gunfire, members of the first group were cut down where they stood.

When the first volley of fire stopped, ostensibly for the troops to reload, survivors who had dropped to the ground stood up and found themselves surrounded by a sea of corpses. The moment they tried to run, the firing started again.

'It was like a bowling game,' recalls one. 'When the ball strikes the pins and everything falls down. There were flashes from the APCs, there were bodies everywhere. I don't think anyone in front of us survived.'

By the time Sardor Azimov and Nodir Mahmudov arrived in the second, larger, group, virtually all of the first group was dead. As the businessmen struggled to take in the scale of the slaughter, a third wave of gunfire started. Mahmudov, with his wife, daughter and son, flung them all to the ground and hugged them tight. Azimov was slower. Beside him, one of his factory workers was shot, first in the leg, then the stomach.

'I saw him go down, and I called someone next to me. We carried him over to the edge of the road and we bound up his leg, but we didn't know what to do about his stomach.' Facing a volley of gunfire, Azimov abandoned his friend and lay down. When the shooting paused, he jumped up and started trying to help again. 'We tried to take them to the sides of the road, but there were so many that we just couldn't help them all. I think about five hundred people died. Some were killed when they were helping the wounded.'

Panicking, survivors now turned right, into Baynalminal Street, and dispersed into the side roads, where they hammered on the doors of locals, begging to be let in. A few opened their doors and agreed to take women and children, warning that snipers were positioned on the rooftops; others simply refused to answer. One witness, looking back at the carnage, saw APCs driving over the bodies of the dead, and government troops apparently executing the wounded.

Anna Neistat, Head of the Emergencies Unit of Human Rights Watch, was at home in Maryland when Sasha Petrov called to inform her that their predictions of the day before had been correct. Something big was happening in Uzbekistan. In fact, it had already happened.

She immediately packed her bags, travelled to the New York office and, together with the Emergencies team, formulated a plan of action. The next day, Neistat and Petrov were on a flight to Russia. From there they flew to Bishkek in Kyrgyzstan and on to Osh, near the Uzbek border. In Osh they conferred with local human rights groups, then picked up a car and drove to the border town of Jalalabad where they found the first batch of Andijani refugees recovering in Suzak Hospital.

'There were about a dozen people wounded,' says Petrov. 'It was bullet wounds; some of them had contusions, but many people had been just in psychological shock.'

Not far from Jalalabad, in a field just across the Uzbek border, the Emergencies Unit found two rows of tents and, inside them, nearly 500 more survivors. The camp was basic to the extreme, with no cooking facilities and no proper sewerage or running water; Kyrgyzstan had never dealt with refugees on this scale and was struggling to cope. The team set about interviewing the refugees one by one, in an attempt to discover what had actually happened to them. Tragically, many had no idea.

'There were women and children who had just showed up at the square near the Hokimiyat, because they heard that there was a big demonstration,' says Neistat. 'These people just left their home at – whatever time it was, ten, twelve in the morning – sat the day on the square and then the shooting started and they were fleeing.'

As the HRW team set about establishing an account of what had actually happened in Andijan, a problem presented itself. The Uzbeks had all left the city together, on the night of 13 May. They had no clue what had happened afterwards, or what was happening now. From discussions with journalists on the border, the team learned that access to Andijan had become near impossible: journalists were being turned away, arrested and held at gunpoint. Cameras, computers and note-books were being confiscated. Telephone lines had been cut, mobile phone networks shut down and Internet access blocked. The entire city had been cordoned off. The question was, how to get in to find out what was going on?

On 21 May, just a week after the shootings, and four days after arriving in Kyrgyzstan, a member of the HRW team succeeded in crossing the border into Uzbekistan, then travelling on to Andijan. The moment she entered town, the researcher realized the situation was worse than she had expected.

'As you enter the town the road goes right past the prison. The moment I saw it, I knew there was absolutely no way I would be able to take pictures,' she recalls. 'I've never seen an institution guarded so heavily.' The prison itself was surrounded by APCs, inside which was a further defensive ring of sandbagged troops scanning the streets with binoculars. 'It was heavily, heavily fortified.'

A brief drive around town was enough to convince her that the prison was not the only area receiving special treatment. Thousands of armed troops and security officers were visible on the streets. Entire districts were cordoned off. Taxi drivers had been instructed not to transport journalists or foreigners across town. No one wanted to talk. Through friends and relatives, however, a picture emerged of the true extent of the damage, and its aftermath.

Recognizing that the Andijan incident was likely to have international repercussions – especially in the United States – President Karimov instructed all proof of the mass killings to be erased. The morning after the shootings, army trucks showed up in the town centre and began disposing of the corpses. The first to be removed were women, children and those killed by heavy-calibre weapons. Fire engines hosed blood from the streets. Many wounded protestors who had survived the night on the streets were killed; hospitals were visited and gunshot victims were murdered; families thought to have taken part in the demonstration received visits from masked SNB officers, who took them into custody for interrogation or, in some cases, shot male members of the family on sight. Numerous Andijanis reported seeing mass graves being dug outside town.

District community groups, known as *mahallas*, were instructed to inform on neighbours who had participated in the protest. Anyone asking too many questions, who might be either a journalist or a representative of a human rights organization, was to be reported to the police. Those who did talk found themselves in trouble. A female doctor who told journalists she had seen 500 corpses piled into the auditorium at School Number 15 the day after the shootings was arrested; another informant who took a Radio Free Europe correspondent to the site of a mass grave in Bogi Shamol was mysteriously stabbed to death four days later. The Uzbek Ministry of the Interior was attempting a cover-up on a vast scale.

Simultaneously, Karimov went out of his way to minimize the damage. Immediately after the shootings, he addressed the nation, announcing that there had been a coup attempt in Andijan, and that he had been forced to step in. Blame for the incident was placed squarely at the feet of the protestors – Islamic fanatics ('extremists' and 'terrorists') trained in Chechnya – who had sought to bring the country to its knees.

Evidence of the insurgents' extremist tendencies was presented: hadn't the jailbreakers shouted '*Allahu akbar!*' moments before they rammed the prison gates? The numbers of the dead were downplayed, killings blamed not on government troops but on the terrorists. The President said 187 people had perished, of whom the majority were either the terrorists themselves or the hostages they had executed. Tragically, sixty civilians had been killed, all by the 'bandits'.

In Kyrgyzstan, HRW staff began the process of putting the information they had gathered into a report, to be distributed around the world.

'I think we all recognized that it was extremely important to get this information out,' says Neistat, 'not just for the sake of creating a record, but also for the sake of the refugees.'

If the Andijanis thought they were safe in Kyrgyzstan, they were wrong. The refugee camp was situated right next to the border. Every day, Uzbeks would cross over to visit them. Some were family members seeking their relatives. Others had shadier motives. The area around the camp was swarming with SNB officers keeping track of who was inside and who was visiting, and trying to persuade refugees to come home. Many of the visitors had already been primed by the SNB to persuade their relatives to return: family members were instructed to tell them that, if they didn't, their relatives would be arrested and tortured in their place. When that failed, SNB officers, aware of the CIA's clandestine programme to snatch and transport al-Qaeda suspects globally, commenced their own extraordinary rendition operations, kidnapping refugees and dragging them back across the border into Uzbekistan.

At the same time, the Uzbek regime deployed more conventional methods, filing extradition requests for the refugees with the Kyrgyz government: these people were terrorists. Uzbekistan wanted them back. Intimidated by its stronger, wealthier neighbour, Kyrgyzstan had some tricky decisions to make.

The United States had some tricky decisions to make, too. In his second inaugural address, the President had sworn that democracy trumped all else ('We will encourage reform in other governments,' Bush promised, 'by making clear that success in our relations will require the decent treatment of their own people') but here was the United States in bed with a dictator who had just killed somewhere between 500 and 2,000 of his own citizens. What was America supposed to do now? It couldn't cut funding to Uzbekistan: it already had. The White House had no carrots or sticks left.

At NATO headquarters in Brussels, US military staff refused to authorize a joint communiqué condemning the Uzbek government's actions for fear of jeopardizing access to K2, but as more and more evidence accumulated it became clear a line had to be drawn. Yes, there had been a jailbreak and, yes, there were armed protestors, but Karimov's response was way beyond proportional.

The State Department and the White House tried to be diplomatic, but, while both refrained from characterizing the Andijan incident as a 'massacre', it was impossible to condone Karimov's actions: as the *Economist* helpfully pointed out, Andijan was probably the worst atrocity by a government against civilian demonstrators since Tiananmen Square in 1989. The day of the shootings, the State Department's Richard Boucher warned the Press that 'the facts are not pretty'; the same day White House spokesman Scott McClellan urged restraint on both sides, but, as evidence amassed of the scale of the killings, this line became harsher. The White House, he said five days later, was 'deeply disturbed'.

This was not what Karimov wanted to hear. The day after the shootings, he made the magnitude of the stakes perfectly clear to his allies, imposing a ban on night flights into K2.[15] Access to the base was now in jeopardy.

'The Uzbeks started restricting our air operations,' says a senior State Department officer working on Uzbekistan at the time. 'That was their way of expressing displeasure about our response to Andijan.' Very quickly it became clear that the Uzbeks were planning to hold the base hostage to try to temper the United States response. The Uzbek regime wanted its refugees back, and was willing to play hardball to get them. 'It put us in a very difficult position.'

The result was a series of frantic conferences. 'There was a tense dialogue at very senior levels,' recalls Colonel Chicky. 'Intense debate within the administration, State Department, National Security Council, Department of Defense, about what to do next.' Chicky, for one, was convinced this story was not going to end happily. 'It was not a good situation. For my mind I knew that we were going to be the bill payer for this.'

Two weeks after the shootings, on 29 May, Senators John McCain, Lindsey Graham and John Sununu visited Uzbekistan. Uzbek authorities refused to meet them. At a press conference in Tashkent, the

[15] Karimov's anger about the US response to Andijan may have a further justification. According to some, on the morning of the Andijan uprising – before troops opened fire on civilians – the Uzbek president requested assistance in handling the situation from the United States in the form of aerial surveillance pictures. The response was a flat 'no'.

senators commented that the events in Andijan were 'shocking, but not unexpected in a country that does not allow the exercise of human rights and democracy', and offered a veiled threat: maintaining a US–Uzbek relationship would be 'very difficult, if not impossible' if the Government failed to reform.

Meanwhile, four Andijanis were handed over to Uzbekistan by Kyrgyz authorities; all immediately vanished into SNB cells, where it appeared they were tortured extensively. A further 121 refugees were charged in absentia with crimes against the state, and extradition requests were filed for another 110. Clearly, if the refugees were handed back to Uzbekistan, their lives would be in danger. The situation was coming to a head.

If one is willing to criticize US policy towards Uzbekistan, one must also be willing to give credit where it's due. Acknowledging the perilous situation of the Andijani refugees, the State Department and the Pentagon now stepped up and showed their true colours.

'The moment of truth took place when it became clear that the only way to keep this base would be if we stood aside and let the refugees be returned to Uzbekistan,' recalls Dan Fried, Assistant Secretary of State for European and Eurasian Affairs at the time. Fried conferred with his opposite number at the Pentagon. 'Is there any way to avoid this dilemma?' he was asked. 'No, not at this point,' he replied. 'The only way to save the base is to send these people back . . . and a lot of them, I suspect, will be tortured.'

'Very rarely in policymaking do you have these kinds of stark moral choices,' says Fried today. 'But this was one of the rare cases where you actually had a clear binary choice. We had to do the right thing . . . I remember my colleague at the Defense Department just groaning and saying, "My God, we've got to get them out and when we do we're going to lose the base."'

The White House put pressure on Kyrgyzstan not to repatriate or extradite the refugees, while at the same time seeking to find them new homes abroad. It then informed the Uzbeks of its decision.

'In the end we told them, "Look, we have serious strategic interests, but we're not going to walk away. We have responsibilities towards refugees,"' says Fried. 'Not a bad moment, if you're interested in human rights.'

The result was a series of tit-for-tat exchanges with the Uzbek regime. On 27 July 2005, Fried announced that the Uzbek refugees would be flown out of Kyrgyzstan to Romania. The next day Karimov responded, delivering a document to the US embassy in Tashkent demanding the termination of the US–Uzbek basing agreement. That the note was not made public suggested it was a threat, to be carried out the moment the United States actually acted. By now, however, the United States' course of action was set. On 29 July, after a two-month stand-off, 439 Uzbek refugees were air-lifted out of Kyrgyzstan to safety.

'That day,' says Fried, 'within an hour, the Uzbek government terminated the base agreement.' The United States had 180 days to pack its bags.

Immediately after the shootings the Uzbek regime launched a wave of arrests of those it deemed responsible for the uprising. Fifteen of the most prominent suspects were paraded in front of the media and a show trial was staged. Government negotiators then contacted the Andijan refugees in Romania and offered them a deal.

'They said, if you keep talking about the events at Andijan,' says Sardor Azimov, 'and keep saying bad things about the Government and keep giving interviews, we will shoot these fifteen people. We will execute them.'

The Andijan refugees went quiet. They were then dispersed around the world to new homes. The story disappeared.

Witnesses effectively silenced, Karimov now shored up his defences. NGOs that had opened as part of the US–Uzbek agreement were hastily ejected from the country – as were the BBC, Radio Free Europe, the American Bar Association and the UNHCR.

The Uzbek president then flew to Moscow, where the nation that had provided the truck that had breached the gates of Andijan Prison on 13 May 2005 was diplomatic enough not to say, 'We told you so.' In a number of press statements, the Uzbek president blamed 'external forces' for the events at Andijan: specifically, the United States.

In September 2005, Uzbekistan announced the cessation of counter-terrorism operations with the United States and, for the first time since 1991, commenced joint military exercises with Russia. Two months later, as US servicemen lowered the flag at K2 for the last time, the republic joined the Eurasian Economic Community, effectively severing US economic influence, and signed a mutual defence pact with the Kremlin. Russian petrochemical giants Gazprom and Lukoil announced that they planned to invest $2.5 billion in the country; shortly afterwards, South Korea's National Oil Corporation and Korea Gas Corporation signed memoranda of understanding that allowed them to develop and exploit oil and gas fields there, too. India then signed seven economic agreements, gaining permission for its companies to explore for oil, gas and other hydrocarbons. China offered $600 million in a parallel oil deal. Uzbekistan, the jewel of the Great Game, had turned away from the West.

At almost this exact moment, the situation in Afghanistan – under-funded, understaffed and under-monitored since the glorious victory in November 2001 – deteriorated: the Taliban was back. The United States moved frantically to shore up relationships with other Central Asian states, offering the kinds of cash, assurances and attention that it should have offered Uzbekistan before it was too late.

Suddenly, it seemed, the United States needed friends in the region after all.

8

The Muslim Disease

How do you deal with an enemy? Muslims, we hate America.
Everything is aggravated now. How can we trust this nation?
Sheikh Muhammed, Waje Central Mosque, Nigeria, 2005

The day before his assassination, Abdul Ghani attended a funeral in Nowshera. On 2 February 2007, a friend, Ikram Ullah Khattak, had been abducted from Lahore. A week later, after an extensive search, police dredged his body from the Upper Chenab Canal in Gujranwala. It was an unfortunate business.

It was also an ominous one. The cinema owner, entrepreneur and billionaire had been a senior member of the Khattak dynasty – about as close to royalty as it was possible to get in Pakistan's North-West Frontier Province (NWFP). The dead man's uncle had been one of the founders of the largest political party in Pakistan, the PPP, and was a former Chief Minister; two of his brothers were prominent MPs. Not long before Dr Ghani's arrival in Nowshera, Pakistan's Minister for Industry had shown up to pay his respects. This was an important occasion.

Ghani wasn't cowed. On the contrary, those who met the fifty-four-year-old doctor that day found him curiously distracted. Bemused by his friend's distant manner, at four o'clock a colleague, Namair Muhammad, took him aside and asked what was wrong. Ghani waved off the question, explaining simply that he was keen to return to work.

Pressed on the matter, however, he opened up a little, admitting that he'd been given an important assignment to undertake the following morning. The Health Ministry had instructed him to drive to the district of Salarzai, fifty kilometres north-east of the main town in Bajaur Agency. Apparently, there was a situation that needed his urgent personal attention.

Ghani's friend immediately commented that the trip sounded dangerous. Salarzai was awash with Taliban. Almost certainly, al-Qaeda was there, too. When Osama bin Laden and his deputy Ayman al Zawahiri had fled Afghanistan for Pakistan in the winter of 2001, they had shown up nearby. There was every possibility that they, and their friends, were still in the area. Travel in and around Salarzai was a lottery. Muhammad suggested that Ghani delay the trip, or at least take a little time to think about it.

'I asked him to stay the night and leave the next morning,' he recalls, 'but he was in a hurry. He wanted to get back to Bajaur before it got dark.' Concerned that his colleague was standing into danger, Muhammad asked whether Ghani was up to date on news of the threats around Salarzai. 'He told me that the security situation was bad. Officers who used official government cars or jeeps were easy targets for the militants.' Noting his friend's pained expression, Ghani leant towards him. 'I know the risks,' he assured him. 'I try not to travel in official cars.' But the doctor was clearly worried.

After the funeral, Ghani paid his respects to the family, bade goodbye, climbed into his car and headed north, back into Bajaur, to prepare for the next day's trip. It was the last time Muhammad ever saw him.

That night, Ghani's second-in-command at Bajaur Agency Hospital had a dream. Hazrat Jamal's son Mohammed Viqar was spending the night with his grandmother; for some reason, this bothered him. At around 2 a.m. on the morning of Friday, 16 February, the EPI Technician awoke with a start.

'I saw my son,' he says. 'He was lying on the road.' The boy appeared to be hanging over the edge of a rocky mountain pass. If he slipped, he would fall into a deep river below. In the dream, Jamal was trying to work out how to retrieve him when he glanced down and realized that something else was horribly wrong. Mohammed Viqar's legs had been ripped apart from the waist down.

Later that morning, when Jamal reported for work, he bumped into Dr Ghani in the hospital foyer. Just the man I wanted to see, the doctor told him. At the request of the Health Ministry, he, Jamal and three others were heading out for a meeting in Salarzai; the driver had already been summoned. For no reason he could decipher, the nightmare suddenly came back to Jamal and a wave of nausea swept over him.

'I got the same feeling. I felt weird.'

Too proud to say anything to his supervisor, the technician suggested that he man the fort while the team was away. Ghani was having none of it. It was highly important that he attend, he told him.

Apparently, the decision revolved around facial hair. Ghani himself was clean-shaven, but Jamal had an impressive beard. This might prove useful, the doctor explained. The village they were heading to, Shehano Bandar, was a Taliban stronghold: the more beards in the car, the better. Jamal found himself unable to disagree, and so at 10 a.m. the five-man team – Ghani, Jamal, another technician, a driver and a political officer – climbed into a white four-wheel-drive pickup and headed north out of Khar.

Jamal was apprehensive. He had been born in the next-door village to Shehano Bandar. What he had heard of the place was not good. 'I knew there were armed militants there. Al-Qaeda, too,' he says. 'There was definitely reason to believe that this was quite dangerous.'

If Dr Ghani was afraid, he did a good job of concealing it. Throughout the hour-long journey, he chatted amiably, laughing, joking and asking the names of villages as they passed. Five kilometres out of Khar, the metalled road disappeared and the pickup traced its way up into the rocky mountain passes that led to Afghanistan.

The moment the team arrived in Shehano Bandar, it became apparent that things were going to be harder than anyone had anticipated. In front of the village's only mosque they met the cleric – a large, dark man with a full beard and a Kalashnikov slung over his shoulder. Taliban.

In his best formal language, Ghani explained that he was a doctor from Khar and that he would like to discuss a few matters relating to the village's health record. Nodding sagely, the cleric led the team into the mosque, where the men of the town were gathering for Friday-morning prayers. He then addressed the crowd. A doctor had come to see them, he said. From Khar. He wanted to speak to them. Abruptly the cleric's tone changed, and he informed his congregation that this 'doctor' was probably a government agent. Everything he said was to be disregarded.

'On the one hand,' he told the crowd, 'the United States is bombing us for no reason.' He turned to the medical team. 'On the other hand, here *you* are – coming here, disguised as health workers to spread vulgarity.'

Ghani winced. It was going to be a long day. Worse, despite his assurance of the day before, he had left home that morning in an official government car.

One of the ironies of human progress is its propensity to create its own obstacles. The emergence of poliomyelitis in the West is a case in point. A hundred and fifty years ago, advances in public health programmes, specifically proper sanitation and clean drinking water, decimated poliovirus reservoirs in industrialized nations. While this might have been expected to improve the health of their populations, when it came to polio the exact opposite happened: as exposure to the virus dropped, natural immunity levels dropped with it, rendering the First World not less but more susceptible to infection.

Further human progress – a revolution in global travel – allowed the virus to spread internationally. By the late 1880s, polio was causing serious problems in Europe. In the early part of the twentieth century, the United States was struck by wave after wave of outbreaks. In 1916, New York City succumbed: 17,000 people were paralysed and 9,000 died.

The result was panic. Cinemas and music halls were shut. People stopped shaking hands to avoid contamination. Parades were cancelled, swimming pools closed and insecticides hosed over the city's streets in an effort to wipe out the infection. Nothing worked. By the 1950s 20,000 Americans were being paralysed by polio each year and images of wasted-limbed children in callipers and adults entombed in iron lungs had seared themselves into the public consciousness: other pathogens may have killed more people, faster and more efficiently, but the suffering inflicted by this disease, together with the fact that its victims were mainly children, earned poliomyelitis a reputation as the most dreaded childhood affliction of the twentieth century.

Such was the level of public fear surrounding polio that, when the Salk vaccine was declared effective in April 1955, 54,000 physicians attended live broadcasts in movie theatres around the country, and department stores set up loudspeakers so shoppers could hear the announcement in real-time. The result was an outbreak of spontaneous celebration. In the streets, motorists honked their horns; criminal trials were suspended; flags were flown and church bells pealed nationwide. Factories observed a moment's silence. In schools, parents and teachers wept openly. Shopkeepers wrote THANK YOU, DR SALK on their windows.

Within two years of the announcement of an effective vaccine, cases of polio were down by more than 80 per cent. The number of new infections dropped consistently until 1979 when, for the first time ever, the sum total of children paralysed in the United States by polio was zero. Pre-emption worked. Here, it seemed, was a disease that could be beaten.

American enthusiasm for polio vaccination was infectious. In 1985, South America's health ministers launched a project to remove the virus from the rest of the continent, too. Three years later, ministers from 166 countries at the World Health Assembly voted unanimously to launch a global programme to wipe the disease from the face of the earth. It was time to ensure the safety of all children from polio forever. The virus' demise, it was declared, would be a fitting gift 'from the twentieth to the twenty-first century'. A date for complete eradication was set: the year 2000.

There was a precedent. In 1959, a similar motion had been passed regarding smallpox. At the time, the virus was killing two million people a year, scarring and blinding millions more. Within twenty years, through a globally comprehensive vaccination and surveillance programme, the virus and the disease were gone.

Saving millions of lives more than justified the smallpox effort, but America's motives were not entirely altruistic. Since the Second World War, the White House had seen fighting infectious diseases as part of its duty to protect its own citizens. The problem was, when it came to smallpox, vaccination at home had not provided a permanent solution. Viruses did not respect international borders. In an increasingly globalized world, where people could move from country to country in a matter of hours, any smallpox virus anywhere was a potential threat. If protection from the disease was to be anything other than a stopgap, the virus had to be hunted down and killed worldwide.

There was also a strong financial motive. If the United States wanted to protect its citizens from smallpox, it had to vaccinate all of its children forever. This was expensive. Global eradication was a cheaper option: once the disease was gone, there would be no need to vaccinate anybody. The global eradication of smallpox cost the world $300 million, of which American voters supplied $32 million. To be sure, this was a lot of money, but within twenty years the United States had saved $17 billion in vaccination costs alone, effectively recouping its entire outlay every twenty-six days since the disease had been eradicated.

To the financially minded, the project had been an incredibly astute investment.

A similar operation for polio promised even greater benefits: the cost of vaccinating American children against the disease was more than $230 million per year. Once polio was gone, that 230 million could be put to better use. Worldwide, the saving would be even larger: approximately $1.5 billion per year.

For all these reasons, when it came to polio it was time for the gloves to come off. In 1988, they did.

From its inception, the WHO Global Polio Eradication Initiative (GPEI) was an epic undertaking. The only means of achieving the goal – saving 200,000 children from paralysis every year – was mind-boggling: the vaccination of every single child under the age of five on the planet. Funded by Rotary International, the US Centers for Disease Control, WHO and donations from various governments, GPEI was the largest public health project in the history of the world. The operation was rather like fighting an immense military campaign constantly, in all countries simultaneously. The challenge was immense.

Initially, planners faced a question of accounting. How could they go about locating all 600 million children in the world under five years old? Ninety per cent of them lived in developing countries with poor infrastructures and poor healthcare facilities: chances were, their own governments didn't know where they were.

Admittedly, smallpox vaccinators had faced the same problem in the 1960s, but they'd had a crucial advantage: a single dose of smallpox vaccine brought lifetime immunity to the disease. Oral Polio Vaccine (OPV) didn't. To guarantee full protection, OPV had to be administered two to four times per child. Finding and vaccinating 600 million children wasn't enough: the WHO had to find and vaccinate them again, and again, and again. That 130 million children were born each year made the task positively Sisyphean: the target was not only moving, it was growing.

The solution for countries in the developing world was to organize National Immunization Days (NIDs), when parents were encouraged to bring their children forward for free vaccination. The scale of the operations was colossal. During India's first NID in December 1995, two million workers manned half a million vaccination posts; 87 million children were vaccinated. Four years later, the country successfully vaccinated 127 million children in three days: the largest health event ever organized by a single country. But that was only part of the picture. To ensure comprehensive vaccine coverage, NIDs were coordinated to take place simultaneously in neighbouring countries. In 1997, 450 million children in 80 countries – roughly two thirds of all the children on earth – were vaccinated against polio. The next January, more than 130 million were immunized in a single day. In the last ten days of May 2009, 222 million children in 22 countries were vaccinated simultaneously.

In areas of political instability there were complications. War zones called for different tactics. Based on operations pioneered in South America, WHO staff called for ceasefires in civil wars during NIDs. The organization shortly found itself arranging not just polio vaccine but armistices. In El Salvador, insurgent guerrillas took part in the programme, themselves vaccinating children in remote areas; in Peru, Shining Path leaders helped to deliver vaccine and gave specific orders that no health workers were to be harmed. 'Days of Tranquillity' were effective in Lebanon, Afghanistan, Sri Lanka, the Democratic Republic of Congo and Somalia. Everywhere, the fighting stopped for the sake of the children. In some areas, combatants actually dug up landmines to allow vaccinators safe access to them.

But vaccination was the easy part. The really tricky task was keeping track of polio's global movements. Where was the disease? Where was it going? How fast? When smallpox had been eradicated, virus surveillance was relatively simple: the disease caused physical scarring, leaving a trail of evidence wherever it went. Polio was harder to pin down. In 199 out of 200 polio cases, victims experienced no more than temporary flu-like symptoms: many had no idea the virus had even passed them by. Entire populations could be infected without knowing it: until a child was actually paralysed, it was unlikely a diagnosis would be made. Even when it was made, for each paralysed child there were another 200 to 3,000 carriers of the virus presenting no symptoms whatsoever. All were capable of spreading the infection.

Poliovirus moved among the people like fish swam in the sea. It emerged, took a few lives, took a few limbs, then vanished. The weakest, the most vulnerable, the most backward, impoverished people in the poorest nations on earth were targeted. Once infected, the virus' victims themselves became reservoirs, machines for producing more virus. Each infected person shed between 10 and 100 million virus particles per day – any one of which was capable of claiming another victim.

Despite the extraordinary levels of international co-operation the GPEI fostered, the WHO was careful with its rhetoric. The organization might well have launched a war on polio, but it wasn't coming out and saying so in quite those terms. It was also rather more circumspect about its ultimate goals. It was quite possible, officials admitted, that the effort might not work. The main thing was that the initiative was used to spread global health advances, rather than focusing simply on one disease. To this end, vaccinators also acted as monitors of infections such as ebola, Marburg disease, yellow fever and cholera. They distributed mosquito nets to young mothers in malarial zones and encouraged parents to vaccinate children against other diseases. They handed out free Vitamin A supplements: a single act that saved the eyesight of millions in the Third World.

Health officials were also reticent when it came to speculating about the future. A common question to senior eradicators was which disease would be next after polio was gone: measles, perhaps? GPEI staff were reluctant to answer. The job was not yet finished.

'It is critical,' US Surgeon-General David Satcher explained in September 1998, 'that the global public health community focus on finishing polio eradication *before* embarking on a more difficult and expensive measles-eradication initiative.'

The message was clear: one war at a time. A global campaign such as the one against polio could be fought effectively – and possibly even won – but only if it was done thoughtfully, methodically and without distraction.

There were lessons to be learned here, if anyone at the White House was listening.

Abdul Ghani knew all about polio. Pakistan was one of the world's leading reservoirs of wild poliovirus, with tens of thousands of cases each year. His home, the North-West Frontier Province, was itself the reservoirs' main reservoir; the young doctor had no shortage of crippled children to attend to. In the 1970s and 1980s, with eradication years away, no one paid the disease much attention. Besides, there were other things to think about.

To strangers, Ghani came across as a quiet, scrupulously polite, diligent individual. Aside from his love of cricket, about which he could become passionate, there was little that appeared to excite him. Like many Pakistanis in the area, he was struggling to better himself. Born in Laki Marwat in southern NWFP to a poor farming family, he and his brother had worked hard at school to get ahead. The brother ended up managing a sugar mill in Charsada, funnelling his wages to Ghani, supporting him through medical school. The process of self-betterment never stopped. After qualifying as a doctor in the early 1980s, his first posting was as a junior Medical Officer at the Rural Health Centre in the village of Manki Sharif, Nowshera. It was here that a fortuitous encounter bore fruit.

In 1985, Ghani treated a local man over a period of months. The treatment was successful, the two became friends and the patient offered to introduce the doctor to his sister, an accomplished poet. Since the man was the *Pir* (spiritual and political leader) of Manki Sharif, this was an opportunity. In Pashtun society, where women are seldom allowed to venture outside the family home, marrying off a sister is a tricky business. More so in this case, since the sister of the *Pir* could not marry just anybody: a marriageable male of suitable social standing had to be found.

Ghani – a Pashtun, a qualified medical man, and one who had proved himself a competent and thoughtful physician to the family – appeared to fit the bill. The two were married, and children arrived soon after-wards: in 1988 Amir Hamza, the following year Rabia Ghani, the next Ali Raza.

Accelerated into the fast stream of conservative Pashtun society, Ghani's rise was now rapid. The family took hiking holidays in the Swat Valley, day trips shopping in Peshawar and mingled with the most influential figures in Nowshera society. There was, however, a cost: as a member of the *Pir*'s family, he was expected to conduct himself appropriately. All the unsuitable friends he had made on the way up were to be discarded. The family had a reputation to uphold.

Ghani was having none of it. He wasn't breaking friendships. 'People would ask him why he was still friends with low-scale workers like us,' says a former colleague, Fazli Raziq. 'He just ignored them.'

The doctor's reasoning was solid. 'I was a poor man myself,' he told Raziq on one occasion. 'My father worked hard to educate me. I don't see what social status has to do with it.' At the risk of alienating his in-laws, Ghani openly visited subordinates at their homes. 'Most of his friends were low-paid workers,' says Raziq.

This egalitarian approach spilled over into his work, too. 'He was a very frank man,' recalls another colleague, Nazirullah Muhmmadzai. 'He never showed that he was our boss. He used to say that, if you wanted respect, you should respect others.'

To those who knew him well, there was a more mischievous side to Dr Ghani. 'He loved parties,' says Azmatullah Jan Faiq, another colleague. 'He never missed an opportunity to get people together.'

Faiq should know. In 2002, when Ghani was promoted to Assistant District Health Officer for Nowshera, colleagues repeatedly suggested that he should organize a surprise party for their boss. 'Only later,' he says, 'did I discover that it was Dr Ghani who had told them to pester me to throw a surprise party.'

When Faiq stepped up and organized a lunch party at an exclusive local restaurant, Ghani acted suitably surprised, but was unable to resist meddling again. 'When it was time to pay the bill, he took me away from the table,' recalls Faiq. 'He said he knew that I didn't have much money.'

Ghani winked at his subordinate. 'Look,' he said, 'we've had a great time, and it's all because of you. Let me cover it.' There was, however, one condition. 'Don't tell anyone that I paid the bill.' Having organized a surprise party for himself, Abdul Ghani covered the cost of the entire event.

The Global Polio Eradication Initiative was so successful that by the late 1990s the WHO was on course to achieve its deadline of eradicating the disease by the end of the year 2000. On 23 September 1998, the US Senate Committee on Appropriations held hearings to determine funding levels for the programme, and to monitor progress. The event, according to its chairman, Senator Dale Bumpers, was 'one of the most enlightening, gratifying hearings I have ever attended in my entire life'.

According to expert testimony, 80 per cent of the world's children were now receiving vaccine. Results were stunning. In a single decade since the commencement of GPEI, global cases of polio had dropped more than 90 per cent. Over fifty nations were now entirely free of the disease. Several million children had been saved from paralysis and more than 100,000 lives had been saved outright.

'This is a dramatic story of success,' the Surgeon-General informed the Committee. 'Hundreds of thousands of children who would have died from polio have been saved.'

More money was required, but if it came on time even Africa would be free of polio by the end of the millennium. 'The goal,' Rotary International's Polio Eradication Advocacy Task Force Chairman, Herbert Pigman, assured the panel, 'is in sight.'

And yet success was by no means guaranteed. As Senator Bumpers noted, fewer than 800 days remained before the 2000 deadline. The programme was at a 'critical stage'. Anything could happen.

Almost three years to the day after the hearing, in September 2001, anything *did* happen. That the 2000 goal for complete eradication had been missed was unfortunate, but by now progress was so meteoric that even 9/11 looked unable to stop it. In 1999, global cases of polio had dropped below 20,000. The next year, the figure was 3,000. A new vaccination initiative, Accelerated Immunization, ensured that vaccine was reaching more children than ever: close on 550 million each year. The entire Western Pacific region had been certified free of polio.

With the end almost in sight, a GPEI technical advisory group released guidelines for laboratory containment of the poliovirus – a condition for certification of global eradication. By the end of 2001, the global number of new polio cases had plummeted from more than 1,000 per day to below 500 for the entire year. From 125 countries, the virus was now endemic in only ten. In 2002, Sudan, Ethiopia and Angola regis- tered no new cases of the disease, leaving just seven countries to go. Poliomyelitis hadn't been eradicated by the turn of the millennium, but the new goal of 2005 was within reach.

And then it all went wrong.

Although the rumour didn't surface until after 11 September, in reality it had been born a year earlier. Its birthplace was Nigeria, one of the last ten reservoirs of wild poliovirus on the planet. In 2000, the emir of one of the country's northern states, Najib Hussein Adamu, had noted a degree of confusion among his rural constituents about vaccination programmes in the country.

Inhabitants of Kazaure wanted to know why the WHO was still vaccinating against polio when there were so few cases of it. Why weren't they concentrating on measles? Adamu, a lawyer, did a little research on the Internet and discovered the answer: according to his sources, all was not as it seemed with the GPEI.

In the United States and Europe, Adamu learned, children received a different vaccine to the one being handed out in Nigeria. His interest piqued, he read on, to discover that Oral Polio Vaccine (OPV), the form in which it was distributed in the Third World, was made using monkey cells. There was a chance, he read, that these might be contaminated with pathogens, including Simian Immunodeficiency Viruses (SIVs). Worse, according to a theory fashionable at the time, OPV manufactured in the Congo during the 1950s using chimpanzee tissue cultures had led to the transferral of SIVs to human beings, causing the outbreak that would later become the AIDS pandemic. The vaccine wasn't safe.

Why would the First World feed African children a vaccine that wasn't safe when it was using a different one at home? Adamu found the answer buried in a secret 1974 US National Security Study Memorandum known as 'NSSM-200'. Signed by Secretary of State Henry Kissinger and declassified in 1989, the document addressed trends in Third World population levels, warning that explosive growth in the world's thirteen 'Least Developed Countries' was unsustainable and could lead them to become security concerns to the United States.

To this end, NSSM-200 recommended that it should be US policy to encourage these thirteen nations to educate their populations in modern family-planning techniques, including contraception (which it included under the euphemism 'actions to reduce fertility'). If the nations were unwilling to listen, the United States should consider acting anonymously via private intermediaries, through which financial coercion could be channelled. The document also mooted making US aid to the thirteen nations dependent on their showing sufficient zeal on the family-planning front. One of them was Nigeria.

To Emir Adamu, the relationship between contaminated OPV and secret United States funding of a fertility-reduction programme was as clear as it was explosive: GPEI was not about eradicating polio at all. It was about the struggle for global resources. It was about depopulating the Third World. It was noteworthy that the populations of six of the thirteen nations listed in NSSM-200 as in need of 'actions to reduce fertility' were predominantly Islamic. In July 2003, the Emir fired a memorandum to an Islamic umbrella group, Jama'atual Nasirul Islam (JNI), warning of the issue of OPV, depopulation and Islam.

Ironically, while Adamu was busy spreading the news of his findings, the Nigerian polio situation was going quite well. In April 2002, Health Minister Alphonsus Nwosu announced that the country was aiming for complete eradication of the disease by the end of the year. Six months later, GPEI launched what it hoped would be a final drive to immunize children in West and Central Africa. But, just as the organization geared up to vaccinate 15 million children, the story found an outlet in the form of the President of the Supreme Council for Shariah in Nigeria (SCSN), Dr Ibrahim Datti Ahmed.

Ahmed concurred with Adamu's reasoning: OPV caused AIDS. It contained female hormones designed to make Muslim men sterile and Muslim women barren.

'Modern-day Hitlers have deliberately adulterated the Oral Polio Vaccine with anti-fertility drugs,' he told the press, 'and contaminated it with certain viruses which are known to cause AIDS.'

In October 2003, three of Nigeria's northern states, predictably those with the highest Islamic populations, stopped vaccinating children against polio.

'It is the lesser of two evils to sacrifice two, three, four, five, even ten children [to polio],' reasoned Ibrahim Shakarao, the governor of Kano Province, 'than to allow hundreds of thousands, or possibly millions, of girl children to be rendered infertile.'

Ignoring protests from the WHO, Nigerian authorities refused to resume vaccination until OPV distributed by the organization had been subjected to scientific testing to prove its purity. In charge of the tests was a Nigerian pharmacologist, Dr Alhassan Bichi, who subjected OPV to photometry and, to the horror of international aid agencies, promptly discovered a low-level contaminant structurally similar to oestradiol, a female hormone. Despite the fact that the quantity of oestradiol was insufficient to cause any significant effects, the compound had not been listed among the vaccine's contents on the bottle's label.

In December 2003, Dr Bichi reported the finding, along with his conclusions: 'Where polio vaccine is seen to contain something that has not been declared, then I find it unethical to recommend that the vaccine be used.'

Further tests were commissioned, but the damage was done. Full vaccination in Nigeria would not recommence for another ten months.

For GPEI officials, the Nigerian ban was more significant than simply a missed deadline for the eradication of polio. At the Senate hearing in 1998, Dr Bill Foege, a former Director of the US Centers for Disease Control and one of the key figures behind the elimination of smallpox in the 1970s, explained why. Smallpox eradication from Ethiopia had taken a month longer than predicted. During that month, the virus had slipped across the border and reinfected Somalia. It took two years to get the disease out of Somalia again. A delay in polio eradication, if it led to further infections, could spell catastrophe for GPEI efforts.

'That is my fear with polio,' Foege told the Senate Panel. 'If it takes one month, six months, one year too long, then we will have reimportations into Brazil or India or Burma.'

The process would have to start all over again.

In a sense, the GPEI had become a victim of its own success. The programme had worked so well, so fast, that the disease was now rare. Villagers in Ethiopia or Yemen – or Nigeria – failed to see why they should continue vaccinating against a disease that appeared already to be gone. The problem was more pronounced in countries that had been cleared of polio altogether: why should precious health care resources be used to support a vaccination programme when the country was not apparently at risk any more? How long would this last?

The answer, of course, was that for the programme to work, each country had to continue vaccinating until *all* countries were free of the disease. By the time of the Nigerian ban, nearly 200 countries were vaccinating against a disease that did not exist within their borders. The longer the eradication programme took, the harder it became to sustain.

There was an even greater risk. Like an incomplete course of antibiotics, GPEI had removed the bulk of the pathogen, but any opportunity for it to return could be catastrophic. This had been the case with the malaria eradication programme started by the United States in 1955. Although $2 billion had been spent and significant progress made, in the late 1960s, the programme had been abandoned for financial reasons. Malaria rushed back into the regions that had formerly been cleared. In some areas, since natural immunity to the disease had now been lost, it caused more damage than it would have done had the programme never been started in the first place.

From the outset, experts had warned of the dangers of a failed polio-eradication campaign. In 1980, Donald Henderson, who had coordinated the smallpox operation, specifically spoke out against the idea of a polio programme. Smallpox, he said, had been eradicated only with a vast quantity of luck. Ten years into the campaign, donors had been as bored of ploughing cash into the operation as Third World countries were of vaccinating. When it came to eradication operations, there was a brief window of opportunity; if it was missed, eradication became ever more difficult and expensive. It was for this reason that the Senate committee in 1998 had declared that, while the programme was 'on the threshold of victory', vigilance was crucial: the last part might be the hardest.

'The consequences of having time run out,' according to WHO's David Heymann, 'are inconceivable.'

Sure enough, almost immediately after the three northern Nigerian states stopped vaccinating against polio, there was a new outbreak. In 2000, Nigeria had seen twenty-eight cases of the disease. By the end of 2003, the number was up to 355. The next year, the figure more than doubled. A second test of the vaccine revealed that it was indeed safe and full immunization resumed in July 2004, but by now it was too late. The virus started reinfecting neighbours formerly declared clear of it: Niger, Sudan, Togo, Ghana, Guinea, Cameroon, the Central African Republic, Burkina Faso and Côte D'Ivoire all saw new cases. One showed up as far south as Botswana. When the Centers for Disease Control in Atlanta analysed wild virus found in each country, all were traceable back to northern Nigeria.

In February 2005, a case occurred in Indonesia. The country had been free of polio for nearly a decade, lulling health authorities into a sense of false security: vaccination programmes had lapsed. Five million children were immediately immunized, but the virus was already up and running. Within a year, WHO had logged 264 new cases in the country – all direct descendants of the Nigerian strain. Eighteen months later, Somalia, clean of the virus for three years, was reinfected: 228 children were crippled.

In the four years following the cessation of vaccination, twenty-seven countries were reinfected with polio – twenty with the Nigerian strain. The country had become the number-one transmitting point for poliovirus in the world.

The WHO was forced to abandon its goal of eradicating polio

worldwide by 2005. By the end of the following year, the cost of mopping up the aftermath of the Nigerian vaccine ban was $450 million, and the number of countries with endemic polio had risen from four to sixteen; 1500 children had been paralysed.

'The world,' noted David Heymann, 'is still paying the price for what happened in Nigeria in 2003.'

Abdul Ghani understood all of these points well. Deputy Medical Superintendent in Nowshera Hospital, he was second-in-charge of vaccination efforts for the region. The way he saw it, Pakistan – until the Nigerian incident one of the last four countries left on earth harbouring reservoirs of wild poliovirus – was going to fight the disease with all it had.

Azmatullah Jan Faiq, who would later organize Ghani's 'surprise' promotion party in 2002, recalls the doctor's devotion to the issue. On the second day of the Muslim festival of Eid in 2001, Faiq received a telephone call from his boss. Ghani informed him that he planned to visit two villages in the region, Taro and Akbarpura, where clusters of children had been missed during the recent NIDs. He needed assistance. Faiq, District Storekeeper for the region, was not amused.

'I told him that it was Eid. I had guests at my home. I was busy.'

Unusually, Ghani insisted, telling his subordinate that this was the perfect time to vaccinate. 'This is a great opportunity,' he said. 'Not only can we spread goodwill on Eid, we can vaccinate the children at the same time.'

The reluctant Faiq was instructed to make apologies to his guests and wait outside his house. Ghani would pick him up.

Faiq and Ghani missed the celebrations and ended up driving home late that night. As they made their way back to Nowshera, Ghani noticed that his companion was unhappy.

'Don't be angry,' he told him. 'We've missed Eid. But look at it this way: we were more successful today than we would have been at any other time. All the parents were at home and in a jolly mood. This is a national cause, and we are responsible for it.'

Faiq grudgingly agreed, but said that the missed holiday still rankled.

'I understand,' Ghani commiserated. 'But remember: Eid will come again next year. If we miss a single child, they won't have that opportunity.'

The Nigerian polio outbreak of 2003 was not simply the result of a vaccine boycott. Many factors were at play. The country's immunization programmes were weak and poorly run: there was every chance of an outbreak anyway. More importantly, the vaccine ban was partly the result of political issues.

In April 2003, Olusegun Obasanjo, a Baptist, had won a second term of office as president over his opponent Muhammadu Buhari, a Muslim. The election had served to crystallize political rancour between the largely Christian, and comparatively wealthy, south of the country and the poorer, largely Islamic, north. Organizations such as the Supreme Council for Shariah became focal points for dissent against what they saw as their elitist, and possibly racist, southern rulers. Refusing to administer polio vaccine had been a simple yet effective means of expressing resistance.

The movement also unwittingly tapped into a groundswell of rage against the United States. With America at war in Afghanistan and angling for war in Iraq, there was a potent belief that what the First World was really engaged in was a crusade against Islam. If the United States could not be trusted in matters of international politics and was willing to invade foreign countries on false premises, why should it be trusted on other issues?

'They claim that the polio campaign is conceived out of love for our children,' explained a leading Nigerian cleric in 2002. 'If they really love our children, why did they watch Bosnian children killed and 500,000 Iraqi children die?'

Interest from the international community in Nigeria had always been suspicious: little was done about measles, little was done about drinking water. Nobody really cared. Yet every year westerners appeared in Land Cruisers insisting that Nigerian children swallow a vaccine for a disease that appeared to be gone. It didn't add up.

'America hates Muslims, and so whatever comes from the United States, no matter how good it is, people will reject it,' said the chief imam at Kano's second largest mosque.

In October 2003, the National Security Council suggested that President Bush write a personal letter to President Obasanjo reminding him of the importance of polio vaccination, but the idea was vetoed: such was the level of distrust in Nigeria that a letter from the US president would have looked even more suspicious, and might have made things worse. In the aftermath of America's reaction to 9/11, the world had lost faith in its last remaining superpower.

'They have always taken us in the Third World for granted,' one member of Nigeria's OPV testing team crowed after oestradiol had been found, 'thinking we don't have the capacity, knowledge or equipments to conduct tests that would reveal such contaminants.' Nigerian technology, Nigerian scientists and Nigerian know-how were proving them wrong.

The problem had been facilitated by technological advances. Globalization – the corrosion of international borders and apparent elimination of distance that had made 9/11 possible and the invasion of Iraq a priority – was dependent on the flow of materials internationally. The United States liked to harp on about the movement of terrorists and weapons, but the most important commodity of all was information. And the driver of the new-found information exchange was, of course, the Internet.

One of the wonders of the World Wide Web was its ability

instantaneously to disseminate vast quantities of unfiltered, often complex, technical information. The availability of this information made it extremely alluring: the Internet provided a licence for those with shadier motives to propagate whatever rumours they felt like propagating, covering their tracks with footnotes and other miscellaneous data that seemingly served to make the arguments not less, but more, credible: Israel blew up the World Trade Centers; America deserved 9/11; the Holocaust didn't happen. All around the world such arguments, peppered with footnotes to prove their authenticity, were disgorged by the Internet, like so much cuttlefish ink. It was this same process that led to Emir Adamu's conclusions about OPV.

It wasn't just the Third World that was duped. At the same time as Nigeria's religious leaders were warning of the dangers of OPV, the United Kingdom was experiencing a vaccine panic of its own. Convinced by erroneous but credible-sounding medical reports that the measles, mumps and rubella (MMR) vaccine caused autism, a swathe of British parents – like the Nigerians – elected to err on the side of caution. In 1996, MMR had been administered to 92 per cent of British children. By 2004, this figure had dropped to 84 per cent – the lowest since reporting began, and far short of the 95 per cent necessary to achieve national immunity. In London, the figure fell below 75 per cent, with some boroughs struggling to break 60.

In the midst of such confusion, it was for the experts – such as those at the WHO and US Centers for Disease Control (CDC) – to establish what was actually going on. Shortly after Nigeria stopped vaccinating against polio and the virus began to spread, CDC scientists analysed data from genetic fingerprinting of wild poliovirus specimens. By correlating information from these specimens, they were able to piece together exactly how the outbreak had moved.

The virus had travelled first to Nigeria's immediate neighbour, Chad, before moving to Sudan. From Port Sudan, it had then crossed the Red

Sea, presumably by ferry, into Yemen. Initially, it was speculated that the virus had simply followed traditional trade routes, skirting the southern Sahara before moving on. Perhaps it had travelled with migrant workers seeking employment, or exporters of Nigerian products to the Middle East.

As details of the routes taken by virus-carriers out of Nigeria into the rest of the world emerged, however, it became clear that many of the routes shared a common goal: Mecca.

Each year, roughly 3 million people congregate in Mecca, half of them from abroad, to participate in the Haj, the largest regularly scheduled mass movement of people on the planet. At the end of the pilgrimage, having mingled with travellers from all over the world, they return home. Modern transport, heavy overcrowding and close contact with individuals from other countries: if an infectious disease makes it to the Haj, odds are high that it will be dispersed globally the moment the pilgrimage is over. In 2004–5, two cases of polio showed up in Saudi Arabia: one in Jeddah, the other in Mecca. From there, the virus travelled onwards: the Indonesian case in spring 2005, for example, was traced back to the Mecca strain.

Saudi Arabia might have been part of the problem. It proved to be part of the solution. The kingdom, which had been polio-free since 1995, had been one of the keenest of the Islamic nations to embrace polio vaccination. Following CDC/WHO intervention, clerics in Saudi announced publicly that OPV was not part of a Western plot, and advised that all Muslims make sure their children received it. They also warned that any child under the age of fifteen who arrived for the next Haj would be forcibly vaccinated unless they could provide proof of previous inoculation.

With some of the most senior and respected clerics in the world now supporting polio vaccination, it became harder for Nigerian hard-liners to maintain their stance regarding the 'contaminated' OPV. The way was clear to start cleaning up the damage created by the Nigerian incident.

And yet commentators noted an alarming trend. Disregarding the recent reinfections from Nigeria, polio was endemic in four countries: Nigeria, Afghanistan, Pakistan and India. Two of the four were overwhelmingly Islamic, and the regions most affected in the other two were those most densely populated by Muslims. Routes taken by Muslims, either on the Haj or in search of work, were the routes the virus was following. The result was that children paralysed by polio were now predominantly Muslim. Poliomyelitis, largely eradicated from the rest of the world, appeared to be becoming a disease that targeted Muslims.

But it wasn't only the virus that was contagious. The African rumour was, too.

Rumours about the safety of OPV appear to have arrived in India in 2004. Like the strains of poliovirus multiplying across Africa and the Middle East at the time, these rumours originated in Nigeria – spread, presumably, by the Internet.

For vaccinators, India had represented one of the major challenges to the GPEI. Poverty, a vast population, a hot climate, heavy overcrowding and poor sanitation combined to make the country a perfect environment for poliovirus. In 1988, at the start of the eradication campaign, the country was facing 25,000 cases each year. The ensuing WHO operation was immense: 150,000 vaccination sub-centres were established and fitted with refrigerators to keep the vaccine cold. Hundreds of thousands of volunteers were trained to administer it.

Immunization days were advertised by town criers, on posters and flags, on television and radio, and in newspapers and public transport hubs. Vaccinators travelled on trains, inoculating passengers. Indians' love of cinema was also harnessed: vaccination was plugged in the lobbies of movie theatres, on the stage before films began and in the films themselves. Bollywood stars, cricketers and pop singers publicly endorsed vaccination. The result was a heavy vaccine uptake as India embraced the GPEI. The country would end up administering a billion doses of OPV every year to an estimated 150 million children under five.

Signs of the programme's success were not long in coming. In 1997, thirty-three Indian states were entirely free of polio and by 2000 cases of the disease had dropped more than 99 per cent, from the tens of thousands to 300. In 2001, the entire country reported just 268 cases, most of them concentrated around two 'hot zones': India's northern states, Bihar and Uttar Pradesh.

There was a reason for this. India's highest-intensity transmission areas were among the biggest, most overcrowded and least-developed regions in the country. Bihar and Uttar Pradesh had a combined population of more than 250 million people. Five million children were born each year in Uttar Pradesh alone, a fact which made vaccination more difficult: each time eradicators returned, another 600,000 children had to be traced.

The states were poor, too. More than 60 per cent of Uttar Pradesh's inhabitants had no access to sanitation. Malnutrition and diarrhoea – factors that not only assist polio infection, but also hinder the efficacy of OPV – were common: 52 per cent of the state's children were malnourished. Problems with logistics and poor local education meant that coverage in these areas, where vaccination was most crucial, was patchy. In richer, southern states, an estimated 90 per cent of children under five received at least three doses of OPV; in Bihar the figure was closer to 10 per cent.

It was thus no great surprise when, shortly after the millennium, Uttar Pradesh experienced a resurgence of the disease. In 2002, the state reported 1,500 new polio cases: 66 per cent of all infections globally that year. Vaccinators stepped in and resolutions were made to improve coverage. Shortly afterwards, however, other problems emerged.

One of the issues that complicated polio eradication in the two northern states was the fact that the majority of their populations was Muslim. Women tended not to leave their homes; there were problems with male vaccinators coming into contact with females. Unlike the southern states, the populations of Bihar and Uttar Pradesh did not come forward to public vaccination booths. The last thing the region needed was a series of community leaders instructing people not to co-operate with vaccinators. But this was what happened.

In 2004 – hot on the trail of an erroneous rumour that children had been killed by the vaccine – came the Nigerian story: OPV contained birth-control agents. The inhabitants of Uttar Pradesh were reminded that India had been one of the thirteen countries targeted for 'actions to reduce fertility' by the secret US memo, NSSM-200. Flags and banners went up instructing Indians not to accept health visitors, who were peddling a mysterious medicine that made Muslim children sterile. In an area already suspicious of foreign medical intervention, this was bad news.

Results were as tragic as they were predictable. By 2006, Uttar Pradesh and Bihar were responsible for nearly 90 per cent of all Indian polio cases. Polio from the two states spread to other regions previously free of the disease. When Nepal and Bangladesh were also reinfected, UN Secretary-General Kofi Annan wrote to the Indian Prime Minister warning of the dangers of not controlling the disease in the region. That year, although Muslims made up just 13 per cent of India's population, they accounted for 70 per cent of the country's polio victims.

If eradicating polio from India's northern states was a struggle, there was one area that presented even more problems. India was at least peaceful. A thousand kilometres to the north-east, the border between Pakistan and Afghanistan was anything but. The area was so politically complicated, so ridden with tribal feuds, that even the British, when they had ruled India, had not known what to do with it.

In 1893, an attempt had been made to pacify the region. The territory had been divided by the Durand Line, creating a border between then British India and Afghanistan. Once the line was in place, instead of trying to rule the region's numerous Pashtun tribes, control had been ceded to autonomous agencies: in return for stability, the area was left well alone. A century later, the 1,500-mile-long border was still disputed and still inconceivably messy. It was also the nexus between two of the remaining four countries harbouring endemic poliovirus.

Conditions that allowed polio to thrive in India and Nigeria – poverty, climate, poor education, poor governance, poor sanitation – were prevalent all along the Pakistan–Afghan border. Rural areas were inaccessible, urban ones overcrowded. Inhabitants of Pakistan's Federally Administered Tribal Areas (FATA) and North-West Frontier Province (NWFP) slipped across into Afghanistan with impunity, then returned just as easily. This was possibly the most porous border in the world: most inhabitants didn't even recognize it existed. The poliovirus certainly didn't. So convoluted were its movements that CDC and WHO staff were unable to work out whether Afghanistan was reinfecting Pakistan with polio, or vice versa.

Perhaps ironically, prior to 9/11, in Afghanistan the Taliban had been willing participants in the GPEI. During the civil war in the 1990s, both the Taliban and their opponents, the Northern Alliance, had ceased hostilities on Days of Tranquillity so that children could receive vaccine. In some areas, vaccination was actually easier on the Afghan side of the border than it was on the Pakistani side. As a result, much of the vaccination in Pakistan's mountainous tribal areas was conducted by Afghan teams, criss-crossing the border and vaccinating at will. Even a diplomatic spat – rumours of Afghan eradicators entering Pakistan to conduct operations without permission – led only to wrist-slapping: officially, they promised to stay on their side of the border. Unofficially, they crossed over and continued to vaccinate anyway.

Results were impressive. 'Nowhere is the achievement of humbling polio more remarkable than in Afghanistan,' wrote UNICEF author Siddarth Dube in a book highlighting the successes of the GPEI in 2003. 'Afghanistan is on the verge of conquering polio . . . its complete defeat in the near-term is almost a certainty.'

Dube's prediction turned out to be premature.

9/11 saw to that.

In 2001, three out of five NIDs were complete before 11 September. The fourth, scheduled for late September, went ahead – bombing had not yet begun – but the fifth, in November, was more problematic. Afghans were fleeing the country in huge numbers. The border areas were unsafe. Nevertheless, 33,000 NID volunteers went ahead with the vaccination plan anyway, immunizing more than 5 million children. It was a testament to the dedication of GPEI staff that such a programme was conducted at all. But the success was not to last.

As the situation in Afghanistan became increasingly chaotic, refugees, desperate to avoid the fighting, flocked across the border. The best connected and best resourced made it into the cities, or sometimes even to foreign countries such as Australia. The rest ended up marooned in Pakistan's border areas, making the already difficult task of tracking down and inoculating children there even harder. The WHO set up vaccination points in refugee camps and at border crossings, but it was impossible to ensure children were not missed. It was also impossible to predict what might happen on this most unstable border.

Vaccination in the autonomous tribal regions was already a tricky business anyway. For a start, there was the issue of accessibility: many of the agencies were so remote that vaccine had to be transported by donkey, packed in blocks of ice. Then there was the culture. Pashtun tribes were among the most conservative of all Islamic societies. Women seldom ventured outside the home at all. As had been the case in Uttar Pradesh and Bihar, they often refused to attend public vaccination booths.

Vaccinators were forced to make the rounds door-to-door, asking parents whether they wished to have their children inoculated, marking each house with chalk to record the number of children inside that had received a dose. But this also created problems.

A Pashtun woman would never allow a strange man into her house. When female health workers teamed up with men, the issue was not resolved: what kind of woman would be seen in public with a man who was not her husband or brother? Sending two women together was little better: females brazen enough to travel around knocking on strangers' doors were often unwelcome.

Because the border regions were off limits to the Pakistani government, asking for assistance there was not likely to help: Pashtun communities didn't trust the Government. They certainly didn't trust foreigners. In these areas, where fighting was common and centuries-old feuds lingered on, a stranger knocking on the door and announcing that he was from any official organization was a reason to reach for the guns – and the one thing there was no shortage of in FATA was guns.

The Pakistani government's schizophrenic policy towards the region made the situation a great deal more difficult. For decades, the military had been supporting the Taliban in Afghanistan. Post-9/11, US pressure to close the door on both Taliban and al-Qaeda fighters achieved little: billions of US dollars supplied to Pakistan went astray, while requests to sweep up insurgents fell on deaf ears. Occasionally, al-Qaeda fighters were handed over, but no senior Taliban members were caught: a clear sign that there was no real interest in neutralizing the organization.

Simply, Pakistan did not believe the Taliban was a threat. The result, as more and more refugees fled Afghanistan for Pakistan, was a series of border regions teeming with civilians, insurgents, foreign fighters, Taliban leaders and al-Qaeda cells. Insurgents fired rockets from Pakistan at US bases in Afghanistan or sneaked across the border, attacked, then retreated back into FATA where they were untouchable. Privately,

American intelligence officials wondered whether the invasion of Afghanistan had achieved anything other than shifting Taliban and al-Qaeda a few miles to the south-east.

Despite US exhortations to clean up the area, Pakistan's government alternated between feigned ignorance of the problem and peace deals with local militia leaders: no violence in Pakistan in return for autonomy, no interference from central government in return for peace. Often Pakistan's Inter-Services Intelligence (ISI) actively assisted insurgents in their cross-border operations. The result was the creeping Talibanization of the border provinces.

Girls' schools were shut down. Barbers were warned not to shave their customers. Sharia law was instituted and madrasas opened by the dozen. By the time the militants turned against the Pakistani government itself and started bombing city centres, they had gained so much power it was too late to rein them in. Troops were sent and beaten back. Towns were destroyed. More refugees fled their homes, further complicating issues: now the area wasn't just dealing with displaced Afghans, but displaced Pakistanis, too. Further peace deals were negotiated and disregarded. The bombings went on. Al-Qaeda strikes around the world were planned here: Bali, London, Madrid. According to Pakistani commentator Ahmed Rashid, all al-Qaeda operations worldwide came with FATA fingerprints on them.

Periodically, when US patience wore thin, the Americans staged cross-border operations themselves, firing missiles at suspected al-Qaeda hideouts. Civilian casualties led to popular outrage: Pakistan was already fighting America's war for it, now the country was being bombed. Even when strikes were accurate, there was rage. In the border areas, mistrust of US and international organizations was such that polio vaccinators were forced to repaint their vehicles. Originally, they had UN stickers on, but when 'UN' came to be read as 'US' this was replaced with 'WHO'. This soon became synonymous with the Americans, too, and was replaced with 'NOPOLIO'.

Still there were problems.

The Afghan Taliban may have accepted Days of Tranquillity in the 1990s, but its modern descendants did not. Travel in the border regions became too dangerous for all foreigners.

The deteriorating situation along the Afghan–Pakistan border made it a perfect hiding place for the poliovirus. Pathogens tend to thrive during war: water systems are wrecked, sanitary infrastructures destroyed. Violence causes health workers to flee. Roads and bridges are destroyed. Transport systems go down. Waves of refugees disperse in all directions, carrying their infections with them. Keeping track of them, let alone offering healthcare, becomes impossible.

Dr Abdul Ghani saw all of this. In the latter part of 2003, looking for a new role, and perhaps a higher salary, he contacted a friend, local politician Abdullatif Bacha.

'He came and requested me to use my influence to transfer him from Nowshera to Bajaur,' Bacha recalls.

The transfer presented a few complications. In Nowshera, Ghani had been the employee of the NWFP administration; in Bajaur, he would be employed by the federal government. But Ghani was a talented, hard-working doctor and the Government wasn't turning away applicants. Bacha called a friend, who arranged the paperwork and on 22 December Dr Ghani was formally transferred. It was to be his last promotion.

At first the doctor was delighted with his new post, inviting former colleagues to visit. Bajaur was beautiful, he told them, with high mountains all around, historic passes into Afghanistan to the west and the Swat Valley – the site of his family's hiking holidays – to the east. It wasn't long before he changed his mind.

The smallest and northernmost of the Federally Administered Tribal Areas, Bajaur was also one of the least secure. Home to a large number of Afghan refugees, mostly Salafists loyal to Gulbuddin Hekmatyar (the warlord who later claimed to have smuggled Bin Laden out of Afghanistan in December 2001), the area was ideally situated for running cross-border operations. In the 1980s, the CIA had used it to equip mujahedin fighters before they attacked Soviet troops in Afghanistan. Twenty years later, Islamic militants used it for the same thing; only this time the targets were American, not Russian, military outposts.

Mountainous, sparsely populated and almost entirely inaccessible to both American and Pakistani militaries, Bajaur was a perfect hiding place for foreign fighters and al-Qaeda operatives – and one in particular.

'Bin Laden loved Bajaur,' says Michael Scheuer, head of the CIA's Bin Laden Unit. 'It was the place he intended to move his family and organization in May of 1997, before he was invited by the Taliban to go to Kandahar.' Ousted from Afghanistan immediately after 9/11, it was highly probable that the sheikh and his acolytes had returned for sanctuary. 'I think, without question, that's the most likely place along the border for them to be,' says Scheuer. This fact did not go unnoticed in US intelligence circles.

On 13 January 2006, two years after Dr Ghani's arrival in Bajaur, the CIA struck a housing complex in one of the agency's main towns, Damadola. Four Predator drones launched Hellfire missiles into the compound. Intelligence sources later explained that there was 'good reporting' that Bin Laden's deputy Ayman al Zawahiri was attending a party in one of the houses. If he was, he was gone by the time the missiles hit. Three homes were razed to the ground, eighteen civilians killed.

'It's terrible when innocent people are killed,' US Senator John McCain explained two days later. 'We apologize, but I can't tell you that we wouldn't do the same thing again.'

Tens of thousands of Pakistanis protested across the country. USAID-funded offices of the NGO Associated Development Construction were burned to the ground; in Karachi, protestors chanted, 'Stop bombing civilians!' and 'Death to America!'

Nine months later, it happened again. This time the target was a madrasa in the village of Chenagai, just outside Bajaur's largest city, Khar. At 5 a.m. on 30 October 2006, several aircraft fired missiles into the building, killing around seventy people. Again, apparently, the target was Zawahiri. Again, he wasn't there. The college's leader, Liaqat Ali, was.

Fury at US actions led to an immediate backlash. Thousands marched in Khar, chanting, 'Death to Musharraf!' and 'Death to Bush!' One of the protest's organizers was a young religious leader from the Swat Valley, Maulana Fazlullah. The son-in-law of the jailed founder of the extremist group Tehreek Nifaz Shariat Mohammed (TNSM), Fazlullah had been a close friend of Liaqat Ali, killed by the United States.

Fazlullah set up an illegal radio station transmitting throughout the region. A barrage of anti-Western, pro-Sharia broadcasts followed, leading to his moniker 'Mullah FM'. The Mullah's broadcasts became required listening for Swat's inhabitants as he castigated both Pakistani and US governments, instructed school administrators not to admit girls, barbers not to shave men, banned music, dancing, television and CDs, advised his audience to burn their evil computers and requested donations. He also handed out lists of provincial and government leaders to be beheaded for their anti-Islamic actions.

Perhaps predictably, after the US airstrike, Mullah FM added another ingredient, exhorting listeners not to allow their children to be vaccinated against polio. The Nigerian rumours were repeated. The 'infidel vaccine' contained female hormones. It spread AIDS. It was unsafe and ineffective. The GPEI was 'a conspiracy of the Jews and Christians', Fazlullah told listeners in January 2007, 'to stunt the population growth of the Muslims'. A new allegation was added: the vaccine was manufactured using pig fat. According to Mullah FM's logic, there was no room in the Koran for the treatment of diseases before they struck, anyway: children who died from polio were martyrs.

Not long afterwards, Fazlullah would strike a bargain with the leader of another Islamist group, Tehreek-i-Taliban Pakistan (TTP), and the two joined forces, making him one of the Taliban's main leaders in the country. He amassed a 15,000-strong army, burned down electrical-goods shops, blew up schools, beheaded village elders, declared war on the country's President Pervez Musharraf and eventually played a key role in the assassination of Musharraf's rival, Benazir Bhutto.

All the while, the anti-polio rhetoric spewed out across the airwaves. According to TTP spokesman Muslim Khan, Pakistan's inhabitants should not trust the United States, which was busy bombing its villagers, with the health of their children.

'There are other diseases,' Khan told listeners, 'hepatitis, typhoid, and so on. Why is everyone concentrating on polio? It's an American conspiracy.'

The organization found an imam willing to declare a fatwah on the UN and WHO workers, and ordered all NGO staff out of the area on the basis that they employed women – promoting vulgarity and obscenity.

'They hire women who work with men, in the field and in offices,' thundered Khan. 'It's totally un-Islamic and unacceptable.'

Ghani was worried. Things had clearly taken a turn for the worse. He stopped inviting his friends to come and stay and started looking for a way out himself.

'He was concerned about the deteriorating security situation,' recalls Azmatullah Jan Faiq. 'On a number of occasions he told us he wasn't happy.'

A month after the US bombing of the Chenagai madrasa, Ghani was supervising a polio-eradication project not far away when his car was surrounded by thirty masked men. They signalled for him to stop.

'Three of them were armed with Kalashnikovs,' the doctor later told his friend Nazirullah Muhammadzai. 'They started threatening me with dire consequences if I didn't stop the anti-polio campaign.' Ghani tried to reason with them. 'I explained that I was both a Muslim and a doctor. I knew how important anti-polio drops were for the life of a child.' When the militants were not persuaded, he shrugged. 'Well,' he told the masked men. 'If you don't believe me, shoot me.' The doctor would later laugh about the incident with friends ('Thank God they let me go!') but it left a scar. Before he was allowed to drive away, the men warned him that, if he ever entered the region again, they would kill him.

Shaken by this confrontation, Ghani told his friends that he was coming home. One more polio-vaccination campaign in Bajaur, and he was finished. He contacted Abdullatif Bacha, the politician who had arranged the posting in the first place.

'He came to me again,' Bacha acknowledges. 'He said he couldn't continue his work in the current hostile situation in Bajaur. He asked me to get him transferred out.'

Bacha agreed, and after the meeting Ghani called Muhammadzai to tell him the news: it was over: 'He was coming back to Nowshera.'

Bacha made some calls to the federal government and wheels were set in motion: the doctor was to be transferred. But first there was one more task he had to complete.

Inside the mosque in Shehano Bandar, when Friday prayers were complete, Ghani and his vaccination team faced their opponents. The numbers were hardly even. There were about twenty health workers and their supporters. Those against OPV numbered more than eighty. A furious debate ensued over the putative merits of polio vaccination. The Kalashnikov-toting cleric took the lead immediately.

'He said that the vaccine was provided by the West, by George Bush and that Western people wanted us all dead,' recalls Hazrat Jamal, the technician recruited by Ghani because of his Islamic-looking beard. 'He said that the vaccine contained pig fat.'

Ghani countered that the vaccine was necessary for the health of the village, that he was himself a Muslim and a doctor and that the allegations were not true. Shouldn't children be left out of this argument, anyway? Surely the War on Terror had nothing to do with kids?

The argument raged back and forth for around two hours. Finally, Jamal lost his temper. 'If you're arguing against this vaccine because it's made in the West,' he told the cleric, 'well, look at your own Kalashnikov. That's made in the West. If you drive a car, that's made in the West, too.' Jamal turned to the assembled crowd. 'And if you go on the Haj, you will fly there on an aeroplane. Where do you think *that* was made?'

At this point, the unimaginable happened. The cleric admitted defeat.

'OK,' he told the vaccinators reluctantly. 'I don't have a family or children myself – but you can come into our village and try to convince the parents here to take the vaccine. I won't stop you.'

The team thanked him, left the mosque, dispersed throughout the village of Shehano Bandar and started vaccinating children immediately.

Two hours later, they met at the white pickup truck.

'Come on,' Ghani told the driver, Abdul Rahim. 'Time to go home.'

Rahim climbed in behind the wheel and Siraj, one of the EPI technicians, sat up next to him. Ghani climbed into the front left-hand seat; the others got into the back. The truck pulled away from Shehano Bandar and began the descent south towards Khar.

Ghani asked how the vaccination had gone and was informed that around 60 per cent of the parents had allowed their children to be inoculated.

'That's good,' the doctor told his staff. 'You've done well.'

There was, however, a problem: 60 per cent was not enough. They needed 100 per cent. They would all have to come back tomorrow. In the back seat, Hazrat Jamal was incredulous.

'I have to be honest,' he told his boss, 'I don't like this place very much. There's something wrong. The people don't seem friendly at all.'

For the next fifteen minutes, the vaccinators argued good-naturedly with Ghani: they didn't want to return; he knew they would all have to.

Then, just as the pickup reached the bottom of the mountain track, it came to a right-hand turn so steep it was forced to slow to a crawl. The driver hauled the wheel over, the vehicle turned sharply and Ghani leant over the seat to speak to Jamal.

'Enough,' he said. 'We *have* to come back tomorrow and get the rest.'

There was no flash. What there was, was a roar so deep and guttural it seemed to suck all the oxygen out of the car, as well as from the lungs of its occupants. So sudden was the detonation that, in the back seat, Jamal thought a rocket must have passed overhead.

'My first reaction was that I was OK, that the rocket had hit somewhere nearby.' At that very instant Jamal realized the pickup truck was ten metres up in the air. 'I realized that it wasn't nearby. That we were the target.' The bearded EPI technician lost consciousness before the truck hit the ground.

When he came round, Jamal found himself lying beside the pickup, unable to move. Looking up, he saw the driver Abdul Rahim trapped behind the wheel of the mangled vehicle. Beside him, in shock, was Abdullah, one of the vaccinators, apparently unharmed. Siraj looked like he was sitting on the ground beside him, but that was impossible: one of his legs was severed. Behind them both was Abdul Ghani, lying on the road, drenched in blood. He had been ripped apart from the waist down.

Unable to move his legs and bleeding profusely, Jamal shouted at the rapidly growing crowd of onlookers for help. Not one stepped forward. He shouted again. Eventually, a voice piped up from the crowd: 'Who are you? Are you foreigners or are you local?'

The full extent of the damage caused by parents in Pakistan's tribal belt not having their children inoculated has yet to be determined.

Perhaps it never will be. GPEI officials are keen to clarify that the problem is more complex than just a question of religious refusal. War, security, paranoia, poor sanitation: all play a role. Vaccinating children in war zones is difficult, dangerous and sometimes impossible. The most common reason why children are missed is not religion but instability.

Privately, officials speculate about what might happen if the programme fails to achieve its goals. In the worst-case scenario, according to Ellyn Ogden of USAID, 'at some point the initiative will run out of money or the spread of virus will simply get too broad to contain'. International commitment and funding will disappear. GPEI will die. The consequences of such a failure would be catastrophic: more than 10 million children will be paralysed in the next forty years.

Even Ciro de Quadros, perhaps more than anyone else the person most responsible for instigating the programme back in the late 1980s, is downbeat.

'We may never eradicate polio,' he admitted to the author Tim Brookes in 2006. 'It was a great adventure that could have been very successful. I feel very sad.'

Perhaps de Quadros should consider what he has achieved. Since 1988, more than 2 billion children in 200 countries have been vaccinated. As a direct result, 5 million of them are not paralysed today. A million more are alive, when they would have been dead. Globally, cases of polio today are as low as they have ever been: just 1,595 in 2009. In 2006, polio from Nigeria was finally cleared from Niger, Egypt, Yemen and Indonesia. The Uttar Pradesh outbreak peaked and has since begun to die down. Pakistan is aiming for eradication of the disease from its borders by the end of 2012. Surely the battle is almost over? Not yet. Now there's polio in Chad, Congo, Kenya, Sudan and Uganda again. The final cut may yet prove to be the hardest.

*   *   *

GPEI staff in FATA are less than optimistic. The programme is in trouble in all seven of the region's agencies.

'We're not moving ahead,' admits one. 'The major issue is inaccessibility. We can't access 53 per cent of the areas in Bajaur.'

The dislocation of millions of people makes the project even harder: refugees want food, shelter and security more than polio drops. 'How can we convince them of the importance of the drops for the children when they are struggling for their very survival?' he asks. The programme is 'at a standstill'.

In neighbouring Mohmand things are little better. 'Three out of seven subdivisions are inaccessible,' says another vaccination official. 'We cannot move there.'

For the Khyber agency, the situation is the same: 'Bara and Terah make up a huge area of the agency, but due to fighting our teams can't go there at all.' Other agencies – Orakzai and Lower Kurrum – are largely inaccessible and ridden with factional fighting. Upper Kurrum can only be accessed via Afghanistan. Vaccine is making it through, but, since there are no monitoring facilities, it's hard to determine how effective the programme is.

'No one knows whether the vaccine was given to children or not,' admits the official.

North Waziristan has been under a military curfew for eighteen months, so no polio vaccination is taking place at all. The whole situation is a lottery.

'Most of the people have migrated to nearby settled districts and frontier regions anyway,' he explains. 'There are no anti-polio campaigns and no valid data on the current status of the disease.'

In South Waziristan, regions under the control of the TTP are no-go areas for anyone, let alone health workers. No vaccination is taking place.

Ongoing fighting along the border creates suspicion, which further fuels the problem. Even in safer areas, polio eradicators are often assumed to be working for the Government or the CIA, collecting information about inhabitants either for new fertility-reduction vaccines or military targeting.

'The military, the militants and the [US] drone attacks have made life miserable for the local communities,' says the official. 'They're caught in a vicious circle and fighting for their survival. Thousands of children are left unvaccinated.' Rumours about vaccinators, and the vaccine itself, abound. 'When Bush was the President of the United States,' he recalls, 'some people even said that his urine was used in the vaccine.'

Such are the levels of suspicion that, although they are willing to talk about the polio-eradication programme, none of the vaccination officials will divulge their real names, even off the record.

To this day, Dr Ghani's friends are unsure about the exact mechanism of the bomb that killed him. Authorities have stated that the explosives were placed under his car seat; Ghani's driver says that he guarded the vehicle the entire time, so it would have been impossible for anyone to place a charge on it. Local villagers, who may know more, maintain that a roadside device was triggered by remote control as Ghani's vehicle passed by. Certainly the location of the detonation, on a sharp turn where the car was forced to decelerate almost to a standstill, would have made this a good place for a bomb; that Ghani was sitting in the left-hand seat might explain why his injuries were so much more severe than the other occupants: if the charge was placed on the outer edge of the turn, he took the brunt of the blast. Next to receive the shockwave would have been Siraj, who lost a leg – then died in hospital a few days later. What seems in little doubt is that it was not a random attack.

'One fact is clear,' says Namair Muhammad. 'He was the target.'

Fazli Raziq was at home when the phone rang at 6 p.m. on 16 February 2007. A colleague informed him that Ghani had been killed near Salarzai.

'It was like a thunderstorm,' he says of the call. 'I couldn't believe it.'

Asked how he knew, the colleague explained there had been a news-flash on local TV. Since Raziq had no television, he called Namair Muhammad, who confirmed the news: Ghani's official car had been travelling away from Shehano Bandar when the bomb went off. His body was on its way home.

Ghani's friends congregated at his family home in Manki Sharif that night. At 11 p.m., the corpse was finally delivered. Medical staff were unable to inspect it because it was in a sealed coffin.

'The lower half of his body had been vaporized by the explosion,' says Raziq. 'But his face and chest were safe.'

Those who inspected the scene of the bomb told his friends that the doctor had been killed instantly. His killers were never identified.

'Nobody ever tried to pressure the Government to bring the perpetrators to justice,' says Nazirullah Muhammadzai. 'It was very discouraging.'

The family was offered a 500,000 rupee award, and a pension of 8,000 rupees per month: about $100. Together they were not sufficient to cover the cost of three children in full-time education, so Ghani's oldest son Ameer Hamza was forced to drop out of college to support the family.

Not long after Ghani's death, a plaque arrived from the Centers for Disease Control in Atlanta. Signed by the Center's president C. Charles Stokes, it announced that – in the light of his 'extraordinary contributions and sacrifices' – Abdul Ghani had been named a 'Polio Eradication Hero'.

He wasn't the only hero, of course. Hazrat Jamal, still unable to use one leg as a result of the explosion, is back on the vaccination trail, still going after twenty-three years. So are the others. Abdul Rahim, the driver, was unconscious for three days. When he woke up, he was told there had been an accident, but everyone had survived. All would be fine. His next recollection, a week later, is of being told this information was incorrect. Actually, the car had been bombed. Dr Ghani was dead.

'I sat and cried for hours. I was just so immensely sad.'

Jamal felt the same. 'A good man,' he says of Dr Ghani. 'We miss him.'

Pakistan's religious leaders are under no illusion as to the scale of the problems in their country. Maulana Rahat Hussain, a religious authority and former parliamentary senator from Swat, first heard rumours about vaccines when he was studying at a seminary in 1988, but immediately dismissed them as scare stories. An educated man, Hussain knows that the OPV rumours are false, though he finds many of the other stories circulating in their wake persuasive.

'US aggression against Iraq and Afghanistan was based on falsified intelligence,' he says. 'And US involvement is creating security problems in the Muslim countries of Pakistan, Afghanistan and Iraq . . . The United States has destabilized the peace of the whole world.'

The failure of Pakistani authorities to restore law and order along the country's north-west border, together with repeated US airstrikes, feeds this notion.

'People are asking why their homes were destroyed by the US forces,' says Rahat. 'Innocent people are being tortured and killed. The whole region is in the grip of violence and uncertainty. What type of peace is this?' The cleric becomes animated. 'What is the US doing here? Apart from killing people in drone attacks, I mean . . . The War on Terror is in fact a war against Muslims and Islam.'

To Rahat's list of allegations, we might add a few more: that Western leaders seized on 9/11 as an opportunity to justify policies they already had in mind, fabricated excuses to sell those policies to their citizens, then ended up falling for their own propaganda. That the United States, a nation so consumed with rage in the aftermath of 9/11 that its own citizens murdered people who simply looked as if they might be Muslims, obeyed the laws it wanted to obey, reinterpreted the laws it did not want to obey and stepped outside the laws it was unable to reinterpret. That it embraced dictators it thought useful, ignored their atrocious human rights records, then abandoned them if they didn't co-operate. That coalition troops fought cowardly campaigns in Afghanistan and Iraq, preferring to drop bombs from the air rather than engaging the enemy on the ground, then lying about the numbers of women and children they killed. That a war declared in the name of human rights, democracy and freedom subverted those very rights and ended up achieving the exact opposite of its stated goals. That the corrosion of international law, international humanitarian law and the laws of war was as irreversible as it was contagious. That wherever the US flag went there was death. That the politicians lied, and lied, and lied.

It doesn't really matter whether you believe these statements or not. What *does* matter is that a huge percentage of people in the Arab world believe them.

'If you are conducting military operations in Pakistan and displacing people from their homes,' says Rahat, 'how can you convince them to use this vaccine? These policies affect the anti-polio campaign.' He sighs. 'People I talk to about this say that the only vaccine they really want is peace.'

Ultimately, vaccine uptake is dependent on trust: in the safety of the vaccine itself and in the people who administer it. Once that trust is lost, it doesn't matter how effective the vaccine or how noble the goal of its administration. If the motives and conduct of the administrators are questionable, why would anyone trust them with the physical welfare of their children?

'It was different before 9/11,' says Hazrat Jamal from his home in Bajaur. 'People used to be co-operative. We would have people come to us and say, "Hey, you missed our village, you missed our children." But after 9/11 and the US invasion of Afghanistan, we are facing all kinds of problems. We might not succeed. People don't trust America. They don't trust anything that comes from America.'

Trust has to be earned. Once lost, it is hard to regain. How to go about doing this – and how long it might take – is anyone's guess.

In the meantime, the virus spreads. Among the poorest, most dissatisfied nations on earth, where life is apparently cheap, education is lacking and word of mouth is strong. In the dark backrooms of tea houses and shops, in mosques and Internet chatrooms and at prayer meetings. Where there is poverty, illiteracy, discrimination, lack of governance, discontent, deprivation, corruption and injustice. The virus may be cornered, but it's hiding in some of the most destitute, poorly governed and war-torn countries on the planet.

That our children have been immunized does not place them beyond risk: globalization works both ways.

On 2 July 2007, Thai Air flight TG999 touched down at Tullamarine Airport, Melbourne. One of its passengers was a foreign-exchange student. A week earlier, at home in Pakistan, he had picked up a dose of what he thought was influenza. It wasn't.

He wasn't an 'illegal'. He wasn't a queue-jumper. He didn't come by boat. He wasn't a terrorist. He had a visa. Everything was above board.

One unvaccinated student turned out to be Australia's first polio case in twenty-one years.

The virus only has to be lucky once. We have to be lucky always.

Epilogue

Polunsky inmate #999409 tries to struggle, but it's no use. He is strapped to a gurney and wheeled in to the chamber. The gurney tilts upright. His arms extend to receive the needles, like a crucifix. He starts to fall.

Stroman dreams a lot, has done since he arrived on Death Row. At night, old friends visit him to talk. Not necessarily about his crimes, but about things that happened long ago: his grandfather, a friend who committed suicide, another who died in a bike crash. It's not spooky, talking with ghosts. It's kind of nice. Friendly. But he doesn't like the gurney dream.

Stroman's not afraid of death. What scares him is the procedure. Like 9/11: it wasn't the planes, the collapsing buildings or the extent of the carnage that horrified him. It was the *process* of death, the suffering on the way there. He doesn't like the idea of a fatal injection. He'd rather be shot. Quicker. More Texan.

Through the glass I ask him about his grandfather, Robert. 'What would he say to you if he was alive today?'

He smiles and shakes his head. 'He'd knock the living shit out of me.'

Stroman is about to become a grandfather himself. One of his daughters is pregnant. The baby, a girl, will be named Madyson. He's excited, loves children.

'Never thought I'd live to see the day,' he says.

*   *   *

On 11 September 2001, a fanatical terrorist organization, al-Qaeda, struck the United States. Three thousand civilians were killed. Western leaders faced a series of impossible decisions: the scale of the attacks was unprecedented. How should we respond? What should we hope to achieve? The answers were unclear.

Today, things are clearer. We have achieved a very great deal. A decade after 9/11, hundreds of thousands more civilians are dead. Iran and North Korea – two of the four nations constituting the 'Axis of Evil' – are either going or have already gone nuclear. The United Nations and NATO have been weakened. International law, the mechanism by which states regulate themselves and each other, is in jeopardy.

Financially, too, the outlook is dire. Joseph Stiglitz, winner of the 2001 Nobel Prize for economics, estimates that Iraq alone will end up costing the United States somewhere in the region of $3 trillion; the rest of the world will end up having to fork out another $3 trillion. After a global financial meltdown, $6 trillion is an outlay we can ill afford.

There are more significant costs. Over the course of the last seven years, the West has proved unable to impose its will on Iraq, a nation with a population a tenth that of the United States. Afghanistan, one of the poorest, most broken states on the planet, appears equally uncontrollable. These two countries were supposed to be the gateways to a new democracy in the Middle East. They may instead prove to be the Vietnams of our generation.

The result has been a crisis of legitimacy. 9/11 brought us together. A decade on, not only is the United States the most reviled nation on earth, but a third of its own citizens believe their government to have been complicit in the bombing of the World Trade Centers.

'Make no mistake about it,' George W. Bush told the American people the day after the attacks. 'We will win.'

We haven't. The world is not less, but more, dangerous.

It's one thing to launch a war with certain goals and not to attain those goals. It's another entirely to declare war and achieve the exact opposite of your stated intentions. If there is anything worse than losing a war, surely this is it?

I meet Alka Patel at the gas station on Big Town Boulevard in Dallas. I want to buy her lunch, but she's too busy to take time off, so we stand by the coffee machine in front of the counter where her husband was gunned down in 2001 and make polite conversation. Her son has just won a scholarship to study medicine at the University of Texas at Austin. Her daughter wants to be a doctor, too. She'll get there: she works hard, makes good grades. Her father would have been proud.

I'm apprehensive. I have a deep aversion to the school of journalism that advocates doorstepping the bereaved to ask them how they feel. Inevitably, that's pretty much what I end up doing. What was Vasudev like? I ask.

Alka thinks for a moment. 'Quiet, pretty quiet, and very generous, and, um . . .' Her voice starts to crack. She takes a breath and tries again. 'Very generous . . . very quiet . . . and . . .' She breaks down. 'Sorry,' she says.

Nine thousand miles away in Melbourne, Australia, Halima al Saadi fixes lunch. 'You know,' whispers Karim the moment his wife is out of earshot, 'some people are crazy after four years on Nauru. They eat tablets [anti-depressants] because of their time there. Our friend S. is completely insane: the police put him in prison because he was walking around with no clothes on.'

Halima, eavesdropping from the kitchen, pipes up. 'Some women are not able to rest,' she says. 'Bad dreams in the night.'

Karim becomes indignant. 'Why did they say we threw our children into the sea? That is not true. Not true. A lie.'

That autumn a group of Uzbek politicians organizes a conference in Belgium. A government-in-exile, of sorts, is formed. The timing is auspicious. For four years, refugees have kept quiet about the Andijan massacre, but on 27 October 2009 the European Union votes to lift sanctions on Uzbekistan. Word is that the move is backed by the United States. The situation in Afghanistan is desperate: America wants back into the K2 airbase. This time, according to experts, things will go better. President Karimov, it seems, is coming back into the fold.

The Uzbeks march outside the EU headquarters in Brussels to protest the resumption of arms trading with one of the world's worst human rights abusers. Only one international broadcaster shows up to cover the issue.

Much of the blame for the failure of the War on Terror lies with the calamitous decision to invade Iraq. Colin Powell, who appears to have been cajoled – and occasionally actively misled – in the run-up to the campaign, was one of a handful of policymakers willing to be upfront about what went wrong. The lack of weapons of mass destruction, he admitted in February 2004, changed the 'political calculus' when it came to the invasion: a cipher, presumably, for the fact that he would not have backed the operation had he known the truth. He was in a minority.

As it became clear there were no WMDs in the country, politicians' reasoning subtly shifted. 'Saddam had WMDs', the main argument for the invasion, became 'Saddam had WMD *programmes*', which then became 'Saddam had WMD-*related programmes*', then 'Saddam had WMD-*related programme activities*'.

Finally, hell, we invaded for other reasons: Saddam was a homicidal dictator who killed civilians. That the coalition of the willing ended up killing more was never mentioned.[16]

Others were less nuanced. 'I still firmly believe,' wrote General Michael

---

[16] According to the *Lancet*, 654,965 'excess deaths' occurred in Iraq from 2003 to 2006 – approximately 2.5 per cent of the entire population. These figures have been disputed. Four years on, other estimates range from 95,000 to well over 1 million.

DeLong in October 2006, 'that Iraq had WMDs and that one day they will be found.' According to DeLong, formerly Deputy Commander at US CENTCOM, the weapons were smuggled to Lebanon and Syria, then hidden.

In the face of such reasoning, one can only conclude that those responsible for the invasion are trapped in a desperate state of denial. Surely they must be aware that the invasion was a failure on a gargantuan scale – that it will go down as one of the worst foreign policy decisions of modern times? Apparently not.

'I can apologize for the information that turned out to be wrong,' Tony Blair told the Labour Party in 2004. 'But I can't, sincerely at least, apologize for removing Saddam.'

Cheerleaders for the invasion look to the future, waiting for the day when their decisions will be vindicated and they will be thanked rather than vilified.

In the meantime, allies that rushed to stand shoulder to shoulder with the United States after 9/11 scheme to remove their troops from harm's way, to disentangle themselves from policies they backed wholeheartedly a few short years ago. Every week, news reports: car bombs, IEDs, ambushes. The bodies come home in bags.

Were we lied to? I'm not certain that we were. To me, it wasn't that the politicians lied more frequently, or that their lies were any grander. It was rather that the truth became inconveniently complex, tangled up with other issues. What we knew. What we believed. What our intelligence agencies promised us. What we told our intelligence agencies to promise us. What was acceptable. What was *necessary*. The issue was not one of dishonesty, but of something far more corrosive: certainty.

Shocked by 11 September, policymakers called for 'moral clarity', but displayed none themselves, instead playing to the cheap seats, appealing to patriotism and to God, while concocting misguided similes linking 9/11 to Pearl Harbor and Bin Laden to Hitler. Mixing their metaphors to fit their audience, they yoked together simultaneously best- and worst-case scenarios to justify policies they had always fancied anyway.

Stuck in a morass of half-baked assumptions and quasi-religious rhetoric, good intentions and misguided concepts of moral rectitude, truth quietly suffocated. Propelled by faith in our cause, our reason superseded by certainty, we didn't even notice.

We never follow up our al-Qaeda contact in Baghdad. Making contact with Tanzhim may well be a journalistic coup, but it's not the story we're after. It's also a good way for all of us to end up on the Internet with masked men chanting Islamic slogans behind us. Abu Shujaa, the bomber, remains in hiding in Syria; Yusuf, the looter who stole much of the HMX from Al Qa'qaa's bunkers, breaks off contact. One of our fixers receives death threats, along with assurances that everything he was shown in Yusifiyah has now been moved. Somewhere, in a potato cellar forty-five minutes south-west of Baghdad, ten tons of crystalline high explosive awaits a purchaser.

A couple of months later, in the village of Deh Rawood, Afghanistan, Abdul Malik receives a visit from an American called Bob, who shows him a photograph. This is the woman, he says, who launched the AC-130 attack on his family. Bob asks if Malik can forgive her.

'No,' he replies. 'Go and kill her in America.' Informed that it's not possible to murder people in the United States, even for revenge, Malik instructs Bob to leave. 'If you can't do this for me,' he tells him, 'we are not friends.'

Malik and Tela Gul still live in the same house. In the afternoons, their two children, Gul Samara and Farid Ahmed, play in the orchard behind the building where, ten years ago, Malik's brother fired his AK-47 to celebrate their engagement. Neither child has ever been told why they have no grandparents. Neither is aware of the fact that their ancestors' remains are all around them, entwined in the branches of the pomegranate trees that reach up towards the sky.

*   *   *

Outspoken liberals like to display their hatred of the lead players behind the War on Terror. Bush, Cheney, Rumsfeld, Blair: the villains of the piece. The truth is that, with a few notable exceptions, nobody covered themselves with glory. Opposition political parties failed to intervene; the military failed to stand behind its beliefs that operations in Iraq and Afghanistan required better resourcing, manpower and planning; the intelligence community failed to insist that caveats in its products were there for a reason. The media failed to inform the public there were serious problems. Perhaps the blame should be shared? There's enough to go round.

Doubtless there is a case to be made that the world changed as a result of 9/11. But *how* it changed was not up to Bin Laden, al-Qaeda or the Taliban. It was up to us. We could have reacted differently. We didn't.

As a result, the situation in which we currently find ourselves is not one that has been thrust upon us. It's one that we have chosen. Al-Qaeda doesn't threaten our existence. It never did. Our reaction to it just might.

Polunsky operates a macabre lottery system. Inmates are allocated numbers on arrival; the higher the number, the longer the wait. Five of the next ten scheduled executions will be of prisoners with numbers greater than Stroman's. Time has almost overtaken him. When it does, #999409 will stop sending me letters plastered with US flags. When it does, the story will be complete: two wives will have been widowed, six children orphaned.

Vasudev Patel was right. 'Whatever revenge they have with each other,' he told Alka on the night of 9/11, 'they're just going to kill innocent people.'

I meet Kevin 'Bear' Hartline at his home in Mesquite. We sit on a battered sofa in his garage drinking beer and reminiscing about Stroman. Bear has stuck by his friend since they first met at school in the 1980s; there's every chance he will be beside him at the end.

It's an uncomfortable meeting. The more Bear drinks, the more despondent he becomes. He looks at his feet and shuffles uncomfortably; at times I wonder if he's about to cry.

'You know,' he muses, 'I'm probably the only person in the world that really gives a damn about that guy. We couldn't have been closer if we were brothers.' It's hot. Outside, the tarmac is melting; above us, a US flag hangs limp. 'I love him. I really do,' he says. 'But I'm just so, so ashamed of what he did.'

Who knows? Perhaps, in the small dark hours of the night, when he's not conversing with ghosts, Stroman is, too.

Suggested Reading

Allawi, Alia A., *The Occupation of Iraq: Winning the War, Losing the Peace* (Yale University Press, 2007)

Anonymous, *Hunting Al Qaeda: A Take-No-Prisoners Account of Terror, Adventure, and Disillusionment* (Zenith Press, 2005)

Bamford, James, *A Pretext for War: 9/11, Iraq, and the Abuse of America's Intelligence Agencies* (Anchor Books, 2005)

Barton, Rod, *The Weapons Detective: The Inside Story of Australia's Top Weapons Inspector* (Black Inc. Press, 2006)

Berntsen, Gary and Pezzullo, Ralph, *Jawbreaker: The Attack on Bin Laden and Al-Qaeda: A Personal Account by the CIA's Key Field Commander* (Three Rivers Press, 2005)

Blix, Hans, *Disarming Iraq: The Search for Weapons of Mass Destruction* (Bloomsbury, 2004)

Bobbit, Philip, *Terror and Consent: The Wars for the Twenty-first Century* (Penguin, 2009)

Booth, Ken and Dunne, Tim, *Worlds in Collision: Terror and the Future of Global Order* (Palgrave Macmillan, 2002)

Bremer, L. Paul and McConnell, Malcolm, *My Year in Iraq: The Struggle to Build a Future of Hope* (Simon & Schuster, 2006)

Brennan, Frank, *Tampering with Asylum: A Universal Humanitarian Problem* (University of Queensland Press, 2007)

Briscoe, Charles H. (ed), *Weapon of Choice: ARSOF in Afghanistan* (Combat Studies Institute Press, 2003)

Briskman, Linda et al., *Human Rights Overboard: Seeking Asylum in Australia* (Scribe Publications, 2008)

Brookes, Tim and Khan, Omar A., *The End of Polio?: Behind the Scenes of the Campaign to Vaccinate Every Child on the Planet* (American Public Health Association, 2006)

Clarke, Richard A., *Against All Enemies: Inside America's War on Terror* (The Free Press, 2004)

Cockburn, Patrick, *The Occupation: War and Resistance in Iraq* (Verso, 2007)

Cole, David, *Enemy Aliens: Double Standards and Constitutional Freedoms in the War on Terrorism* (The New Press, 2005)

Coll, Steve, *Ghost Wars: The Secret History of the CIA, Afghanistan, and Bin Laden, from the Soviet Invasion to September 10, 2001* (Penguin, 2005)

Cook, Robin, *The Point of Departure: Why One of Britain's Leading Politicians Resigned over Tony Blair's Decision to Go to War in Iraq* (Simon & Schuster, 2007)

Croft, Stuart, *Culture, Crisis and America's War on Terror* (Cambridge University Press, 2006)

Davis, Walter A., *Death's Dream Kingdom: The American Psyche since 9/11* (Pluto Press, 2006)

DeLong, Lt. Gen. Michael with Lukeman, Noah, *A General Speaks Out: The Truth about the Wars in Afghanistan and Iraq* (Zenith Press, 2007)

Dobbins, Ambassador James F., *After the Taliban: Nation-Building in Afghanistan* (Potomac Books, 2008)

Drogin, Bob, *Curveball: Spies, Lies and the Man Behind Them – The Real Reason America Went to War in Iraq* (Ebury Press, 2007)

Drumheller, Tyler, *On the Brink: An Insider's Account of How the White House Compromised American Intelligence* (Politico's Publishing, 2007)

Dudziak, Mary L. (ed), *September 11 in History: A Watershed Moment?* (Duke University Press, 2003)

Eisner, Peter and Royce, Knut, *The Italian Letter: How the Bush*

Administration Used a Fake Letter to Build the Case for War in Iraq (Rodale, 2007)

Ferguson, Charles H., *No End in Sight: Iraq's Descent into Chaos* (Public Affairs, 2008)

Franks, General Tommy with McConnell, Malcolm, *American Soldier* (HarperCollins, 2004)

Galbraith, Peter W., *The End of Iraq: How American Incompetence Created a War without End* (Simon & Schuster, 2006)

Gannon, Kathy, *I is for Infidel: From Holy War to Holy Terror in Afghanistan* (Public Affairs, 2006)

Gordon, Michael, *Freeing Ali: The Human Face of the Pacific Solution* (University of New South Wales Press, 2005)

Gordon, Michael and Trainor, Bernard, *COBRA II: The Inside Story of the Invasion and Occupation of Iraq* (Atlantic Books, 2006)

Grey, Stephen, *Ghost Plane: The Inside Story of the CIA's Secret Rendition Programme* (C. Hurst & Co., 2006)

Halberstadt, Hans, *War Stories of the Green Berets* (Zenith Press, 2004)

Hersh, Seymour M., *Chain of Command: The Road from 9/11 to Abu Ghraib* (Penguin, 2005)

Isikoff, Michael and Corn, David, *Hubris: the Inside Story of Spin, Scandal, and the Selling of the Iraq War* (Three Rivers Press, 2006)

Jackson, Robert J. and Towle, Philip, *Temptations of Power: the United States in Global Politics After 9/11* (Palgrave Macmillan, 2006)

Johnson, Chris and Leslie, Jolyon, *Afghanistan: The Mirage of Peace* (Zed Books, 2004)

Jones, Seth G., *In the Graveyard of Empires: America's War in Afghanistan* (W. W. Norton & Co, 2009)

Kampfner, John, *Blair's Wars* (The Free Press, 2003)

Kevin, Tony, *A Certain Maritime Incident: the Sinking of SIEV X* (Scribe Publications, 2004)

Kiriakou, John, *The Reluctant Spy: My Secret Life in the CIA's War on Terror* (Bantam Books, 2009)

Langewiesche, William, *American Ground: Unbuilding the World Trade Center* (Scribner, 2003)

Leonard, Mark (ed), *Re-ordering the World: The Long-term Implications of 11 September* (Foreign Policy Centre, 2002)

Lusher, Haslam, *Yearning to Breathe Free: Seeking Asylum in Australia* (The Federation Press, 2007)

McClellan, Scott, *What Happened: Inside the Bush White House and What's Wrong with Washington* (Public Affairs, 2008)

Mares, Peter, *Borderline* (University of New South Wales Press Ltd, 2002)

Marr, David and Wilkinson, Marian, *Dark Victory: The Tampa and the Military Campaign to Re-elect the Prime Minister* (Allen & Unwin, 2003)

Mayer, Jane, *The Dark Side: The Inside Story of How the War on Terror Turned into a War on American Ideals* (Doubleday, 2008)

Meyer, Christopher, *DC Confidential: The Controversial Memoirs of Britain's Ambassador to the US at the Time of 9/11 and the Run-up to the Iraq War* (Weidenfeld & Nicholson, 2005)

Meyerowitz, Joanne (ed), *History and September 11th* (Temple University Press, 2003)

Muñoz, Heraldo, *A Solitary War: A Diplomat's Chronicle of the Iraq War and Its Lessons* (Fulcrum Publishing, 2008)

Murray, Craig, *Murder in Samarkand: A British Ambassador's Controversial Defiance of Tyranny in the War on Terror* (Mainstream Publishing, 2006)

Obeidi, Mahdi and Pitzer, Kurt, *The Bomb in My Garden: the Secrets of Saddam's Nuclear Mastermind* (John Wiley and Sons, 2004)

Olcott, Martha Brill, *Central Asia's Second Chance* (Brookings University Press, 2005)

Packer, George, *The Assassins' Gate: America in Iraq* (Faber & Faber Ltd, 2006)

Paglen, Trevor and Thompson, A. C., *Torture Taxi: On the Trail of the CIA's Rendition Flights* (Icon Books, 2007)

Phillips, David L., *Losing Iraq: Inside the Postwar Reconstruction Fiasco* (Basic Books, 2007)

Plame Wilson, Valerie, *Fair Game: My Life as a Spy, My Betrayal by the White House* (Simon & Schuster, 2007)

Poole, Steven, *Unspeak: Words are Weapons* (Little, Brown, 2007)

Power, Samantha, *Chasing the Flame: Sergio Vieira de Mello and the Fight to Save the World* (Penguin, 2008)

Rashid, Ahmed, *Descent into Chaos: The United States and the Failure of Nation Building in Pakistan, Afghanistan, and Central Asia* (Allen Lane, 2008)

Rich, Frank, *The Greatest Story ever Sold: The Decline and Fall of Truth from 9/11 to Katrina* (Penguin, 2006)

Ricks, Thomas E., *Fiasco: The American Military Adventure in Iraq* (Allen Lane, 2006)

Risen, James, *State of War: The Secret History of the CIA and the Bush Administration* (The Free Press, 2006)

Rothstein, Hy S., *Afghanistan and the Troubled Future of Unconventional Warfare* (Naval Institute Press, 2006)

Runciman, David, *The Politics of Good Intentions: History, Fear and Hypocrisy in the New World Order* (Princeton University Press, 2006)

Salgado, Sebastiao, *The End of Polio: A Global Effort to End a Disease* (PixelPress, 2003)

Sands, Philippe, *Lawless World: Making and Breaking Global Rules* (Penguin, 2006)

Scanlon, Jennifer, *The Selling of 9/11* (Palgrave Macmillan, 2005)

Scheuer, Michael, *Imperial Hubris: Why the West Is Losing the War on Terror* (Potomac Books, 2004)

Schroen, Gary C., *First In: An Insider's Account of How the CIA Spearheaded the War on Terror in Afghanistan* (Presidio Press, 2005)

Schulz, William, *Tainted Legacy: 9-11 and the Ruin of Human Rights* (Thunder's Mouth Press, 2003)

Scraton, Phil (ed), *Beyond September 11: An Anthology of Dissent* (Pluto Press, 2002)

Short, Clare, *An Honourable Deception?: New Labour, Iraq, and the Misuse of Power* (The Free Press, 2004)

Sifry, Micah L. and Cerf, Christopher, *The Iraq War Reader: History, Documents, Opinions* (Touchstone, 2003)

Simpson, David, *9/11: The Culture of Commemoration* (The University of Chicago Press, 2006)

Solomon, David (ed), *Howard's Race: Winning the Unwinnable Election* (Harper Collins, 2002)

Stafford Smith, Clive, *Bad Men: Guantanamo Bay and the Secret Prisons* (Weidenfeld & Nicholson, 2007)

Stiglitz, Joseph, and Bilmes, Linda, *The Three Trillion Dollar War: The True Cost of the Iraq Conflict* (Allen Lane, 2008)

Suskind, Ron, *The Way of the World: A Story of Truth and Hope in an Age of Extremism* (Simon & Schuster, 2008)

———, *The One Percent Doctrine: Deep inside America's Pursuit of Its Enemies since 9/11* (Simon & Schuster, 2006)

Tenet, George and Harlow, Bill, *At the Center of the Storm: My Years at the CIA* (Harper Press, 2007)

Weller, Patrick, *Don't Tell the Prime Minister* (Scribe Publications, 2002)

Whitney, Craig R. (ed), *The WMD Mirage: Iraq's Decade of Deception and America's False Premise for War* (PublicAffairs, 2005)

Wilkie, Andrew, *Axis of Deceit: The Story of the Intelligence Officer Who Risked All to Tell the Truth about WMD and Iraq* (Black Inc Agenda, 2004)

Woodward, Bob, *Bush at War* (Pocket Books, 2003)

———, *Plan of Attack* (Pocket Books, 2004)

———, *State of Denial* (Simon & Schuster, 2006)

Other sources

'Adrift in the Pacific, the Implications of Australia's Pacific Refugee Solution', Oxfam (February, 2002)

Akiner, Shirin, 'Violence in Andijan, 13 May 2005. An Independent Assessment', CACI Silk Road Paper (July 2005)

Albright, David, *Iraq's Aluminium Tubes: Separating Fact from Fiction*, ISIS (5 December 2003)

Assessing Damage, Urging Action, Report of the Eminent Jurists' Panel on Terrorism, Counter-Terrorism and Human Rights (2009).

Beehner, Lionel, *Documenting Andijan*, Council on Foreign Relations, 26 June 2006

Bennett, Scott, et al., *Commonwealth Election 2001*, Research Paper 11, 2001–2, Law and Bills Digest Group, Australian Parliamentary Library

Blank, Stephen J., *US Interests in Central Asia and the Challenges to Them*, Strategic Studies Institute, March 2007

Boven, Theo van, 'Civil and Political Rights, Including the Questions of Torture and Detention', Report of the Special Rapporteur on the Question of Torture (3 February 2003)

Bullets were Falling like Rain: The Andijan Massacre, May 13, 2005, Human Rights Watch, Vol. 17, No. 5 (D) June 2005

Burying the Truth: Uzbekistan Rewrites the Story of the Andijan Massacre, Human Rights Watch, September 2005

By Invitation Only, Human Rights Watch, 10 December 2002

Clyne, Michael, 'Words Excusing Exclusion', University of Melbourne, Monash University Conference, 2005

Comprehensive Report of Charles A. Duelfer, Special Adviser to the DCI and Leader of the Iraq Survey Group on Iraq's WMD, 30 September 2004 ['Duelfer Report']

Cordesman, Anthony H., 'Al Qa'qaa and the Military Realities in Iraq',

Center for Strategic and International Studies, 28 October, 2004

Daly, John C. K. et al. (eds.), *Anatomy of a Crisis: US–Uzbek Relations 2001–2005*, CACI Silk Road Studies Programme (February 2006)

Feldbaum, H. and Kaufmann, J. R., 'Diplomacy and the Polio Immunisation Boycott in Northern Nigeria', *Health Affairs*, 28 (6) (November–December 2009)

Final Report of the National Commission on Terrorist Attacks Upon the United States ['9/11 Commission Report'], July 2004

GAO: Operation Iraqi Freedom: DoD Should Apply Lessons Learned Concerning the Need for Security over Conventional Storage Sites to Future Operations Planning (March 2007)

GAO: Radiological Sources in Iraq: DoD Should Evaluate its Source Recovery and Apply Lessons Learned to Future Recovery Missions (September 2008)

Gibney, Matthew, 'A Thousand Little Guantanamos' in K. Tunstall (ed), *Displacement, Asylum, Migration* (Oxford University Press, 2006)

'Global Eradication of Polio and Measles', Hearing before the Senate Subcommittee on Appropriations, 23 September 1998

Iraq: Looting, Lawlessness and Humanitarian Consequences, Amnesty International, 10 April 2003

Leach, Michael, *Disturbing Practices: Dehumanising Asylum Seekers in the Refugee Crisis in Australia, 2001–2*, Deakin University, Melbourne. Refuge, 21 (3) 2003

Lester, Paul Martin, *Visual Symbolism and Stereotypes in the Wake of 9/11* in *Images that Injure: Pictorial Stereotypes in the Media* (Praeger Publishers, 2003)

McLachlan, Debi, 'A Certain Maritime Incident', *Counterpoints*, Vol. 3, No. 1 (September 2003)

Marty, Dick, 'Alleged Secret Detentions and Unlawful Inter-state Transfers of Detainees involving Council of Europe Member States', *Special Rapporteur* (12 June 2006)

National Security Study Memorandum NSSM-200: 'Implications of Worldwide Population Growth for US Security and Overseas Interests'

('Kissinger Report'), 10 December 1974 (http://pdf.usaid.gov/pdf_docs/)

Parliament of Australia Senate Select Committee for an Inquiry into a Certain Maritime Incident [CMI], 23 October 2002

Pillar, Paul, 'Intelligence, Policy and the War in Iraq', *Foreign Affairs* (March/April 2006)

Polat, Abdumannob, *Reassessing Andijan: The Road to Restoring US–Uzbek Relations*, Occasional Paper, Jamestown Foundation (June 2007)

Pollack, Kenneth M., 'Spies, Lies and Weapons: What Went Wrong', *The Atlantic* (January/February 2005)

Preliminary Findings on the Events in Andijan, Uzbekistan, OSCE, 13 May 2005

Refugees, Asylum Seekers, Migrants and Internally Displaced Persons, Human Rights Watch Press Kit

Report of the Select Committee on Intelligence on the US Intelligence Community's Pre-war Intelligence Assessments on Iraq ['Rockefeller Report'] 9 July 2004

Report on Whether Public Statements Regarding Iraq by Public Officials were Substantiated by Intelligence Information, Senate Select Committee on Intelligence, June 2008

Rosenstein, Scott and Garrett, Laurie, 'Polio's Return: A WHO-Done-It?', *The American Interest*, Vol. 1 (3) (Spring 2006)

'Senate Select Committee on the Scrafton Evidence', Report, December 2004

Spinning the Tubes, ABC *Four Corners*, 27 October 2003

Steyn, Lord, *Our Government and the International Rule of Law since 9/11*, Annual Lecture of the Law Reform Committee of the Bar Council, 29 November 2006

Still Drifting – Australia's Pacific Solution becomes a 'Pacific Nightmare', Oxfam, August 2002

Stroman Trial Papers: 292nd Judicial District Court (Frank Crowley Courts Building, Dallas). Trial Court Cause No. FOI-40949-V

The Commission on the Intelligence Capabilities of the United States

Regarding Weapons of Mass Destruction, 31 March 2005 ['Robb-Silberman']

Uzbekistan: Progress on Paper Only. Analysis of the State Department's Certification of Uzbekistan, Human Rights Watch, 3 June 2003

Wark, McKenzie, *Globalisation from Below: Migration, Sovereignty, Communication* (January 2002)

We are Not the Enemy: Hate Crimes against Arabs, Muslims and those Perceived to be Arab or Muslim after September 11, Human Rights Watch, November 2002

World Report 2002, Human Rights Watch

Yahya, Maryam, 'Polio Vaccines – Difficult to Swallow: the Story of a Controversy in Northern Nigeria', Institute of Development Studies (March 2006)

Notes

Introduction

3   **as sharp and clear as Pearl Harbor:** George W. Bush, German Bundestag, 23 May 2002.

3   **Not only is the Cold War over:** Colin Powell, Remarks at a business event, Shanghai, 18 October 2001.

3   **we are all Americans:** Jean-Marie Colombani, *Le Monde* (12 September 2001).

3   **History starts today:** Richard Armitage to General Mahmood Ahmed, Head of Pakistani intelligence, 12 September 2001 (PBS *Frontline*, 'Campaign against Terror', 19 April 2002).

5   **The kaleidoscope has been shaken:** Tony Blair, 2 October 2001.

7   **I hate them:** Interview with Haki Mohammed (name changed), Hamra Hotel, Baghdad, 22 March 2009.

8   **No:** Interior Ministry official, Baghdad, 4 April 2009.

9   **a new and different war . . . on all fronts . . . different type of mentality:** George W. Bush press conference, 11 October 2001.

9   **may never end:** Bob Woodward, 'CIA Told to Do "Whatever Necessary" to Kill Bin Laden', *Washington Post* (21 October 2001).

9   **Our responsibility:** George W. Bush, Washington National Cathedral, 14 September 2001.

1: Rage

13   **I don't care what the international lawyers say:** Clarke, *Against All Enemies*, p. 24.

14   **like I was floating:** Interview with Stroman, Livingston, Texas, 26–7 June 2008.

14   **I see that gun:** CCTV tape.

14   **Sam Bradley:** opening statement, Greg Davis, 1 April 2002, *Reporter's Record*, cause No. FOI-40949-V, Vol. 18. Bradley police statement, also Vol. 18.

16   **I did what every other American:** KDFW-TV interview, 12 February 2002.

17   **in their own world:** testimonies of Tina Stroman, Teressa Christine Talamantez, Brenda Sue Carlson, *Reporter's Record*, Vol. 20, 3 April 2002.

17   **came unglued . . . I'm sorry, Doyle but . . . these children:** Brenda Carlson.

17   **$50 away from having an abortion:** testimony, Dr Mary Connell, Vol. 20, 3 April 2002.

18   *I WOULD HAVE PICKED MY OWN COTTON:* evidence presented by Detective Steven Richards (Chevrolet suburban), Officer Brady Snipes (Thunderbird), Vol. 19.

18   **racist dog:** Jim Oatman closing speech, 4 April 2002, Vol. 21.

19   **100 per cent hardcore racist:** Interview with Kevin 'Bear' Hartline, Sheila Hartline, Dallas, 21 June 2008.

19   **Yeah, he was pretty much prejudiced:** Interview with Stroman friend, Dallas, 25 June 2008.

19   *Fuck you:* Exhibit 120, Vol. 19.

20   **You just want them to:** Interview, Stroman friend, Dallas, 23 June 2008.

20   **These people . . . :** Interview with Ronnie 'Shy' Galloway, Dallas, 20 June 2008.

21   **Look at the hotels!:** Interview with Stroman former employer, Dallas, 25 June 2008.

22   **I didn't want money:** Interview with Alka Patel, Dallas, 28 June 2008.

23   **You got a second chance:** Interview with Tom Boston, Dallas, 23 June 2008.

24   **He'd get all wound up:** Interview with George Dodd, Dallas, 25 June 2008.

24   **Not good:** Stroman, 26–7 June.

25   **There were two sides:** Boston, 23 June.

26   **303rd District Court:** *Reporter's Record*, Vol. 20, 3 April 2002.

27   **That was just a bad time:** Boston, 23 June.

27   **He became real distant:** Hartline, 21 June.

28 **See if he needs a place:** Interview with Bob Templeton, Carolyn Templeton, Dallas, 22 June 2008.

28 **14 July 2001:** trial testimony, Robert McMillin (Dallas Police), Vol. 19.

29 **That month, two months!:** Boston, 23 June.

29 **That's not my style.** trial testimony, Vol. 19; interview, Ronnie Galloway, 20 June. Stroman denies that this conversation ever took place. In the light of what happened next, however, and how Tom Boston came to be involved, it seems that he is probably mistaken.

29 **I saw Mark:** Boston, 23 June.

30 **Something's happened:** Patel, 28 June.

30 **Have you SEEN this?:** Bob Templeton, 22 June.

31 TRUE AMERICAN: 19 January 2002.

32 **This will be a monumental struggle:** George W. Bush, statement, 12 September 2001.

32 **Every nation in every region:** George W. Bush, address to a joint session of Congress, 20 September 2001.

33 **a patriotic bonanza:** See Paul Martin Lester, *Visual Symbolism and Stereotypes in the Wake of 9/11*; Department of Sociology, College of William and Mary, *Who Flies the Flag? Findings from the World and Change in American Research Project on Patriotism after 9/11* (April, 2002); Jennifer Scanlon, *The Selling of 9/11*. According to the website, www.entrepreneur.com, flag purchases went up from 20 million to 50 million in 2001; one flag tie-pin manufacturer told *Newsday* that sales had leapt from 1,000 a month to 300,000. It wasn't only flags. Patriotic merchandising included exclusive 9/11 Beanie Babies (a bear, 'America', and a dog, 'Courage'); 'Liberty' pillows ('speak our heart and belief in country and freedom'); firearms (a Beretta 'United We Stand' pistol), pet accessories (Petsmart's 'Patriotic Cat Toy Value Pack' – including a stars-and-stripes catnip mouse) and childcare items. The appeal of most of these products proved short-lived. 'Little Patriot' nappies, featuring a stars-and-stripes design, were removed from the market when it was pointed out that defecating on – or disposing of – the US flag, was a federal offence.

33 **How dare Senator Daschle . . . :** Helen Dewar, 'Lott Calls Daschle Divisive', *Washington Post* (1 March 2002).

33   **This is no time to be precious:** Ann Coulter, 'This is War', *National Review* (13 September 2001); **They hate us?:** Coulter, 'Why We Hate Them', *Jewish World Review* (26 September 2002).

34   **I say bomb the hell out of them:** Zell Miller, speech on Senate floor, 12 September 2001.

34   **Kill the Arabs!:** *We Are Not the Enemy: Hate Crimes against Arabs, Muslims and Those Perceived to be Arab or Muslim after September 11*, Human Rights Watch, November 2002; *Middle East Report* 224, *No Longer Invisible: Arab and Muslim Exclusion After September 11* (Fall, 2002). 'Deluge of Hate Crimes after September 11', *Los Angeles Times* (6 July 2003).

34   *Kill all Muslims:* Langewiesche, *American Ground*, p. 14.

35   **Opinion polls at the time:** *No Longer Invisible* (op. cit.).

35   **He's gonna take care:** Galloway, 20 June.

36   **We were all talking about:** Dodd, 25 June.

36   **There's a man:** Patel, 28 June.

37   **I can sit there and lay back:** Hartline, 21 June.

37   **In the days after 9/11:** Mick North, 'Dangers of the Armed Response at Home' in Scraton, *Beyond September 11*.

37   **The best defence:** Donald Rumsfeld, *Fox News*, 16 September 2001.

38   **The only path to safety:** George W. Bush, graduation speech, West Point, 1 June 2002.

38   **Is my husband OK?:** Patel, 28 June.

39   **If you see Shy:** Interview with Jesse Garcia, Dallas, 20 June 2001; Stroman, 26–7 June.

40   **Damn!:** Boston, 23 June; also Clerk's Record, Trial Court Cause FOI-40949 NV, which contains the police records of Boston's 'anonymous' tip to Paul Macaluso and Sgt J. DeCorte (Defense Exhibit 2), then for some reason goes on to name him.

41   **For legal reasons:** Stroman's attorney has requested that no information be divulged about his alleged role in these crimes.

41   **Waqar Hasan . . . Raisuddin Bhuiuian:** Police documents on these shootings are filed under FOI-40949 NV.

41   **in none of these crimes:** During Oatman's cross-examination, Bhuiuian revealed that he had placed the cash drawer on the counter, then taken

a number of steps backwards. His assailant had not reacted. 'Did the man reach for the money?' asked Oatman. 'No,' replied Bhuiuian. 'He didn't even look towards the money. Rather he asked me a question . . . then he shot me.'

42 **all that same stuff:** Trial transcript, Vol. 21, 4 April.

44 **Stroman was suffering:** Dr Judy Stonedale, trial transcript, Vol. 21, 4 April.

44 **in extreme distress:** Dr Mary Connell, trial transcripts, Vol. 21, 4 April. Prior to 9/11, Stroman was 'paranoid, suspicious, guarded, incredibly distressed, angry, agitated. In short . . . he was virtually out of control'.

44 **The jury didn't care:** Prior to the salute, there was a brief exchange with the judge, Henry Wade Jr, whom Stroman clearly admired. 'Mr Stroman, good luck to you,' Wade told him after reading the sentence. 'Have a good one,' Stroman replied. 'Thank you, sir.'

2: For Those Who Come across the Seas

45 **Abu Badr sent me:** Interview with Karim and Halima al Saadi (names changed), Melbourne, 1 November 2008.

46 **He looked at the engine:** Interview, Saadi, 1 November.

46 **This is dangerous . . . We didn't have any experience:** Interview with Rashid and Soham Kahtany, Sydney, 29 October 2008.

47 **a tatty Indonesian flag . . . fixed course of 174 degrees:** 'Immediate, restricted' cable from Adelaide *Subject Operation Relex – SIEV 04 List of Chronological Events.*

48 **simply unelectable:** Commonwealth Election 2001, Bennett et al.

48 **Parliament House was . . . :** Interview with Liberal Party adviser, Melbourne, 2 November 2008.

48 **surf into office:** Commonwealth Election 2001, Bennett.

48 **It looks as though we can't lose:** Solomon (ed), *Howard's Race*, p. 145.

49 **She started vomiting:** Interview with Ali and Widad Alsaai, Melbourne, 2 November 2008.

49 **Very bad . . . We had one lady:** Kahtany, 29 October.

50 *Mariner 1:* testimony, Norman Banks, *Inquiry into a Certain Maritime Incident* (hereafter 'CMI') 25, 26 March 2002, 4 April 2002.

50 **Some Australian navy people spoke Arabic:** Kahtany, 29 October.

51   **They shouted 'Stop! Stop!':** Saadi, 1 November.

52   **whole villages in Iran:** Leach, *Disturbing Practices*; Mares, *Borderline*, p. 28.

52   **those who are prepared to break our law:** *Borderline*.

53   **We are a humane people:** Marr and Wilkinson, *Dark Victory*.

53   **Stop your vessel!:** Immediate, restricted cable from Adelaide.

53   **We could see their faces:** David Leser, 'Children Overboard, Two Women, Two Stories', *Australian Women's Weekly*, August 2007, cited Briskman (ed), *Human Rights Overboard*.

54   **Some people went down:** Kahtany, 29 October.

54   **They said, 'Go back!':** Saadi, 1 November.

55   **He said that he didn't:** Alsaai, 2 November.

55   **Some people on the boat:** Kahtany, 29 October.

55   **What are you doing?:** Saadi, 1 November.

56   *Vessel disable the steering:* Testimony of Brigadier Silverstone before CMI, 4 April 2002, p. 329 onwards.

57   **A number of people . . . The sorts of children . . . :** Comments from Ruddock, Howard and Reith can be found at www.youtube.com/watch?v=E3WJ10xGkas. For timing, see Senate CMI majority report, Chapter 4.

57   **Clearly planned and premeditated:** www.youtube.com/watch?v=E3WJ10xGkas.

58   **These people are criminals:** cited *Borderline*, p. 28.

58   **who did what happened in New York . . . quaint:** *Dark Victory*, pp. 194–5.

58   **How many . . . are sleepers?:** *Borderline*, p. 134.

58   **We shouldn't make assumptions:** *Dark Victory*, p. 201.

58   **There is a possibility:** *Disturbing Practices*.

59   **There's something to me incompatible:** www.youtube.com/watch?v=E3WJ10xGkas.

60   **Most likely unrepairable:** Sitrep HMAS *Adelaide* 110002ZOct01, Senate CMI majority report, Chapter 3.

60   **We turned a lot:** Saadi, 1 November.

60   **I think we're going to lose this one:** Banks testimony (CMI) 4 April 2002, p. 294.

61 **The worst – or most feared – order:** Banks testimony (CMI), 25 March 2002, p. 187.

61 **The soldiers told us:** Saadi, 1 November.

61 **The ocean was dark!:** Kahtany, 29 October.

62 **The weight of the engine:** Saadi, 1 November.

62 **I was particularly proud:** Banks testimony (CMI), 25 March 2002, p. 165.

63 ASYLUM SEEKERS THROW: *Daily Telegraph*; 'BOAT PEOPLE THROW: *Melbourne Herald Sun*; CHILDREN OVERBOARD: *Sydney Morning Herald*.

63 **Any civilized person:** cited Clyne, 'Words Excusing Exclusion'.

63 **It was clearly:** *Children Overboard: View from the Sea* on *Sunday*, Channel 9, 29 August 2004.

63 **This kind of emotional blackmail:** Weller, *Don't Tell the Prime Minister*, p. 2.

63 **There are those who wish to breach:** *To Deter and Deny*: ABC *Four Corners*, 15 April 2002.

64 **Should boat people:** 'Words Excusing Exclusion'.

64 **At 9.30 a.m.:** Banks testimony (CMI), 25 March 2002, p. 166.

64 *You* **may want to question:** www.youtube.com/watch?v=E3WJ10xGkas.

65 **there was a clear misrepresentation:** Banks testimony (CMI), 26 March 2002, p. 202.

66 **The whole show was wrong:** *Don't Tell the Prime Minister*, p. 20.

66 **An interpreter came in:** Saadi, 1 November.

66 **Some Iraqi people said, 'Don't go!':** Kahtany, 29 October.

66 **It was a cargo plane:** Alsaai, 2 November.

67 **We were in the middle of a jungle!:** Saadi, 1 November.

67 **Soldiers:** Alsaai, 2 November.

68 **Mister, where are we? . . . There was nothing there:** Saadi, 1 November.

68 **We're going to live** *here?* **. . . cried and cried . . . Every day we killed maybe five:** Kahtany, 29 October.

69 **Everyone got sick:** Saadi, 1 November.

69 **The Department of Immigration:** 'Experts Claim Malaria Risk for Asylum Seekers on PNG Island', ABC News, 19 February 2002. 'Detainees Struck Down by Malaria', *Sydney Morning Herald* (22 December 2001). 'Australia's Latest Refugee Policy: Cages, Armed

Guards, and Imprisonment on a Remote Island', *Independent* (7 February 2002). The President of the Royal Australasian College of Physicians, Professor Richard Larkins, was unequivocal: 'The responsible course of action is to immediately evacuate the detention centre.' ('Australia's MDs Throw Support behind Asylum Seekers', *Canadian Medical Association Journal* 14 May 2002; 166 (10): 1325.)

70 **The courts here in Australia . . . It was at about this time:** Interview with Philip Ruddock, Sydney, 28 October 2008.

71 **In September 2001:** Australian Government Fact Sheet 81, 2009: 'Australia's Excised Places'.

71 **Over the next four years:** *Still Drifting*, p. 7.

71 **In September:** CMI, Chapter 10.

72 **unmitigated bribe:** 'Phantom Aid Never Leaves our Shores', *Sydney Morning Herald* (28 May 2007).

72 **Australia has taken its own policy:** *By Invitation Only*, p. 70.

72 **an attempt by Australia:** *No Safe Refuge*, HRW, p. 11.

73 **Not consistent with:** *The Australian* (2 August 2002).

73 **Typical were the governments . . . anti-terrorist fight:** *No Safe Refuge*, p. 10.

73 **shamelessly manipulated xenophobic fears:** HRW World Report 2002: *Refugees, Asylum Seekers, Migrants and Internally Displaced Persons*.

73 **excessively harsh . . . unprecedented:** HRW World Report, 2002.

73 **'Surely there are better ways':** 'UNHCR Head Condemns Politicization of Issue', UNWIRE, 2001. 'It is hard to see,' agreed the *Economist*, '[the Pacific Solution] as anything but a populist attempt to gain votes' (cited, *Howard's Race*).

74 **a sharp upsurge in Liberal popularity:** Commonwealth Election 2001, Bennett et al.

74 **The atmosphere changed:** Interview, Liberal Party adviser, 2 November.

75 **there goes the election:** Interview with Kim Beazley, Canberra, 7 November 2008.

75 **We can't take a trick . . . we're competing:** *Howard's Race*, p. 224.

76 **Whatever you hear:** 'Overboard incident "never happened"', *The Australian* (7 November 2001).

77 **All hell's broken loose . . . The Prime Minister wants . . . In my view . . . I**

think the best you can say: Interview with Mike Scrafton, Castlemaine, 2 November 2008.

78   **In my mind there is no uncertainty:** 'Senate Select Committee on the Scrafton Evidence', p. 18.

78   **Nobody rang my office . . . at no stage:** 'Scrafton Evidence', p. 19.

78   **I have not received . . . I'd make it public:** 'Scrafton Evidence', p. 20.

78   **My understanding:** 'Scrafton Evidence', p. 19.

79   **lying through his teeth:** Despite discrepancies in his evidence, Scrafton later took – and passed – a polygraph examination, then challenged the Prime Minister to do the same. Howard refused to participate in such 'gimmicks'. As had been the case with the CMI Inquiry before it, the inquiry into the Scrafton evidence was controversial: Liberals viewed it as sour-faced politicking after a catastrophic election defeat.

79   **This is fantastic! . . . We had the most dramatic:** Interview, Beazley, 7 November.

80   **Yeah. We were going to win . . . From our point of view . . . No:** Interview, Beazley, 7 November.

81   **Were they found to be refugees?** Interview, Ruddock, 28 October.

82   **I thought that if I told them:** Interview, Saadi, 1 November.

3: The Wedding Party

83   *We did not start this war:* US Department of Defense news briefing, 4 December 2001.

83   **What are you doing? . . . It's you:** Interview with Abdul Malik, 8 March 2010.

85   **She's good, a perfect match . . . On the afternoon of . . . It was a great moment:** Interviews with Haji Abdul Khaliq (Malik's brother), Haji Mohammed Anwar (Malik's uncle), Haji Khalifa Sadat (Deh Rawood district governor), Haji Saheb Jan Agha (Malik's neighbour), Khalifa Jan Mohammed (Popalzai tribal chief, Deh Rawood) and Jan Mohammed (former governor, Oruzgan) – all conducted in March 2010.

86   **Nine months earlier:** 'Seeking a Blend of Military and Civilian Decision Making', *New York Times* (24 October 2001); *Air Power against Terror, America's Conduct of Operation Enduring Freedom*, Benjamin Lamben,

National Defense Research Institute, 2005.

86   **origins of the SPECTRE programme:** For general history of the AC-130s, see the Spectre Association's excellent website: www.spectre-association.org. The 16th Special Operations Squadron also have information at www.canon.af.mil. Current and former AC-130 operators were specifically instructed not to co-operate with research for this book.

87   **Masirah Island:** Charles Miller, 'Low, Slow and Deadly', *National Review Online*, 18 October 2001. *Masirah, Oman* at www.globalsecurity.org, etc.

88   **With regret I have to say:** Woodward, *Bush at War*, p. 103. The CIA officer was Cofer Black. Numerous Soviet generals warned of the dangers of an Afghan invasion. 'They're wolves, these people,' General Alexander Lebed told the *Washington Post* ('Soviet Generals Warn of Sea of Bloodshed', 19 September 2001), noting that for every town razed by the Soviet military 'perhaps one mujahedin was killed – the rest were innocent'.

88   **The Soviets introduced:** PBS Frontline, *Campaign Against Terror*, 8 September 2002.

89   **If you do go in, don't stay:** Interview, *Face the Nation*, 18 November 2001.

90   **initial success, followed by:** Speech at Virginia Military Institute, 17 April 2002.

90   **He said to Franks:** Interview with a senior UK diplomat who declined to be named, 21 March 2010.

90   **It became clear not immediately:** Interview with Ambassador James Dobbins, 3 March 2010.

91   **The idea that Afghans:** Dobbins, *After the Taliban*, p. 103. 'Washington's setting geographical limits on ISAF,' writes Dobbins, 'was my first exposure to a mind-set that excluded local security as a post-conflict mission for US forces.'

91   **The rhetoric from Washington:** Interview, Ambassador Robert Finn, 3 March 2010.

91   **I was told to take . . . No Bondsteel . . . So I concluded from that:** Interview, General Dan McNeill, 24 February 2010.

92   **It can't be a lie:** Interviews, Abdul Malik, Abdul Khaliq, Mohammed Anwar, March 2010.

92 **(ODA) 574:** For a great account of the mission, see Eric Blehm, *The Only Thing Worth Dying For* (HarperCollins, 2009).

93 **We were told . . . They were filtering . . . When more Americans:** Interview, Abdul Malik, March 2010.

93 **When President Karzai started:** Interview, Jan Mohammed, March 2010.

93 **People were very optimistic . . . We were pretty sure:** Interview, Abdul Khaliq, March 2010.

93 **America is a very developed country:** Interview, Jan Mohammed, March 2010.

94 **undisclosed location:** www.canon.af.mil.

94 SPECTRE: These slogans, and more, can be viewed at www.spectre-association.org.

94 **three aircraft and three crews . . . 1,300 rounds . . . 225 missions:** www.canon.af.mil.

95 **Extremely competent:** Interview with anonymous US Special Forces officer, 16 February 2010.

95 **Angel of Death:** 'Mark' of ODA 595, PBS Frontline, *Campaign Against Terror* (8 September 2002).

95 **clandestine AC-130 strike:** *9/11 Commission Report*, p. 135.

96 **It would kill *everything*:** Interview with Michael Scheuer, 26 March 2010.

96 **It *looked* like nothing was happening:** US Department of Defense press briefing, 27 November 2001.

97 **Jack Straw ridiculed:** Kampfner, *Blair's Wars*, p. 143.

97 **Bin Laden was there:** Interview with CIA officer, 14 March 2010.

98 **Marginalized:** White House Press Conference, 13 March 2003.

99 **the heart of the Taliban:** Special Forces officer, 16 February 2010.

99 **I knew him when . . . We would put up a cigarette . . . I went into hospital . . . Come and join:** Interview, Haji Mohammed Anwar, March 2010.

101 **They will be helping them:** Carlotta Gall, 'Seeking Mullah Omar in a Land of Secrets', *New York Times* (22 May 2002).

101 **Norway, Germany, Australia . . . :** Details of Special Forces operations in the valley come from Anonymous, *Hunting Al Qaeda*, Chapters 8 and 9.

101 **CONOP:** *Hunting Al Qaeda*, p. 99 displays the plan.

101–19 Details of the first Deh Rawood operation come from *Hunting Al Qaeda*.

103 **The groom never stays:** Interview, Abdul Khaliq, March 2010. Details of the rest of the preparations come from Abdul Malik's family.

103 **Tela Gul's uncle:** 'On the Hunt for Mullah Omar', *TIME* (5 August 2002). Confirmed by family members.

104 **three raids:** 'Seeking Mullah Omar in a Land of Secrets' (op. cit.)

105 **Operation Full Throttle:** *Hunting Al Qaeda* contains an account of the various errors of the operation. An alternate view is reported by a Special Forces officer 'John Andersen' in his piece 'Afghan T&A' in Hans Halberstadt's *War Stories of the Green Berets*. Both accounts agree that the operation was compromised; both contain versions of the 'would you like to have some tea' incident. A final, official, summary ('US Military Report Says Taliban Hid Guns in Civilian Areas') was released by the Pentagon on 8 September 2002.

108 All accounts of the bombing itself are from interviews with those present, apart from those of Laik, Nassema and Ahmed Jan Agha – all of whom were quoted in the Press at the time.

109 **They blindfolded us . . . They asked if we knew Mullah Omar:** Interview, Abdul Bari, March 2010.

111 **At least one bomb was errant:** Andrew Buncombe and Kim Sengupta, 'Scores Killed by US Bomb at Afghan Wedding', *Independent* (2 July 2002); Luke Harding and Matthew Engel, 'US Bomb Blunder Kills 30 at Afghan Wedding', *Guardian* (2 July 2002).

112 **It does seem as though:** NPR, *Talk of the Nation* (2 July 2002).

112 **the result of anti-aircraft artillery:** 'Scores Killed by US Bomb at Afghan Wedding' (op. cit.).

112 **I read in the paper:** Luke Harding, 'No US Apology over Wedding Bombing', *Guardian* (3 July 2002).

112 **there isn't any reason:** Marc Herold, *Crashing the Wedding Party*, 8 July 2002.

112 **Taliban and al-Qaeda manuals:** US Department of Defense news briefing, 2 July 2002.

112 **Something was fishy:** *War Stories of the Green Berets*.

112 **Describe for me:** Interview, Dan McNeill, 24 February 2010.

113 **Why do you assume there was a wedding party?:** Packer, *The Assassins' Gate*, p. 117. Wolfowitz believed that the victims were Taliban fighters dressed as partygoers.

113 **Let's not call them innocents:** US Department of Defense news briefing, 21 February 2002.

113 **All the evidence suggests:** Wolfowitz and Dr Abdullah, press briefing, Kabul, 15 July 2002.

114 **cleaned the area:** Dumeetha Luthra, 'Draft Report Indicates US Cover-up of Afghan Wedding Attack', *The Times* (29 July 2002).

114 **It never was:** 'UN Keeps Damning Report of Afghan Massacre Secret', *Independent* (31 July 2002); 'UN Revises Afghan Wedding Attack Report', CNN, 30 July 2002.

114 **The more it drags on:** 'Draft Report Indicates US Cover-up' (op. cit.)

115 **I don't think this was necessarily:** Interview, Ambassador Dobbins, 3 March 2010.

116 **There was a moment:** Interview, unnamed UK diplomat, 21 March 2010.

116 **mostly on editorial boards:** Rashid, *Descent into Chaos*, p. 200.

116 **1.6 troops per thousand:** Dobbins, Jones et al., *Europe's Role in Nation-Building, from the Balkans to the Congo* (RAND, 2008), cited Jones, *In the Graveyard of Empires*, p. 119.

117 **8,000 troops:** Dobbins, p. 140; **Bosnia had received 2,000** Dobbins, p. 127.

117 **None of the countries:** Interview, Ambassador Robert Finn, 3 March 2010.

118 **The idea that we'd liberated a country:** Interview, Ambassador James Dobbins, 3 March 2010.

118 **$577 per civilian:** Jones, p.122.

118 **In Bosnia they had:** Interview, Ambassador Robert Finn, March 2010.

119 **There was no planning:** Interview, British diplomat, 21 March 2010. One reason for the lack of planning was the speed of the operation. 'Everything happened so quickly,' he admitted. Only later did potential problems emerge: 'After the Afghan government was established, I was certainly then thinking to myself, "What we've got here is totally inade-

quate. It doesn't look like a government at all. Now we'd better start doing something." . . . I think there were things that we could have done – and quickly – which would have changed the scene. Now, whether that would ultimately have led to success or not, I don't know. But we would have given ourselves a better chance.'

119   **We three brothers . . . The presence of Americans . . . When you see . . . I hate Americans:** Interviews with Abdul Malik's family, March 2010.

120   **We had very elaborate administrative structures:** CIA source, 14 March 2010.

120   **At that time:** Interview, General Dan McNeill, 24 February 2010.

120   **In March 2002:** Interview with Michael Scheuer, 26 March 2010.

121   **But we haven't caught Bin Laden yet!** CIA source, 14 March 2010.

121   **Afghanistan was really:** cited Jones.

121   **When we succeeded:** Fox News, 9 July 2002.

4: Groupthink 7075-T6

123   *Simply stated, there is no doubt:* 26 August 2002.

123   *Fuck Saddam:* First reported by Daniel Eisenberg, 'We're Taking Him Out', *TIME* (5 May 2002).

123   ASSISTANCE REQUIRED: Interview, Sami Ibrahim, Baghdad, 30 February 2009.

124   **In 1984:** Background on the Nasser 81 mm project comes from Sami Ibrahim, various IAEA sources and weapons technicians in Iraq. An excellent summary appears in the Iraq Survey Group's final report ('Duelfer Report'): 'Aluminium Tube Investigation'.

124   **They weren't very successful:** Interview with anonymous weapons inspector, 1 July 2009.

126   **It was severely corroded . . . Corrosion is a bit like a disease . . . We classified them . . . not usable at all:** Interview, Ibrahim, 30 February 2009.

127   **We can extrude aluminium . . . That's a hard alloy . . . He screwed me down:** Interview with Garry Cordukes, Sydney, 29 October 2008.

127   **Kamel put in place:** Original correspondence, contracts and paperwork provided by Cordukes.

129   **A signal had been picked up . . . There were a lot of meetings . . . All we were going off:** Interview with Geoff Wainwright, 13 August 2010.

132   **It was a top secret signal:** Details of meetings between Cordukes and
      Wainwright come from interviews with both men. Corduke's collection
      of these meetings is somewhat different. According to the aluminium
      trader he was aware from the outset of what Wianwright was up to.

135   **President's Daily Brief . . . Senior Executive Intelligence Brief:**
      'Rockefeller Report', p. 88.

136   **I happened to be in town . . . They just didn't work:** Interview with
      Houston Wood III, 2 July 2009.

136   **not consistent with a gas centrifuge:** 'Rockefeller Report', p. 89.

136   **the key thing:** Interview, Geoff Wainwright, 13 August 2010.

137   **Fuck. Are you serious? . . . Happy to . . . You're from the Defence . . . I
      thought it was dodgy . . . For Christ's sake! . . . We've got a big problem
      . . . You've obviously fed me bullshit:** Interview, Garry Cordukes, 29
      October 2008.

139   **'Joe T'** has been publicly named as Joe Turner. He still works at the
      CIA. Through intermediaries he has refused to comment on this
      chapter.

139   **to manufacture chambers:** Daily Intelligence Highlight, 9 May 2001,
      cited 'Rockefeller Report', p. 89.

139   **less likely:** 14 June 2001, Senior Publish When Ready (SPWR), cited
      'Rockefeller Report', p. 90.

139   **The specifications for the tubes far exceed:** 2 July intelligence assess-
      ment, cited 'Rockefeller Report', p. 90.

140   **At the Nassr facility . . . The assessment was made:** Interview with Bob
      Kelley, 18 February 2009.

140   **We were aware of all these tubes:** Interview with George Healey, 1 July
      2009.

141   **'The [tubes'] walls were way too thick . . . It wasn't hard . . . about half
      an hour . . . You would talk to him:** Interview with unnamed IAEA
      officer, 18 February 2009.

142   **A so-called expert . . . practically a layman:** Interview with unnamed
      IAEA officer, 17 February 2009.

142   **If we wait for threats:** Remarks by the President at the Graduation
      Exercise of the US Military, West Point, 1 June 2002.

143   **This is not the time to err:** Blair in Sedgefield, 5 March 2005.

143 **It's hard to overstate:** Interview with unnamed senior US intelligence official, 30 June 2009.

143 **That sense – worldwide – of vulnerability:** Interview with unnamed CPD officer, 3 July 2009.

143 **People were working . . . It was unlike anything:** Interview with unnamed CTC officer, 14 March 2010.

143 **I thought we had put the issue to rest . . . The tubes were purported by the CIA . . . That's when I began to get angry:** Interview, Houston Wood III, 2 July 2009.

145 **compelling:** *Spinning the Tubes*, ABC *Four Corners*, 27 October 2003.

145 **little gem:** *Lateline*, ABC, 18 July 2003.

145 **I wasn't aware:** Interview, Geoff Wainwright, 13 August 2010.

145 **a mood of great accomplishment . . . They were very proud:** Interview with unnamed Australian intelligence officer, 3 July 2009.

146 **There were all kinds of reasons:** Interview with Carl Ford, 30 June 2009.

147 **Oh Wayne! . . . Maddening! This was the kind of logic:** Interview with Wayne White, 10 July 2009.

148 **I blame that on 9/11 . . . Carl, what are you guys:** Interview, Carl Ford, 30 June 2009.

148 **Basically, they had all disappeared:** Interview with unnamed British intelligence official, 27 January 2009.

149 **Having leaked the information:** Cheney, *Meet the Press*; Rice, CNN, *Late Edition with Wolf Blitzer*; Rumsfeld, CBS *Face the Nation;* Powell, *Fox News Sunday*. All broadcast 8 September 2002.

149 **Is this something new?:** Interview, Houston Wood III, 2 July 2009.

149 **There's Dick Cheney on** *Meet the Press***:** Interview with CPD officer, 3 July 2009.

149 **It was very skilfully done:** Interview with Greg Thielmann, 21 September 2009.

150 **Now there's new evidence:** BBC *Panorama*, *The Case Against Saddam*, 23 September 2002.

150 **There's nothing that frightens:** Interview, Wayne White, 10 July 2009.

150 **The way the information was presented:** Interview, Greg Thielmann, 21 September 2009.

151   **highly unlikely to be intended:** cited 'Robb-Silberman', p. 73.

151   **Only if you believed it before:** Interview, Carl Ford, 30 June 2009.

152   **will be forced either to demonstrate:** cited Cook, *Point of Departure*, p. 246.

152   **[T]his resolution contains no hidden triggers:** UN Security Council, Meeting 4644, 8 November 2002. **There is no 'automaticity':** Sir Jeremy Greenstock, Meeting 4644, also 8 November 2002. **There is nothing in the resolution:** 'UK Expects Iraq to Fail Arms Tests', *Guardian* (11 November 2002).

153   **OK, what was it you were doing . . . They literally stood on their heads . . . Bent over backwards . . . Tubes guys had . . . We went through the manufacturing process:** Interview, George Healey, 1 July 2009.

153   **Stop burying them!:** Interview with two Iraqi scientists from Al Qa'qaa, Baghdad, 4 April 2009.

154   **Look, you know our [old] centrifuge programme:** Obeidi and Pitzer, *The Bomb in My Garden*, p. 193. Interview, George Healey, 1 July 2009.

154   **He was absolutely right . . . There was no question:** Interview, George Healey, 1 July 2009.

155   **When we got done:** Interview, Bob Kelley, 18 February 2009.

155   **With the Iraqi record:** cited *Blair's Wars*, p. 256.

156   **From March 2002:** Interview, Michael Scheuer, 26 March 2010.

156   **When intelligence does not:** Interview with Larry Johnson, 29 March 2010.

157   **There was another staple in it:** Interview with Rod Barton, Canberra, 7 November 2008.

157   **You couldn't be sure:** Interview with unnamed British intelligence official, 27 January 2009.

157   **Bugging was also rife:** See Short, *An Honourable Deception*, as well as numerous press reports at the time. Chile was a particular target. See Muñoz, *A Solitary War*.

158   **We knew absolutely:** Interview with unnamed British intelligence official, 27 January 2009.

158   **I think Mr ElBaradei, frankly, is wrong:** NBC *Meet the Press*, 16 March 2003.

159   **The not-so-good intelligence:** Interview with unnamed IAEA officer, 17 February 2009.

159   **We found nothing:** Interview, Rod Barton, Canberra, 7 November 2008.

159   **slam dunk:** The most famous comment of all, first reported in Woodward, *Plan of Attack*.

160   **Five tests were performed:** For spin tests and their results, see 'Rockefeller Report', pp. 105–8.

160   **[My analysts] went directly:** Interview, Carl Ford, 30 June 2009.

160   **According to WINPAC:** Tables displaying rotor specifications can be found in 'Rockefeller Report', pp. 109–12.

161   **considerably more expensive:** 'Rockefeller Report', p. 98.

161   **Cheap as chips:** Interview, Garry Cordukes, Sydney, 29 October 2008.

161   **This fact was not presented:** 'Rockefeller Report', p. 110.

161   **When it came to rocket production . . . twenty-five pages . . . bicycle-seat posts:** 'Rockefeller Report', p. 102.

162   **[We] explained to him . . . After he returned from his visit to Vienna:** Interview, IAEA official, 18 February 2009.

163   **That speech!** Interview, Houston Wood III, 2 July 2009.

163   **If anyone had tested [the tubes]:** Interview, Garry Cordukes, 29 October 2008.

164   **I thought that they had the goods:** Interview, Rod Barton, 7 November 2008.

164   **What he was saying was not matching:** Interview, unnamed CPD officer, 3 July 2009.

164   **I had a serious problem:** Interview, Wayne White, 10 July 2010.

165   **The biggest load of crap:** Interview, Geoff Wainwright, 13 August 2010.

165   **I just couldn't believe it:** Interview, George Healey, 1 July 2009.

165   **Somebody mis-briefed Powell:** Interview, Bob Kelley, 18 February 2009.

165   **It was all very convincing . . . A counterpart in an allied country . . . Powell had heard . . . The damage was done . . . he was lied to:** Interview with Lawrence Wilkerson, 3 September 2009.

166   **France:** Wilkerson was reluctant to name the nation responsible, but in a speech before the New American Foundation American Strategy Program Policy Forum on 19 October 2005 he named France. An article in the *Financial Times* (4 July 2003) reported the spin test allegation before Colonel Wilkerson's speech.

166   **The issue of having the tubes spun:** Baute, correspondence, 2 October
       2009.

166   **The secretary got led . . . I could not believe:** Interview, Carl Ford, 30
       June 2009.

167   **It's hard to think of a more odious:** Interview, Greg Thielmann, 21
       September 2009.

5: Stuff Happens

169   *Freedom's untidy:* US Department of Defense news briefing, 11 April
       2003.

169   *I really do believe:* NBC *Meet the Press*, 16 March 2003.

169   **Are you true Arabs? . . . Take it:** Interview, Haki Mohammed (name
       changed), Baghdad, 27 February 2009.

171   *Huge:* Interview with unnamed British weapons intelligence expert,
       February 2009.

171   **Just enormous:** Interview with unnamed weapons inspector, 18 February
       2009.

173   **On a whim, one enterprising inspector:** It was Bob Kelley of the IAEA.

173   **We thought it might be:** Interview, Haki Mohammed, 27 February
       2009.

174   **The Americans came in:** Interview with Ali (name changed), Baghdad,
       4 April 2009.

174   **Lots of people went in:** Interview, Haki Mohammed, 27 February 2009.

175   **In the images of falling statues:** Televised address, USS *Abraham
       Lincoln*, 1 May 2003.

175   **traffic jams of looters:** Robert Fisk, 'Baghdad, the Day After',
       Independent (11 April 2003).

175   **Imagine the frustration:** CNN, 'Rampant Looting Across Iraq', 9 April
       2003.

175   **The images you are seeing . . . Stuff happens:** US Department of
       Defense news briefing, 11 April 2003.

176   **Lathes, machine tools:** Interview, Haki Mohammed, 27 February 2009.

177   **It was astonishing:** Interview, Ali, 4 April 2009.

177   **In the mosques:** Interview with Ahmed (name changed), Baghdad, April
       2009.

178   **It was a sightsee:** Interview with Joe Caffrey, 20 February 2009.

179   **There was just row after row . . . The 101st Airborne . . . These guys were like kids:** Interview with Dean Staley, 21 February 2009.

180   **There were these round cardboard cylinders . . . It was very flour-like:** Interview, Joe Caffrey, 20 February 2009.

180   **Prior to the invasion:** In January 2003, ElBaradei personally reported on Al Qa'qaa to the United Nations Security Council.

180   **Two weeks after the start:** According to the IAEA, Jacques Baute regularly expressed his concerns about the security of materials stored at Al Qa'qaa – specifically the high explosives – in the months following the war. IAEA had been in and out of Qa'qaa prior to the invasion – partly to try to sort out the issue of the aluminium tubes (the propellant for the Nasser 81 mm rockets was made there). IAEA inspectors checked the explosives on 14 and 15 January and 8 and 15 March 2003.

181   **the greatest explosives bonanza:** The memo was actually written by George Healey.

182   **Buildings just disappeared before our eyes:** Interview, Rod Barton, 7 November 2008.

182   **You'd end up with just granules:** Interview with unnamed British intelligence official, 27 January 2009.

183   **Write this down:** Bush at the White House, 20 September 2002, cited McClellan, *What Happened*. Six months later, Paul Wolfowitz drew a direct analogy to the liberation of Paris: 'Like the people of France in the 1940s,' he told Veterans of Foreign Wars on 11 March 2003, '[the Iraqis] view us as their hoped-for liberators.'

183   **[This war] could last:** Address to US troops in Aviano, Italy, 7 February 2003. Cheney agreed: 'weeks, rather than months' he told NBC's *Meet the Press* on 16 March 2003.

183   **It's hard to conceive:** US Congress Committee on the Budget, Department of Defense Budget Priorities for Fiscal Year 2004, 1st Session, 27 February 2003.

184   **I remember a representative:** Interview, unnamed CIA officer, 14 March 2010.

184   **Chief of the Agency's Bin Laden Unit:** Interview, Michael Scheuer, 26 March 2010: 'The Chief of the whole Bin Laden Unit at the time

directly told Tenet that, whatever the threat is from Saddam, if we invade Iraq we will give the entire Muslim world the perfect Koranic predicate for a defensive jihad.'

184   **No progress is possible:** *Iraq: What's Going Wrong?* Cable sent 11 May 2003, cited Gordon and Trainor, *COBRA II*, p. 471.

185   **At the Tuwaitha nuclear plant:** Actually, the looters weren't interested in yellow cake at all. They wanted the yellow plastic drums the uranium was stored in for use as water butts. See Security Council Report, S/2003/711, 14 July 2003. On yellow cake discoveries abroad, see, for example 'IAEA Confirms Yellowcake Found in Rotterdam Likely from Iraq', *USA Today* (16 January 2004).

185   **black fever, cholera, HIV:** Galbraith, *The End of Iraq*, p. 102.

185   **My cousins came to me . . . We allowed the Arabs in to our homes . . . They told us they had come:** Interview with Yusuf (name changed), Baghdad, March 2009.

185   **After the invasion we started seeing:** Interview, Haki Mohammed, 27 February 2009.

186   **I saw loads of munitions:** Interview with Abdul (name changed), Baghdad, March 2009.

187   **There was a rush . . . There were bunkers . . . We found something:** Interview, Yusuf, March 2009.

188   **The biggest trade I ever did?:** Interview with Abu Sultan, Iraq, March 2009.

188   **People from Yusifiyah:** Interview, Haki Mohammed, 27 February 2009.

189   **a classified Defense Intelligence Agency report:** 9 November 2003, cited US News and World Report, 31 October 2004. The 'Joint Department of Defense/Intelligence task force' special analysis is cited in the same piece.

189   **We had a map . . . I had a couple of Marine buddies:** Interview, Lawrence Wilkerson, 3 September 2009.

189   **All these things were there:** Interview, Ali, 4 April 2009.

189   **There was a bridge:** Interview, Haki Mohammed, 27 February 2009.

190   **UN Building in Baghdad:** Al-Kurdi's questioning at the hands of the United Nations is cited in Power, *Chasing the Flame*, p. 513. Apparently, Power's revelation caused problems. Asked about the interview, and

given the code of the cable in which it is apparently transcribed (CZX-251), staff refused to be drawn. 'No one is prepared to discuss this sensitive matter,' I was informed on 22 September 2008. 'Especially after the reference to that cable in Ms Power's book.' A more concrete link between Kurdi, the UN bomb and Yusifiyah can be found in 'Abu Ghraib Attack Planner Caught' (American Forces' Information Service, 8 May 2005). According to this article, Kurdi's associate Abu al Abbas stole his explosives from 'a weapons facility in Yusifiyah', then stored them on his farm, also in Yusifiyah. At least ten car bombs were made there. Al Kurdi was estimated to have been responsible for 75 per cent of the car bombs in Baghdad until his capture. Yusifiyah is fifteen kilometres from Al Qa'qaa.

190   **We told him we had lost 40,000 tonnes:** Interview, Ali, 4 April 2009. '[The Americans] only had to do simple things: imposing a curfew and not let people move from their houses to protect both the people and the country. But they did nothing. They are responsible for the chaos that ensued,' he recalled. 'They didn't care.'

191   **suicide-bomb belts:** Interview, Ali, 4 April: 'We got the order to make the explosive belts in February 2003, a month before the war. It was not my job, but I heard from the other engineers that they managed after a month or so to manufacture them. But I don't think they made more than a thousand.'

191   **Virtually every single report was the same:** Interview, Wayne White, 10 July 2009.

191   **It was being dismissed:** Interview, Lawrence Wilkerson, 3 September 2009.

191   **One of the operations we did:** Interview with Abu Shujaa, Baghdad, July 2008. Shujaa named three specific attacks in which munitions looted from Al Qa'qaa were used: October 2003 (Al Amyria Police Station), February 2004 (al Jihad Bridge) and May 2004 (roadside bombs on Route Irish, the main road to Baghdad Airport). Although he gave details of the bombings, he was unable to recall their exact dates – making it difficult to pinpoint the specific attacks, or the exact number of casualties in each one. The clearest of the three is the Amyria blast: there was a blast at the police station in the month he indicated and

casualties concur approximately with his recollections of the incident. For details of the Amyria bomb, see *The Times* (28 October 2003).

193 **The IAEA officially informed:** Security Council letter, 21/10/S/2004/831

193 **Then, suddenly, the story leaked:** Interview with Chris Nelson, 16 February 2009.

194 **Rove came and screamed at me:** Interview with David Sanger, 10 February 2009.

195 **Al Qa'qaa was an Iraqi problem:** CNN, 'Tons of Iraq Explosives Missing', 26 October 2004.

195 **There weren't, for instance, 141 tons:** 'The quantity of explosives of a particular type, this so-called RDX material, was actually much different than what was initially reported . . . on the order of more than 100 tons of difference. We've learned that since these initial reports.' *Special DoD Briefing on Al Qa'qaa Munitions Facility in Iraq,* 29 October 2004.

195 **Saddam had moved them:** Photographs of trucks were released on 28 October 2004. They had been taken on 17 March 2003. See www.globalsecurity.org/wmd/world/iraq/images.

195 **highly improbable:** Interview with Reporters, US Department of Defense news transcript, 27 October 2004.

195 **Picture all of the tractor trailers:** WHPT Radio, Philadelphia, 29 October 2004.

196 **which we may provide later:** Special Department of Defense briefing on Al Qa'qaa Munitions Facility, 29 October 2004.

196 **John A. Shaw:** 'Russia Tied to Iraq's Missing Arms', *Washington Times* (28 October 2004). According to Shaw, Russian Special Forces descended on the plant in January 2003 to shred all evidence of complicity with Iraqi weapons programmes. Arms were shipped to Syria and Lebanon.

197 **cast his vote:** This story apparently emerged in the *Wall Street Journal.* Mohammed ElBaradei called it 'total junk'. See 'ElBaradei Dismisses Revenge Claim', BBC News, 30 October 2004.

197 **The stories have pretty much been discredited:** Fox, *The O'Reilly Factor,* 28 October 2004.

197 **bogus:** 'Munitions Issue Dwarfs the Big Picture', *Washington Post* (29 October 2004).

197   **an embarrassment:** Tony Snow made this suggestion on Fox News.
        For a full examination of the ins and outs of media presentation of
        the Al Qa'qaa allegations, see Eric Boehlert, 'Iraq Explosive's Story
        Detonates under Bush Campaign', Salon.com, 30 October 2004.

197   **0.06 per cent:** First to cite this figure appears to have been Anthony
        H. Cordesman, 'Al Qa'qaa and the Military Realities in Iraq', Centre
        for Strategic International Studies, 28 October 2004.

198–9   Bush and Cheney's speeches in Sioux City, Michigan, Wisconsin,
        and Ohio can be accessed at www.georgewbushlibrary.gov/white-
        house.

198   **Accusing the IAEA:** The original holding of RDX was 141.23 tonnes.
        In 2003 IAEA inspectors verified the existence of 128 (the Iraqis said
        10 tonnes had been used for non-military purposes from 1998–
        2002); 3 tonnes were never accounted for. Vice President Cheney's 3
        ton figure was wildly off the mark.

200   **[The Pentagon] was trying to compare:** Interview with unnamed
        weapons inspector, 18 February 2009.

200   **Joe, I think we've been to the place . . . It was clear:** Interview, Dean
        Staley, 21 February 2009.

201   **I think it's game, set and match:** CNN, *Newsnight with Aaron Brown*,
        28 October 2004

201   **Osama bin Laden succeeded:** That the al-Qaeda leader's message
        might prove politically useful to the Republican Party was not lost on
        the CIA. 'Bin Laden certainly did a nice favour today for the
        President,' commented the former acting Director of Central
        Intelligence, John McLaughlin. 'Certainly,' replied Deputy Director
        for Intelligence, Jami Miscik. 'He would want Bush to keep doing
        what he's doing for a few more years.' The reporter of this exchange
        noted the irony of the moment: 'What did it say about US policies
        that Bin Laden would want Bush re-elected?' Suskind, *The One
        Percent Doctrine*, p. 336.

201   **The second operation:** It is entirely possible that this attack was less
        successful than Shujaa portrays it. Al Jihad Bridge spans Route Irish,
        the main highway leading to Baghdad Airport – possibly the most
        common target of the insurgency. Whether or not the attack inflicted

the damage he claims is a matter for debate; the fact that he failed to name a specific date (other than a month and a year) makes it almost impossible to pin down with any certainty which American troops, if any, were injured or killed.

202 **I met him:** Interview, Yusuf, March 2009.

202 **Those guys started ruling:** Interview, Haki Mohammed, 27 February 2009.

202 **We had a firing range:** Interview, Ali, 4 April 2009.

203 **We were making up rumours . . . We realized that al-Qaeda didn't come:** Interview, Yusuf, March 2009.

203 **We hadn't seen anything like this:** Interview, Haki Mohammed, 27 February 2009.

204 **wants to get to the bottom of this:** David Sanger, 'Iraq Explosives Become Issue Campaign', *New York Times*, 26 October 2004.

204 **detailed investigation:** Interview with Bill Cunningham, 700 WLW-AM, Cincinnati, Ohio, 26 October 2004

204 **important and ongoing:** President's remarks in Vienna, Ohio, 27 October 2004.

204 **Impossible:** Interview, Ali, 4 April 2009.

205 **The explosives were available everywhere . . . I would say 98 per cent:** Interviews with bomb disposal experts who declined to be named, 4 April 2009.

206 **You want to do Iran for the next one?:** cited *The Assassins' Gate*, p. 145.

6: The Egyptian

207 **The war against terrorism:** Memorandum from George W. Bush on 'Humane Treatment of Taliban and Al-Qaeda Detainees', 7 February 2002.

207 **They caught the Egyptian:** Since Khaled el Masri is currently incarcerated and refusing to communicate even with his lawyer, this account of his arrest, detention, rendition, incarceration and release is taken almost entirely from:
Declaration of Khaled el-Masri in Support of Plaintiff's Opposition to the United States' Motion to Dismiss or, in the Alternative, for Summary Judgement, 6 April 2006.

www.aclu.org/pdfs/safefree/elmasri_decl_exh.pdf.

Complaint, for the Eastern District of Virginia, Alexandria Division. Khaled el Masri v George J. Tenet; Premier Executive Transport Services, Inc; Keeler and Tate Management LLC, Aero Contractors Ltd, Does 1–20. 6 December 2005.

Declaration, Exhibit F, English Translation www.aclu.org/pdfs/safefree/elmasri_decl_exh.pdf.

James Meek, 'They Beat Me from All Sides', *Guardian* (14 January 2005).

Don Van Natta Jr and Souad Mekhennet, 'German's Claim of Kidnap Brings Investigation of US Link', *New York Times* (9 January 2005).

Dana Priest and Julie Tate, 'Wrongful Imprisonment: Anatomy of a CIA Mistake', *Washington Post* (4 December 2005).

Stephen Grey, *Ghost Plane.*

207   **I don't know. A hotel?:** *Declaration of Khaled el-Masri*, p. 3.

209   **In the winter of 1998:** *9/11 Commission Report*, 5.3: *The Hamburg Contingent.* The Khaled el Masri encounter appears on pp. 165–6.

212   **We're staying here . . . Am I under arrest?:** *Declaration of Khaled el-Masri*, p. 6. *Declaration*, Exhibit F, p. 3.

212   **We got him! . . . She briefed all of us:** Interview with unnamed CTC officer, 14 March 2010.

213   **You know, it would scare the shit . . . :** *9/11 Commission Report*, p. 189.

213   **Afghan Eyes:** Details of the project, including early Predator deployments, are also in the *9/11 Commission Report*, starting at p. 189. See also Grey, *Ghost Plane*, Clarke, *Against All Enemies* and Coll, *Ghost Wars.*

214   **National Security Directive 207:** Margaret Satterthwaite, *The Story of el Masri versus Tenet: Human Rights and Humanitarian Law in the 'War on Terror*, New York University School of Law, Public Research Paper 08–64 (December 2008).

214   **George Bush Snr had reauthorized . . . So had Clinton . . . Directive 62:** *The Story of El Masri versus Tenet.*

215   **The rendition operations they did:** Interview, Michael Scheuer, 26 March 2010.

215   **These renditions have shattered:** Statement of DCI George J. Tenet before the Senate Select Committee on Intelligence: *The Worldwide*

Threat in 2000 Global Realities of Our National Security (2 February 2000).

215   'exceptional' authority . . . Great job!: *Bush at War*, pp. 76–8, 97, 101.

216   There can be no bureaucratic impediments: Tenet, *At the Center of the Storm*, p. 179.

216   Call the German embassy!: *Declaration of Khaled el-Masri*, p. 6. Don van Natta, 'Germany Weighs if it Played Role in Seizure by US', *New York Times* (21 February 2006).

216   They don't want to talk to you: *Declaration of Khaled el-Masri*, p. 8; *Declaration*, Exhibit F, p. 4. Don van Natta, 'Germany Weighs if it Played Role in Seizure by US'.

217   What kind of a deal?: *Declaration*, Exhibit F, p. 4.

218   I then felt a stick: *Declaration of Khaled el-Masri*, p. 9.

219   We can see British Airways . . . You want to get: Interview with Josep Manchado, 23 October 2010.

220   It was quite a boring day . . . It's not a good time . . . It was a very new: Interview, Josep Manchado, 23 October 2010.

222   That's the question I wanted to ask you: *Declaration*, Exhibit F, p. 7.

222   You attended terrorist . . . You're in a country where . . . If the charges here weren't correct . . . Everyone claims that when we start interrogating: *Declaration*, Exhibit F, pp. 7–8.

223   The snatch is something that: Interview with Professor John Radsan, 22 March 2010.

224   We said very clearly . . . We had no permission: Interview, Michael Scheuer, 26 March 2010.

225   That's something from the dark side: Interview, Professor John Radsan, 22 March 2010

225   For some reason: Interview, Michael Scheuer, 26 March 2010.

228   I am a German: *Declaration*, Exhibit F, p. 10.

228   The passport was genuine: Lisa Myers, 'CIA Accused of Detaining Innocent Man', MSNBC, 21 April 2005; Dana Priest and Julie Tate, 'Wrongful Imprisonment: Anatomy of a CIA Mistake', *Washington Post* (4 December 2005). James Meek, 'They Beat Me from All Sides', *Guardian* (14 January 2005).

229   From the very beginning people had doubts . . . We'll get our proof . . .

The guy was an innocent: Interview, unnamed CTC officer, 14 March 2010.

229   Jailers at the Salt Pit . . . Even the rendition team: Mayer, *The Dark Side*, p. 283.

230   This is not the appropriate place: *Declaration*, Exhibit F, p. 11.

230   I don't think you belong here: Lisa Myers, 'CIA Accused of Detaining Innocent Man', MSNBC, 21 April 2005.

230   Is that guy still locked up in the Salt Pit?: *The Dark Side*, p. 285.

230   The Agency was already in a state of quiet panic: Details of the Salt Pit's existence, and the tragic death that took place there, were revealed in Dana Priest, 'CIA Avoids Scrutiny of Detainee Treatments', *Washington Post* (3 March 2005).

231   It's the wrong Khaled el Masri: *The Dark Side*, p. 285.

231   Are you telling me we've got an innocent guy: *The Dark Side*, p. 286.

231   deny everything: If the 'reverse rendition' was handled correctly, CIA officers reasoned, the el Masri problem would vanish. 'There wouldn't be a trace. No airplane tickets. Nothing. No one would believe him,' one former official told the *Washington Post* ('Wrongful Imprisonment', 4 December 2005). There was even a chance that Masri might benefit: perhaps he could be paid to shut up. According to Jane Mayer, Deputy Director of Operations James Pavitt found this notion amusing: '[T]he guy will earn more money in five months than he ever could have any other way!' The ruse was vetoed by Condoleezza Rice. 'Your plan won't work,' she told Tenet. 'We have to tell the Germans.' *The Dark Side*, p. 286.

232   I can't answer those questions: *Declaration*, Exhibit F, p. 13. *Declaration of Khaled el-Masri*, p. 18.

232   Please don't. Give me two days: *Declaration*, Exhibit F, pp. 13–14.

235   The exposure of the CIA's rendition programme: For details about the investigative processes involved, see Grey, *Ghost Plane*.

236   They were Germans . . . They told me they wanted to talk: Interview, Josep Manchado, 23 October 2010.

236   Germany's ZDF Television showed . . . There it was: The ZDF researcher responsible was Jorg Hendrik Brase – who happened to have excellent contacts in Macedonia ('I knew some guys who knew the boss of flight control'). '[Manchado] could prove through his photo that this

plane with this registration number, had been seen in Palma,' he recalls. 'But the confirmation actually we finally got through the database on Skopje Airport. They had all the flight details, the arrival of the plane. They confirmed that he came from Palma, that he arrived in Skopje that certain day and stayed there a certain number of hours and then took off . . . and from there he went to Kabul.' Interview with Jorg Hendrik Brase, 21 June 2010.

237 **An enterprising Mallorcan journalist:** Matias Valles, 'La CIA usa Mallorca como base para sus secuestros por avion', *Diario de Mallorca* (12 March 2005).

237 **Gran Melia Victoria . . . Marriott Son Antem:** *Ghost Plane*, Chapter 4: 'Mistaken Identity'.

237 **On 31 May 2004, Daniel R. Coats:** According to Jane Mayer, Otto Schilly was livid: 'Why are you telling me this?' he demanded. 'My secretary is here – taking notes!' Schilly was of the opinion that the CIA's original plan – sending el Masri home and shutting up – would have been preferable: 'Why didn't you just let him go, give him some money and keep it quiet?' *The Dark Side*, pp. 286–7. See also Dana Priest and Julie Tate, 'Wrongful Imprisonment: Anatomy of a CIA Mistake', *Washington Post* (4 December 2005).

237 **She didn't know. She just had a hunch:** 'Wrongful Imprisonment: Anatomy of a CIA Mistake'.

238 **There is no rendition that was ever . . . I was there:** Interview with an unnamed CIA official involved with the rendition programme, 26 March 2010.

240 **I'm able to say:** Press Availability with Secretary of State Condoleezza Rice and German Chancellor, Angela Merkel, 6 December 2005.

240 **We're not sure what was in [Merkel's] head:** Joel Brinkley, 'Rice is Challenged in Europe over Secret Prisons', *New York Times* (7 December 2005).

240 **the local government can make . . . to work with us:** Secretary of State, *Remarks upon Departure for Europe*, 5 December 2005.

241 **All of the Europeans:** Interview, Michael Scheuer, 26 March 2010.

241 **Credit records, phone records:** Interview with unnamed CIA official involved with the rendition programme, 26 March 2010.

242   **speculative and unfounded:** Dick Marty, 'Alleged Secret Detentions and Unlawful Inter-state Transfers of Detainees involving Council of Europe Member States', *Special Rapporteur* (12 June 2006), p. 26.

242   **Let me make it clear:** 'CIA Received German Files on German Captive', Reuters, 17 December 2005.

242   **I would say if you wrote that:** Interview with unnamed CIA official involved with the rendition programme, 26 March 2010.

242   **I do not underestimate . . . laws such as these:** *Opinions of the Lords of Appeal for Judgement in the Cause*, 16 December 2004, pp. 52–3.

243   **perhaps one of the most serious challenges . . . governments depart from their obligations in this way:** *Human Rights Council's Eminent Panel of Jurists*, Forward (v).

243   **States tamper with this framework . . . It is difficult to exaggerate:** *Human Rights Council's Eminent Panel of Jurists*, pp. 16–17.

243   **In operating the system . . . international law:** Annual Lecture of the Law Reform Committee of the Bar Council: 'Our Government and the International Rule of Law since 9/11', 29 November 2006, p. 7.

244   **twenty-six CIA operatives:** 'Italy Convicts CIA agents in CIA Kidnap Trial' CNN, 4 November 2009. 'CIA Agents Convicted in Italy Unlikely to Serve Time', *TIME* (4 November 2009).

244   **I probably wouldn't travel:** Interview, Professor John Radsan, 22 March 2010.

244   **Eric Robert Hume . . . wife's name was Janet:** See, for example, '"Ghost Pilots" of the CIA's Rendition Team', *Los Angeles Times* (18 February 2007). For details on these individuals, go to www.source-watch.org/index.php?title=Extraordinary_rendition.

245   **Eleven American men and two women:** 'Germans Charge 13 CIA Operatives', *Washington Post* (1 February 2007).

245   **This isn't something where:** Interview with unnamed CTC officer, 14 March 2010.

245   **Don't believe this was some devious operation . . . approving it . . . we don't run secret prisons:** Interview, Professor John Radsan, 22 March 2010.

245–8   **The Executive Branch . . . Not only were they ordered . . . we would get sold out at some point:** Interview, Michael Scheuer, 26 March 2010.

246   **What we want you to do:** Interview with unnamed CTC officer, 14
        March 2010.

247   **The appearance didn't do much good:** Margaret Satterthwaite, 'The
        Story of el Masri versus Tenet: Human Rights and Humanitarian
        Law in the "War on Terror"', New York University School of Law,
        Public Research Paper 08-64 (December 2008).

247   **all fair-minded people must:** 'The Story of el Masri versus Tenet:
        Human Rights and Humanitarian Law in the "War on Terror"'.

247   **The case of Khaled el Masri is exemplary:** Dick Marty, 'Alleged Secret
        Detentions and Unlawful Inter-state Transfers of Detainees involving
        Council of Europe Member States', p. 33.

248   **central facts [of the case]:** 'The Story of el Masri versus Tenet:
        Human Rights and Humanitarian Law in the "War on Terror"'.

248   **The only place in the world:** 'The Story of el Masri versus Tenet:
        Human Rights and Humanitarian Law in the "War on Terror"'.

248   **Do whatever you want:** 'German CIA Rendition Victim Sentenced to
        Jail for Assault', *The Local* (31 March 2010).

249   **CIA shell company:** European Parliament, Giovanni Claudio Fava,
        'Working Document No. 8 on the Companies Linked to the CIA,
        Aircraft Used by the CIA and the European Countries in which CIA
        Companies have Made Stopovers', *Rapporteur*, 16 November 2006.

7: Friends in Low Places

251   *All who live in tyranny:* George W. Bush's Second Inaugural Address,
        January 2005.

251   *Ozodlik!:* Shirin Akiner, 'Violence in Andijan, 13 May 2005. An
        Independent Assessment', CACI Silk Road Paper (July 2005). Akiner
        concludes that the raiders shouted '*Allahu akbar!*' (p. 14). Human
        Rights Watch disagrees: 'Protestors were shouting *ozodlik* ('freedom'),
        not, as reported, *Allahu akbar.*' *Bullets were Falling like Rain: The
        Andijan Massacre, May 13, 2005.*

251-2   **I heard these very loud noises . . . You're free! . . . I was very
        emotional . . . What are we supposed to do *now*?:** Interview with
        Sardor Azimov (name changed), 6 November 2009.

253   **boiled alive:** Khusnuddin Alimov (24) and Muzafar Avazov (35),

serving sentences for involvement in Hizb-ut-Tahrir, were murdered, apparently for refusing to stop praying in Jaslyk. Their bodies were returned to Tashkent for burial on 8 August 2002. Avazov's body was photographed. Forensic analysis of the photographs at Glasgow University led to the conclusion that 'The pattern of scalding shows a well-demarcated line on the lower chest/abdomen, which could well indicate the forceful application of hot water whilst the person was within some kind of bath or similar vessel.'

253   **Every year when our conversations . . . They basically said:** Interview with Sasha Petrov, 8 September 2009.

254   **There's going to be a crisis in Central Asia:** Interview with Alison Gill, 2 September 2009.

255–6   **The main focus was on quality . . . When we started . . . We never advertised:** Interview with Nodir Mahmudov (name changed), 26 October 2009.

256   **We understood that we had to:** Interview, Sardor Azimov, 6 November 2009.

256   **We started building schools . . . They saw that what we were making:** Interview, Nodir Mahmudov, 26 October 2009.

257   **We told them all about:** Interview, Sardor Azimov, 6 November 2009.

257   **We offered our system to the President:** Interview, Nodir Mahmudov, 26 October 2009.

258   **This region is probably the most:** Interview with a senior Pentagon official, 13 October 2009.

258   **You look at the map:** PBS Frontline: *Campaign Against Terror*, 19 April 2002.

259   **CSAR:** Woodward, *Bush at War*.

259   **Very swiftly after [9/11]:** Interview with David Merkel, 10 September 2009.

259   **Uzbekistan will be vital:** Franks, *American Soldier*, p. 254.

259   **geographical and political keystone:** Lt-Col Kurt Meppen, 'US–Uzbek Bilateral Relations: Policy Options', p. 14, in Daly et al. (eds.), *Anatomy of a Crisis: US–Uzbekistan Relations 2001–2005*.

260   **I don't know what H-Hour was:** Interview with Colonel Jon Chicky, 2

September 2009. Colonel Chicky would like it made clear that all opinions expressed here are his own, not those of the National Defense University, the Department of Defense or the US government.

260 **Travel well into the night:** Interview, senior Pentagon official, 13 October 2009.

260 **secret deal:** The 'initiative' began in 1999. Covert aid to Uzbekistan was endorsed by the Deputies Committee in April. From the outset things looked bad. The Uzbeks needed equipment and at least six months' training; chances of success were estimated at just 10 per cent. Predator flights took over, but also ran into trouble (see Chapter 6, 'The Egyptian'). *9/11 Commission Report*, pp. 142, 203, 488. The footnote **the ethnicity was wrong** comes from an interview with an unnamed CIA source.

261 **The US and Uzbek positions on this:** Interview, senior Pentagon official, 13 October 2009.

262 **the jumping-off point:** *At the Center of the Storm*, p. 177.

262 **They weren't very easy to deal with:** Interview with Pentagon negotiator, 2 September 2009. Tommy Franks agreed: 'Horse-trading was underway all across the region' (*American Soldier*, p. 269).

262 **the kinds of people you found yourself:** *Bush at War*, p. 77. Tommy Franks likewise noted that Karimov's human rights record was 'tarnished, at best'. But then, '[Rumsfeld would] probably have shaken hands with the devil if that had furthered our goals in the war on terrorism.' (*American Soldier*, p. 374).

262–3 **You need to be exactly clear . . . We have to be sure . . . We need to get al-Qaeda:** *Bush at War*, pp. 128–9.

263 **Our delegation is not senior enough:** *Bush at War*, p. 160.

264 **As soon as the agreement was signed:** Interview, Colonel Jon Chicky, 2 September 2009.

265 **He told us that we should pay . . . I could take this phone:** Interview, Sardor Azimov, 6 November 2009.

266 **There was optimism:** Interview, senior Pentagon official, 13 October 2009.

267 **The base gave us some equity:** Interview, Colonel Jon Chicky, 2 September 2009.

267   **On 27 January 2002:** Michael Anderson, 'Base Motives', *Spectator* (21 May 2005).

267   **At a certain stage:** cited Shahram Akbarzadeh, *Uzbekistan and the United States: Authoritarianism, Islam and Washington's Security Agenda* (Zed Books, 2005), p. 88.

267   **Two days later, Elizabeth Jones:** Michael Anderson, 'Base Motives', *Spectator* (21 May 2005).

268   **shot in the forehead . . . I'm prepared to rip off the heads:** 'Torture, an Iron Fist and Twisted Logic Set Stage for Islam Karimov's Landslide Victory', *The Times* (21 December 2007).

268   **9/II changed the picture:** Interview, Alison Gill, 2 September 2009.

268   **It wasn't only the Uzbeks:** 'Opportunism in the Face of Tragedy, Repression in the Name of Anti-terrorism', Human Rights Watch, 20 January 2002.

268   **we were right from the beginning:** cited 'Opportunism in the Face of Tragedy'.

268   **We agree with President Bush:** 'Lots of Wars on Terror: The Bush Doctrine is now a Template for Conflicts Worldwide', *Guardian* (10 December 2001).

268   **How do you balance . . . I thought it was going to be:** Interview with Tom Malinowski, 7 October 2009.

269   **habitual, widespread and deliberate:** UN Economic and Social Council, 'Report of Special Rapporteur on the Question of Torture, Mission to Uzbekistan', 3 February 2003.

270   **A lot of stuff in there:** Interview, unnamed senior State Department official, 28 September 2009.

270   **Just stay quiet:** Interview, Nodir Mahmudov, 26 October 2009.

271   **There were loads of people:** Interview, Sardor Azimov, 6 November 2009.

271   **President Karimov was woken . . . 7.30 onwards:** Abdumannob Polat, *Reassessing Andijan*, p. 13.

272   **People started joining us:** Interview, Nodir Mahmudov, 26 October 2009.

273   **Do not spill any blood!:** 'Video of Ill-Fated Uzbek Rising offers Haunting, Complex View', *New York Times* (22 June 2006).

273 **Dear Andijanis!:** Bukharbaeva and Azamatova, 'No Requiem for the Dead', Institute for War and Peace Reporting, 16 May 2005.

273 **we are not going to teach you:** Lt-Col Kurt Meppen, 'US–Uzbek Bilateral Relations: Policy Options', p. 21, in Daly et al. (eds.), *Anatomy of a Crisis: US–Uzbekistan Relations 2001–2005.*

274 **They did a pretty good job . . . It sure as hell was:** Interview, unnamed senior State Department official, 28 September 2009.

275 **Very few cases:** Interview, Alison Gill, 2 September 2009.

275 **(footnote) So far as we can tell:** cited Durukan Kuzu, *Andijan Uprising*, PhD thesis, Bilkent University, Ankara (September 2008). **Rotary club:** cited Lionel Beehner, *Documenting Andijan*, Council on Foreign Relations, 26 June 2006. Interview with Professor Frederick Starr, 27 August 2009.

275 **textbook conditions:** Zeyno Baran of the Nixon Centre. House of Representatives Subcommittee on Middle East and Central Asia, Committee on International Relations, 15 June 2004. Baran was clear that things were going wrong: 'The United States and Uzbekistan are losing the battle for the hearts and minds of the Uzbek people.'

276 **a hub for CIA rendition:** According to the European Parliament, from the end of 2001 to the end of 2005, forty-six suspect plane stopovers occurred in Uzbekistan, placing it fifth in line for most popular rendition hub. Jordan, Azerbaijan, Turkmenistan and Egypt saw more CIA flights; Iraq, Afghanistan, Morocco, Libya and Guantanamo Bay all saw fewer. European Parliament, Giovanni Claudio Fava, 'Working Document No. 8 on the Companies Linked to the CIA, Aircraft Used by the CIA and the European Countries in which CIA Companies have Made Stopovers', *Rapporteur*, 16 November 2006, p. 7.

277 **When you stand for your liberty:** George W. Bush, Inaugural Address, 20 January 2005.

278 **[Karimov] had signed . . . It's hard to argue . . . We're not the kind of country:** Interview, Tom Malinowski, 7 October 2009.

279 **For us, at the DoD:** Interview, Colonel Jon Chicky, 2 September 2009.

280 **You had the State Department:** Interview with Dr Stephen Blank, 21 July 2009.

280 **You've got the bureaucratic technique:** Interview, Lawrence Wilkerson, 3 September 2009.

280 **That will screw the State Department!:** Reported by Danish journalist Michael Andersen, who was present.

281 **like watching a train wreck:** Interview, Pentagon negotiator, 2009.

281 **Karimov wrote to the United States:** 'Over a period of time stretching from late 2003 to early 2005, Tashkent presented no less than six drafts of a permanent agreement for the US use of Khanabad. Each draft was carefully considered in Tashkent, as the leadership attempted to divine which words and concepts were necessary to convince the US to come to the bargaining table . . . [T]he State Department's sanguine views were summed up in one senior staffer's comment that, "Uzbekistan needs us more than we need them. They'll come around."' Lt-Col Kurt Meppen, 'US–Uzbek Bilateral Relations: Policy Options', p. 14, in Daly et al. (eds.), *Anatomy of a Crisis: US–Uzbekistan Relations 2001–2005*.

281 **These letters from the Uzbek side:** Interview with a senior Pentagon official, 13 October 2009.

282 **The moment we went through . . . There was a hole through both sides:** Interview, Nodir Mahmudov, 26 October 2009.

283 **From the APCs:** Human Rights Watch video interview transcript: Lutfullo Shamsuddinov (chair), Independent Organization for Human Rights in Andijan. The interview was conducted by Alison Gill. Shamsuddinov returned to the site of the shootings the next morning at 5.30 a.m.: 'There were slippers belonging to those who were killed. There was blood everywhere. There were human brains on the ground. And a lot of blood. Like a puddle. And there was an odour of meat on the asphalt – a really awful meat-like odour.'

283 **It was like a bowling game:** Human Rights Watch interview with 'Marat M', 28 May 2005, cited *Bullets were Falling like Rain*.

284 **I saw him go down . . . We tried to take:** Interview, Sardor Azimov, 7 November 2009.

285 **There were about a dozen:** Interview, Sasha Petrov, 8 September 2009.

285 **There were women and children:** Interview with Anna Neistat, 4 September 2009.

286   **As you enter the town:** Interview with the HRW team member who entered Andijan.

286   **The morning after the shootings:** 'Around 5 a.m. five KAMAZ trucks arrived and a bus with soldiers. The soldiers would ask the wounded, "Where are the rest of you?" When they would not respond, they would shoot them dead and load them into the trucks. There were no ambulances there. Soldiers were cleaning the [area of] bodies for two hours,' Human Rights Watch interview with 'Rustam R', Kyrgyzstan, 20 May 2005, cited *Bullets were Falling like Rain*. See also *Burying the Truth*.

287   **I think we all recognized:** Interview, Anna Neistat, 4 September 2009.

289   **the facts are not pretty:** CNN, 'Uzbek Relatives Search for Bodies', 15 May 2005.

289   **The Uzbeks started restricting our air operations:** Interview, Senior State Department official, 13 October 2009.

289   **There was a tense dialogue:** Interview, Colonel Jon Chicky, 2 September 2009.

290   **shocking, but not unexpected:** John C. K. Daly, 'Chronology of US–Uzbekistan Relations, 2001–2005, in Daly et al. (eds.), *Anatomy of a Crisis: US–Uzbekistan Relations 2001–2005*.

290   **The moment of truth . . . Is there any way . . . Very rarely in policy-making . . . In the end we told them . . . That day, within an hour:** Interview with Dan Fried, 13 October 2009.

291   **They said if you keep talking:** Interview, Sardor Azimov, 7 November 2009.

8: The Muslim Disease

293   *How do you deal with an enemy?*: 'Muslims Fears Pose Barrier to Fighting Polio in Nigeria', *Boston Globe* (11 January 2004).

294   **I asked him to stay the night . . . He told me . . . I know the risks:** Interview with Namair Muhammad, 3 December 2009.

294–5   **I saw my son . . . I got the same feeling . . . I knew there were armed:** Interview with Hazrat Jamal, 5 April 2010.

296   **On the one hand:** 'Official Leading Polio Drive Killed', *Pakistan Daily Times*, 17 February 2007.

298 **The global eradication of smallpox cost:** Smallpox eradication started in 1967 and took eleven years, costing $300 million; the United States gave $32 million. If polio is eradicated, 'the US alone will reap annual savings of over $230 million'; worldwide savings will be more than $1.5 billion. 'Global Eradication of Polio and Measles', Hearing before Senate Subcommittee on Appropriations, 23 September 1998.

299 **From its inception:** GPEI information can be found at www.polioeradication.org. Also see Salgado, *The End of Polio*, and Brookes and Khan, *The End of Polio?*.

300 **two million workers:** NID statistics from Salgado, *The End of Polio*; 'Global Eradication of Polio and Measles', Hearing before Senate Subcommittee on Appropriations, 23 September 1998; Progress against Polio (the Bill and Melinda Gates Foundation).

300 **Days of Tranquillity:** 'We had wars in El Salvador, we had civil war in Nicaragua, we had Sendero in Peru, we had guerrillas in Colombia,' recalls Ciro de Quadros, who has been credited with the establishment of GPEI. 'People had Days of Tranquillity where the fighting stopped and everybody was vaccinated – government and anti-government forces. This was done in Afghanistan not so long ago, this was done in Lebanon in the 80s . . . You *can* broker with the people. It's a tremendous undertaking, but it's possible. It requires lots of planning, lots of collaboration, lots of different groups and so on. *Everything* is possible.' Interview with Dr Ciro de Quadros, February 2010.

302 **It is critical:** 'Global Eradication of Polio and Measles', Hearing before Senate Subcommittee on Appropriations, 23 September 1998. Ciro de Quadros agreed. 'In the Americas all the politicians were, like, when we eradicated one they said, "Look, we want to eradicate measles now" . . . We had even to stop them for two, three years, because we thought it would be very difficult to have two eradications at the same time . . . "We can eradicate measles, but let's finish polio first."' Interview, Ciro de Quadros, February 2010.

303 **People would ask him . . . I was a poor man:** Interview with Fazli Raziq, 2 December 2010.

303 **He was a very frank man:** Interview with Nazirullah Muhammadzai, 2 December 2010.

304   **'He loved parties . . . Only later . . . When it was time . . . Look, we've had a great:** Interview with Azmatullah Jan Faiq, 2 December 2010.

304   **one of the most enlightening . . . 80 per cent . . . Over fifty nations . . . This is a dramatic . . . The goal . . . critical stage:** 'Global Eradication of Polio and Measles', Hearing before Senate Subcommittee on Appropriations, 23 September 1998.

305   **With the end almost in sight:** Salgado, *The End of Polio*, p. 149.

305   **Although the rumour didn't surface:** The best account of the evolution of the contaminated OPV rumour appears in Rosenstein and Garrett, 'Polio's Return: A WHO-Done-It?'.

306   **NSSM-200:** National Security Study Memorandum NSSM-200: 'Implications of Worldwide Population Growth for US Security and Overseas Interests' ('Kissinger Report'), 10 December 1974. Ibrahim Datti Ahmed was under no illusions as to what the memo was really saying: 'Just look at the Internet,' he told a reporter. 'There's strong proof that the US government, dating back to thirty-five years ago, with Kissinger and Nixon, believed that population is the most important factor for US hegemony in the world. Since they cannot rapidly increase the US population, the only way for them to dominate is to depopulate the Third World. That is the motive.' 'Muslims Fears Pose Barrier to Fighting Polio in Nigeria', *Boston Globe* (11 January 2004).

307–8   **Modern-day Hitlers . . . It is the lesser of two evils . . . Where polio vaccine is seen to:** cited 'Polio's Return: A WHO-Done-It?'.

308   **That is my fear with polio:** 'Global Eradication of Polio and Measles', Hearing before Senate Subcommittee on Appropriations, 23 September 1998.

309   **In 1980, Donald Henderson:** Smallpox was certified eradicated in 1980. One year later a new disease emerged: HIV. In 1984, an HIV-positive US military recruit was vaccinated against smallpox. The vaccine triggered the HIV to convert to AIDS. 'If the smallpox eradication campaign had dragged on for another five years, then, vaccination . . . would have had to stop, and the disease would have been able to rebound. Nobody knew how small the window of opportunity actually had been.' Brookes, *The End of Polio?*, pp. 40–1.

310 **The consequences:** David Heymann, Foreword to Brookes, *The End of Polio?* (October 2006).

310 **In February 2005:** 'Polio Detected in Indonesia', *New York Times* (2 May 2005).

311 **The world is still paying:** 'Rumors Cause Resistance to Vaccine in Nigeria', Associated Press, 25 September 2006. 'Nigeria exported cases to countries that had no vaccination, and then the cases went out again into countries that were already free,' says Ciro de Quadros. 'A disaster.' Interview, Ciro de Quadros, February 2010.

311 **I told him that it was Eid . . . This is a great . . . Don't be angry . . . I understand:** Interview, Azmatullah Jan Faiq, 2 December 2009.

312 **They claim that the polio campaign:** 'Polio's Return: A WHO-Done-It?'.

313 **America hates Muslims:** 'Muslims Fears Pose Barrier to Fighting Polio in Nigeria', *Boston Globe* (11 January 2004). A number of anti-OPV campaigners later admitted that they had urged Nigerians not to vaccinate their children despite knowing it was safe – simply to express their anger at American policies in the Middle East and towards Islam.

313 **In October 2003:** J. R. Kaufmann and H. Feldbaum, 'Diplomacy and The Polio Immunisation Boycott in Northern Nigeria', *Health Affairs*, 28 (6) (November–December 2009).

313 **They have always taken us:** Yahya, 'Polio vaccines – Difficult to Swallow: The Story of a Controversy in Northern Nigeria', p. 14.

314 **92 per cent:** 'MMR Uptake Falls to Record Low', BBC News, 26 September 2003; House of Commons, 'Measles and MMR Statistics', 10 February 2009.

316 **And yet commentators noticed:** 'African Strain of Polio Found to Have Spread to Indonesia', *New York Times* (3 May 2005): 'Polio is now found almost exclusively in Muslim countries or regions.' 'I think that's true,' says de Quadros, 'because most of the population in Uttar Pradesh and Bihar in India are Muslim, and Pakistan and Afghanistan and Nigeria – you see, all these are Muslim areas. But it's not because they are Muslims that they have polio! It's that they are not vaccinated.' Interview, Ciro de Quadros, February 2010.

318 **In 2004 – hot on the trail:** 'What's behind India's Outbreak of Polio

Paranoia?', *TIME* (28 September 2006). 'In U.P. the War on Polio Stumbles', *India Together* (31 December 2006).

318 **When Nepal and Bangladesh:** 'In U.P. the War on Polio Stumbles'.

319 **As a result, much of the vaccination:** Brookes, *The End of Polio?*, p. 79.

320 **Nowhere is the achievement:** Siddarth Dube, cited in Salgado, *The End of Polio*, p. 127.

320 **In 2001, three out of five:** Dube, cited in Salgado, *The End of Polio*, p. 131.

322 **According to . . . Ahmed Rashid:** 'FATA had become terrorism central,' writes Rashid. 'Almost all latter-day al-Qaeda terrorist plots around the world had a FATA connection.' Al-Qaeda was so safe there, it even set up a media production arm, As Sahab ('The Clouds'). Pakistani authorities disagreed with Rashid's assessment: '[Al-Qaeda] no longer has any command, communication and programme structure in Pakistan,' President Pervez Musharraf declared in July 2005. 'It is absolutely baseless to say that al-Qaeda has its headquarters in Pakistan and that terror attacks in other parts of the world in any way originate from our country.' *Descent into Chaos*, pp. 278–9.

323 **He came and requested me:** Interview with Abdullatif Bacha, 28 December 2009.

324 **Bin Laden loved Bajaur:** Interview, Michael Scheuer, 26 March 2010.

324 **On 13 January 2006:** 'Airstrike Misses Al-Qaeda Chief', *The Times* (15 January 2006).

324 **It's terrible when:** CBS *Face the Nation*, 15 January 2006.

325 **Nine months later, it happened again:** 'Pakistan School Raid Sparks Anger', BBC News, 30 October 2006. 'US Carried out Maddrassah Bombing', *Sunday Times* (26 November 2006).

325 **a conspiracy of the Jews:** 'Impotence Fears Hit Polio Drive', BBC News, 25 January 2007.

326 **There are other diseases:** 'Anti-US Views Fuel Polio Growth', *San Francisco Chronicle* (5 October 2008).

326 **They hire women:** 'Taliban Orders NGOs to Leave Swat', *Pakistan Daily Times* (23 March 2009). 'I'm forty-five and have never had a drop of the vaccine,' Khan said. 'I am still alive.'

326 **He was concerned:** Interview, Azmatullah Jan Faiq, 2 December 2009.

326   **Three of them were armed . . . I explained . . . Thank God they let me go!:** Interview, Nazirullah Muhammadzai, 2 December 2009.

327   **He came to me again:** Interview, Abdullatif Bacha, 28 December 2009.

327–8   **He said that the vaccine . . . If you're arguing . . . OK. I don't have a family:** Interview, Hazrat Jamal, 5 April 2010.

328   **Come on:** Interview with Abdul Rahim, 5 April 2010.

328–9   **That's good . . . I have to be honest . . . Enough:** Interviews, Hazrat Jamal, Abdul Rahim, 5 April 2010.

329   **My first reaction was . . . Are you foreigners?:** Interview, Hazrat Jamal, 5 April 2010.

330   **at some point the initiative:** 'We're not ready to give up,' Ogden told Brookes. '[But] we believe it'll take longer and cost more than anyone is currently predicting . . . I worry about 2003 happening again.' Brookes, *The End of Polio?*, p. 196

330   **We may never eradicate polio:** Brookes, *The End of Polio?*, p. 196. I asked de Quadros about this quote. 'That was years ago,' he said. 'Five or six years ago when the programme was a real disaster. It was very, very sad. Today it looks a little bit better. Now that the Gates Foundation has got involved and Mr Gates and his group are pushing WHO and CDC and UNICEF on this issue. There is a window of opportunity here. I have a little hope now.' Bill Gates, who has ploughed hundreds of millions of dollars into GPEI, explained the implications of failure in 2009. 'The harsh mathematics of polio makes it clear,' he said. 'We cannot maintain a level of 1,000–2,000 cases a year. Either we eradicate polio or we return to the days of tens of thousands of cases a year.' 'Funds for Polio Eradication Drive', BBC News, 21 January 2009. There may be other side effects. 'If there is a failure of the polio eradication,' says de Quadros, 'it will be very difficult for WHO to push for any other major global initiative . . . If the programme fails, WHO will bear the burden and it will take some years for them to recover. I cannot predict the consequences, but they will not be nice.' Interview, Ciro de Quadros, February 2010.

331–2   **We're not moving ahead . . . Three out of seven subdivisions . . .**

Bara and Terah . . . No one knows . . . Most of the people . . . The military: Interviews with health officials in NWFP, 10–12 January 2010.

332 **One fact is clear:** Interview, Namair Muhammad, 3 December 2009.

333 **It was like a thunderstorm . . . The lower half of his body:** Interview, Fazli Raziq, 2 December 2009.

333 **'Nobody ever tried to pressure:** Interview, Nazirullah Muhammadzai, 3 December 2009.

334 **I sat and cried:** Interview, Abdul Rahim, 5 April 2010.

334 **A good man:** Interview, Hazrat Jamal, 5 April 2010.

334 **US aggression against Iraq . . . People are asking . . . If you are conducting military operations:** Interview with Maulana Rahat Hussein, 19 January 2010.

335 **It was different before 9/11:** Interview, Hazrat Jamal, 5 April 2010.

Epilogue

337 **He'd knock the living shit . . . Never thought I'd live:** Interview, Mark Stroman, 27 June 2008.

338 **$6 trillion:** Stiglitz and Bilmes, *The Three Trillion Dollar War*.

338 **a third of its own citizens:** Polled by Scripps Howard/Ohio University, 36 per cent of more than 1,000 respondents declared it 'somewhat likely' or 'very likely' that US Federal officials either participated in the attacks or took no action to stop them, 'because they wanted the United States to go to war in the Middle East'. 'Third of Americans Suspect 9-11 Government Conspiracy', Scripps Howard News Service, 1 August 2006.

338 **Make no mistake about it:** Remarks by the President in photo opportunity with the National Security team, 12 September 2001.

339 **Quiet, pretty quiet:** Interview, Alka Patel, 28 June 2008.

339 **You know, some people are crazy . . . Some women are not able to rest . . . Why did they say:** Interview, Karim and Halima al Saadi, 1 November 2008.

340 **political calculus:** 'Powell Rows Back on Doubts over Invasion', *Guardian* (4 February 2004).

340   **I still firmly believe:** Lt. Gen. Mike DeLong, *A General Speaks Out*, Introduction.

341   **I can apologize for the information:** 'Why Can't More People Just Say Sorry?' *The Times* (29 October 2008).

342   **No. Go and kill her . . . If you can't do this for me:** Interview, Abdul Malik, 8 March 2010.

344   **You know:** Interview, Kevin Hartline, 21 June 2008.

Acknowledgements

Interviews

JA; Dr Jalaa Abdelwahab; Haji Saheb Jan Agha; 'Ahmed'; 'Ali' and his friend from Al Qa'qaa; David Albright; the Alsaai family; Haji Mohammad Anwar; 'Sardor Azimov'; Andrew Bartlett; Rod Barton; Jacques Baute; Ambassador Kim Beazley; Andrea Berg; Dr Stephen Blank; Eric Blehm; Matilda Bogner; Tom Boston; Peter Bouckaert; Jorg Hendrik Brase; Julian Burnside QC; RC; Joe Caffrey; Colonel Jon Chicky; Mary Connell; Garry Cordukes; JD; Ambassador James Dobbins; George Dodd; Elias Durry; Azmatullah Jan Faiq; Ambassador Robert Finn; Carl Ford; Ambassador Daniel Fried; Tom Fuentes; Ronnie 'Shy' Galloway; Jesse Garcia; Alison Gill; Kevin 'Bear' and Sheila Hartline; George Healey; Marc Herold; Melissa Hooper; Sami Ibrahim; JH; Russell Hogg; Roland Jabour; Jan Mohammed Khan; Lai-Ling Jew; Larry Johnson; Dr Brian Jones; HK; JK; Bob Kelley; MS; NM; Tom Malinowski; General Dan McNeill; David Merkel; the Kahtany family; Haji Abdul Khaliq; JM; 'Nodir Mahmudov'; Abdul Malik and Tela Gul. Josep Manchado; David Manne; Khalifa Haji Jan Mohammad; 'Haki Mohammed'; Namair Muhammad; Nazirullah Muhammadzai; Abu Nazir; Anna Neistat; Chris Nelson; Martha Brill Olcott; JP; VP; Khalid Pashtoon; Alka Patel; Sasha Petrov; Abdumannob Polat; Dr Ciro de Quadros; Asim Qureshi; Professor John Radsan; Maulana Rahat Hussein; Haji Abdul Rahim; Fazli Raziq; Rachel Reid; Philip Ruddock; Dr Michael Rwykin; MS; 'Karim' and 'Halima al Saadi'; Haji Khalifa Sadat; Hazrat Jamal Salarzai;

David Sanger; Michael Scheuer; Mike Scrafton; Abu Shujaa; John Sifton; Dean Staley; Professor Frederick Starr; Mark Stroman; Bob and Carolyn Templeton; Greg Thielmann; AW; Geoff Wainwright; Wayne White; Monica Whitlock; Colonel Lawrence Wilkerson; Richard Wood; Professor Houston Wood III; Tim Wyatt; 'Yusuf' and Sam Zarifi.

Thank you

For time, advice and contacts: Sidney and Roland Alford; Michael Andersen; Iroda Askarova; Moazzim Begg; Mike Coldrick; Patrick Cook at the Spectre Association (sorry it didn't work out) and the indefatigable Pamela Curr in Melbourne. Cath Davis; Mark Dowd; Marsha Emerman; George Fulton; Manfred Gnjidic; Hans Halberstadt; Charlie Hawes; Shahzeb Jillani; David Leser; Kirstine Lumb; Peter Mares; Grant Mitchell; Umida Niyazova; the Polio Eradication Heroes' Fund; Samantha Power; Peter Rickwood; Margaret Satterthwaite; Gerald Schumacher; Sarah Sewall; Zahid Shah; Jack Smit; Mary Snider; Rudi Tangermann; Jessie Taylor; Stephen Watt; Andy Worthington; Shahida Yakub; Assistant DA Shelly O'Brien Yeatts and the staff at the Dallas County District Attorney's Office.

To the various individuals who shepherded me through their countries or went to meet the people I was hunting: in Iraq, Haider al Safi, Gailan and al Mutalibi. In Pakistan, Shaheen Buneri. In Afghanistan, Ali Ahmad. In Australia, Chris and Fiona Whitwell – who sent me to the doctor when I thought pneumonia was a chesty cough – Henry and Polly (who smells), and Helen Collier (who doesn't).

On the bookish side, thank you to Julian at LAW for putting up with the crises; Pete Beatty at Bloomsbury and Toby Mundy at Atlantic – who came up with the idea, the title and everything else, then had to wait . . . and wait. Sorry. Margaret Stead and Ian Pindar. And a massive thank you to Simon Berthon, for wise advice when all appeared lost.

To my parents for listening patiently; to Rollo (any chairs left?); to Chris Gair for his relentless computer-based chivvying; and, of course, to Diesel – who has had more than enough of book-writing, and debt, for a while. Thank you. Oh, and Zoe Elton, who didn't help at all but wants a mention.

Index